ETHICS
A UNIVERISTY GUIDE

ETHICS

A UNIVERSITY GUIDE

Edited by Richard H. Corrigan & Mary E. Farrell

PROGRESSIVE FRONTIERS PRESS

GLOUCESTER

Ethics: A University Guide
Edited by: Richard H. Corrigan & Mary E. Farrell

Progressive Frontiers Press
1A Leonard Road
Gloucester
GL1 4PQ
www.frontierspublications.com

All rights reserved. No part of this publication may be reproduced, stored in a retrival system, or transmitted, in any form or by any means, electronic, photocopying, recording, or otherwise, without the prior written permission of the publisher.

Printed in the USA.

A Catalogue of this title is available from the British Library.

ISBN-13: 978-0-9563288-2-3

*For Peter Farrell
Father and Friend*

Acknowledgements

We would like to acknowledge the efforts expended by all those who contributed to this volume. We would also like to thank all those great thinkers that have left us a legacy so rich and diverse that a book like this can be produced.

Contents

Preface   i

Authors and Editors   iii

Chapter 1. A Brief History of Ethical Thought   1
Richard H. Corrigan and Mary E. Farrell

Chapter 2. Animal Ethics   21
Constantine Sandis

Chapter 3. Business Ethics   41
John F. Humphrey

Chapter 4. Ethics of Care   79
Treasa Campbell

Chapter 5. Contractualism: History, Theories and Critiques   109
Sebastian Schleidgen

Chapter 6. Egoism and Ethics   135
Andy Cochrane

Chapter 7. Environmental Ethics   157
Steven Bond

Chapter 8. Global Ethics   185
Sylvie Loriaux

Chapter 9. Kantian Ethics   207
Joyce Lazier

Chapter 10. Law and Rights   221
Claudio Corradetti

Chapter 11. Normative Ethics   241
Owen Anderson

Chapter 12. Utilitarian Ethics   267
Joakim Sandberg

Chapter 13. Virtue Ethics   289
Richa Yadav

Chapter 14. Ethics and Well-Being 309
Mark Piper

Index 335

Preface

The intention of this book is to fill a significant gap that currently exists in academia. There is a huge volume of books devoted to ethics as an academic discipline, including numerous 'introductions' and 'guides'. However, these are primarily targeted at the philosopher who has already become competent in his/her ability to comprehend philosophical language and modes of expression. In other words, in order to be able to understand these texts one would require significant tertiary education. Alternatively, there are the series of broadly philosophical guides common as popular culture tasters of the field of ethics. These are aimed at a broader audience that does not need a significant depth of detail. However, neither of these areas is of much value to the undergraduate student who is looking for a resource that will provide him/her with the fundamentals that they require to complement their studies. This is where this particular volume will prove indispensible.

In deciding what to include in the contents, we surveyed a large number of university courses, compiled a database of the particular areas of ethics most frequently studied and proceeded to secure contributions for the most popular modules. It is our belief that via this process we have ensured that the most important areas have been covered and that the needs of the majority of students have been addressed.

The writing styles evident in the individual chapters vary greatly in their approach. This, however, is a particular strength of this book. The authors of each of the chapters are experts in the fields that they discuss and many have extensive experience of teaching undergraduate courses in the areas of their contribution. Each philosopher is unique and therefore it is often prudent to adopt a unique approach that is appropriate to the nature of their work. With this in mind, the way in which different individual philosophies and schools of thought are explained has been largely left to the discretion of the authors.

This book may be read continuously from start to finish and will, in itself, provide the reader with a comprehensive guide to the study of ethics. However, it can also be read as individual chapters that stand in isolation from the remainder of the book. In this way, it is possible to 'pick and choose' those areas that are pertinent to one's particular needs at the time of reading. Undergraduates can therefore use it as a resource to support their lectures, assist essay writing and term papers and point them towards further reading materials. One book will never be sufficient to fully accommodate the study of any particular discipline, but this volume will certainly help to establish the fundamentals of ethics as an academic field for the active student.

This volume is the first in a series, which is specifically designed to facilitate the study of undergraduate students in their respective fields. The coming years will see the publication of additional volumes in diverse areas including Animal Ethics, Religious Philosophy and Business Ethics.

Richard H. Corrigan

Mary E. Farrell

Authors and Editors

Owen Anderson

Owen Anderson received his Ph.D in Philosophy from Arizona State University in 2006. Dr. Anderson began teaching at ASU at the West campus in 2002 and is currently working as Assistant Professor in the Philosophy of Religion. His research areas include the Ethics of Belief, World Religions and Common Ground, and the Problem of Evil. His book *Benjamin B. Warfield and Right Reason* examines the Princeton Theological tradition and its roots in Scottish Common Sense Philosophy. He is a regular contributor to *Reviews in Religion and Theology*, and has published articles on Aristotelian and Thomistic concepts of law, and on contemporary natural law theory.

Mark E. Blum

Mark E. Blum is Professor of History at the University of Louisville in Kentucky. He earned his Ph.D. in Austrian history at the University of Pennsylvania. He was Fulbright Fellow at the University of Vienna and Visiting Fellow at Carl Rogers' Center for Studies of the Person in La Jolla, California. He is the author of *The Austro-Marxists 1890-1918: A Psychobiographical Study* (1985) and *Continuity, Quantum, Continuum, and Dialectic: The Foundational Logics of Western Historical Thinking* (2006). His interest in phenomenological history and stylistics stems from his studies of Austrian and German culture.

Treasa Campbell

Treasa Campbell is an IRCHSS Scholar in the Department of Philosophy at Mary Immaculate College, University of Limerick (Ireland). She is a member of the department's ethics subcommittee and lectures on ethics to undergraduate philosophy students. She also teaches ethics to students completing the honours degree in Applied Social Studies in Social Care at Limerick Institute of Technology. She has presented work at national and international conferences, and has published on Hume. Her current research looks at the difficulties surrounding the introduction of empirical facts into normative reasoning.

Andrew Cochrane

Andrew Cochrane teaches part-time for the Department of Philosophy and Inter-Disciplinary Ethics Applied, a Centre for Excellence in Teaching and Learning, at the University of Leeds. His research interests are in a variety of areas within applied ethics, metaethics, and normative ethics, particularly with relation to theories of practical reasons. He is currently working on a number of papers that deal with various problems that theories of morality and objective rationality face in accounting for rational and moral options.

Claudio Corradetti

Claudio Corradetti is a researcher in political philosophy and bioethics at the European Academy and temporary lecturer at the University of Rome 'Tor Vergata'.

Richard H. Corrigan

Richard H. Corrigan gained his Ph.D. from University College Dublin in 2007. He has published numerous books, articles and magazine entries on a wide variety of philosophical areas. His areas of specialisation are religious philosophy, freedom and control, ethics and metaphysics. He is the Chief Editor of *Philosophical Frontiers: A Journal of Emerging Thought* and the Managing Director of the Progressive Frontiers Press.

Mary E. Farrell

Mary Farrell is a lecturer at The University of the West of England, Hartpury College. She is the Assistant Chief Editor of the *Philosophical Frontiers* academic journal. Her current research interests include animal ethics, human-animal interactions, reproductive behaviour and animal welfare. She is currently editing a book on Animal Ethics that will serve as core University reading and is working on several articles for publication.

John Humphrey

J. F. Humphrey is an Assistant Professor with a joint appointment in the North Carolina Agricultural and Technological State University, Department of Liberal Studies and the Division of University Studies. His research interests are in the history of philosophy. He has published articles in ancient philosophy, nineteenth century philosophy, and critical theory.

Joyce Lazier

Joyce Lazier received her Ph.D. from the University of Nebraska. Her dissertation work concentrated on Kant's Duties of Right in the *Metaphysics of Morals*. She has articles and book chapters on Kantian ethics in all stages of publication. Currently, she is teaching at Indiana University, Purdue University Fort Wayne (IPFW) as a Limited Term Lecturer.

Mark Piper

Mark Piper is Assistant Professor of Philosophy at James Madison University. He specializes in normative ethics, especially debates concerning autonomy, well-being, and virtue. He also researches issues in applied ethics, the philosophy of education, and the philosophy of religion (especially the problem of evil). His recent work has focused on the normative warrant for the principle of respect for autonomy and the relation between autonomy and well-being.

Joakim Sandberg

Joakim Sandberg is Research Fellow in Practical Philosophy at University of Gothenburg, Sweden. He is currently also Honorary Research Fellow in Global Ethics at University of Birmingham, UK, and Associate Researcher at the Centre for European Research on Microfinance at Université Libre de Bruxelles, Belgium. His main academic interests are moral philosophy and applied ethics, especially business ethics. Joakim is president of the Philosophy Society at University of Gothenburg and a member of the Gothenburg Animal Research Ethics Committee.

Constantine Sandis

Constantine Sandis is a senior lecturer in philosophy at Oxford Brookes University and NYU in London. He is the editor of *New Essays on Action Explanation* and (with Timothy O' Connor) *A Companion to the Philosophy of Action* (Wiley-Blackwell) and has published widely in the philosophy of action, moral psychology, and the history of ideas (including human-animal relationships).

Sebastian Schleidgen

Sebastian Schleidgen studied philosophy and sociology at the University of Constance (Germany). His research interests mainly are normative ethics, meta-ethics, political philosophy, action and decision theory.

Richa Yadav

Richa Yadav completed her Ph.D in philosophy of mind in IIT, Kanpur, India. Her dissertation focussed on individuation of mental states, with especial reference to the individualist and the non-individualist debate. She now works as an independent scholar. Her research interest lies in ethics, epistemology, and philosophy of language. She is also interested in creative writing.

1

A Brief History of Ethical Thought

Richard H. Corrigan and Mary E. Farrell

1. Introduction

Ethics is the particular school of philosophy that is concerned with questions of morality, and which seeks to establish a solid foundation upon which to prescribe what ought to be done. Often also referred to as moral philosophy, it engages with issues such as rights, obligations, virtue, duty, what is good and bad, justice and what is most beneficial to society. It seeks to establish standards for action that are supported by comprehensive and consistent reasoning. In this introductory chapter, we will not attempt to fully delineate the various forms of ethical thought and practice that dominated different cultures in different epochs; we will rather offer a very brief history of the most important philosophical systems that have influenced our understanding of the moral order.

2. Early Greek Philosophy

Socrates (470 – 439 BC) and Plato (427 – 347 BC)

Ethics, as a systematic philosophical pursuit, first emerged in ancient Greece in the teachings of Socrates (470-399 BC), a figure who proved hugely influential in the shaping of ethics – right to the present day. Our knowledge of the thought of Socrates is derived from the dialogues of his greatest student – Plato. Plato presents us with two contrasting depictions of Socrates. In the aporetic dialogues Socrates himself claims no knowledge of what it is to be ethical, and proceeds to ask the other protagonists probing questions that seek to uncover moral truths (for example in the *Apology*, *Charmides*, *Laches*, *Crito*, *Euthydemus*, and *Euthyphro*). Often, in these texts, the solutions offered to key questions are tentative and indecisive. However, in the didactic dialogues, we are confronted with a character that is knowledgeable and resolute, offering insight and deduction (see for example the *Republic*, *Phaedo*, and *Phaedrus*). Various scholars have expounded theories about which texts most aptly reflect views of the historical personage, but here we will focus on what has commonly become known as Socratic ethics, which is an admixture of the aporetic, didactic and mixed texts (which include the *Protagoras*, *Meno*, and *Gorgias*).

The Socratic system is intellectualist – moral practice is completely dependant upon a species of theoretical knowledge. The implication is that it is fundamentally a cognitive state that motivates any action. If you have knowledge of that which is good you will proceed to do it, and if you are lacking in this knowledge and do what is bad it is because you mistakenly believe your action to be good. In order to act virtuously one must have knowledge of virtue itself. Socrates believed that the ultimate object of human pursuit is lasting happiness (eudaimonia), and consequently it is a fundamental human desire. He further believed that the only means of achieving it is through virtue. He encouraged people to focus on their own personal development rather than the accumulation of material riches and the lure of fame. Everyone ultimately desires to be happy and no one would deliberately deprive themselves of that which they want the most. If a person does not achieve happiness, it is because he has failed to recognize the means of attaining it. Corruption and evil are not the products of deliberate intention, but are rather the result of ignorance, as no one would knowingly desire what is bad (*Meno*, 78a-b and *Protagoras*, 258c-d). By 'bad' he intends in this context those things that are harmful to the subject. Ignorance is fundamentally rooted in error, and so knowledge is what is necessary to ensure that good prospers. All vices are forms of ignorance and knowledge of what is good is a form of virtue. The ultimate conclusion is that virtue is sufficient for happiness (*Euthydemus*), and that virtue always corresponds to just action.

Aristotle (384-322 BC)

Aristotle was perhaps the greatest and most influential of Plato's students. His work was one of the first attempts to construct a comprehensive system of philosophy, and the impact of his writings have firmly established him as one of the most important founders of Western thought. He dedicated himself to establishing the conditions that would allow us to attribute moral responsibility to individual agents, the nature of vice and virtue and the path that would lead to lasting happiness. The most complete acocunt of his ethical thought is to be found in his *Nicomachean Ethics*.

For Aristotle, happiness or *eudaimonia* meant human flourishing – a state in which the individual thrives, which he describes as 'living well and doing well.' This happiness is the principal object of desire of our rational natures. The happiness in question should not be confused with an emotional state – it is rather concerned with the matter of doing well, which can be objectively established.

Moreover, it is concerned with the flourishing of the soul rather than the thriving of the body. Happiness, so understood, is not a static state – it is rather an activity of the soul that conforms with virtue.

Virtues, simply explained, are those attributes of character that promote eudaimonia. Virtues are of two distinct varieties: intellectual, which involve the rational or intellectual part of the soul, and moral, which involve the rational and appetitive elements of the soul. To be an ethical individual requires that the appetitive passions and desires be under the control of the intellect. A virtue is the perfectly mediated avoidance of extremes (although Aristotle did not claim that the ideal mean was mathematically calculable). Thus, the virtue of bravery would lie between the deficiency of cowardice and the excess of rashness. Virtues are not inherent in the individual but are acquired through a process of habituation. Moral virtues cannot be obtained merely through instruction, as their acquisition requires practice. Part of the process of establishing moral virtue requires the imitation of those that we deem to be of noble character – through the practice of those traits that we recognise as superior, virtue will eventually become entrenched in our nature and become evident in our activities.

Aristotelian ethics differs from many modern moral theories in one essential respect. His intention is not to prescribe how one should act when confronted with a particular concrete situation; it is rather to build virtuous character so that the ultimate end (*eudaimonia*) of the individual might be achieved.

3. Later Greek and Roman Philosophy

Democritus (C. 460 – 370 BC)

It is difficult for us to construct an exact theory of ethics from our extant knowledge of the writings of Democritus because most of what has survived is fragmentary and non-systematic. However, there is common consensus on a number of themes that can be confidently attributed to him. It appears that he was perhaps the first proponent of a form of enlightened hedonistic ethics (edone – pleasure). He believed that the good consisted in an internal state of mind rather than in some external metaphysical principle or reality. He refers to the good in many terms including euthymia, which can be translated as 'cheerfulness'. A continually cheerful and contented disposition was considered to be the greatest good for man and thereby led to the greatest happiness. The way to attain this personal temperament is through the pursuit of virtue, which is a means to freeing ourselves from slavery to external goods by moderating our desires. Virtue, at least in part, consists in the ability to discriminate between those pleasures which are beneficial and worthy of pursuit, and those that are harmful and should be avoided. Therefore, the means to leading a virtuous and moral life was grounded in the moderation and appropriate direction of desire. Living an ethical life was likened to the art employed by the physician when caring for the body, but its object lay in caring for the soul (Vlastos, 1975, 386-94). Because most of what we know of the thought of Democritus is found in non-systematized platitudes this is perhaps the best account we can construct of his theories.

Diogenes (412 – 323 BC)

The Cynic school was founded in Athens in approximately 400 B.C. by Antisthenes and continued until roughly 200 B. C. Although it had its origins in the thought of Socrates regarding the role of moderation and freedom from material pleasures, it greatly reinterpreted the significance of the insights of Socratic ethics. The Cynics rejected the conventions of 'polite society' and exploited the methods of the Sophists for their personal goal – showing contempt for common conceptions of knowledge, decency and refinement.

Diogenes is perhaps the most famous of the Cynics due to the way in which he lived his private life and conducted himself in public. He is reported to have taken as his permanent residence a wine jar, and spent a considerable amount of his time in the streets of Athens looking for one 'uncorrupted man'. Unfortunately, it is principally through the reports of others that we know the theories of the Cynics, as little of their writings have survived (in those few cases where they did in fact set their ideas down for posterity). The lifestyle of Diogenes is illustrative of his principal contention – that a life lived in accordance with nature was far superior to that which assimilated to current convention. He believed that the natural life was one of simplicity and happiness, where striving was minimized and the pursuit of superfluous (and evil) luxury was unnecessary. He was not so foolish as to believe that the transition was an easy one, but he did believe that with sufficient effort and training it was achievable.

Diogenes counselled denial of those things that society would have us believe are good, so that a state of detached happiness can be achieved. Such a simple and natural state, free from petty concerns, was the ideal state for virtue to flourish. Unfortunately, he leaves us with no explicit account of virtue, although he did advise pursuit of the virtuous life. The ethical life was therefore one of virtue, in which the pursuits of society were denied in favor of the happiness of simplicity, and freedom from strife. Diogenes taught that we should satisfy the simple needs of our desires and instincts. We will soon see how this particular strand of his thought was later taken up and developed by the Epicureans.

The development of the ideas of the Cynic school has left it open to accusations of haughtiness, contempt for the laws of men and outright arrogance. However, it is not unreasonable to counter that the principle endeavor of the Cynics was to undermine the conventions of a society which they perceived as corrupt and to challenge the prevailing notions of goodness and justice.

Epicurus (341-270)

Epicurus was convinced that the principle purpose of life was the pursuit of personal happiness. By 'happiness' he intended something completely in contrast to the definitions offered by many of his predecessors. Happiness was not conceived of as eudaimonia in the Aristotelian sense, but rather as pleasure itself. It is therefore not a transcendent pleasure of the soul or mind, but rather a pleasure particular to our condition as embodied individuals – the only type of pleasure that Epicurus believed humanity could attain in this life. However, he did not condone a life that lacked virtue for he believed that it is through virtue that the most pleasurable state could be achieved – a state of being that was free from physical pain and mental stress or anxiety. Thus, virtue leads to a persevering state of tranquility – and it is this state that should be the ultimate object of human pursuit. Virtue is not conceived as an end-in-itself but rather as a means to an end – the end of pleasure. Virtue should be considered as a medicine that we employ for no other reason than to further our health, and a state of health is a life of pleasure. The greatest virtue for Epicurus is prudence, for it is through prudence that we achieve our ultimate good – excess leads to anxiety and pain.

4. The Stoics

The Stoic school, founded by Zeno of Cittium (350-258 BC) believed that good should be always understood in terms of virtue. In this instance 'virtue' should be understood as identical to 'moral virtue' – which include ideals such as justice, courage, moderation and prudence. However, the highest purpose of human pursuit is not the philosophical contemplation of Plato, but is rooted in actual practice. Thus, virtue and its application is central to the attainment of the happy life, which is the good life - the morally superior life. Zeno and his disciples believed that man should live in accordance with nature. However, the nature in question is not that of the particular nature of man, but rather the eternal divine law which is evident in the processes of the natural world. Therefore, for man to be happy he must exercise his reason in order to live in accord with the divine will. This is a duty from which nobody is exempt.

Reason leads to virtue, and only that which is ultimately rational can have the elements of harmony and order which are essential features of goodness. Vice, or evil, becomes manifest when there is a rejection of reason. Virtue and vice are polar opposites and the existence of either one in a single instance excludes the possibility of the existence of the other in the same occurrence. Virtue is demonstrated in action and all actions are deemed either good or bad. Virtue and vice do not occur in various degrees, and cannot be increased or decreased – therefore it does not make sense to claim that one action is more or less virtuous than another. Zeno was convinced that even mental states, desires and impulses that are not regulated by reason are immoral and give rise to vice – which usually takes the form of activity that stems from one or more of the negative emotions: desire, fear, pleasure and pain. The only way to ensure correct moral living is to eradicate all error and substitute in its place the correct exercise of reason.

As the exercise of virtue gives rise to happiness, and as bodily and material goods are not essential to virtue, the pursuit of physical pleasures are not necessary for the moral, happy life. Nevertheless, the Stoics differed from the Cynics in that they did not believe that material goods and social conventions should be treated with scorn – they merely believed that such pursuits are in no way constitutive of the good. Passion and physical affectations are not desirous and the enlightened and moral man is independent of them. As the divine law is discerned through reason, this system has become known as rational deontologism (duty based on reason).

5. The Skeptics

Pyrrho (C. 360 – 270 BC)

The classical Greek philosopher Pyrrho is generally acknowledged as the father of the first school of Skepticism, known as Pyrrhonism, which was established by Aenesidemus in the first century B.C. The skepticism of Pyrrho had a particularly ethical focus and was devoted, like the other systems of his peers, to discovering the path to attaining happiness. His theory was that there was no ultimate truth to be found through philosophy, and that therefore all philosophical systems were ultimately and equally false. If there is an underlying truth to things then it cannot be acquired through a process of rational investigation and postulation.

The core of Pyrrho's theory is kernelized in the idea of acatalepsia, which asserts that at the core of all things is incomprehensibility, and that all scientific and philosophical claims to truth are nothing more than deception and verisimilitude. Unlike the Stoics, who as we have seen were convinced that a divine order could be apprehended in the nature of things, the Skeptics were convinced that all claims to truth were nothing more than smoke and mirrors. In light of this fact the Skeptics proposed that we should maintain an attitude of doubt. This is not just because they held that the senses could be deceptive, but also because they contended that in and of themselves things are never more one thing than another – more beautiful than ugly, more good than bad, more bright than dark and so forth. The wise man therefore commits himself to epoche; abstaining from judging the nature of reality. This is also the foundation of happiness, for we can only be happy if we achieve a state of complacency that frees us from the turmoil of futile endeavors. When we accept that we can never know the truth this will bring with it a happy calm. When we apply their ideas explicity to ethics we can see that the Skeptics have a critical epistemological view about what constitutes knowledge and the justification of belief – this in turn leads to doubt about the very existence of moral knowledge or justified moral belief.

6. Christian Ethics: A New Beginning

Augustine (384 – 386)

Augustine believed that man's primary focus should be on achieving ultimate happiness, the summum bonum. However, he was convinced that the only way in which this can be accomplished is through the active love of God, the ultimate exemplification of all moral virtue. His philosophy is an exercise in the reinterpretation of the idea of eudaimonia within the framework of Christian theology. The free will of mankind is best exercised when it is focused on the love of God, and true virtue is achieved when we live rightly in the eyes of the Almighty. But due to the deviant activity of our forebears (the Fall of Adam and Eve) and the negative effect it had on their progeny, we are no longer capable of virtuous intention and action without assistance. We therefore must rely on the merciful beneficence of God to assist our endeavors through the unwarranted gift of grace (we do not deserve to be saved). Due to our finitude and fallen nature, we are incapable of perceiving moral principles with any significant degree of certitude and therefore all truths to which we are privy are a consequence of the illuminating power of God.

In order to be an ethical individual we are dependent on revealed knowledge, which he contended was only possible through Christianity and its Church, which is the sole means of procuring revealed truth. To be an ethical individual requires one opening oneself to the divine law that is revealed in conscience and the teachings of the Church, and thereby receive God's saving grace. Man's sinful nature can be overcome by the mercy of the divine which is channeled through the individual's inner life including his attitudes, motivations and intentions. However, as was revealed in Augustine's refutation of the teachings of the heretical monk Pelagius and his followers, man does not have the capacity to save himself – to become moral and righteous through his own power; God alone chooses who will benefit from grace, who will be chosen as the elect (the saved) and who will be left to the deserved fate of sinners.

Aquinas (1225 – 1274)

Aquinas was inspired by the ideas of Aristotle and the Stoics and sought to use their insights to provide a grounding for Christian morality. In his monumental *Summa Theologiae* he argued that the good could be equated to the correct exercise of rationality. The world is a place of order, meaning and purpose and through the correct application of our faculty of reason we can discern the role that we have been ordained (by God) to play in it. This is what he defined as our 'final cause' (a term borrowed from Aristotelian metaphysics), or our ultimate purpose. Once we have apprehended our final cause it is then possible to correctly deduce the way in which we should act in order to be moral.

Aquinas ethical system makes use of a concept called Natural Law. Natural Law stems from the idea that God is the ultimate being and creator of the world. In the process of his creative act he established within the world an order and meaning that is indicative of his divine will. Given that the world is a creation with an established purpose, mankind should be able through the application of reason to judge how to fulfill that purpose. Acts that compliment this purpose correspond to ethical action. This is not an elitist system, as the purpose of the universe is there to be observed by anyone who has a mind to do so. It is God's will that is of absolute importance. Given that man can discover what that will consists in he must take complete responsibility for acting in accordance with it, or for failing to do so.

7. 1500s and 1600s

Thomas Hobbes (1588 – 1679)

Hobbes postulated that mankind originally existed in a primitive condition which has become known as 'The State of Nature' (status naturae). This state was man's primordial situation before the advent of society. In this natural state man was unfettered in his freedom and could act in any way that pleased him. There were no universal rights and each individual was entitled to anything that he could successfully secure for himself. From this circumstance arose a condition of continual strife in which everyone was constantly at war with everyone else in the pursuit of their own interests and the preservation of their possessions. Obviously, this state of nature was far from satisfactory and man was in constant fear that he would lose everything that he had possessed, including his life. It was therefore rational to abandon this state in favour of something more stable and enduring. On this basis, it was commonly agreed that each individual would be subject to a common ruler in exchange for fundamental rights to property and protection. This is what has become known as Hobbes' 'Social Contract' – a binding agreement that is implicitly or explicitly consented to by all the constituent members of a state. It is solely the ruler of the state that dictates what is to be deemed good or evil. It is only in relation to the decrees of the ruler that there is a significant distinction established between good and evil which has any legitimate claim to universalisation for the members of the state.

Hobbes has been described as a 'psychological egoist' as he holds that human nature is fundamentally selfish and self-motivated. In its most extreme form psychological egoism holds that people cannot do other than act in their own self-interests and any endeavour to claim altruistic moral action is an attempt to disguise the true motivation of the act.

Baruch Spinoza (1632-1677)

Spinoza was an ethical relativist. He held that moral concepts such as good and evil have no intrinsic value and that all value is relative to the particular individual. Thus, traditional notions of moral value are nothing more than reflections of what was good or bad for humans during particular epochs. He was also a pantheistic monist, in that he held that there was no dualism between God and the world (they were essentially the same – a single entity).

Spinoza believed in a deterministic universe in which the idea of contingency was a mere fabrication. All things progress along causally predetermined lines and there was no element of chance or randomness. Everything that comes about is the product of its essential nature coupled with the laws of Nature/God. Therefore, human free will is an impossibility. Spinoza's was a pantheistic metaphysics in which all things are but part of a single infinite substance. It follows that man is not an independent substance composed of body and soul, but is rather a mode of the attributes of God – where spirit is a mode of thought and body a mode of extension.

Reality in itself is perfection and all judgments regarding our interpretations of it, be they good or bad, suffer from our inability to fully conceive the complete nature of things. It is not that human beings are incapable of comprehending the nature of cause and effect; it is rather that we are limited in our capacity to see the greater complex of which any occurrence is but an infinitesimal part. Science is not yet developed to an extent where the whole mechanism of the world can be empirically conceived.

Spinoza's ethical theory was devoted to the question of how perfect happiness can be achieved. Given that we are part of a determined world, it follows that Spinoza's ethical theory is one that is devoted to the idea of liberation – and this liberation is closely related to the idea of the promotion and nurturing of reason. The liberation in question is liberation from our passions, where he understood the passions as a mode of being in which man is passive in his relation to things. It is as a consequence of passion that man believes that there is a multiplicity of discrete human beings upon which he can act and exert control. However, this is an error as all things are not in opposition and separate to man, because they are all held in relation to the eternal – God. When we come to this realization we become liberated from the passions and can be more active in the moral sphere.

Spinoza was not committed to delineating the nature of morality, or to defining the basis of moral duty, he was much more interested in what constituted the ideal human existence. He believed that it was only the 'Free Man' that was capable of such a life, as he is an individual that is guided by reason rather than being held in the thrall of the passions. For Spinoza, the highest form of virtue is the intellectual love of knowledge of God, Nature and the world in which we find ourselves (all manifestation of one holistic being). It is through intuition that we come to know that all things are unified in the infinite essence of God. When we come to realize that we are but manifestations of an aspect of God, in a pantheistic sense, we can come to a perfect moral state. This is achieved through knowledge that the love we have for God will be returned - for the love of God for man, and the love of man for God, is nothing more than the love of God for himself.

8. 1700s

Immanuel Kant (1724 – 1804)

The moral philosophy of Kant caused a huge shift in the focus and direction of ethics and exerted an influende that is still evident today. Central to his theory of ethics is the principle of duty. Therefore, Kant's ethics are deontological (duty based). He proposed that we have certain inalienable duties to oneself and others, such as promise keeping. In order to ensure that one is acting in the correct moral way, one must act from one's sense of duty (deon). It is better, according to Kant, to act from a sense of moral duty than it is to act solely because it brings one a sense of pleasure to act morally.

However, in his consideration of practical reason, he discovered a more fundamental universal, categorical moral law that encompassed all particular instances of duty. He believed that this principle must be a priori - discovered exclusively through a process of philosophical reasoning without recourse to the external world. He believed that through the exercise of reason alone one could come to apprehend this principle as self-evident and fully applicable in all circumstances. He called this principle the 'categorical imperative'. A categorical imperative differs significantly from a hypothetical imperative in that the latter always involves some particular personal desire that we harbor. Thus, the proposition 'If you want to be a good ethicist, you ought to learn the history of ethics' is a hypothetical imperative, whereas a categorical imperative is a universal maxim that transcends any particular person's desire. Thus, 'You ought not to X' is without exception and does not take into consideration any specific circumstances. Moral commands are always unconditional and not subject to mitigating qualifications.

Kant proposes at least four formulations of the categorical imperative, but the most influential of these are perhaps the following (i) treat all people as ends in themselves, and not merely as means to an end (treat people as though they have inherent value which is not dependant on your personal projects) (ii) act such that you would have that action apply as a universal law (never perform an action that you would not have all others perform also). Through the pursuit and application of the categorical imperative we strive to attain the highest good. The highest good is a world that consists in maximal virtue and maximal happiness. For Kant, maximal virtue and maximal happiness are co-dependent. Happiness is only good when it is accompanied by the appropriate degree of virtue, and virtue – although unconditionally good – can never fill the void of a lack of happiness.

9. 1800s

John Stuart Mill (1806 – 1873)

Mill's is one of the most popular formulations of utilitarianism. Utilitarianism is an ethical system that asserts that the moral worth of any action can be evaluated in terms of its utility (or usefulness) in providing happiness or pleasure (versus suffering or pain) for the greatest number of human beings. Thus, it is a form of consequentialism, which means that its principal ethical focus is on the direct and indirect consequences that any particular action gives rise to.

Mill's argument is based on the belief that each individual desires his own personal happiness. The 'general happiness' is then the sum of each of the discrete ends that constitute each individual's personal happiness. It can therefore be postulated that the general happiness is what is most desired by everyone, and that this provides a standard against which individual moral actions can be assessed.

Mill went further than his utilitarian predecessor Bentham, in claiming that it was not just the quantity of happiness produced by an action that had to be taken into moral consideration, but also the quality of the resultant happiness/pleasure. He contended that the intellectual and moral pleasures are superior to the more base physical pleasures. He proceeded to qualify two distinct categories of pleasure – higher and lower. Higher pleasures include mental, aesthetic and moral pleasures and lower all other forms of pleasure. Mill is adamant that higher pleasures should be accepted as superior to lower pleasures purely in virtue of their nature and the faculties that they involve. Thus, when calculating the aggregate sum of pleasure that will be derived from a particular action the higher pleasures must be given greater weight in the assessment than their inferior counterparts. Exactly how this calculation can be successfully made however is a matter that has given rise to much contention. Finally, Mill held a theory of association which theorized that actions which have been repeatedly found to give rise to significant pleasurable or painful consequences have been generally endorsed as being good or bad respectively. After a time, we no longer give actual consideration to the agreeable or disagreeable results of an action and come to believe that it is in fact good or bad in itself.

Friedrich Nietzsche (1844 – 1900)

Nietzsche was an outspoken critic of the moral systems that prevailed in his day

– Christianity, Kantianism and Utilitarianism. He believed that exceptional men of creativity and power are exempt from the conventional dictates of the moral law. He held that the concept of goodness was originally associated with power and position, where a man endowed with these attributes acted on his personal inclinations and whatever proclivity he possessed was good. Those who were oppressed and subjugated were by comparison weak, coarse and inferior – which Nietzsche held to be 'bad'. These were the majority of the public that comprised the proletariat. Those who were ignoble envied and hated those of superior position and rank and it was due to this resentment that moral distinctions were originally born. They came to associate the characteristics displayed by their superiors as morally 'bad' and their own obsequious behaviors as morally 'good'. Thus, we had the emergence of what Nietzsche called the master-slave morality. Traits that were common to the base herd which furthered their prospects of survival such as meekness, obedience and humility were generally considered morally laudable. However, Nietzsche held that these supposed 'virtues' were nothing more than a deceptive mask to cover weakness and cowardice. It follows that in his ideology the entire moral system needed to be re-evaluated, as it was nothing more than the vehicle of deception.

The intellectual superiority of the noble should not be subject to the prevailing ideas of good and evil that have been established through a dubious process by the ignoble proletariat. There is no transcendent or binding moral order to which these men are universally subject. The 'over-man' or 'super-man', as the idea has been frequently translated, is his own end and creates his own morality. Those with a 'slave mentality' must be obliterated. The super-man is not a product of breeding or bloodline, but is rather an intellectual aristocrat that has a 'will to power' – who is willing to emancipate himself from conventional understandings of the moral order, to stand independently and to do as he sees fit. It should be noted that Nietzsche did not endorse a complete abandonment of all traditional morality – he believed that it was suited to the herd and was useful in some sense to them in appropriating their lives. However, he encouraged those of exception to not be ashamed of their individuality and unique powers and to free themselves from moral constraints that could only be detrimental to their creativity – they should therefore follow their own 'inner law'.

Karl Marx (1818 – 1883)

It is difficult to exactly define what Marx's particular views on ethics might have been as there is a general tendency to believe that he rejected the concept of morality and ethics on the basis that the communism that he endorsed would obviate both. There can be no doubt that Marx wished to escape from what he called the 'impotence' of many of the moral systems that dominated his era. In essence, Marx's ethical method was a restrained rejection of the liberal thesis that morality is grounded in suppressing natural desires that are self-serving and egotistical. He believed that all moral and ethical concepts were merely the product of historical, social and economic conditions and their effect on men. However, these conditions are not static and therefore the ideas associated with them are also subject to change. Therefore, the idea of an eternal, divine or universally binding moral code is a fabrication, as each generation modifies its ideals in relation to its factual circumstances.

We will continue by examining what has become known as Marxist Ethics, which are grounded in his thought but have been expanded by his successors. Marxism believes in a concept called 'class morality'. This morality is grounded in the idea that all things are in flux and that history will ultimately ensure the abolition of class discrimination and distinction. This destruction will make way for a classless society in which each individual is considered equal. An act is considered moral if it facilitates or directly assists this process. The 'Old Moralities' of traditional philosophy have merely provided a means for the bourgeoisie to oppress the proletariat and thereby ensure their own personal position of privilege and power in society. The idea of religion has also become a tool that is utilized towards this end and Christian ethics is a means through which the rich and advantaged can control the working class who live in poverty. Religion is an 'opiate' that makes the suppressed malleable by justifying the oppressive and inhumane regime in the name of God – a source of supposed ultimate justification. Marxist ethics is therefore not a normative system that proscribes particular actions in particular situations, it is rather a theory regarding the beneficial evolution of humanity towards the end of individual flourishing.

10. 1900s

G. E. Moore (1873 – 1958)

Moore was an 'Ethical Non-Naturalist' which means that he believed that one could not define morality in terms of any natural phenomena. Thus, function and performance are not sufficient justifications for an assertion that something is 'good' or 'bad'. Moore takes these terms to be descriptors that we attribute to particular objects and actions, and are not actually to be found residing in the objects or actions themselves. What follows is the assertion that an ethical statement cannot be reduced to non-ethical terms. Any attempt at such a reduction suffers from what Moore calls the 'naturalistic fallacy'. This fallacy occurs when we state facts and then assume an essential correlation to moral values. This is a mistake frequently made by ethicists, but for which they can give no justificatory grounding. This is an argument that is redolent of David Hume who concurred that a moral term like 'good' is properly basic and cannot be reduced to any simpler terms.

Moore went on to claim that since moral terms refer to things that cannot be further defined, they can be recognized by us through the faculty of intuition and in this way we can comprehend and appropriately utilize them. It follows that the truth or falsity of moral judgments are entirely self-evident. Moore likened our ability to intuit moral values to our ability to recognize the colour yellow. We all have an idea of the meaning of the word, yet we cannot reduce it or explain it without reference to the colour itself – however, this does not mean that the word lackd content or cannot be correctly employed.

A. J. Ayer (1910 - 1989)

Ayer was a proponent of what has become known as 'Emotivism'. He was convinced that are no moral truths that can be definitively known and therefore it is impossible to verify moral propositions. From this he concludes that moral propositions lack cognitive content and significance. He believed that there is a relation between our motivations and feelings and the supposedly moral utterances that we issue when faced with particular situations. From this connection he theorized that our moral utterances are nothing more than an expression of our feelings – when we state them we are effectively 'emoting'.

He was however careful to qualify that our utterances are not descriptions of our feelings, which would allow for subjective truth-evaluation, but are rather an expression of positive or negative feelings about a particular state of affairs. Thus when we say 'It is wrong to kill the innocent' we are in essence actually expressing a negative feeling that we harbor regarding the killing of those who do not deserve it. Similarly, all statements of moral approbation are mere expressions of positive feelings regarding the state of affairs involved. Ayer later went on to believe that our emotive moral utterances also contained a prescriptive component. Thus, when we say 'Torture is wrong' we are not only expressing our own emotional reaction to the idea, but are also implicitly encouraging and expecting others to share our feelings and to govern their actions accordingly.

Jean-Paul Sartre (1905 – 1980)

Sartre was an existentialist (emphasized freedom and personal responsibility) and a phenomenologist (studied the structure of our consciousness from the first-person point of view). Sartre employed phenomenology to investigate the issue of ethics. Freud had postulated that the unconscious mind has a huge influence on human consciousness and that this is a mitigating factor when considering certain types of behavior. This is because the unconscious is not under the direct control of the individual and is the product of various environmental and structural factors. Thus, Freud maintained that our psychological constitution provided the potential for being excused from certain deviant behaviors. Sartre vehemently refuted this and developed a theory of the ego which claimed that it is not prior to consciousness and experience in the world, but is in fact produced by them in conjunction with our intentional reactions. Thus, there is no antecedent ego that determines the particular actions of the individual. Man must accept full responsibility for all that he does – he is condemned to be free. His choices are what constitutes the individual that he becomes and he has the power of governance over those choices. Of course Sartre is not so naïve as to deny that there are factual constraints on our particular circumstance in any situation, but he claims that we are always free to make a choice regarding how we interpret an occurrence. Thus, we can always choose to surrender to the idea that our facticity determines us completely and deny responsibility for who we are and what we do. This is what Sartre calls living in 'bad faith' – it is a refusal to live authentically – to live as though we have freedom and responsibility in every situation.

Existentialism was not concerned with developing a normative ethics, but was far more concerned with the moral value of self-making and authentic existence. Generally speaking, existentialists believe that conventional values are groundless and are merely the product of particular human projects in an indifferent and meaningless world. We often feel an anxiety when confronted with the true nature of reality, the absurdity of the world. However, the idea of value is necessary for the completion of any human project (for if there was no concept of value there would be no point) and it is through the notions of free personal commitment and engagement that we create a moral meaning that is relevant to us.

11. Present Day

Peter Singer (1946 -)

Singer is a utilitarian, who believes that the morally superior action is that which provides 'the greatest good for the greatest number'. He is best known for his writings in the field of applied ethics. He has expanded on Bentham's and Mill's ideas regarding the most effective formulation of the principle of utility. He believes that the suffering of individuals is one of the most important factors that needs to be considered when considering the greatest good.

He popularised the idea of 'speciesism' (originally proposed by Richard D. Ryder), which is defined as the practice of giving the interests of humans preference over similar interests of other beings. He has likened the moral indefensibility of speciesism to that of sexism or racism and has been credited with the founding the modern day animal rights movement. However, he does not believe that all individuals are equally valuable and some of his most controversial work centres on his definition of two different classes of life: 'persons' and 'nonpersons'. For him, personhood is integrally linked to essential cognitive capabilities including the capacity to feel, self awareness and the ability to imagine a future. Singer believes that all those who qualify as persons, be they human or not, have an approximately equal moral status and are morally more significant than non-persons.

Singer's theses regarding the quality of life in the face of suffering, and the moral status of individuals with limited cognitive capacities, has led to the exposition of several controversial arguments. Singer has always kept a strong commitment to utilitarianism and believes that animals may be used for various purposes as long as they conform to utilitarian principles and this view has brought him into conflict with some proponents of animal rights. He proposes that if an experiment is for the greater good, then animals may be used (as this conforms to his principle of utility), but that researchers should also be prepared to carry out their experiments on humans that are at a similar mental level to the animals that would be used. He also argues that people should be allowed to die with dignity if their suffering warrants it but does distinguish between voluntary, involuntary, or non-voluntary euthanasia. He further states that arguments for or against abortion should be based on a utilitarian calculation which weighs the preferences of a mother against the preferences of the foetus. He believes that although a foetus can suffer, it lacks the ability to plan and anticipate its future and therefore has no preferences. Therefore, he concludest that the choice should be left to the mother.

He has also considered the issue of poverty and has highlighted the fact that it is morally indefensible for some people to live in rich abundance while others live in absolute deprivation. He argues this on the basis that we can provide for those most in need without sacrificing anything of comparable moral significance.

12. Conclusion

It is at this juncture in the history of ethics that we will finish our current discussion. The following chapters will further delineate many of the ethical positions briefly outlined here. They will also investigate ethical theories that have sought to use the insights of the philosophers we have discussed, through reformulation or refutation. Once again we would briefly comment that the above account is concise and lacks critical analysis and development (as this was not the intention of this introductory chapter). Each of the philosophers had much more to say on ethical issues than it has been possible to recount here. We would therefore encourage readers to examine the bibliography and to pursue greater exploration of the ideas outlined. The history of ethical philosophy constantly expands with the progression of time. Not only do new thinkers add their theories to the sum of knowledge, but new modes of interpretation of previous philosophers also emerge and add to the way in which we think about ethics, its role and validity.

BIBLIOGRAPHY

Ashby, W. A. and Ashby, W. (1997). *A Comprehensive History of Western Ethics: What do we Believe?* Amherst, Prometheus.

Banner, M. (2009). *Christian Ethics: A Brief History.* Oxford, Wiley-Blackwell.

Becker, L. C. and Becker, C. B. (eds.) (2003). *A History of Western Ethics (Second Edition).* New York, Routledge.

Cahn, S. M., and Markie, P. (2002). E*thics: History, Theory, and Contemporary Issues (Second Edition).* New York, Oxford University Press.

Cavalier, R. J., Gouinlock, J., and Sterba, J. P. (eds.) (1989). *Ethics in the History of Western Philosophy.* New York, St. Martin's Press.

Copleston, F. (2003). *History of Philosophy: Logical Positivism and Existentialism.* London, Continuum.

Kain, P. J. (1991). *Marx and Ethics.* Oxford, Clarendon Press.

Klemke, E. D. (1999). *Defense of Realism: Reflections on the Metaphysics of G. E. Moore.* New York, Humanity Books.

Long, A. A. (2006). *From Epicurus to Epictetus: Studies in Hellenistic and Roman Philosophy.* Oxford, Clarendon Press.

May, S. (2003). *Nietzsche's Ethics and his War on 'Morality'*. Oxford, Oxford University Press.

Morrisson, R. (ed.) (2010). *The Cambridge Companion to Socrates*. Cambridge, Cambridge University Press.

Parkinson, G. H. R. (2003). *The Renaissance and Seventeenth Century Rationalism*. Oxford, Routledge.

Plato. (Cooper, J. M. ed.) (1997). *Complete Works*. Cambridge (MA). Hackett Publishing.

Sharples, R. W. (1996). *Stoics, Epicureans and Sceptics: Introduction to Hellenistic Philosophy*. Oxford, Routledge.

Singer, P. (2001). *Animal Liberation (2nd Edition)*. New York, Eco Press Books.

West, H. R. (2003). *An Introduction to Mill's Utilitarian Ethics*. Cambridge, Cambridge University Press.

Wood, A. W. (2007). *Kantian Ethics*. Cambridge, Cambridge University Press.

Wright, M. R. (2009). *Introducing Greek Philosophy*. Durham, Acumen.

2

Animal Ethics

Constantine Sandis

1. Introduction

The history of Western thought has been cruel to non-human animals (from here onwards 'animals'[1]), for the most part allotting them a relatively low status, both cognitively and ethically. Some philosophers, possibly including Descartes (but see Baker and Morris 1993 and 1649 letter referred to in § 3 below), have even insisted that animals are non-conscious machines, incapable of any sensation whatsoever, let alone perception, belief, emotion, or reason. Most,

---

1   The view that biological classification is to some extent interest-dependent is easily applicable to the issue of human-animal relationships. Wishing to emphasise the similarities between humans and (other) higher order animals, we may choose to do so by saying that human beings are animals too. If by contrast we wish to highlight general dissimilarities between humans and (other) higher order animals - perhaps while also emphasising similarities between the latter and lower order animals - we might find it more effective to do so by reserving the term 'animal' for non-human creatures. Yet a person who at one time takes the first approach and at another the second need not be contradicting herself. Having said this, I believe that Derrida was right to suspect any attempt to us the catch-all term for purposes of delineation: 'A critical uneasiness will persist;in fact a bone of contention will be incessantly repeated throughout everything that I wish to develop. It would be aimed in the first place, once again, at the usage, in the singular,of a notion as general as "the Animal," as if all nonhuman living things could be grouped without the common sense of this "commonplace," the Animal, whatever the abyssal differences and structural limits that separate,in the very essence of their being, all "animals," a name that we would therefore be advised, to begin with, to keep within quotation marks. Confined within this catch-all concept, within this vast encampment of the animal, in this general singular, within the strict enclosure of this definite article ("the Animal" and not "animals"), as in a virgin forest, a zoo, a hunting or fishing ground, a paddock or an abattoir, a space of domestication, are all the living things that man does not recognize as his fellows, his neighbors, or his brothers. And that is so in spite of the infinite space that separates the lizard from the dog, the protozoon from the dolphin, the shark from the lamb, the parrot from the chimpanzee, the camel from the eagle, the squirrel from the tiger or the elephant from the cat, the ant from the silkworm or the hedgehog from the echidna. I interrupt my nomenclature and call Noah to help insure that no one gets left on the ark.' (Derrida 2002:402; Cf. Tyler: forthcoming).

however, are happy to allow that animals feel pain, though they stop short of attributing any kind of rationality to them, usually on the grounds that they lack any sophisticated form of language. This has potential ethical consequences, for according to many popular Kantian systems of ethics, if a being is to be of moral concern, it is *necessary* for it to possess rationality. Against this view, utilitarians such as Jeremy Bentham and Peter Singer have argued that sentience is *sufficient* to render animals worthy of moral consideration. This has lead to the recent movement of animal liberation whose aim is to defend the interests of animals. Some of its proponents go as far as to talk of animal rights (for example, the right to a peaceful life), yet on the whole the West continues to believe that some animals are more equal than others, with exceptions occasionally being made only in cases of extreme cruelty to animals for the sake of 'pure' luxury or 'mere' entertainment: witness the increasing establishment resistance to the fur-trade industry and fox hunting.

In much Eastern thought, by contrast, the principle of non-injury to *all* living creatures ('*Ahimsa*') has long been widespread among many religions and philosophies such as Buddhism, Hinduism, and Jainism. The relation between this ancient Eastern principle and more recent Western ones will be examined further below (in § 3) through an overview of Mahatma Gandhi's vegetarianism, formed under the joint influence of Ahimsa and shall be presented in the light of both this ancient Eastern principle, and some of the more modern Western thoughts which influenced him during his time in London.

2. Antiquity to the Middle Ages

The ancient Egyptians (2686 BC – AD 395), not unlike many people around the globe today, had a variety of strikingly different and often inconsistent relationships with animals. They used them as help in the field, kept them as pets, worshipped them as manifestations of deities, and ate their meat for food. They also mummified them, a practice whose results tell us much about ancient attitudes towards animals, and could have told us even more had most of them not been destroyed, recycled, peddled, and even used as fuel during the 18th and 19th centuries.

There are four basic categories of animal mummies, each of which reveals a little more about human-animal relationships in the ancient world: (i) pets, (ii) 'sacred' animals, (iii) offerings, and (iv) preserved foods (what follows is a shortened, modified, account of material first presented in Sandis 2007):

> (i) Pets (including gazelles, monkeys, and hunting dogs) were preserved so that they might be reunited with their owners after death. They were frequently given elaborate burials and, though the possibility that

when their owners died the animals were killed in order to be buried with them cannot be ruled out, it is more likely that they were only added to their tomb after their own natural deaths. As I write this, pet-animal mummies from the Cairo museum are being X-rayed in order to determine the cause of their death, which would in turn help to clarify the above question.

(ii) So-called sacred animals were thought to be live incarnations of Egyptian gods. So, while the Egyptians didn't worship animals per se, they often gave them elaborate burials upon death. Examples of Gods worshipped as beasts (which would invariably be turned into 'sacred mummies' after their death) include Horus (falcon or hawk), Anubis (dog, fox, or jackal), Khephir (scarab), Bastet (cat), Sobek (crocodile), Hathor (cow), Atum (eel), Khnum (ram), and Apis (bull). Mummified votive offerings include cats, shrews, snakes, dogs, raptors, and ibises, while typical examples of victual mummies would be geese and cow ribs.

(iii) Votive offerings (to honour the dead, or, alternatively, some deity associated with the animal in question). Archaeologists have also discovered a number of fake sacred and votive mummies (some of which may be found in the British museum), most probably sold as genuine offerings to unsuspecting pilgrims.

(iv) Preserved as food for use by the dead in the afterlife. Alongside the genuine votive offerings, this confirms that the ancient Egyptians were, generally speaking, happy to use animals as a means to their own ends, while (i) and (ii) above suggest that they would have held back from using them merely as a means (compare to Kant's views in § 3 below).

Egyptians clearly treated animals differently to both plants and humans. While there is little evidence of any systematic biological or philosophical taxonomy at play, their attitudes generally conform to the sort of account that would come to be favoured by the Greek philosopher Aristotle (384-322 BC).

On Aristotle's view, plants, animals, and humans all have a 'psuche' (often translated as 'soul'), where this is understood as the function-related *form* in which any material body is arranged. Thus, the same lump of matter may become *living* if it is arranged in such a way that it becomes capable of performing certain (biological) functions. Aristotle argued further that what distinguishes animals from plants is therefore not the possession of a 'soul' but, rather, sense-perception and locomotive powers to *cause* (or *refrain* from causing) movement as well as to move (plants only lacking the former). By contrast what distinguishes humans from other animals, on Aristotle's model, is the faculty of *reason* whose mark is the ability to engage in theoretical and practical thought leading to rational belief and choice.

This intuitive picture seems more or less right, but it leaves many questions unanswered. Do animals have language? Do they have beliefs, desires, and emotions? Can they make choices? Do we have any moral duties towards them? Aristotle believed that their lack of rationality entitled us to use them for our own purposes. Once challenged, however, Aristotle's claim soon collapsed into the view (defended by both Stoics and Epicureans) that it is okay to eat animals because they don't have syntax (cf. Osborne 2007: Ch.4 who makes a helpful comparison to the role of language in modern debates, as discussed in § 5 below). This was attacked by one of Aristotle's own pupils: Theophrastus (d. 287) of the Peripatetic school, and by many Pythagoreans and Neoplatonists, the most notable of the latter being Porphyry (233-309) who in his Treatise *On Abstinence from Animal Food* argues that animals *do* have reason (even if they don't have syntax) and, more importantly, that even if they didn't their sensitivity would still provide sufficient justification for abstinence (Cf. Sorabji 1993). Although many modern day Aristotelians (such as the contemporary philosopher Rosalind Hursthouse) also stray from Aristotle on this point, the evenly balanced Ancient debate would eventually die out, not to reappear in full swing until the nineteenth century. Of chief influence here was Augustine (354-430), who in his *City of God* sought to justify the killing of animals by appealing - contra to earlier Church Fathers - to the contested ancient view that animals lacked rationality. The Augustinian return to Aristotle and the Stoics more or less formed the standard Western account for most of the next 1500 years influencing. Islamic philosophers such as Ibn Sina (980-1037) and Ibn Rushd (1126-128) as well as Christian thinkers such as Thomas Aquinas (c. 1225-74) all accepted the basic Aristotelian tenet that animals have (i) souls and (ii) sensitive and locomotive powers, but not (iii) *reason*. External senses attributed to animals (in either potentiality or actuality) included touch, taste, smell, hearing and sight while internal ones (attributed to 'higher' animals such as dogs and wolves but not 'lower' ones such as worms or flies) were typically limited to imagination, memory, and Aristotle's infamous 'common sense' (viz. a power to collect objects of the external senses). To these Ibn Sina would come to add estimative and representational powers too, but the resulting faculties were still thought to fall short of reason.

3. Early Modern Philosophy

According to Descartes, animals are non-conscious automata which only differ from manmade machines, such as clocks, in their degree of complexity. This view was the result of a (dualistic) division of the world into two kinds of substance: mind and matter. Human bodies, he believed, were made of matter and functioned according to Newtonian mechanics. Human minds, by contrast, were made of an entirely different substance, and their primary function was not movement, but thought. Since Descartes did not believe that animals could think, he did not attribute minds to them. But given his additional belief that it was the human mind (and not the human body) that was conscious, Descartes could not allow animals any ability which requires consciousness, such as perception, sensation, recognition, intention, emotion, attention, imagination, and so on. Now this may well be true of shrimps and worms, but to maintain that, say, monkeys cannot feel pain is nothing short of absurd. Indeed, in February 1649, a before he died, Descartes wrote the following to the Cambridge Platonist Henry More (1614–1687): "to animals I do not even deny sensation, in so far as it depends upon a bodily organ" (in Cottingham et. al 1991). So we might best interpret Descartes as suggesting that animals have sensations but no judgments about them. Yet it remains unclear how Descartes can consistently maintain this unless he is working with far narrower notions of mind and consciousness than critics have supposed.

Another so-called rationalist thinker, Baruch (Benedict) de Spinoza (1632-1673) allowed that animals were sentient but claimed that their lack of rationality prohibited them from qualifying as members of our moral community. This view is not dissimilar from that of the materialist Thomas Hobbes (1588-1679) whose bleak view of human nature (we are all brutish and power-seeking) lead him to believe that morality is *constructed* only when human beings of roughly equal strength and intelligence enter into agreements or social contracts with each other whose 'moral' rules help ensure their mutual security, and the better life which follows. If animals lack rationality (as Hobbes and Spinoza believed) they cannot enter into any mutual agreements with us (or indeed each other), and consequently remain in a state of war with both humans, and themselves. Hobbes' metaphorical talk of 'war' seems extreme when conceiving of the typical relation between a pet-owner and her pet (though it rather neatly describes my first relationship with a non-human animal). Still, one might plausibly argue most (if not all) animals are amoral, that is to say, incapable of acting either morally or immorally. This would entail that they are not moral *subjects*, but not that they cannot be *objects* of moral consideration.

The equally empiricist philosophers, John Locke (1632-1704) and David Hume (1711-1776) found it easier to endow animals with not only perception and sensation, but also *some* degree of rationality, maintaining that there was no great gulf between humans and animals, a belief found also in Chinese Neo-Confucian philosophers such as Chu Hsi (1130-1200), as well as with native American peoples. Despite this philosophical liberalism (not to mention their political one), both Locke and Hume condoned the killing of animals, because they were not said to have a *high* degree of reason, and, more importantly, although mutual benefit rationally prevented humans from harming each other, there were no benefits to be gained from our not harming animals. This argument is bears many similarities to that of Hobbes and Spinoza. For example, although Locke believed that the laws of any given society are entered upon by public consent, he argues that these agreements are only made to enable the weak to defend their rights and duties which are literally given to them by God. Indeed, Locke's view regarding animals ultimately stems from the Christian view (defended by Augustine and much later by Aquinas) that God placed animals on earth for human use.[2]

Hume's belief that Reason alone cannot tell us what we ought to do but only inform us of which actions would best fulfill our passions, and his further claim that these desires lead us to develop an *artificial* system of rules base on conventions which aim to propagate our overall well-being, is more amenable to a Hobbesian reading. Yet Hume also believed, *contra* Hobbes, that we have a natural disposition 'to sympathize with others, and to receive by communication their inclinations and sentiments', not least when these are useful or agreeable to us, , it being a moot point whether we share any of them with non-human animals.

4. Late Modern Thought

Immanuel Kant (1724-1804) also maintained that the suffering of animals does not matter because *mere* animals are not rational beings and so, unlike human animals, lack the related freedom (of the will to act according to, or against, reason) required for creatures to be considered as ends-in-themselves: 'if only rational beings can be ends in themselves, that is not because they have reason, but because they have freedom. Reason is merely a means' (Kant 1900-2009, 27, 1321). In principle, then, Kantian morality seems to allow people to use animals *merely* as a means, that is to say they may be treated as means to our own ends with no concern for any harm that may be inflicted upon them (as opposed to, say, the practice of relying upon a baker as a means to obtain bread). In practice, Kant actually concedes that cruelty to animals is often wrong, but this is only because he believes that repeated cruelty will give rise to cruel habits and dispositions which may well affect our behaviour towards each other. While the associations in question are undeniable, anybody who sees animals as ends-in-themselves will find Kant's reasoning perverse.

Many of the views outlined above seem motivated by a kind of *rule-consequentialism* which maintains that laws ought to be implemented whenever following them would advance the overall benefits to members of any given society. Yet the arguments of utilitarians such as Jeremy Bentham (1748-1832) and John Stuart Mill (1806-1873) after him, which simply count as a benefit or

---

2   It is worth noting here, however, that the RSPCA was formed by an Anglican clergyman in 1824, and almost all of its first supporters were Christian. Indeed, Christian theologians (such as Andrew Linzey) have recently made a strong case in favour of rights for animals whose welfare God is said to have entrusted us with.

a good the presence of pleasure and absence of pain, have had an enormous influence on our thinking about animals. This approach dispenses with any connection between being rational and being the object of moral concern. Even so, Bentham did not hesitate to add that 'a full-grown horse or dog, is beyond comparison a more rational, as a more conversible animal, than an infant of a day, or a week, or even a month, old'. This was not because he took rationality and language to play an important moral role, but, on the contrary, because he wanted to show that our moral intuitions may be contaminated by unrelated factors revealing despicable motives. By way of illustration, Bentham notes with approval that the French do not see skin colour as a reason to abandon someone to torment.

Later that same century, Mohandas Karamchand - later 'Mahatma'- Gandhi (1869-1948) would reach the same conclusions through a related – but ultimately distinct – chain of reasoning (what follows is a shortened, modified, account of the narrative given in Sandis, 2007). Like all devout Hindus, Gandhi's family were strict vegetarians. In an 1891 interview with *The Vegetarian*, however, Gandhi revealed that in his youth he had been 'betrayed into taking meat about six or seven times' at a period when he allowed his friends (in particular a vicious boy called Mehtab) to do his thinking for him. In the end he gave up meat-eating because he could not go on lying to his mother, and before leaving Gujarat for London in 1888 Gandhi vowed never to touch meat again.

Once in London, determined to keep his promise, Gandhi ignored the advice of new acquaintances who told him that he could not survive its cold climate without eating meat and went searching for a vegetarian restaurant in London, finally finding one on Farringdon street (the 'Central') a few months later. He there picked up some vegetarian literature, including the essay 'A Plea for Vegetarianism' by animal *rights* activist and social reformer Henry Salt (1851-1939) which helped him to firmly give up the idea that eating 'flesh food' might be better for one's diet, converting to vegetarianism as a matter of principle. Gandhi would have been particularly struck by the following statement:

> If it can be shown that men can live equally well without flesh-food or, rather, unless it can be shown that the contrary is the case (for the burden of proof must always rest with those who take on for themselves the responsibility of wholesale slaughter), it must surely seem unjustifiable, on the score of humanity, to breed and kill animals for merely culinary purposes (1886, 10).

Salt (who contrasted mere *'utilitarian'* arguments for vegetarianism with his own *moral* ones) would also introduce Gandhi to the Work of the American slave abolitionist and animal food objector Henry David Thoreau (1817-1862) as well as the *Vegetarian Society of Manchester* (publishers of the *Vegetarian Messenger*) and the *London Vegetarian Society* (LVS), which he joined in 1890 and in whose weekly journal (*The Vegetarian*) he would soon come to publish his first pieces of work in 1891.

Gandhi's first writings focused on Indian Vegetarians and their festivals, distinguishing between those whose vegetarianism was voluntary and strict ('pure vegetarians') from those who were willing to take meat but were too poor to buy it, and those (in Britain) who followed a V.E.M (vegetables, eggs, milk) diet. Pure vegetarians, he pointed out 'argue that to eat an egg is equivalent to killing life; since an egg, if left undisturbed would, *prima facie*, become fowl' adding that he is sorry to say that he himself had recently been eating eggs. Unlike 'extreme vegetarians' (i.e. vegans) he added, they do not abstain from eating dairy products, because they do not believe that cows - an object of worship among Hindus *because* of their dairy produce - suffer when milked. Needless to say, such truths are contingent upon the specific methods used to milk cows and the conditions in which hens are kept (not to mention the question of how one goes about maintaining an 'all-female' workforce). Salt's influential essay (whose target is flesh-foods) speaks of 'how cruel to animals, and how degrading to men, is the institution of the slaughterhouse' (1886,11) but is largely unconcerned with eggs and dairy. This is most likely because farming conditions in the eighteenth century were considerably more humane than those typical of the industry today (cf. Foer 2009). To return to such conditions today we would all have to, at the very least, seriously reduce our consumption of both eggs and dairy. Buying organic or free range whenever possible is insufficient, given current quantities of demand. Fortunately, the range of easily accessible dairy alternatives - such as soya-based ones - is far wider today than anything Gandhi would have ever encountered (indeed, this is also true of meat-replacement products), though soya farming is not without environmental complications that cannot be ignored.

Gandhi also argued that the cause of the physical weakness of Indian vegetarians could not be attributed to their diet, using the example of certain Indian shepherds to argue that, if anything, a vegetarian diet was 'conducive to bodily strength'. As for mental strength, Gandhi pointed out that Buddha, Pythagoras, Plato, Porphyry, John Ray, Daniel (from the Old Testament), John Wesley, John Howard, Percy Bysshe Shelley, Sir Isaac Pitman, Thomas Edison, and Sir W. B. Richardson were all vegetarian (as was George Bernard Shaw whom he would soon befriend). Later that year, he started the Bayswater branch of the *LVS*, and would continue to support the Society when he briefly returned to India, and upon his subsequent move to South Africa a couple of years later. In 1931, he gave a talk at the *LVS* on *The Moral Basis of Vegetarianism* which would form the inspiration for a posthumously published collection of related writings.

Gandhi's vegetarianism nicely compliments - and might even be thought to have motivated - his general advocacy of non-violence which was to mark India's struggle for independence from British colonial rule. His philosophy of compassion clearly extended beyond people to all creatures and it is noteworthy that apart from vegetarianism Gandhi also championed humane farming, and in the 1920s protested against vivisection, believing it to be his duty to speak out on behalf of animals.

Be that as it may, there is considerable tension between Gandhi's writings on the non-killing of animals from the 1920s and those from the late 1940s. In the former he takes a rather extreme pacifist view (though he does allow for mercy killing, see *Young India* newspaper, 18 November 1926, p. 396). For example, in his 1925 *Autobiography* (translated in 1927) he writes :

> To my mind the life of a lamb is no less precious than that of a human being. I should be unwilling to take the life of a lamb for the sake of the human body (p.172, Cf. Article in *Young India* newspaper, 18 May 1921, p. 156).

And in a 1927 newspaper article:

> I do not want to live at the cost of the life even of a snake. I should let him bite me to death rather than kill him…If in not seeking to defend myself against such noxious animals I die, I should rise again a better and fuller man. With that faith in me, how should I seek to kill a fellow-being in a snake?' (*Young India* newspaper, 14 April, p. 121).

As noted above, the Gandhi of the 1920s was also a stern critic of vivisection:

> I abhor vivisection with my whole soul. I detest the unpardonable slaughter of innocent life in the name of science and humanity so-called, and all the scientific discoveries stained with innocent blood I count as of no consequence. If the circulation of blood theory could not have been discovered without vivisection, the human kind could well have done without it (*Young India*, newspaper, 17 December 1925, p. 40).

In the late 1940s, by contrast, Gandhi appears to have abandoned the view that it is always wrong to kill an animal no matter what. Thus, in the second volume of his book *Non-Violence in Peace and War* (published posthumously in 1949) he writes:

> I am not able to accept in its entirety the doctrine of non-killing of animals. I have no feeling in me to save the life of these animals who devour or cause hurt to man. I consider it wrong to help in the increase of their progeny. Therefore, I will not feed ants, monkeys or dogs. I will never sacrifice a man's life in order to save theirs. Thinking along these lines, I have come to the conclusion that to do away with monkeys where they have become a menace to the well-being of man is pardonable. Such killing becomes a duty. The question may arise as to why this rule should not also apply to human beings. It cannot because however bad, they are as we are. Unlike the animal, God has given man the faculty of reason (Vol. II, 67; reprinted in Gandhi 1959-1994).

And in two newspaper articles from 1946:

> The emphasis laid on the sacredness of sub-human life in Jainism if understandable. But that can never mean that one is to be kind to this life in preference to human life. While writing about the sacredness of such life, I take it that the sacredness of human life has been taken for granted. The former has been over-emphasized. And while putting it into practice, the idea has undergone distortion. For instance, there are many who derive complete satisfaction in feeding ants. It would appear that the theory has become a

wooden, lifeless dogma (*Harijan* newspaper, 9 June, p. 172).

True Ahimsa [non-violence] demands that, if we must save the society as well as ourselves from the mischief of monkeys and the like, we have to kill them (*Harijan* newspaper 7 July, p. 213).

Despite such changes of opinion, one underlying view remains clear and constant in Gandhi's thought and that is that 'the greatness of a nation and its moral progress can be judged by the way its animals are treated' (1954).

5. Current Concerns

Modern day utilitarians such as Peter Singer (1946-) argue that anybody who favours the well-being of, say, a baby with a serious mental illness over that of an advanced animal like an ape or even a pig is guilty of *speceism*, a frame of mind analogous to racism and sexism. Some have accused Singer of attempting to provide a utilitarian justification of infanticide, yet the argument is not intended to persuade that infanticide is as harmless as eating a steak, but rather that eating meat (or indeed fish) is as morally repugnant as infanticide. The comparison implies that *even if* suffering is all that matters, levels of cognition remain relevant to moral debate.

Recent research on the question of whether or not animals possess the power of cognition has done much to combat the view that animals have no thoughts at all. Cognitive Ethologists, such as Marc Bekoff and Jane Goodall, have advanced evidence in support of animal displays of consciousness, cognition, memory, intelligence, passion, emotion, devotion, jealousy, playfulness, anger, and more. Christine Nicol and John Webster, for example, maintain that cows have a 'complex mental life in which they bear grudges, nurture friendships and become excited by intellectual challenges' and are 'capable of strong emotions such as pain, fear and even anxiety about the future'. According to their research, 'even chickens might have to be treated as individuals with needs and problems'. Evidence for these claims includes documentation of 'how cows within a herd form friendship groups of between two and four animals with whom they spend most of their time, often grooming and licking each other. They will also dislike other cows, and can bear grudges for months or years'.

Likewise, Donald Broom demonstrates, through tasks where cows had to find how to open a door to get some food (whilst an electroencephalograph measured their brainwaves) that 'their brainwaves showed their excitement; their heartbeat went up and some even jumped into the air', from which he concludes that cows 'become excited by solving intellectual challenges. we called it their "Eureka" moment'. Keith Kendrick similarly claims that sheep can remember up to fifty bovine faces and are able to recognise other sheep after as long as a year.

According to Kendrick, sheep also form strong affections for humans, showing signs of depression after lengthy separations, and enthusiasm during subsequent reunions. Webster explains that 'people have assumed that intelligence is linked to the ability to suffer and that because animals have smaller brains they suffer less than humans' but that this is 'a pathetic piece of logic' for 'sentient animals have the capacity to experience pleasure and are motivated to seek it. You only have to watch how cows and lambs both seek and enjoy pleasure when they lie with their heads raised to the sun on a perfect English summer's day. Just like humans'.[3]

The precise assessment of such claims requires a conceptual investigation which no amount of scientific research - or even the existence of talking lions - could possibly settle. Do animals act for reasons or does rational agency require conceptual, cognitive, and/or linguistic capacities beyond the reach of all non-human animals? Such questions continue to attract philosophical controversy over how to *interpret* empirical findings (for very recent examples see Finkelstein, 2007; Glock, 2009; Steward, 2009, and Stoecker, 2009). There is much debate, for example, over the extent to (and sense in) which various animals might be said to have minds. The arguments typically revolve around what it *is* to have a mind, and in particular what it is to have a so-called 'mental state' such as a belief or desire. For example Donald Davidson (1917-2003) maintains, contra behaviourism, that animals lack the conceptual capacities necessary for having the sorts of thoughts, beliefs, or intentions at work in intentional agency. According to Davidson, a dog cannot believe that the cat is at the top of the oak tree unless it has the concept of an oak tree, where a concept is a linguistic representation of some kind:

> Can the dog believe of an object that it is a tree? This would seem impossible unless we suppose that the dog has many general beliefs about trees: that they are growing things, that they have leaves or needles, that they burn. There is no fixed list of things that someone with the concept of a tree must believe, but without many general beliefs there would be no reason to identify a belief as about a tree, much less an oak tree (Davidson, 1975; cf. Davidson, 2001, 97).

On the other hand, we might think that, if a cat runs up a tree and the dog starts barking at it, there is a legitimate sense in which the dog may be said to think, believe, or know that the cat is on the tree (cf. Malcolm, 1977, 49), and to mistakenly keep thinking so if it continues to bark at it after the cat has snuck away. Our everyday concept of belief, it would seem, is tied to both behavioural and linguistic capacities:

> We say a dog is afraid his master will beat him; but not: he is afraid his master will beat him tomorrow. Why not? (Wittgenstein, 1951, § 650, cf. 'part II', i)

Keith Frankish (2004) helpfully contrasts a behaviour-based concept of mind

---

[3] Quotations sourced from Leake (2005); for further detail see Webster (2005). See also Bekoff (2007b).

with the language-involving concept of 'supermind'. Frankish accordingly also distinguishes between two strands of belief, associated with two distinct kinds of mental processing and, more generally, two conceptions of mind. The first ('basic belief') is typically nonconscious, passive, 'non-occurrent', and attributable on purely behavioural grounds to most (if not all) animals. The second ('superbelief') may be held consciously, typically requires linguistic conceptualization, is frequently 'occurrent', and arguably absent from most (if not all) animals.

We might ask whether having super-beliefs and super-desires is a necessary condition of being treated as an (ethical) end or whether a behaviourally-ascribed mental life is sufficient. Opting for the former is effectively claiming that you only matter ethically if you can form *concepts* (a view not all that far removed from the syntactic criterion dismissed above as absurd). Opting for the latter is no better, for it leads to the equally ludicrous view that non-conscious machines matter ethically if they behave in suitably complex ways (possessing artificial intelligent). Science-fiction films like Ridley Scott's *Bladerunner* and Stephen Spielberg's *A.I.* may succeed in eliciting empathy from audiences towards human-made machines, but the 'machines' in question do not just *behave* as if they have thoughts they also have – by stipulation –a consciousness which encompasses sensations, emotions, and even self-consciousness. At the end of the day it is *this* criterion, as opposed to that of thought or reason, that seems necessary, which is not to deny *all* links between rational ability and ethical value.

To think otherwise is to be guilty of *speceism*. The term was first introduced by animal activist and philosopher Tom Regan (1938-) who argues against utilitarianism and, inspired by Gandhi, in favour of the *deontological* view that animals have *rights* (based on their inherent value) that we have a duty to respect no matter what the consequences. There has been much talk as to whether it even makes sense to talk of animals having moral or legal rights. For example, according to Roger Scruton (1996, 80) the attribution of rights is at least partly determined by the possession of the ability to make a justifiable claim, which animals lack. But even if this were the case, we can presumably make a claim on their behalf (Ibid). Recent debate amongst constructivists has centred on contractualist accounts, such as that of T. M. Scanlon, who argue that humans can act as *trustees* of animals, representing them whenever a new moral contract is called for. Scanlon claims that pain –whether that of rational creatures or non-rational ones - is something we have '*prima facie* reason to prevent, and stronger reason not to cause'. Both suggestions are promising, but nothing has been said about why humans who were motivated to find general regulative principles of behaviour could not reasonably reject the proposal to enter such contracts with animals (by proxy), and consequently also the claim that they have any (contract based) reasons not to cause animals pain. Scruton (1996) argues further that *if* animals can have moral and/or legal rights it must also make sense to ascribe moral and/or legal duties to them (which would be absurd), yet it is far from clear that our ordinary conception of a right is anywhere near as stringent as

Scruton's Kantian incarnation.

No matter what our moral theory though, there is no escape from the dawning reality that humans must alter their perspective and accept that, as custodians of the planet, they have serious moral responsibilities towards animals. These duties regarding animals ought to affect our thoughts and actions relating to a variety of human exploitative practices including (but not exhausted by) commercial agriculture, animal experimentation, the use of animals in and/or for travel, entertainment (including circus acts and blood sports), arts and crafts, clothing, upholstery, zoo-keeping, space exploration, and the management of wildlife. This is largely the case in India, although other nations are finally following in its steps. There are now over four million vegetarians and 300,00 vegans in the UK alone; yet even with a further 20,000 turning vegetarian each month, it has a long way to go yet.

As with any ethical movement that does not peak in revolution, laws of nations relating to animal rights and welfare have reluctantly yet steadily (though by no means uniformly) followed. Fox hunting with dogs has now become illegal in England and Wales after the Labour Party brought a ban on the activity into force in February 2005. This does not, however, mean that all hunting (or even all fox hunting) is illegal. It is still legal, for example, for hunters to 'flash out' foxes, as long as they shoot them rather than set their hounds on them. Alternatively, if the fox hunter so desires, he or she may mount a hunt for an artificial scent.

While opinions vary widely, the details of this relatively new law and the arguments surrounding it on both sides reveal some fairly common assumptions behind our moral thought regarding animals. What people *primarily* appear to be objecting to is the intensity and duration of the *pain* which certain methods of killing may cause the hunted animal in question. Many pro-hunters, for example, argue - erroneously as it happens - that setting dogs onto a fox is a relatively quick and painless way of killing them.

This raises the question 'is it acceptable to kill animals in a painless fashion'? According to Aristotle's pupil Theophrastus (discussed in § 2 above), what is wrong with killing animals is the very fact that in doing so we are robbing them of life. Yet we rightly do not feel the same way about each and every plant. What Theophrastus (who was no fruitarian) had in mind, no doubt, was that we were robbing them of a *sentient* life. On this proto-Reganian view, it is the fact that animals have *consciousness* that makes it wrong to kill them. This is because he (in my opinion rightly) assumes that a conscious life is, at least typically, of great value. What makes a conscious life valuable is the *experiences* which the being in possession of it undergoes. Utilitarians argue that these experiences are only valuable when they are pleasurable, but we need not agree with them on this detail to see the general value of sentience. Be that as it may, a prolonged and painful death is undoubtedly worse that a quick, painless one. This is certainly the case for humans, and there is no reason why it should be any different for animals. By the same token, killing someone in a slow and painful fashion is morally worse than say, poisoning them in their sleep. Reasons for this (be they based on rights, consequences, or virtue) may vary from one moral theory to another, but all are in agreement about which action would be morally worse. Once, again, there is no reason why this should be any different with respect to animals. Indeed the point can be couched in truistic terms: a merciless killing is worse than a merciful one.

What *is* contested , however, is the claim that in the case of animals merciful killing is wrong at all. Those who cannot see anything wrong with it are committed to the view that mere sentience is not enough for a life's being valuabe. Others, such as Scruton, maintain that although all sentient life is valuable, in the case of some animals this value is outweighed by other values (such as those of alleged dietary and environmental benefits, or the mere pleasure humans experience when participating in blood sports, or eating meat). It is the lack of consensus on such issues that makes it difficult to ban (rather than simply morally criticise) fox hunting altogether without, say, banning the subsistence hunting of duck, or indeed, the mass slaughtering of cows, pigs, and sheep. It is far from clear, however, that we should see this as an argument in favour of keeping fox hunting, rather than (at the very least) banning the factory killing of animals, if not all unnecessary killing of animals or fish. As with other legislation with drastic socio-economic consequences, it would of course be of utmost importance to do this gradually, accompanied by appropriate subsidy measures and redeployment opportunities.

6. Bad Arguments Against Vegetarianism

The number of fallacious arguments against vegetarianism is legion. In this final section I wish to expose four of the most popular ones. I shall not concern myself here with the harder choice between vegetarianism and veganism though I have tried to suggest above that, at the very least, we have an ethical duty to not only care about the *source* of any lacto-ovo consumption, but about the *quantity* too. Either way, in what follows the the word 'vegetarian' may be substituted by the word 'vegan' (or indeed 'pescatarian') with no change in reasoning.

(i) The Perfectionist Fallacy

It is often claimed that since being vegetarian will never put an end to animal cruelty, vegetarianism could never accomplish its intended goal. While the (one and only) premise of this argument might be true, its conclusion simply does not follow. This is because no vegetarian (or group of vegetarians) has the single goal of eliminating *all* animal cruelty (or pain). Rather, the primary goal of vegetarianism is to *reduce* animal cruelty as much as is humanly possible. What was wrong with the above argument is that it made what is sometimes known as the *perfectionist* fallacy, namely the mistake of thinking that only plans that *completely* solve the problems they are intended to solve should be pursued (the fallacy is most frequently made by those critiquing charity work aimed at the reduction of poverty).

(ii) The Life-Giving Fallacy

People are also correct to point out that were it not for the meat industry fewer animals would have come into existence in the first place, since most animals are bred especially for it. Once again, though, they make an invalid inference from this obvious point to an absurd conclusion. In this instance the irrelevant conclusion is that this somehow promotes animal welfare and/or that it is ok to kill animals bred for this purpose since they would otherwise have not existed anyway. If you cannot immediately see the absurdity of this reasoning simply replace 'animals' with 'humans' in the above argument and try again! Moreover, the grain required to feed the animals which (in turn) feed those humans who can afford meat is, at any given time, alone sufficient to feed all populations dying of starvation. As if this wasn't bad enough, livestock are responsible for 18 per cent of the greenhouse gases thought to cause *global warming* (more than any single method of transport). This is not a reason to eat them and breed more but to stop breeding so many in the first place.

(iii) The 'Already Dead' Fallacy

Another common error of reason is to think that since the meat one buys in the supermarket (or at the butcher's) is from an animal that is already dead, consumers are in no way contributing to the death of any animals. We might represent this argument slightly more formally, as follows:

> **Premise 1:** Whenever I buy meat in a supermarket the animal it came from is (always) already dead.
>
> **Premise 2:** I cannot contribute to the death of animals by eating animals that are dead already.
>
> **Conclusion:** In buying this meat from the supermarket I am not contributing to the death of animals.

Here the conclusion *does* follow from the premises (i.e. is entailed by them). This is because *if* it is true that (a) whenever I buy meat from a supermarket the animal it came from is already dead and that (b) I cannot contribute to the death of animals by eating animals that are dead already then it *must* also be true that when I buy meat from a supermarket I am not causing any animals to die. However the second premise is dubious to the extreme. What is wrong with it is that it harbours the implicit assumption that one can only contribute to the death of something by killing it. This assumption (which we might call a *hidden premise*) is clearly false. Imagine a butcher shop where the animals are killed on demand for you. You call in on Monday and order however many chickens you want the butcher to 'prepare' for you by Wednesday, yet if you don't order any somewhere down the line fewer chickens will need to be 'supplied' (within the meat 'industry' doublespeak is ubiquitous). Do you not play some part in the chicken's death by ordering two chickens on Monday? The obvious answer is 'yes'. You are certainly not *the only one* responsible for the chicken's death (there is also the butcher), but you nevertheless play a role, because had it not been for your demand, the dead chicken would have never been supplied. While supermarkets don't work in quite so straightforward a manner, their basic mode of operation is *supply and demand*. Supermarkets do not like to make a loss: if they find that they are repeatedly ordering more chickens than they are managing to sell, they will start ordering less chickens. Consequently, less chickens will be killed for them. So each person alone can save a considerable number of chicken lives (indeed an entire menagerie of animals), even if nobody else does the same, (simultaneously increasing the demand for vegetarian alternatives). The second premise is therefore false since my buying meat from a supermarket would indirectly cause more animals to be slaughtered (cf. Sandis, 2007b). This is not to say, of course, that there might not be special situations in which not eating flesh-food would cause it to be wasted (with no indirect benefit), but such cases are few and far between, especially once you keep in mind the possible consequence of its consumption creating an appetite and/or need for more of the same, a point often emphasized by virtue ethicists.

(iv) The Design Fallacy

Finally, there are those who claim that we are 'meant', 'designed', or otherwise 'intended' to eat meat, as 'evidenced' by our sharpish teeth (which would have been razor-sharp had we not developed the ability to fashion useful tools and weapons). Leaving aside the more general worry of whether evolution may be legitimately thought of as a vehicle of 'nature's intentions' (whatever that might mean), the most basic understanding of how evolution works reveals that, if anything, our teeth are sharp *because* we eat meat, and not the other way around (cf. Mayell 2005; note also that gorillas, who are folivores, have similar teeth to us). More importantly, many vegetarian humans have proven that you can be a vegetarian and have a perfectly healthy mind and body (see § 3 above) and (c) too much meat and dairy has been proven to be bad for our health. Of course there will be exceptions: people might occasionally need to eat (some) meat or fish for reasons related to health. But this gives us no more license to abstract a general rule than extreme scenarios of human survival would license cannibalism. Let us not forget, moreover, that enough animals die of natural causes (unrelated to disease) to cater for all basic *needs* as opposed to *comforts*.[4]

---

4 This essay much expands material from Sandis (2006).

BIBLIOGRAPHY

Baker, G. P. and Morris, K. J. (1993). Descartes Unlocked. *British Journal for the History of Philosophy*, 1, 5-27.

Bekoff, M. (ed.) (2007). *Encyclopedia of Human-Animal Relationships (2nd Edition)*. California, Greenwood Press.

_____ (ed.) (2009), *Encyclopedia of Animal Rights and Animal Welfare (2nd Edition)*. California, Greenwood Press.

_____ (2010). Action in Cognitive Ethology. In Sandis, C. and O' Connor, T. (2010).

Bekoff, M., Allen, C., and Burghardt, G. (eds.) (2002). *The Cognitive Animal*. Cambridge MA, MIT Press.

Bekoff, M. and Jamieson, D. (eds.) (1996). *Readings in Animal Cognition*. Cambridge, MA. MIT Press.

Cottingham, J., Murdoch D, Stoothoff, R., and Kenny, A. (eds). (1991). *The Philosophical Writings of Descartes*, Vol. 3: Correspondence. Cambridge, Cambridge University Press.

Davidson, D. (1975). Thought and Talk. In Guttenplan, S. (ed.) *Mind and Language*. Oxford, OUP.

_____ (2001). Rational Animals. In his *Subjective, Intersubjective, Objective*. Oxford, Clarendon Press, 95-105.

Derrida, J. (2002). *The Animal That Therefore I Am (More to Follow)*. Translated by Wills, D., *Critical Inquiry*, 28, 2, 369-418.

Dupré, J. (2002). *Humans and Other Animals*. Oxford, Clarendon Press.

Finkelstein, D. (2007). Holism and Animal Minds. In Crary, A. (ed.). *Wittgenstein and the Moral Life: Essays in Honor of Cora Diamond*. Cambridge MA, MIT.

Foer, J.S. (2009). *Eating Animals*. London, Little Brown and Co.

Frankish, K. (2004). *Mind and Supermind*. Cambridge, CUP.

Gaita, R. (2003). *The Philosopher's Dog*. London, Routledge.

Gandhi, N. K. (1925, trns. by Desai, M. 1927 and 1929). *Autobiography: The Story of My Experiments with Truth*. Washington DC, Public Affairs Press.

_____ (1959). *The Moral Basis of Vegetarianism*. Ahmedabad, Navajivan

Publishing House.

_____ (1959-1994) *Collected Works Vols. 1-100* (in which all newspaper articles are reprinted). New Delhi, Publications Division, Ministry of Information and Broadcasting, Government of India and at http://www.gandhiserve.org/cwmg/cwmg.html and on CD-Rom.

Glock, H-J. (2000). Animals, thoughts and concepts. *Synthese*, 123, 35–64.

_____ (2009). Can Animals Act For Reasons? *Inquiry*, 52, 232-254.

_____ (2010). Animal Action. In O' Sandis and O' Connor (2010).

Hursthouse, R. (2000). *Ethics, Humans, and Other Animals*. London, Routledge.

Ikram, S. (2004) (ed.). *Divine Creatures: Animal Mummies in Ancient Egypt*. Cairo, American University in Cairo Press.

_____ (2006). *Beloved Beasts: Animal Mummies from Ancient Egypt*. Cairo, American University in Cairo Press.

Jamieson, D. (2002*). Morality's Progress: Essays on Humans, Other Animals, and the Rest of Nature*. Oxford, Clarendon Press.

Kant, I. (1900-2009). *Gesammelte Schriften (Collected Works)*. Berlin, Royal Prussian (subsequently German, then Berlin-Brandenburg) Academy of Sciences.

Leak, J. (2005). The Secret Life of Moody Cows. *Sunday Times*, 27 February.

Lindzey, A. (1976). *Animal Rights: A Christian Assessment of Man's Treatment of Animals*. London, SCM Press.

Malcolm, N. (1977). Thoughtless Brutes. In his *Thought and Knowledge*. Ithaca, Cornell University Press, 40-57.

Mayell, H. (2005). "Evolving to Eat Mush": How Meat Changed Our Bodies. *National Geographic News*, Feb 18.

Midgley, M. (1980). *Beast and Man*. London, Penguin.

Osborne, C. (2007). *Dumb Beasts and Dead Philosophers: Humanity and the Human in Ancient Philosophy and Literature*. Oxford, Oxford University Press.

Regan, T. (1983). *The Case for Animal Rights*. Berkeley, University of California Press.

Rowlands, M. (2002). *Animals Like Us*. London, Verso.

_____ (2008). *The Philosopher and the Wolf*. London, Granta.

_____ (2009). *Animal Rights: Moral Theory and Practice (2nd Edition)*. Basingstoke, Palgrave Macmillan.

_____ (2010). Contingent Vegetarianism. *Times Literary Supplement*, March 3, 4.

Salt, H. (1886). *A Plea for Vegetarianism and Other Essays*. Manchester, The Vegetarian Society.

Sandis, C. (2006). Animals. In Cohen, M. (ed.). *Essentials of Philosophy and Ethics*. USA, Hodder Education/Oxford University Press.

_____ (2007a), 'Animal Classification', 'Gandhi', 'Animal Mummies', and 'Animals in Space' in Bekoff (2007b).

_____ (2007b). Bad Arguments: They Live Amongst Us. *Dialogue*, 29, Nov.

Sandis, C. and O' Connor, T. (2010) (eds.). *A Companion to the Philosophy of Action*. Oxford, Wiley-Blackwell.

Scruton, R. (1996). *Animal Rights and Wrongs*. London, Demos.

Searle, J. (1994). Animal minds. *Midwest Studies in Philosophy*, XIX, 206–19.

Singer, P. (ed.) (1985). *In Defence of Animals*. Oxford, Basil Blackwell.

_____ (2001). *Animal Liberation* (2nd Edition). New York, Eco Press Books.

_____ (ed.) (2005). *In Defense of Animals: The Second Wave*. Oxford, Wiley-Blackwell.

Sorabji, R. (1993). *Animals Minds and Human Morals: The Origins of the Western Debate*. London, Duckworth.

Steward, H. (2009). Animal Agency. *Inquiry*, 52, 217-231.

Stoecker, R. (2009). Why Animals Can't Act. *Inquiry*, 52, 255-271.

Taylor, A. (1999). *Magpies, Monkeys, and Morals*. Ontario, Broadview Press.

Tyler, T. (forthcoming). *CIFERAE: A Bestiary in Five Fingers*. Minneapolis, MN, Minnesota University Press.

Webster, J. (1995). *Animal Welfare: A Cool Eye Towards Eden* (2nd Edition). Oxford, Wiley-Blackwell.

Wittgenstein, L. (1951). *Philosophical Investigations*. Oxford, Blackwell.

3

Business Ethics

John F. Humphrey

Business is an ethical activity. ... The search for excellence, whatever else it may be, begins with ethics. – Robert C. Solomon (1997)

1. Introduction

This chapter is devoted to ethics in the context of business. The topic is a difficult one because many believe that there is no such thing as ethical behaviour in business. Others believe that business ethics is the way in which businesses do act, not the way that they should act. Still others argue that while businesses ought to act ethically, business people are so unethical that ethics in business is either very unlikely or an impossibility. Business is about making money – profit – not about doing good. This picture is complicated by the fact that even many people who are involved in business do not believe that ethics and business have anything to do with one another; ethics and business do not mix. While the prudent business person may not be unethical, they argue, he or she would be foolish to be wholly ethical either; indeed, those who work in business would be well – advised to be amoral.

In this chapter, I will begin by considering some of the definitions scholars have given for the term 'ethics.' Once 'ethics' has been defined, the way in which various ethicists have thought about business ethics will be considered. I will proceed by looking at the way in which the discipline has evolved and developed – the history and the origins of business ethics. Finally, I will consider the question: How can we hold a corporation responsible for its actions? While this question is not the only question considered by business ethicists, in some respects, everything hangs on the way in which one answers it. In considering moral responsibility, I will consider Peter A. French's analogical argument that just as you can be responsible for the decisions you make, so too a corporation can be responsible for the decisions that it makes.

2. What is 'Ethics'?

"The word 'ethics,'" Robert C. Solomon explains, "is derived from the Greek word *ethos*, meaning character or custom" (1984, 3). Expanding on Solomon's etymology, William H. Shaw and Vincent Barry add, "Today we use the word ethos, to refer to the distinguishing disposition, character, or attitude of a specific people, culture, or group (as in, for example, 'the American ethos' or 'the business ethos')" (1998, 4). While ethics is usually focused on "individual character" or individual actions, "including what we blandly call 'being a good person,'" the fact that 'ethics' is derived from ethos reminds us that ethics also involves "the effort to understand the social rules which govern and limit our behaviour, especially those ultimate rules – the rules concerning good and evil – which we call morality" (Solomon 1984, 3). The emphasis on individual character (what it means to be a good person) points to the fact that ethics is concerned with the actions of individuals, while the stress on social rules that govern and limit the actions of individuals reflects the fact that ethics is concerned with the society, culture, group, or community within which individuals act.

Ethics may be defined as a philosophical discipline in which the theories and principles of good and bad or good and evil actions are considered. Or, as G. E. Moore holds, "Ethics" is concerned with "human conduct" and is "the general enquiry into what is good" (1965, 2). "The field of ethics (or moral philosophy)," James Fieser states, "involves systematizing, defending, and recommending concepts of right and wrong behaviour" (2006, 1). According to Brooke Noel Moore and Kenneth Bruder, ethics is also concerned with the question, "Which moral judgments are correct?" (1998, 10). Surely Louis Pojman is correct, however, when he emphasizes the connection between ethics and action. "Ethics has a distinct action guiding aspect, and as such, belongs to the group of practical institutions that include religion, law, and etiquette" (1998, 2). Certainly, Pojman is not suggesting that ethics, religion, law, and etiquette are equivalent terms; one may act according to religious principles, legal principles, or the principles of proper behaviour and still be acting immorally or unethically. Clearly, believers in many of the world's religions have committed unfathomable atrocities in the name of their various faiths and sects. Just because something is legal does not mean that it is ethical; indeed, some, Martin Luther King, Jr. for instance, have argued that there are times when one has a moral obligation to break unethical laws. Hence, King argues, had he been living in Hitler's Germany he would have had a moral obligation to disobey the laws of the Third Reich against protecting Jews, and in the United States he openly advocated breaking segregation laws ecause they were immoral (1964, 70-74).[1]

---

1   In the fifth chapter of *Why We Can't Wait* (1964) entitled "Letter from Birmingham Jail," King asserts, "I would be the first be the first to advocate obeying just laws, One has not only a legal but a moral responsibility to obey just laws. Conversely, one has a moral responsibility to disobey unjust laws" (70).

In answer to the question: "What is Ethics?" Claire Andre and Manuel Velasquez conclude that "ethics is two things."

> First, ethics refers to well based standards of right and wrong that prescribe what humans ought to do, usually in terms of rights, obligations, benefits to society, fairness, or specific virtues. Ethics, for example, refers to those standards that impose the reasonable obligations to refrain from rape, stealing, murder, assault, slander, and fraud. Ethical standards also include those that enjoin virtues of honesty, compassion, and loyalty. And, ethical standards include standards relating to rights, such as the right to life, the right to freedom from injury, and the right to privacy. Such standards are adequate standards of ethics because they are supported by consistent and well founded reasons (1987, 2).[2]

Notice that ethical actions are based on standards. Ethical standards, however, are not thought to be arbitrary or subjective; they are considered to be objective; they are universal and consistent – they apply to everyone alike in the same way; and they are based on good reasons or arguments. If an alleged ethical principle is not supported by good reasons, however, we are not bound by it.

> Secondly, ethics refers to the study and development of one's ethical standards, … feelings, laws, and social norms can deviate from what is ethical. So it is necessary to constantly examine one's standards to ensure that they are reasonable and well-founded. Ethics also means … the continuous effort of studying our own moral beliefs and our moral conduct, and striving to ensure that we, and the institutions we help to shape, live up to standards that are reasonable and solidly-based (2).

We have an obligation to examine our own motives and actions to make certain that our own behaviour is consistent with the same ethical principles we believe others are obligated to follow. Should our actions not conform to ethical principles, it is incumbent on us to change our behaviour.

James Rachels concurs with Andre and Velasquez; ethics must be founded on rational principles and ethics demands that we reflect on our own actions, but he adds "the requirement of impartiality" (2003, 13). "We may note two main points: first, that moral judgments must be backed by good reasons; and second, that morality requires the impartial consideration of each individual's interests" (11). If moral judgments are to be guided by good reasons, we cannot allow our actions to be guided by emotions, feelings, or sentiment. We must also consider the reasons that criticize or oppose our own decisions to act. If moral judgments are to be impartial, "each individual's interests are equally important; from within the moral point of view, there are no privileged persons. … each of

---

2 This piece was first published by Clair Andre and Manuel Velasquez (Fall, 1987). "What is Ethics?" in *Issues in Ethics*, 1, 1, 1-2, http://www.scu.edu/ethics/publications/iie/v1n1/whatis.html . Later, a revised and edited version, attributed to Manuel Velasquez, Claire Andre, Thomas Shanks, S.J., and Michael J. Meyer, appeared on the Markkula Center for Applied Ethics' website: http://www.scu.edu/ethics/practicing/decision/whatisethics.html.

us must acknowledge that other people's welfare is just as important as our own" (13). Even though my own interests are extremely important to me, they are no more important than other's interests are to them. We cannot favour or disfavour individuals because they happen to belong to a particular racial or ethnic group, nation state, religious group, or gender. The requirement of impartiality, then, guards against "arbitrariness in dealing with people" and "forbids us from treating one person differently from another when there is no good reason to do so" (14). But what would count as a "good reason" to treat others differently? Rachel's gives an example of a child blind from birth. While one might support the position that all careers should be open to everyone, a blind person would not qualify to be a referee in football or soccer or an umpire in baseball. This does not mean that blind people should be prevented from working or participating in all sports; it simply means that blindness is a good reason to treat an individual differently.

"Ethics," Solomon writes, "is the study of a way of life, our way of life – its values, its rules and justifications. It involves … thinking about 'good' and 'evil' and what they mean" (1984, 2). Ethics may also include the question: What is the good life? As many have observed, this is precisely the question that Socrates asks.[3]

> Whether the just also live better than the unjust and are happier … must be considered. And now, in my opinion they do also look as though they are … Nevertheless, this must still be considered better: for the argument is not about just any question, but about *the way one should live* (Plato 1968, 352d; italics added).

Some have argued that the good life is the life of pleasure, the life of parties, drink, and promiscuity. Still, if one parties too much, one will not be successful; too much drink and one wakes up with a headache; promiscuity may lead to sexually transmitted diseases – where is the pleasure in that? Perhaps the good life is not the life of the flesh at all, but the life of the mind – good books, good friends, and good conversation. Or perhaps the good life is the life of service, a life exemplified, for example, by Mother Theresa and her service to poverty stricken people. Of course, Socrates argues for the life of contemplation, the philosophic life. But does the philosophic life necessarily exclude the life of service? David Hume, on the other hand, reminds us that since humans are "reasonable," "sociable," and "active" creatures, "a mixed kind of life … [is] most suitable to [the] human race" (Hume, 1999 [1748], 89).[4]

---

3   See, for example, James Rachels (2003), *Elements of Moral Philosophy*, ix and Bernard Williams (1985), *Ethics and the Limits of Philosophy*, 1.
4   Hume writes:

> Man is a reasonable being; and as such, receives from science his proper food and nourishment: But so narrow are the bounds of human understanding, that little satisfaction can be hoped for in this particular, either from the extent or security of his acquisitions. Man is a sociable, no less than a reasonable

3. 'Business Ethics'?

Nonetheless, if ethics is the study of good and bad actions and the study of the good life, the question is: How do these ways of thinking about ethics relate to business? After all, business is about making money, buying at the lowest possible price and selling at the highest - whatever the market will bear! But isn't this taking advantage of people? How can this be ethical behaviour? Many argue that business is amoral; business and ethics, like oil and water, do not mix. In his article, "Is Business Bluffing Ethical?," Albert Z. Carr, for example, compares doing business to a poker game; "the ethics of business are not those of society, but rather those of the poker game" (1968, 148). Carr wants to distinguish clearly between the way people act in their private lives and the way they act in business; business is a game that one plays to win at all costs. Richard T. De George, however, is critical of the way that many business people think of business and view themselves and their professional roles; he cautions against "the myth of amoral business" according to which "businesses and people in business are not explicitly concerned with ethics. They are not unethical or immoral; rather they are amoral insofar as they feel that ethical considerations are inappropriate in business. After all, business is business" (1995, 5). Paul F. Camenisch argues that while making money is important because it allows businesses to function, business is not just about making money; rather, he observes, "there are two essential elements in any adequate definition of business, the provision of goods and services, and the fact that this is done with the intention of making a profit (1981, 62).[5]

Solomon extends this line of reasoning in arguing against the "myth of the profit motive" (1993, 356) and in another place Solomon adds:

> Business on the other hand, has nothing to do with jingles, survivalism, and Darwin, whatever the mechanisms of the market may be. The 'profit motive' is

---

being: But neither can he always enjoy company agreeable and amusing, or preserve the proper relish for them. Man is also an active being; and from that disposition, as well as from the various necessities of human life, must submit to business and occupation: But the mind requires some relaxation, and cannot always support its bent to care and industry. It seems, then, that nature has pointed out a mixed kind of life as most suitable to human race, and secretly admonished them to allow none of these biases to draw too much, so as to incapacitate them for other occupations and entertainments. Indulge your passion for science, says she, but let your science be human, and such as may have a direct reference to action and society" (Hume (1999), 89).

5   Camenisch is aware that many business people would not accept his definition of business when he writes: "Admittedly this understanding of the relation between the production of goods and services and the making of a profit does not reflect the perception of many persons currently engaged in business. They might argue that the relation is precisely the reverse. But is not just such a reversal of ends and means the rock which has wrecked a good many commendable human enterprises?" (1981, 63-64).

an offensive fabrication by people who were out to attack business, which has curiously – and self-destructively – been adopted by business people themselves. Business isn't a single-minded pursuit of profits; it is an ethos, a way of life. It is a way of life that is at its very foundation ethical. What is more central to business – any kind of business – than taking contracts seriously, paying one's debts, and coming to mutual agreements about what is a fair exchange? Ethics isn't superimposed on business. Business is itself an ethics, defined by ethics, made possible by ethics (11-12).

Clearly by business ethics, Solomon does not mean the ethical principles that some corporations *do* have, but the ones that businesses *ought* to have. And in yet another place, he argues that profits are not the end, but the means for doing business.

Profits are not as such the end or goal of business activity; profits get distributed and reinvested. Profits are a means to building the business and rewarding employees, executives and investors (1993, 354).

Still, business people seem to forget about providing goods and services and focus on short term gain. 'Show me the money!' has entered the language and become a common saying. Think of Ivan Boesky's speech of 1986 in which he said to students at the University of California, Berkeley: "I think greed is healthy. You can be greedy and still feel good about yourself".[6] Indeed, the public has witnessed many scandals perpetrated by business people. The savings and loan debacle of the 1980s and 1990s cost U. S. taxpayers billions of dollars; Michael Milken's 1990 guilty plea to six felony charges involving junk bonds ended the career of an extremely talented individual; the 2001 Enron scandal destroyed several corporations and left many employees and investors without pensions; and most recently the world-wide banking and mortgage crisis has brought the global economy to a halt. While many are struggling today to keep their jobs and their homes, taxpayers are forced to divert much needed tax revenues from education, health, and welfare to businesses that are failing because business executives, thinking only of immediate gain, made extremely poor choices. Not surprisingly, many believe that business people are self-serving, corrupt, selfish, and greedy. Perhaps it is for these reasons some have jested that business ethics, like military intelligence, is an oxymoron - a contradiction in terms. Scholars working in ethics, however, recognize that business ethics has become a well-established discipline.[7] As De George writes, "business ethics is neither a fad as some claimed early on, nor an oxymoron, as so many lamely joked. It is a vibrant,

---

6   In 1986, Ivan Boesky was convicted of insider trading and served approximately two years of a three and one-half year prison sentence, paid over one hundred million U. S. dollars in fines, and can no longer work on Wall Street. His name has become associated with corruption, for example in the film *Wall Street*.

7   In the "Preface" to the seventh edition of their *Moral Issues in Business*, William H. Shaw and Vincent Barry write: "Yet some people still scoff at the idea of business ethics, jesting that the very concept is an oxymoron" Shaw and Barry (1998), viii.

complex enterprise developing on many levels" (2005, 10).

According to De George, however, "the term 'business ethics'" is used in many "different ways" (1). Some argue that business ethics has been around from the time that humans began to buy and sell. Solomon points to the Sumerians (1993, 355), but Alexei Marcoux, for example, writes "construed broadly as moral reflection on commerce, business ethics is probably as old as trade itself." He cites "the Code of Hammurabi (1700s B.C.), prescribing prices and tariffs and laying down both rules of commerce and harsh penalties for noncompliance" as indications of "civilization's earlier attempts to identify the moral contours of commercial activity" (2006, 1). In "Teaching Business Ethics," Jeffrey Gandz and Nadine Hayes define "Business Ethics ... as the study of those decisions of managers and corporate management which involve moral values" (1988, 657). In his "Business Ethics," Marcoux, who distinguishes between the concept and the practice of business ethics, explains the breadth of the discipline.

> In concept, business ethics is the applied ethics discipline that addresses the moral features of commercial activity. In practice, however, a dizzying array of projects is pursued under its rubric. Programs of legal compliance, empirical studies into the moral beliefs and attitudes of business people, a panoply of best-practices claims (in the name of their moral merit or their contribution to business success), arguments for (or against) mandatory worker participation in management, and attempts at applying traditional ethical theories, theories of justice, or theories of the state to firms or to the functional areas of business are all advanced as contributions to business ethics (2008, 1).

Surely Marcoux is correct; business ethics is a broad interdisciplinary field of research and study.

Solomon, too, notes that business ethics belongs to the field of applied ethics[8],

---

8   In his "Ethics," James Fieser distinguishes metaethics, normative ethics, and applied ethics,

> Philosophers today usually divide ethical theories into three general subject areas: metaethics, normative ethics, and applied ethics. Metaethics investigates where our ethical principles come from, and what they mean. Are they social inventions? Do they involve more than expressions of our individual emotions? Metaethical answers to these questions focus on the issues of universal truths, the will of God, the role of reason in ethical judgments, and the meaning of ethical terms themselves. Normative ethics takes on a more practical task, which is to arrive at moral standards that regulate right and wrong conduct. This may involve articulating the good habits that we should acquire, the duties that we should follow, or the consequences of our behavior on others. Finally, applied ethics involves examining specific controversial issues, such as abortion, infanticide, animal rights, environmental concerns, homosexuality, capital punishment, or nuclear war.

> By using the conceptual tools of metaethics and normative ethics, discussions in applied ethics try to resolve these controversial issues (1).

but it holds

> ... a peculiar position in the field of 'applied' ethics. Like its kin in such professions as medicine and law, it consists of an uneasy application of some very general ethical principles (of 'duty' or 'utility' for example) to rather specific and often unique situations and crises. But unlike them, business ethics is concerned with an area of human enterprise whose practitioners do not for the most part enjoy professional status and whose motives to put it mildly, are often thought ... to be less than noble. 'Greed' (formerly 'avarice') is often cited as the sole engine of business life, and much of the history of business ethics, accordingly, is not very flattering to business (Solomon, 1993, 354).

Yet another way of understanding business ethics, Wayne Norman argues, is that it belongs as much to political philosophy as to personal ethics.

> The short answer is that business ethics ... is as much a branch of political philosophy as it is a branch of personal ethics. Of course, business ethics aims to give individuals the tools to solve ethical dilemmas at work. But it must also be concerned with evaluating the institutional structures and the organizational cultures within which individual managers identify problems, make decisions, and summon their moral courage.

The problem, however, is that the discipline "is too vast" to be left "to moralists who are confident that business ethics merely requires that individual business people rediscover the virtues or their fathers or grandfathers." Since the market occupies such a central place in "our individual lives and ... in the political system," Norman calls for "political philosophers" to "devote more attention to evaluations of both the market system and to the broad range of activities that take place in the conduct of everyday business." One consequence, he continues,

> ... of this conception of the field of business ethics is that it is necessarily an interdisciplinary enquiry – not least because of the need to grasp the social sciences that make up contemporary management studies, from economics, finance and accounting, to operations research, organizational behaviour, marketing and corporate law ://www.philo.umontreal.ca/prof/wayne.norman.html .

Still, if theory is distinguished from application within the philosophical discipline of ethics, then common to these uses of the term, 'business ethics,' is the conception that business ethics is a subdiscipline of applied ethics in which ethical theories and principles are applied to the actions of both for-profit and not-for-profit businesses, corporations, and organizations and to the actions of those practitioners involved in the various aspects of conducting business.

4. The Origins and History of Business Ethics

Both De George (1987) and Thomas F. McMahon (2002) hold that business ethics in the United States had its origins in European philosophical and religious traditions.⁹ McMahon distinguishes "six successive stages" in the development of business ethics by identifying the underlying ideologies of each stage.

1. The religious underpinnings and underlying ideologies of English origins (1700-1776)
2. The early American business ethics in development (1777-1890)
3. A mature concept of business ethics (1891-1963)
4. The rise of social issues in business ethics (1962-1970)
5. Perceiving business ethics as a specific discipline
6. Recognizing American business ethics as global (2002, 342).

Since the dates above are only approximate, McMahon says some of these periods overlap. Solomon, however, distinguishes "three … levels of business and business ethics" – macro-ethics, micro-ethics, and molar-ethics (1993, 359). "Macro-ethics in business" he notes, belongs to:

> ... traditional ethics – the nature of promises and other obligations, the intentions, consequences and other implications of an individual's actions, the grounding and nature of various individual rights. What is peculiar to business micro-ethics is the idea of a fair exchange and, along with it, the notion of a fair wage, fair treatment, what counts as a 'bargain' and what instead is a 'steal'. Aristotle's notion of 'commutative' justice is particularly at home here.

"Macro-ethics" tries "to take in the 'big picture', to understand the nature of business world and its functions as such." Macro-ethics in business, Solomon observes, includes:

> ... those large questions about justice, legitimacy and the nature of society that constitute social and political philosophy. What is the purpose of the 'free market' – or is it in some sense a good of its own, with its own telos? Are private property rights primary, in some sense preceding social convention … or is the market too to be conceived as a complex social practice in which rights are but one ingredient? Is the free market system 'fair'? Is it the most efficient way to distribute goods and service throughout society? Does it pay enough attention to cases of desperate need (where a 'fair exchange' is not part of the question)? Does it pay enough attention to merit, where it is by no means guaranteed that virtue will be in sufficient demand so as to be rewarded? What are the legitimate … roles of government in business life, and what is the role of government regulation?

Finally, Solomon states that the "corporation is "the definitive 'molar' unit of modern business" and represents the third level of business and business ethics. The salient questions concerning business and business ethics are

---

9 De George writes, "Business ethics, which grew out of religion's interest in ethics in business and management education's concern with social issues, has become an interdisciplinary academic field" (De George 1987, 201).

... aimed at the directors and employees of those few thousand or so companies that rule so much of commercial life around the world. In particular, they are questions that concern the role of the corporation in society and role of the individual in the corporation.

However, instead of examining McMahon's six stages of business ethics or Solomon's three levels of business and business ethics in detail, I shall briefly consider three different but related senses of business ethics, – "the 'ethics in business' sense of business ethics," "business ethics as an academic field," and "business ethics as a movement" – contained in De George's "A History of Business Ethics."

De George relates each sense of the term, 'business ethics,' to a different historical thread. The first "strand," according to De George, is "the 'ethics in business' sense of business ethics" (2005, 2). By "ethics in business," De George does not mean the application of philosophical theories and concepts to business; rather, by "ethics in business" he understands "the application of everyday moral or ethical norms to business" (2). For example, those who embrace religious texts such as the Bible, the Koran, or the Talmud or particular principles derived from such texts like the Ten Commandments, The Sermon on the Mount, commandments to be truthful, honest, not to steal, not to be envious, and some concept of "stewardship" for the allocation of resources to guide their business dealings. McMahon concurs with De George on this point and notes "two basic ideologies" in this context that have their roots in the earliest days of the founding of the United States:

> The first viewed wealth as divine favour. Cotton Mather and Benjamin Franklin ubscribed to this idea. The second viewpoint was expressed by John Woolman, a lawyer and a merchant, who incorporated William Penn's precept that merchants are stewards or trustees for the public good (2002, 342).

Beginning with the discussion of justice in Plato's *Republic*, De George traces the evolution of philosophical and religious thinking about ethics in relation to business up to the September 4, 1993 Parliament of the World's Religions, "Declaration Toward a Global Ethic"[10] in order to identify specific important concepts in the development of business ethics. Thomas Aquinas (1225-1274), for example, discusses trade and "selling articles for more than they are worth and selling them at a higher price than was paid for them" (2005, 2). Although Aquinas, like Aristotle, condemns "usury," he defends borrowing for good causes if there is one who is willing to lend at a reasonable rate of interest. De George attributes "the development of the Protestant work ethic" to Protestant Reformation leaders like Martin Luther, John Calvin, and John Wesley, and

---

10 First drafted by Hans Kung, in 1992: http://astro.temple.edu/~dialogue/Antho/kung.htm , the adopted version of the Parliament of the World's Religions, "Declaration Toward a Global Ethic (September 4, 1993) may be found at http://www.parliamentofreligions.org/_includes/FCKcontent/File/TowardsAGlobalEthic.pdf.

citing R. H. Tawney's *Religion and the Rise of Capitalism*, he emphasizes the importance of religion to the emergence of "individualism and commerce as it developed in the modern period" (2). At the same time, the modern period also separates "the religious from the secular and politics from religion."[11] Think of Thomas Hobbes' injunction to follow the laws of the state instead of the dictates of one's conscience (1974 [1651], 1, 15). John Locke contributes the conception that individuals have a natural right to property if they mix their labor with nature's gifts. Adam Smith, who was concerned with economics (*An Inquiry into the Nature and Causes of the Wealth of Nations*) and thought about moral philosophy (*The Theory of Moral Sentiments*), transforms "Locke's notion of labor into a labor theory of value" (De George 2005, 3). Karl Marx criticizes capitalism because it was founded on "the exploitation of labor." Marx grounds his claim, De George explains,

> ...on his analysis of the labor theory of value, according to which all economic value comes from human labor. The only commodity not sold at its real value ... is human labor. Workers are paid less than the value they produce. The difference between the value the workers produce and what they are paid is the source of profit for the employer or the owner of the means of production. If workers were paid the value they produced, there would be no profit and so capitalism would disappear. In its place would be socialism and eventually communism, in which all property is socially (as opposed to privately) owned, and in which all members of society would contribute according to their ability and receive according to their needs. The result would be a society (and eventually a world) without exploitation and also without the alienation that workers experience in capitalist societies (3).

In *Imperialism: The Highest Stage of Capitalism*, De George argues, Lenin takes Marx's analysis of the class war between bourgeoisie and the proletariat one step further. The interests of the capitalists and proletariat have become allied in imperialist nations; hence, exploitation of the working class has decreased as menial labor and the exploitation that goes with labor have been exported to the colonies.

In response to Marx's claims, Pope John Paul II (1891) and the U. S. Catholic Bishops (1984)[12] in the Catholic tradition, and Reinhold Niebuhr (*Moral Man and Immoral Society*) in the Protestant tradition argue for "a just wage, which was one sufficient 'to support a frugal and well-behaved wage-earner,' his wife and his children" (3).[13] Unlike Marx's critique of capitalism, De George insists, the nature

---

11 Solomon also notes that while business ethics condemned business and in particular the practice of usury, in the early modern period business ethics began to take a more positive view of business in the person of John Calvin, the English Puritans, and Adam Smith (1993, 359).

12 The 1984 *Pastoral Letter on the U. S. Economy* is published as *Economic Justice for All: Pastoral Letter on Catholic Social Teaching and the US Economy* (1986).

13 De George cites the *Rerum Novarum: Encyclical of Pope Leo XIII on Capital and Labor* (1891), which, as he asserts, was "the first of the papal encyclicals on social

of these criticisms was not to endorse or condemn any one economic system, but to argue that any economic system had to be based on ethical principles of justice and fairness, i.e., they should be based on "Christian moral principles and should improve the conditions of the masses of humanity, especially of the poor and the least advantaged" (3). Such criticisms of business and capitalism have continued to the present and have led to the more recent 1993 Parliament of the World's Religions where a "Declaration of a Global Ethic," patterned on the 1948 United Nations, "Universal Declaration of Human Rights," was adopted, condemning "'the abuses of the Earth's ecosystems,' poverty, hunger, and the economic disparities that threaten many families with ruin" (4).[14] Still, the emphasis in this first sense of business ethics – the *ethics in business* sense of business ethics – is on the individual and the individual's compliance with basic moral principles.

The origin of the second sense of the term 'business ethics,' "business ethics as an academic field," De George connects to the enormous social, economic, and political transformations in the United States of the 1960s. Emerging from the Second World War to become embroiled in the Cold War, the United States government had become engaged in the Viet Nam War – a war that many around the world opposed. Opposition to the war created criticism of and opposition "to official public policy and to the ... military-industrial complex, which came in for increasing scrutiny and criticism" (4). Additionally, De George argues, large business concerns and multinational corporations were replacing small and medium sized businesses. In particular, advances in "the chemical industry" and air and water pollution caused by these concerns increased public suspicion of large corporations. "The spirit of protest led to the environmental movement, to the rise of consumerism, and to criticism of multinational corporations" (4). "Ethicists," McMahon writes, "began to see the environment as something more than land, air and water, and business ethicists began to see environmental protection as human protection" (2002, 349). Public scrutiny, disapproval, and censure led businesses to embrace the concept of "social responsibility"; at the same time, corporations began to promote the view that they were contributing to the common good. "But whether it was reforestation or cutting down on pollution or increasing diversity in the workforce, social responsibility was the term used to capture those activities of a corporation that were beneficial to society and usually, by implication, that made up for some unethical or anti-social activity with which the company had been charged" (De George, 2005,

---

justice" (3): http://www.vatican.va/holy_father/leo_xiii/encyclicals/documents/hf_l-xiii_enc_15051891_rerum-novarum_en.html .

14 De George sites the 1993 Parliament of the World's Religions, *Declaration of a Global Ethic*. "We condemn the abuses of Earth's ecosystems. We condemn the poverty that stifles life's potential; the hunger that weakens the human body, the economic disparities that threaten so many families with ruin" (1) ://www.parliamentofreligions.org/_includes/FCKcontent/File/TowardsAGlobalEthic.pdf.

4). Business departments in professional schools, colleges, and universities also began to offer courses on "social responsibility and social issues in management" (4). During the 1960s, De George holds, these courses stressed "law, and the point of view of managers prevailed, although soon that of employees, consumers and the general public were added" (4). Business ethics texts, however, "paid no systematic attention to ethical theory, and tended to be more concerned with empirical studies than with the development or defense of norms against which to measure corporate activity" (4-5).

As an example of those who have been working on social responsibility De George cites Archie B. Carroll's pyramid of social responsibility, according to which corporations have economic, legal, ethical, and philanthropic responsibilities (5).[15] In his "Pyramid of Corporate Social Responsibility," Carroll argues that corporations have economic responsibilities which form the base of a pyramid. "All other business responsibilities are predicated upon the economic responsibility of the firm because without it the others become moot considerations" (1991, 41). Legal responsibilities form the next level of Carroll's pyramid; "law is society's codification of right and wrong" (42). Clearly, businesses are obligated to follow the laws of the existing societies within which they do business; corporations must "play by the rules of the game." Furthermore, Carroll writes, corporations have ethical responsibilities that have not been codified into law.

> Although economic and legal responsibilities embody ethical norms about fairness and justice, ethical responsibilities embrace those activities and practices that are expected or prohibited by societal members even though they are not codified into law. Ethical responsibilities embody those standards, norms, or expectations that reflect a concern for what consumers, employees, shareholders, and the community regard as fair, just, or in keeping with the respect or protection of stakeholders' moral rights (41).

Briefly, corporations have ethical responsibilities "to do what is right, just, and fair" (42); most importantly, they ought to "avoid harm." Finally, Carroll argues that corporations also have "philanthropic responsibilities," to respond to "society's expectations that businesses be good corporate citizens," including making charitable contributions of "resources to the community ... [to] improve [the] quality of life" (42). Still, Carroll maintains that the first responsibility of businesses is their economic ones; "philanthropy is icing on the cake" (42).

McMahon cites three significant changes occurring in the late 1950s and early 1960s that led to the maturation of business ethics in the United States. The first change occurred when the federal government convicted people working in the "electrical industry" for a "price fixing conspiracy." The second change occurred

---

15 Although De George does not mention the article, he is probably referring to Archie B. Carroll, (July-August, 1991). "The Pyramid of Corporate Social Responsibility: Toward the Moral Management of Organizational Stakeholders," *Business Horizons*.

when Raymond C. Baumhart published a survey in the *Harvard Business Review* (1961) under the title "How Ethical are Businessmen?" showing, "contrary to business's claims that only the electrical industry behave illegally and unethically, … that most businesses, if not all, had unethical practitioners." Finally, McMahon cites the Civil Rights movement that brought social, political, and economic injustices to light, and that enjoyed the support of many citizens for changes in policy and legislation. Specifically in this context, McMahon mentions the 1954 U.S. Supreme Court case, *Brown vs. the School Board of Topeka, Kansas* – the case that overturned the 1896 U. S. Supreme Court case *Plessy vs. Ferguson*, the case that had written 'separate but equal' into law (2002, 348). Additionally, McMahon observes, it was the "the 1964 Civil Rights Act and subsequent social legislation" that led to a change in "the emphasis of business ethics from the individual business executive and manager to corporate activity" (346). The Civil Rights Act created the awareness that evils like racism could be systemic and, hence, had to be addressed not only at the individual level but also at the institutional or structural level.

De George, however, connects the emergence of "business ethics as a specific 'academic field'" to two events. The first event, according to De George, agreeing with McMahon's second point, was the Baumhart survey. Although Baumhart's survey did not answer his own question, "How Ethical Are Businessmen?," it did reveal areas where business leaders needed to improve their awareness of the necessity of and the possibilities for including ethical principles in business. Baumhart's study led to the conclusion that

> … the desire for change permeates executive belief from the top to the bottom of the corporate structure. But this change will not come about, say executives, merely by hoping for it, instituting half-measures, or issuing platitudes. The time has come for courageous top-management leadership to implement executives' desires to raise the level of business ethics (1961, 176).

While most people dealing with ethical issues in this period were from theological and religious backgrounds, De George insists that business ethics came into being because of the application of ethical theory to empirical studies about business like Baumhart's; however, "the new ingredient and the catalyst that led to the field of business ethics as such was the entry of a significant number of philosophers, who brought ethical theory and philosophical analysis to bear on a variety of issues in business" (2005, 5). "Business ethics as an academic field," however, De George cautions, "depends not on the number of undergraduate courses taught in it or on its influence on business, but on the quality and quantity of research done in it" (1987, 206). Citing Norman Bowie, De George identifies the second event as the first business ethics conference in November, 1974 at the University of Kansas, and he notes that a number of anthologies appeared in the years following this conference. [16] Additionally, with the publication of his

---

16 De George mentions Tom Beauchamp and Norman Bowie, *Ethical Theory and*

A Theory of Justice John Rawls demonstrated the connection between ethical, political, social, and economic issues; this connection and his notion of contract theory had an enormous influence on a number of disciplines including business ethics. Yet, De George asserts, while "most of those who wrote on social issues were professors of business, most of those who wrote initially on business ethics were professors of philosophy, some of whom taught in business schools" (2005, 5).

De George emphasizes three factors that distinguish the social responsibility and social issues in business and management position from business ethics orientation.

> 1) The fact that business ethics sought to provide an explicit ethical framework within which to evaluate business, and especially corporate activities (5).

As previously mentioned, corporations had used the notion of social responsibility to promote the view that they were contributing to the common good and that because of this, their less than ethical actions were justified. Business ethicists claim that corporations could not justify unethical behaviour by claiming that they were contributing to the common good. The academic discipline of business ethics, De George asserts, focused on ethics first.

> 2) The field [of business ethics] was at least potentially critical of business practices – much more so than the social responsibility approach had been (5).

While those promoting social responsibility want businesses to be, or at least to appear to be, more socially responsible, they still tend to hold that the corporation's economic responsibilities are most important and cannot be compromised. De George reminds us of Carroll's pyramid the base of which was formed by the corporation's economic responsibilities; legal, ethical, and philanthropic responsibilities were relegated to second, third, and fourth place of importance respectively. Those promoting business ethics, on the other hand, want ethics to take the first place of importance. After all, as Solomon asserts, "Ethics isn't superimposed on business. Business is ... an ethics." Since businesses and corporations are often ahead of the law, pushing into new and uncharted territory with the creation of new goods and services - surrogate motherhood, selling human sperm and eggs, human cloning, genetic engineering, genetically modified foods, and stem cell research, for example – economic and legal responsibilities must conform to ethical constraints. While ethical considerations may justify existing law, they may also demonstrate the need for adopting new legislation to restrain business. Such considerations, as De George emphasizes, however, have led "the business community" to view business ethics "as a

---

Business; Thomas Donaldson and Patricia Werhane, *Ethical Issues in Business*; and Vincent Barry, *Moral Issues in Business*, all of which first appeared in 1979 and all of which have been published for classroom use in various editions since that time. Many other texts are currently available.

threat" because they could not accept "preaching by the uninformed who never had to face a payroll" (5-6). Additionally, the academy was critical of business ethics; indeed, some philosophers have questioned whether business ethics is an appropriate area of research for philosophers.

> 3) Although the field was concerned with managers and workers as moral persons with responsibilities as well as rights, most attention was focused on the corporation – its structure and activities, including all the functional areas of business, including marketing, finance, management, and production (6).

Business ethicists were also concerned with basic moral theories that could be used to help students think about ethical issues in business. Arguments for and against capitalism were examined as were "the ethical foundations of business, of private property, and of various economic systems" (6). Skimming through any current business ethics text reveals the kinds of issues that business ethicists have been considering – responsibility to stakeholders, hiring and firing, plant relocation, environmental problems caused by industry, discrimination, globalism, and multinational and transnational corporations to name a few. "As a field," Dr George notes, "business ethics included a good deal, but not all, of what was covered in social issues courses ... as well as giving structure to discussions of ethics in business" (6).

While many business schools and business departments in universities and colleges now have business ethics courses, there are still those who resist including business ethics courses in their curricula, believing that a common sense approach to morality and social responsibility in their programs is sufficient. What value, then, De George asks, does the academic discipline, business ethics, add to the business curriculum? Answering his own question, he argues that business ethicists have introduced students to "the basic techniques of moral argumentation," appealing to the two most important ethical theories "utilitarianism," which claims "that an action is right if it produces the greatest ... good for the greatest number" and "deontology," which asserts "that duty, justice and rights are not reducible to considerations of utility" (6). Business ethicists have also explored contributions other ethical theories might make to the field, e.g., social contract theories, virtue ethics, feminist ethical theories, and libertarianism. More recently, Solomon holds, the importance of "new applications and renewed sophistication in game theory and social choice theory have allowed the introduction of more formal analysis in business ethics" (1993, 354).

While ethical theory had essentially not been included in courses and discussions of social responsibility, business ethicists brought "a theoretical framework" to business ethics that included both individual moral responsibility found in the ethics in business sense of business ethics, and corporate social responsibility, "which they pushed explicitly into the ethical realm by applying ethics to economic systems, to the institutions of business, and especially to corporations" (De George 2005, 6). As De George observes, no one needs business ethicists to determine whether stealing or cheating are unethical; everyone knows such actions are wrong. "Common sense morality and the ethics in business approach ... are fine for the ordinary, everyday aspect of ethics in business" (6). If business ethics only dealt with these kinds of issues, it would be a trivial venture indeed.

> What the business ethicists could add is not only arguments that show why most common sense judgments are indeed correct, but also the tools by which the morality of new issues could be intelligently debated. They could and did also join that debate – the debate for instance on whether affirmative action is justifiable, and even more basically, what affirmative action means. Ethicists analyzed and defended worker's rights, the right to strike, the ethical status of comparable worth in the marketplace, what constitutes bribery and whistle blowing, and so on (6-7).

Business ethicists brought the tools and the methodology for considering ethical issues in a business context.

Besides the increase of business ethics courses in business schools, colleges, and universities, and the textbooks for these courses, De George notes that a number of additional developments have contributed to the progress of the discipline, including the founding of business ethics journals, scholarly books in the field, and business ethics centers, e.g., the Bentley University Center for Business Ethics, Bentley University, Waltham, Massachusetts (1976) and the Markkula Center for Applied Ethics, Santa Clara University, Santa Clara, California (1986). A number of organizations devoted to business ethics, such as the Society for Business Ethics (1980), have also contributed to the advancement of the academic field of business ethics. By the 1980s, business ethics had become an international phenomenon; Europeans also became interested in this field and in 1987 held the first conference of the European Business Ethics Network.[17] Currently, the Bentley University Center for Business Ethics website lists over 125 links to professional business ethics organizations in Canada and the United States alone and more than 70 links to international business ethics organizations.

In the third strand of the history of business ethics, De George discusses "business ethics as a movement" (8). By "business ethics as a movement," De George means all those "structures" that have been introduced into businesses and corporations that encourage and support ethical behaviour by the employees and the institutions, businesses, and corporations that employ them. Among the measures taken by businesses to incorporate an ethical culture, De George mentions: "clear lines of responsibility, a corporate ethics code, and ethics training program, an ombudsman or a corporate ethics officer, a hot or help line, a means of transmitting values within the firm and maintaining a certain corporate

---

17 For a discussion of business ethics in Europe, see Henk van Luijk's (2002) "Business Ethics in Europe: A Tale of Two Efforts."

culture" (8). Johnson and Johnson, for example, already had its *Credo*, written in 1943 by Robert Wood Johnson, chairman of the company from 1932-1963, before most corporations even thought of the importance of such a document.[18] In essence, the *Credo* "challenges" Johnson and Johnson "to put the needs and well-being of the people [they] serve first." McMahon also emphasizes the importance of the Johnson and Johnson *Credo* to that corporation's actions during the Tylenol disaster when seven people died in the Chicago area on Wednesday, September 25, 1982 after taking extra-strength Tylenol that, unbeknownst to the company, had been laced with poison.

> Some businesses, such as Johnson and Johnson, developed codes of ethics to assist employees in resolving problems in which ethics had considerable weight in the final outcome (Johnson and Johnson expressed their values in a *Credo*, which became their guideline in dealing with the now-famous Tylenol disaster that required total recall of the product. One of the vice-presidents of this division stated that, when they were informed of the disaster, one of the first things they did was to apply the mandates of the company's *Credo*.) (2002, 347).

As more and more corporations began to listen "to growing public pressure, media scrutiny, their own corporate consciences, and, perhaps most importantly, to legislation," De George observes, business ethics "became a movement" (2005, 8). Following Johnson and Johnson's example, most corporations have introduced some sort of corporate code. Remarking on the popularity of the codes of ethics in business, McMahon estimates that "about 95 percent of larger corporations have them today" (2002, 347). De George dates corporations' interest in ethical codes to the 1980s as public awareness of business scandals led to the insistence on incorporating ethics into the business practices. Typically, corporate codes deal with employee behaviour and clarify the corporation's expectations of employees' behaviour to one another, the corporation, customers, and the community.

Additionally, both De George and McMahon mention a number of important pieces of legislation that served to raise ethical standards in business. De George credits the 1964 U. S. Civil Rights Act which "prohibited discrimination on the basis of race, color, religion or national origin" with being "the first piece of legislation to help jump start the business ethics movement" (2005, 8). McMahon also points to the importance of President Johnson's "Executive Order 11246 whereby any corporate entity" desiring "a government contract had to engage in affirmative actions to accelerate the movement of minorities, including women, into the workforce" (2002, 348). Responding to this Act, large businesses and corporations have created "equal opportunity offices," usually housed in "their human resources offices," that serve to guarantee the company's compliance with government regulations. While the 1964 Civil Rights Act also raised awareness of employee's rights, the U. S. Occupational Safety and Health Act, 1970, directed

---

18 The Johnson and Johnson *Credo* may be found at: http://www.jnj.com/connect/about-jnj/jnj-credo/.

corporations to take worker's rights to a safe working environment seriously. In 1977 when U. S. corporations' involvement in bribery in other countries came to light, the U. S. Congress passed the Foreign Corrupt Practices Act. "The Act was historic," De George argues, "because it was the first piece of legislation that attempted to control the actions of U. S. corporations in foreign countries" by prohibiting U. S. corporations from participating in bribery to further their business dealings in and with foreign states (2005, 9). Believing that the best way to avoid government regulation was for corporations to regulate themselves, some corporations, e.g., IBM and Motorola, took the position of refusing to pay bribes even before the Foreign Corrupt Practices Act was passed.

Another example of corporate self-regulation is the 1971 Sullivan Principles, authored by the Reverend Leon H. Sullivan while serving on the board of General Motors and originally meant to provide guidelines for corporations doing business in South Africa under the racial policies of apartheid, but now concerned with ethical business practices in all parts of the world. The Sullivan Principles have been endorsed by many U. S. corporations, including General Motors, the Hershey Company, and the Chevron Corporation. "The objectives of the Global Sullivan Principles," Sullivan asserts, describing his principles,

> ... are to support economic, social and political justice by companies where they do business; to support human rights and to encourage equal opportunity at all levels of employment, including racial and gender diversity on decision making committees and boards; to train and advance disadvantaged workers for technical, supervisory and management opportunities; and to assist with greater tolerance and understanding among peoples; thereby, helping to improve the quality of life for communities, workers and children with dignity and equality (Sullivan, http://www.thesullivanfoundation.org/gsp/principles/gsp/default.asp).

"The Principles," as De George notes, "have become a model for other voluntary codes of ethical conduct by companies in a variety of other ethically questionable circumstances" (2005, 9).

Responding to the 1984 Union Carbide catastrophe in Bhopal, India that killed thousands of people and drew criticism from all corners of the world, De George explains, the chemical industry adopted "a voluntary code of ethical conduct known as Responsible Care, which became a model for other industries" (9). Another important example of corporations' attempts to regulate themselves is the Defense Industry Initiative (DII) on Business Ethics and Conduct. As De George notes, originally there were 32 signatories, but the number soon increased to 50. The Defense Industry Initiative describes its organizational efforts in the following way:

> Established in June 1986, DII consists of companies that provide systems, professional services, weapons, technology, supplies and construction to the U.S. Department of Defense. DII Signatory Companies are united in their commitments to adopt and implement the highest standards of business ethics

and conduct. Not a lobbying organization, DII seeks to promote and nurture a culture of ethical conduct within every company in the defense industry ://www.defenseethics.org/).

The Defense Industry Initiative is important, De George argues, because it became the model "for what has been the most significant governmental impetus to the business ethics movement, namely, the 1991 U. S. Federal Sentencing Guidelines for Corporations" (9). The 1991 law, De George continues:

> ... took the approach of providing an incentive for corporations to incorporate ethical structures within their organizations. If a company could show that it had taken appropriate measures to prevent and detect illegal and unethical behaviour, its sentence, if found guilty of illegal behaviour, would be reduced considerably. Appropriate measures included having a code of ethics or of conduct, a high-placed officer in charge of oversight, an ethics training program, a monitoring and reporting system (such as a 'hotline'), and an enforcement and response system. Fines that could reach up to $290 million could be reduced by up to 95 percent if a company could show bona fide institutional structures that were in place to help prevent unethical and illegal conduct (9).

One of the difficult problems that the public faces is how do we promote ethical behaviour in corporations. The Act indicates the importance of using government to both force and encourage ethical behaviour in business. The 2002 Sarbanes-Oxley Act was passed in response to the Enron scandal, involving the Arthur Andersen accounting firm, WorldCom, and several other corporations. Sarbanes-Oxley proscribes transparency in financial dealings with employees and stockholders. As De George notes, "the Act requires among other things, that the CEO and CFO certify the fairness and accuracy of corporate financial statements (with criminal penalties for knowing violations) and a code of ethics for the corporation's senior financial officers, as well as requiring a great deal more public disclosure" (10).

One way that corporations have responded to public pressure and governmental regulation is to adopt what John Elkington calls "win-win-win business strategies for sustainable development" or the "triple bottom line" that attempts to take into account people, the planet, and profits (1994, 90). Elkington purposefully argues against pitting the economy against the environment; indeed, if businesses are successful in the future, corporations will have to embrace sustainable development. They will have to take into account all those who have a stake in business – consumers, employees, and employers.

> We must hope that business people will be actively involved in shaping and implementing such projects [sustainability]. In contrast to the anti-industry, anti-profit, and anti-growth orientation of much early environmentalism, it has become increasingly clear that business must play a central role in achieving the goals of sustainable development strategies (91).

Businesses and corporations will have to cease being the problem and will have to contribute to the solution. Among other things, Elkington argues, citing Stephan

Schmidheiny, Chair of the Business Council for Sustainable Development, corporations will have to attend to "the entire life cycles" of their "products and to the specific and changing needs of ... customers."[19] Nonetheless, "the challenge facing individual companies," Elkington continues, "will be to work out new ways of co-operating with their suppliers, customers, and other stakeholders – including competitors – in this key area of business activity, while ensuring that they benefit not only in corporate citizenship terms, but also in terms of competitive advantage. ... emerging win-win-win strategies will be a major feature of the business environment" (99).

One thing that is clear, while many businesses and corporations complain of regulation, their own actions have created public suspicion and scrutiny, the demand to include openness and transparency in business dealings, and the need for regulation. One would be justified, I think, in holding that businesses and corporations have created the need for business ethics. In the current banking and mortgage crisis, already the U. S. government has discussed regulating executive remuneration structures because the same people who caused and contributed to these problems are intent on giving themselves enormous bonuses. It will be interesting to see the kinds of legislation that emerge from the current banking and mortgage crises as citizens and taxpayers around the world bailout financial institutions whose thoughtless actions have created an international economic crisis.

5. How Can a Corporation Be Responsible?

Corporate Social Responsibility

One of the most important issues in business ethics has been the question of corporate social responsibility. Those in business management positions tend to understand corporate social responsibility in the narrowest possible terms, arguing that business has few if any social responsibilities. Milton Friedman, for example, has argued that "the social responsibility of business is to maximize its profits" (1970).[20] Business ethicists, however, want to extend the notion of corporate responsibility. But just what do we mean when we use the word, 'responsibility'? Typically, the word 'responsibility' refers to individual

---

19   Elkington cites Stephan Schmidheiny and the Business Council for Sustainable Development (1992). *Changing Course: A Global Business Perspective on Development and the Environment.* Cambridge, MA, The MIT Press.
20   Milton Friedman (September 13, 1970). "The Social Responsibility of Business is to Maximize its Profits." *The New York Times Magazine*, New York, New York, USA, The New York Times Company. Although Friedman's article has been anthologized many times, it may be found online at: http://www.colorado.edu/studentgroups/libertarians/issues/friedman-soc-resp-business.html .

responsibility. Some argue that we have natural duties or responsibilities to other human beings simply because we are human. Some would even argue that the political community ought to provide all members with health, education, and welfare; others, however, argue for a more limited understanding of individual rights. Certainly, we have a responsibility to treat others with respect, but what does having respect for others require of us? Are we obligated to sell all of our possessions and give the proceeds to the poor? Most would argue that we are not; although, if we wish, we are free to do so. Most would agree that being ethical does not mean we have a responsibility to perform supererogatory acts; we are not obligated to be saints or even to act like saints. If being ethical required this of us, most of us could not or would not be ethical. On the other hand, what if you are walking down the street and you meet someone who is begging for money? Do you have a responsibility to give that person some change? Obviously, she needs the money or she would not be begging. Will she use the change to buy food? Will she try to get back on her feet and become a productive citizen? Or will she use the money to buy drugs or alcohol? Instead of giving her money, would the responsible action be to find her professional help? But are you responsible to give up the time it would take to assist this person? While many would agree that you do not have a responsibility to intervene in the beggar's life, most would agree that you have a responsibility not to harm her; indeed, most ethicists assume that we have a minimal obligation to act according to the principle of harm, i.e., we should not cause harm.[21]

According to Shaw and Barry (1998, 192), we use the word 'responsibility' in at least three senses. First, to be responsible, one must be able make rational

---

21   The classical statement of the harm principle is found in John Stuart Mill's *On Liberty*, where Mill states:

> The object of this Essay is to assert one very simple principle, as entitled to govern absolutely the dealings of society with the individual in the way of compulsion and control, whether the means used be physical force in the form of legal penalties, or the moral coercion of public opinion. That principle is, that the sole end for which mankind are warranted, individually or collectively, in interfering with the liberty of action of any of their number, is self-protection. That the only purpose for which power can be rightfully exercised over any member of a civilized community, against his will, is to prevent harm to others. His own good, either physical or moral, is not a sufficient warrant. He cannot rightfully be compelled to do or forbear because it will be better for him to do so, because it will make him happier, because, in the opinions of others, to do so would be wise, or even right. These are good reasons for remonstrating with him, or reasoning with him, or persuading him, or entreating him, but not for compelling him, or visiting him with any evil in case he do otherwise. To justify that, the conduct from which it is desired to deter him, must be calculated to produce evil to some one else. The only part of the conduct of any one, for which he is amenable to society, is that which concerns others. In the part which merely concerns himself, his independence is, of right, absolute. Over himself, over his own body and mind, the individual is sovereign" (1975 [1859], 10-11).

choices and decisions. Indeed, Hobbes refers to those who can make rational decisions and can represent themselves or others as persons. "A person," Hobbes explains, "is he whose words or actions are considered, either as his own, or as representing the words or actions of an other man, or of any other thing to which they are attributed, whether Truly or by Fiction" (1974 [1651], 217). Since children, people who are mentally handicapped, and people who are in comas cannot represent themselves, they are technically not persons. A child, for instance, becomes a person when he or she reaches the age of majority. This does not mean that children are not human or that parents can treat them any way they wish; rather, parents have increased responsibilities for their young children.[22] If a child should throw her ball through your window, her parents are responsible for replacing the window – the child cannot be held responsible. In most countries, the child is protected by the laws of the state. Despite the parents' irritation with the child, the parent cannot abuse the child. Unfortunately, the concept of personhood is far from straightforward. In the United States, for example, there have been a number of cases in which a child who committed a murder has been tried as an adult; in such cases the state based its decision on the fact that the child was old enough to know right from wrong.[23] Just as children are represented by their parents or guardians, mentally handicapped people and people in comas are represented by their guardians or caregivers because they are unable to represent themselves.[24] Again, we must be clear – mentally handicapped people and people in comas are human but they are not able to represent their best long term interests.

Second, provided that we are able to represent ourselves and make decisions for ourselves, we are responsible for our own actions. If you borrow money from

---

[22] Notice that this means that not all human beings are persons. Indeed, this is one of the important issues in the abortion debate – the question is: Is the fetus a person? not Is the fetus human? To conflate the terms 'human' and 'person' is to commit what Peter A. French calls "an anthropomorphic bias" (1975, 207).

[23] In "Juveniles and the Death Penalty," *FindLaw* reports a 2005 U.S. Supreme Court ruling established that states could not execute juveniles who were under the age of sixteen when they committed their crime. In a sensitive and controversial case that had repercussions well beyond the bench, a very divided (5-4) U.S. Supreme Court ruled in 2005 that executing a convicted murderer whose capital crime was committed at the age of 17 constituted "cruel and unusual punishment" under the Eighth Amendment. The decision in *Roper v. Simmons*, overruled an earlier Court decision (*Stanford v. Kentucky*). Further, as applicable to the states under the Fourteenth Amendment, the decision rendered several state laws unconstitutional, causing those states (12 in all) to reverse sentences for 72 prisoners on death row who were under 18 at the time of committing capital crimes. As of 2005, at least 20 of 38 states with the death penalty had permitted its application to offenders less than 18 years old ://criminal.findlaw.com/crimes/juvenile-justice/juveniles-and-the-death-penalty.html .

[24] Presumably, this is the reason health care facilities recommend that one have a living will in place before one enters the hospital for surgery.

a friend and promise to repay him on payday, you have a responsibility to do so; you have created an obligation by promising to pay the money to your friend. If I am driving my car after taking my medication on the bottle of which there is a warning against operating a motor vehicle while taking this particular drug, and if I hit and kill a pedestrian, I am responsible for my actions. While I may not be punished for premeditated murder, I may be prosecuted for manslaughter; certainly, I am responsible for having made the very poor decision to drive while taking my medicine. On the other hand, if you are driving and you see an accident, and if you stop to rescue people from the burning vehicle, you deserve recognition for your courageous action. In short, people who do something good are praised for their actions, while people who do something evil are condemned for theirs, because in each case they are assumed to be responsible for their own actions (1998, 192).

Third, one is responsible for "the specific social role that one plays" (Shaw and Barry 1998, 192). If one is a medical doctor, for example, one does not have responsibility for the health and treatment of every ill person on the planet; however, one does have responsibility for his or her patients precisely because as a doctor one has taken those people who are his or her patients under his or her care. Similarly, a teacher has a responsibility for his or her students. This does not mean that a teacher is required to give every student top marks, but a teacher must create an environment conducive to learning, have realistic and attainable expectations, present material as clearly as possible, and be available to his or her students.

If individuals are responsible because they have the ability to make rational moral decisions, because they are able to take responsibility for their actions, and because of the social roles they play, how can we argue that a corporation is responsible for its actions? After all, a corporation is significantly different from an individual; corporations are not, as Peter A. French would say, "biological human beings" (1979, 207). Indeed, Milton Friedman and Peter Drucker both argue that while individuals may be held morally responsible, corporations cannot be. In his *New York Times Magazine* article, "The Social Responsibility of Business is to Maximize its Profits" (1970), Friedman argues that business has a social responsibility to increase profits from a *laissez faire* position. Although some have argued that Friedman's position is unethical, this is not quite correct. It is not intellectually honest to reject a philosophical or ethical position merely because one does not happen to like it. One cannot simply reject a position just because it does not agree with one's own preferred ethical stance; rather, one must offer good reasons and good arguments for why the position with which one disagrees is unacceptable or is inferior to another position and why the preferred position is superior to the rejected position. As indicated by the title of his essay, Friedman actually does have a conception of corporate responsibility, i.e., corporations have a social responsibility to maximize profits. While Friedman does not expound on this point, it stands to reason that if a corporation is attempting to maximize its profits, it can only do this by providing quality goods and services to its customers at the best possible price. Furthermore, if a corporation is providing quality goods and services, demand, in keeping with the laws of capitalism, should be high and that means that the business will need employees to produce these goods and services. Although the corporation does not necessarily intend to provide jobs – that is not its purpose – it will inadvertently do so in pursuing its goal to maximize profits. Presumably, those who work for the corporation will purchase the necessary goods and services to feed, clothe, shelter, and generally make themselves and their families comfortable; hence, the corporation's attempt to maximize its profits will, at least in theory, impact customers and the community positively. If the corporation is maximizing its profits, it will be able to pay dividends to the owners, namely, the stockholders; and if stockholders are receiving dividends, the corporation should be able to attract investors. Additionally, Friedman, like Carroll, stipulates that businesses are obligated to follow the existing laws of the community; the pursuit of profits cannot be compromised by illegal activity. Consequently, a more accurate way to understand Friedman, is to read him as a proponent of the "narrow view" of corporate responsibility (Shaw and Barry 1998, 195).

Moreover, Friedman argues, managers of businesses have specific responsibilities to the stockholders. If the mangers of the business use the corporation's monies and resources for any other reasons than to maximize profits, Friedman insists, the manager is taxing stockholders without allowing them to participate in deciding how to allocate funds. "Taxation without representation!" (1970, 2). Of course, many, like Carroll, believe that corporations should be involved in making philanthropic contributions to the community; corporations should donate monies to education, the arts, and sports programs for youth. Friedman disagrees; the only legitimate reason to contribute to the community beyond providing goods and services for a profit, is if a specific contribution would benefit the business in some way.

> In practice the doctrine of social responsibility is frequently a cloak for actions that are justified on other grounds rather than a reason for those actions.
>
> To illustrate, it may well be in the long run interest of a corporation that is a major employer in a small community to devote resources to providing amenities to that community or to improving its government. That may make it easier to attract desirable employees, it may reduce the wage bill or lessen losses from pilferage and sabotage or have other worthwhile effects. Or it may be that, given the laws about the deductibility of corporate charitable contributions, the stockholders can contribute more to charities they favour by having the corporation make the gift than by doing it themselves, since they can in that way contribute an amount that would otherwise have been paid as corporate taxes (4).

To make Friedman's point about taxation clearer, however, suppose that you have purchased stock in a particular corporation; presumably you have bought stock to make money; you wish to realize a return on your investment. Moreover, suppose that the CEO of that particular corporation decides to make a charitable donation to a radical hate group – an organization that you would be loathe to support. Certainly, you would be offended by the CEO's decision to divert monies to an immoral organization that could have been used to improve the business, to pay dividends to the stockholders, or to make the products available to customers at a lower price, thus making the corporation more competitive. The CEO would be making a political decision on the stockholders' behalf. Friedman believes that if this notion of social responsibility is allowed to take hold, we will end up with socialism because political principles not market principles are determining the CEO's decisions for the corporation.

> This is the basic reason why the doctrine of "social responsibility" involves the acceptance of the socialist view that political mechanisms, not market mechanism, are the appropriate way to determine the allocaton of scarce resources to alternative uses (2).

Furthermore, Friedman asks,

> What does it mean to say that "business" has responsibilities? *Only people can have responsibilities.* A corporation is an artificial person and in this sense may have artificial responsibilities, but "business" as a whole cannot be said to have responsibilities, even in this vague sense (September 13, 1970, 1; http://www.colorado.edu/studentgroups/libertarians/issues/friedman-soc-resp-business.html; italics added).

Corporations cannot have moral responsibilities; only human beings have responsibilities; individuals within the corporation have specific responsibilities defined by the roles that they play within the institution, but the corporation itself is not a biological human being. In particular, Friedman emphasizes management's responsibility to the stockholders of the corporation.

Although Peter Drucker (1981) has been credited with coining the term 'business ethics,' like Friedman, he has been critical of expanding the notion of the social responsibility of business, preferring to understand the role of business very narrowly. Drucker agrees with Friedman that ethics has to do with "individual behaviour" when he writes:

> All authorities of the Western tradition – from the Old Testament prophets all the way to Spinoza in the 17th century, to Kant in the 18th century, Kierkegaard in the 19th century and, in this century, the Englishman F. H. Bradley (*Ethical Studies*) or the American Edmond Cahn (*The Moral Decision*) – are however, in complete agreement on one point: There is only one ethics, one set of rules of morality; one code, that of individual behaviour in which the same rules apply to everyone alike (1981, 19).

On the next page, Drucker continues, "But – and this is the crucial point … There is only one code of ethics, that of *individual behaviour,* for prince and pauper, for rich and poor, for the mighty and the meek alike" (20; italics added). And a few pages further on, he adds, "Ethics, almost anyone in the West would have considered axiomatic, would surely always be ethics of the *individual* and independent of rank and station" (30; italics added).

Peter A. French, however, demurs; people like Friedman and Drucker are mistaken.

> Methodological individualism blinds its adherents to significant differences between types of human organizations. Individualists insist that only individual human beings can qualify as basic moral units and intentional agents. Talk of group, collective, or corporate action, intention, goals, decisions, etc. is, when properly analyzed, reduced to or exposed as disguised talk about the actions, intentions, goals, decisions, etc. of individuals. The individualist program applied to theories of corporate economic behaviour and corporate criminal liability treats corporations as market reactors and is blind to their function as major elements in the broader social environment (1982, 271).[25]

In another place, French accuses the adherents of this position of having "an anthropomorphic bias" because they hold that a person must be a biological human being and that means "that corporations just cannot be moral persons" (1979, 207-08). In keeping with French's concern with corporations' "function as major elements in the broader social environment," business ethicists have attempted to address the question of corporate responsibility by considering just how corporations make decisions.

Typically, individuals make decisions by considering the various possible options in a particular situation, weighing the consequences of choosing one option over the other available possibilities, and finally settling on the one that either best serves the individual's own self-interest or is the least repugnant. Consider your decision to attend the college or university in which you are now enrolled. Perhaps you had some idea of your career path; you wanted an institution that could meet your needs. It would be counterproductive, however, to enter an art school if you intended to become a physician. Perhaps there were financial considerations; your family could not afford an expensive private institution. Or perhaps generations of your family have gone to this particular private institution and your family is willing to do whatever it takes for you to carry on the family tradition. On the other hand, you could work for a year to save money before entering the university. Perhaps you did not make top marks and you were not offered a scholarship. Or perhaps you have a number of scholarships being offered to you; you must decide which one best suits your needs. Perhaps your parents are not wealthy and you need to go to a college or university close to home so that you can live at home to save money on room and board. Still, if you attend the university and receive training for your chosen

---

25 Note that Friedman specifically says, "Society is a collection of individuals and of the various groups they voluntarily form" (1970, 4).

career, you will probably be able to make more money in your life time than if you had not received a university education. Perhaps the best institution for your chosen career is across the county or in another country. Possibly you could apply for a government guaranteed student loan. Or maybe there is a wealthy relative who would consider a low interest loan to help you get through school. All of these factors and more might play into your choice of a college or university. The important point here is that you have made a rational choice by considering the various options open to you in relation to your best long term self-interest; your best long term self-interest and your goals establish a standard that allows you to process the various possibilities open to you. There is a procedure according to which you arrived at your decision.

Now consider a student organization of which you are a member. Is the process of making a decision in such a group really that different from the way in which you arrived at your decision to attend the college or university in which you are currently enrolled? Suppose that some members of the organization want to undertake a service project to assist elementary pupils in a local school with their homework. Suppose that others would like to solicit donations for cancer patients in a local hospital. Suppose that still others would like to hold a fair to raise money to fund scholarships for individuals who cannot afford to attend the university. How do you reach a decision about which project your student organization will undertake? Most likely members will discuss the positive and negative features of the three proposals. Often during such discussions, the proposals are revised and altered. Perhaps the membership will adopt one of the proposals, but it is just as likely that some combination of the proposals will be adopted, or that a completely new proposal will emerge from the discussion. Perhaps the membership will reach consensus regarding which plan seems best to everyone; if not, the membership will, in accordance with the by-laws of the student organization, vote on the various proposals that emerged from the discussion. Most importantly, there are by-laws that establish a procedure for making decisions and identifying positions or offices within the organization – for example, the president who chairs the meeting, the secretary who records minutes, the treasurer who is responsible for the finances, etc. Those who hold these offices are responsible for making certain that the organization follows its stated processes for making decisions. Typically, we say that the members came to a decision. That does not mean that everyone has voted for the same proposal; nor does it mean that everyone voted for one of the three original proposals that were presented at the beginning of the meeting. It simply means that the majority voted for a particular proposal and in so doing, the student organization has made a decision to act in a particular way; hence, we say, 'our student organization decided to … .'

Similarly, corporations make decisions. "It is obvious," French writes, "that a corporation's doing something involves or includes human beings doing things and that the human beings can be described as having reasons for their behaviour" (1979, 212). But what French wants to show "is that there is sense in saying that corporations and not just the people who work in them, have reasons for doing what they do"; hence, corporations can be held responsible for their actions. To demonstrate this, French notes that every corporation, like your student organization, has a procedure, stipulated by corporate policy, for making decisions. French calls this "a Corporation's Internal Decision Structure" or the "CID Structure" (11). The CID Structure has two features: First, the CID Structure stipulates "an organizational or responsibility flow chart that delineates station levels within the corporate power structure." Just as your student organization has a president, a vice-president, a secretary, a treasurer, etc., so too corporations have officers – corporate executive officers, corporate fiduciary officers, presidents, and vice-presidents, for example – who are responsible for running the business. These positions and the attendant responsibilities are clearly defined. In other words, a specific position or office is not particularly dependent on the individual – the biological human being – who holds that position. Those who hold these positions do not intend for their actions to serve their own personal self-interests; they intend their actions to serve the goals and interests of the corporation.

Second, according to French, the CID Structure specifies "corporate decision recognition rule(s) (usually embedded in something called 'corporation policy')." Not only does the CID Structure delineate the offices, the responsibilities that belong to those offices, and the hierarchy within an organization, but it also defines the rules whereby decisions are made. The CID Structure determines how decisions are made from the lowest levels of the corporate hierarchy to the highest, how the departments at the lowest level have input into the corporate decision making process, who has the final decision making authority, and whose authority is greater and as a consequence who can override whom. In other words, the CID Structure delineates power relations within the corporation. As French explains:

> The CID Structure is the personnel organization for the exercise of the corporation's power with respect to its ventures, and as such its primary function is to draw experience from various levels of the corporation into a decision-making and ratification process. When operative and properly activated, the CID Structure *accomplishes a subordination and synthesis of the intentions and acts of various biological persons into a corporate decision* (212; italics added).

French asks us to imagine a situation in which three Gulf Oil Corporation executives are tasked with determining "whether or not Gulf Oil will join a world uranium cartel" (213). The three executives have an enormous number of papers before them to consider.

> Some of the papers will be purely factual reports, some will be contingency plans, some will be formulations of positions developed by various departments, some will outline financial considerations, some will be legal opinions and so on. In so far as these will all have been processed through Gulf's CID Structure system, the personal reasons, if any, individual executives may have had when

writing their reports and recommendations in a specific way will have been diluted by the subordination of individual inputs to peer group input.

Thus, each relevant department in the hierarchical structure of the Gulf Oil Corporation will contribute to the decision of whether or not the corporation will participate in the uranium cartel. Because of the number of diverse positions, personal interests, opinions and beliefs, "personal reasons ... will have been diluted by the subordination of individual inputs to peer group input"; they should not play a role in the final outcome. The three executives will work through the documents, weigh the various positions presented to them, and finally vote on the matter. "Their taking of a vote, French argues, "is authorized procedure in the Gulf CID Structure, which is to say that under these circumstances the vote" of the three executives "can be redescribed as the corporation's making a decision." Thus, French argues, we can speak of the corporation as having made a decision and can hold the corporation morally and legally responsible for its actions. "Simply, when the corporate act is consistent with, an instantiation or an implementation of established corporate policy, then it is proper to describe it as having been done for corporate reasons, as having been caused by a corporate desire coupled with a corporate belief." If businesses and corporations make decisions, businesses and corporations – just like individuals, i.e., biological human beings – can be held responsible for the good that they do and they can also be punished for the evil that they do.

Many say that the purpose of business is to make money. Clearly, there is something to this; a business or a corporation cannot survive without making money. But as mentioned above, Camenisch emphasizes that making a profit in business is tied to producing goods and services. "In looking for the essential or definitive element in business," Camenisch suggests "that it is necessary and helpful to see business as one form of that activity by which humans have from the beginning sought to secure and / or produce the material means of sustaining and then of enhancing life" (1981, 61). In the past, Camenisch reminds us, societies have provided goods and services for their members in a variety of ways. Typically, in hunting and gathering cultures, for example, women who gathered nuts, berries, insects, small game, etc. provided most of the food for the community, while men hunted. If the men were successful, everyone ate well, but storing game was difficult if not impossible; hence, it was either feast or famine. While hunting and gathering is one way to distribute goods and services, it is not the way that we distribute goods and services today – hunting and gathering is not the way that we sustain and enhance our lives. Most people who participate in industrial countries do not hunt or gather to keep themselves and the members of their societies alive. Instead, business involves industry, international trade, and market economies whereby goods and services are distributed.

While this fact may have a number of consequences, let us consider two. First, this means that business is not merely about making money; clearly,

Camenisch notes, there is a significant difference between doing business and robbing banks; robbing banks is not about producing goods and services; it is merely about making or at least acquiring money; business is about providing goods and services to human communities for a profit.

> What if profit is present but the provision of goods and services is entirely absent as in a bank robbery. Most ... would deny that here we have just another instance of business, or even an instance of business of a rather unusual sort. Most would simply want to deny that the bank robber was engaged in business at all (63).

Business is not theft! If business exists to provide goods and service, then business plays a social, economic, and political role in the life of human communities. It may be true that many individuals are attracted to business because there is a great deal of money to be made in business careers, but we must distinguish between the reasons that individuals are attracted to business and the social, economic, and political role that business plays within society.

Second, if business exists to provide goods and services to human communities, then businesses must be bound by certain ethical and moral standards. Any action by a business or those involved in conducting business that causes harm to the social, political, or economic fabric of the community, to individual members of the community, specific groups within the community, to the practitioners or stakeholders of the business, or to the enterprise itself must be rigorously scrutinized. However, therein lies the problem. If we think of business as something that is separate from the complexities of the social, economic, and political spheres of human communities, if we think of "us" (the citizens, the people, and the consumers) as opposed to "them" (businesses, corporations, and business people), we are ignoring the important social role that these institutions play in our world. On the other hand, if we think of business as part of the social, economic, and political fabric of the community, citizens, consumers, and stakeholders have the right and the obligation to demand ethical behaviour from businesses, corporations, and those conducting business. With the intensity of globalization, the former is not really an option at all; we cannot afford to think of businesses and corporations as being separate from society; we must expand the moral community to include these institutions. Once we think of business not as separate from but an important part of the social, political, and economic fabric of society, the truth of Solomon's claim becomes evident. "Business is itself an ethics, defined by ethics, made possible by ethics."

6. Conclusion

Although there are a number of ways to think about business ethics, perhaps the various approaches to the discipline can be understood as falling between two poles. At one extreme is the view that business ethics is exclusively an academic discipline in which one studies ethics and ethical behaviour as they pertain to business. Business ethics, according to this view, is descriptive and not prescriptive. Philosophy, including philosophical ethics has as its task to reflect on what is already there - what has already taken place; it is the task of business ethics to study what businesses, corporations, and business people *have done*, not to tell them what they *ought* to do. At the other extreme is the view that business ethics is a discipline that will bring radical change to business as it is actually practiced by being involved in developing policy, offering workshops and training sessions on business ethics for business people, teaching business ethics courses in professional schools, universities, and colleges, serving as ethical consultants to businesses, and so on. As Aristotle holds, ethics is not just a study of good and evil; rather, ethics is the study of good and evil actions; ethics is about how one should act and as such ethics belongs to practical philosophy. It is probably true that we cannot totally adopt either one of these two extremes to the exclusion of the other; fortunately, most ethicists fall somewhere between these two poles. The difficulty here is that those who tend to cluster around the latter view are often disappointed. At the International Business Ethics Conference, entitled "Business Ethics in a Global Economy," held at the Markkula Center for Applied Ethics, Santa Clara University, Santa Clara, California (February 16-20, 2005), I was fascinated by how many people in the field were extremely disappointed that so little progress had been made in actually changing business and corporate behaviour. Additionally, they could not understand how businesses that had once had a reputation for ethical decision making and ethical behaviour had compromised themselves.

We can ill afford superficial idealism or negative cynicism here; we must remain optimistic and yet realistic. The stakes in business are extremely high; there are enormous amounts of money to be made and to be lost. Still, we are clearly being naïve if we expect that businesses, corporations, and business people will reach some sort of utopian state where everything and everyone will be perfect and where we can be finished with business ethics once and for all. If ethics has to do with action, as long as we are living we will act and as long as we act, we will be required to make ethical decisions; we are unlikely to attain stasis – a state of equilibrium where no ethical decisions and no actions are required of us. That means that it is always possible to make better or worse decisions; just as it is possible for us and for business institutions to act more ethically, it is also possible to act less ethically. This means that ethics in general and business ethics in particular are important because all stakeholders in business – consumers, the community, business people, and business institutions themselves – need to keep the discussion of ethical issues alive in public debate. While philosophers and business ethicists may have taken the lead in bringing these issues to the public arena, in democratic forms of government participation in public debate is required of all citizens; hence, citizens must be educated not only about the issues but also about how to think about and how to discuss the issues.

In some important respects, however, we are in uncharted waters here. We have incredible wealth and incredible poverty and an enormous gap between the haves and the have-nots. Globalization has forced us to become aware of the limits of our environment and natural resources. While we have made remarkable progress in curing disease and lengthening life spans, we live with immense population pressures due in part to our successes; statisticians tell us that these pressures will continue to increase in the foreseeable future. Surely Thomas Friedman is correct; planet Earth has become "hot, flat, and crowded" (2008). Given the economic, political, and social fabric of much of the world, it seems unlikely and unrealistic to think that businesses and corporations will not be players in one form or another as we make the difficult transition from a fossil fuel based energy economy to more sustainable energy sources, whether these new energy sources will be solar, tidal, wind, bio-fuels, hydrogen fuel cells, methane, nuclear, or, as is more likely, some combination of all of these. Corporations have enormous resources to develop these technologies.

Business ethicists, too, will have a role to play in defining the agenda for the 21st Century as we move forward to address these enormous social, political, economic, and environmental problems. Obviously, business ethicists will argue against compromising our basic civil rights and our freedoms, and at the same time they will insist that all stakeholders have a duty to others and to future generations to become responsible for the environment and the use of natural resources. It will be especially important to develop new models for development of underdeveloped countries – models that avoid the incredible waste of natural and human resources that has been the by-product of Western development. Business ethicists will become more involved in the question of plant relocation, exporting industries to countries with cheap labor, sustainability, the triple-bottom line, and forcing corporations to internalize their externalities.[26]

---

26 In his "Ethical Issues in Plant Relocation," John P. Kavanagh defines "externalities."

The term "externalities" is common enough in the literature of economics. It refers to unintended side effects – good or bad – which an operation produces along with its intended product. In recent years environmentalists have emphasized externalities which affect the quality of air or water in the vicinity of manufacturing plants. A firm really interested in producing paper, for example, also produces physical and chemical waste products which may affect the surrounding environment adversely if not properly controlled. The company has no interest in producing these products nor any direct intention of doing so, but in doing what it does intend –making paper – it also perforce produces these unwanted products (Shaw and Barry, 1998, 231).

Even though some members of the community do not purchase or use the product, the costs of making the product are passed on to all members of the community. By challenging corporations to internalize their externalities, ethicists are encouraging

They will be involved in analyzing policies, proposing legislation to regulate businesses, and proposing strategies to encourage corporations to become good citizens without regulation.

While many still sneer at the idea of business ethics, we must ask ourselves, what are the alternatives here? One possibility is a totalitarian state – left or right - that would stand any unethical business person before the firing squad. The problem with this solution is that totalitarian regimes are corrupt. Who will watch the watchers? Who will watch the totalitarian state? Another solution proposed by some is to return to more traditional forms of communal societies. Like it or not, this seems rather unlikely. Indeed, citizens of developing nations, not surprisingly, seem to want the freedoms that we in the West enjoy, including the freedom to purchase desired goods and services. If this is true, and if it is true that we value our democratic institutions and our civil liberties, then the only solution is ethics in some form or other. Indeed, we need to educate autonomous citizens who are able to participate in public life, who are able to analyze, criticize, and debate the important problems that we face and the proposed solutions to those problems. Clearly, self regulation based on ethical standards would be best; then, perhaps government regulation would even become unnecessary. In democratic societies, is there any other choice?

BIBLIOGRAPHY

Ahner, G. (2007). *Business Ethics, Making a Life, Not Just a Living.* New York, Orbis Books.

Andre, C. and Velasquez, M. (1987). What is Ethics? *Issues in Ethics*, 1, 1 (Fall), 1-2. http://www.scu.edu/ethics/publications/iie/v1n1/whatis.html.

Anon (1986). *Economic Justice for All, Pastoral Letter on Catholic Social Teaching and the US Economy.* Washington, D.C., National Conference of Catholic Bishops.

Baumhart, R. (1961). How Ethical are Businessmen? *Harvard Business Review*, 39 (July-August), 4, 6-8, 10, 12, 16, 19, 156,158, 160, 163-64, 166, 168, 170-72, 174, 176.

Beauchamp, T. L. and Norman E. B. (eds.) (2001). *Ethical Theory and Business*

---

businesses and the consumer of their products to take complete responsibility for all actual costs of production and not to pass some costs, e.g., negative environmental consequences of production, on to those who are not involved in the buying or selling of the product.

(6th Edition). Upper Saddle River, New Jersey, Prentice Hall.

Camenisch, P. F. (1981). Business Ethics, On Getting to the Heart of the Matter. *Business and Professional Ethics Journal*, 1, 1 (Fall), 59-68.

Carr, A, Z. (1968). Is Business Bluffing Ethical? *Harvard Business Review*, 46, 1 (Jan/Feb), 143-53.

Carroll, A. B. (1991). The Pyramid of Corporate Social Responsibility, Toward the Moral Management of Organizational Stakeholders. *Business Horizons*, 34, 4 (July-Aug), 39-48. http://www-rohan.sdsu.edu/faculty/dunnweb/rprnts.pyramidofcsr.pdf).

Anon. (1986). *Defense Industry Initiative on Business Ethics and Conduct*. http://www.defenseethics.org/home.html.

De George, R. (Feb 19, 2005). A History of Business Ethics. A talk delivered at "The Accountable Corporation Conference" the third biennial global business ethics conference sponsored by the Markkula Center for Applied Ethics, Santa Clara University, Santa Clara, California, USA. http://www.scu.edu/ethics/practicing/focusareas/business/conference/presentations/business-ethics-history.html .

De George, R. (1982). What Is the American Business Value System? *Journal of Business Ethics*, 1, 4, 267-75.

_____ (1987). The Status of Business Ethics, Past and Future. *Journal of Business Ethics*. 6, 3, 201-11.

_____ (1995). *Business Ethics*. Englewood Cliffs, New Jersey, Prentice Hall.

_____ (1999). *Business Ethics (6th Edition)*. Upper Saddle River, New Jersey, Prentice Hall.

DesJardins, J. R. and John J. McCall (2004). *Contemporary Issues in Business Ethics (5th Edition)*. Kentucky, Cengage Learning.

_____ (2008). *Introduction to Business Ethics (3rd Edition)*. New York, McGraw-Hill Companies.

Donaldson, T., Werhane, P. H. and Cording, M. (2002). *Ethical Issues in Business, A Philosophical Approach (7th Edition)*. Upper Saddle River, New Jersey, Prentice Hall.

Drucker, P. (1981). "What is Business Ethics?" *The Public Interest*, 63 (Spring), 18-36.

Elkington, J. (1994). Towards the Sustainable Corporation, Win-Win-Win Strategies for sustainable Development. *California Management Review*, 36, 2

(Winter), 90-100.

Fieser, J. (2006). Ethics. *The Internet Encyclopedia of Philosophy*. http://www.iep.utm.edu/e/ethics.htm, 1-14.

FindLaw (2009). Juveniles and the Death Penalty. Egan, Minnesota, Thomson Reuters: http://criminal.findlaw.com/crimes/juvenile-justice/juveniles-and-the-death-penalty.html.

Frederick, R. E. (ed.) (2002). *A Companion to Business Ethics*. Oxford, Blackwell Publishing.

French, P. A. (1979). The Corporation as a Moral Person. *American Philosophical Quarterly*, 16, 3 (July) 207-15.

_____ (1982). Crowds and Corporations. *American Philosophical Quarterly*, 19, 3, 271-77.

Friedman, M. (September 13, 1970). The Social Responsibility of Business is to Maximize its Profits. *The New York Times Magazine*, New York, New York, USA, The New York Times Company: http://www.colorado.edu/studentgroups/libertarians/issues/friedman-soc-resp-business.html .

Friedman, T. L. (2008). *Hot, Flat, and Crowded, Why We Need a Green Revolution and How It Can Renew America*. New York, Farrar, Straus and Giroux.

Gandz, J. and Hayes, N. (1988). Teaching Business Ethics. *Journal of Business Ethics*, 7, 9 (September), 657-69.

Hobbes, T. (1974 [1651]), *Leviathan* (ed. C. B. Macpherson). Harmondsworth, Middlesex, England, Penguin Books Ltd.

Hume, D. (1999 [1748]). *An Enquiry Concerning Human Understanding* (Beauchamp, T. L. (ed.)). Oxford, Oxford University Press.

Kavanagh, J. P. Ethical Issues in Plant Relocation. In Shaw, W. H. and Barry, V. (1998). *Moral Issues in Business. 7th Edition*. Belmont, California, USA, Thomson Wadsworth Publishing Company, 230-35.

King, M. L., Jr. (1964). *Why We Can't Wait*. New York, New American Library, Signet Classic.

Kung, H. (1992). Declaration of the Religions for a Global Ethic. http://astro.temple.edu/~dialogue/Antho/kung.htm.

Luijk, H. van (2002). Business Ethics in Europe, A Tale of Two Efforts. In Frederick, R. E. (ed.) (2002). *A Companion to Business Ethics*. Oxford, Blackwell Publishing, 353-65.

Marcoux, A. (2006). The Concept of Business Ethics. *Journal of Private Enterprise.* http://findarticles.com/p/articles/mi_qa5477/is_200604/ai_n21406562/.

_____ (2008). Business Ethics. *Stanford Encyclopedia of Philosophy*, 1-16. http://plato.stanford.edu/entries/ethics-business/.

McMahon, T. F. (2002). A Brief History of American Business Ethics. In Frederick, R. E. (ed.) (2002). *A Companion to Business Ethics.* Oxford, Blackwell Publishing, 342-52.

Mill, J. S. (1975 [1859]). *On Liberty* (Spitz, D. ed.). New York, W. W. Norton and Company.

Moore, B. N. and Bruder, K. (1998). *Philosophy, The Power of Ideas (2nd Edition).* Mountain View, California, Mayfield Publishing.

Moore, G. E. (1965). *Principia Ethica.* London, Cambridge University Press.

Newton, L. H. (2002). *Ethics and Sustainability, Sustainable Development and the Moral Life* (Basic Ethics in Action). Upper Saddle River, New Jersey, Prentice Hall.

Newton, L. H. and Ford, M. M (2007). *Taking Sides, Clashing Views on Controversial Issues in Business Ethics and Society (10th Edition).* New York, McGraw-Hill / Dushkin.

Norman, W. (n. d.). http://www.philo.umontreal.ca/prof/wayne.norman.html.

Parliament of the World's Religions (September 4, 1993). *Declaration of a Global Ethic.* Chicago, Illinois. http://www.parliamentofreligions.org/_includes/FCKcontent/File/TowardsAGlobalEthic.pdf.

Plato (1968). *The Republic* (Bloom, A. trans.). New York, Basic Books.

Pojman, L. P. (1998). *Ethical Theory, Classical and Contemporary Readings (3rd Edition).* California, Wadsworth Publishing Company.

Pope Leo XIII (1891). *Rerum Novarum, Encyclical of Pope Leo XIII on Capital and Labor.* Vatican, Libreria Editrice Vaticana. http://www.vatican.va/holy_father/leo_xiii/encyclicals/documents/hf_l-xiii_enc_15051891_rerum-novarum_en.html .

Rachels, J. (2003). *Elements of Moral Philosophy (4th Edition).* New York, McGraw Hill.

Roberts, R. (2001). *The Invisible Heart, An Economic Romance.* Cambridge, Massachusetts, Massachusetts Institute of Technology Press.

Shaw, W. H. and Barry, V. (1998). *Moral Issues in Business (7th Edition).* Belmont,

California, Thomson Wadsworth Publishing Company.

Singer, P. (ed.) (1993). *A Companion to Ethics*. Oxford, Blackwell Publishing.

Solomon, R. C. (1984). *Morality and the Good Life, An Introduction to Ethics through Classical Sources*. New York, McGraw-Hill Book Company.

_____ (1993). Business Ethics. In Singer, P. (ed.).

_____ (1997). *It's Good Business, Ethics and Free Enterprise for the New Millennium*. Maryland, Rowman and Littlefield Publishers, Inc.

Stackhouse, M. L., McCann, D. P., and Roels, S. J. with Williams, P. N. (eds.) (1995). *On Moral Business, Classical and Contemporary Resources for Ethics in Economic Life*. Michigan, William B. Eerdmans Publishing Company.

Sullivan, L. H., Reverend (1971). *The Global Sullivan Principles*. http://www.thesullivanfoundation.org/gsp/default.asp).

Tawney, R. H. (1926). *Religion and the Rise of Capitalism*. New York, Harcourt, Brace and Company.

Velasquez, M. G. (2006). *Business Ethics (6th Edition)*. Upper Saddle River, New Jersey, Prentice Hall.

Velasquez, M; Andre, C; Shanks, T. S. J.; and Meyer, M. J. (Fall, 1987). What is Ethics? http://www.scu.edu/ethics/practicing/decision/whatisethics.html.

Weiss, J. W. (2009). *Business Ethics, A Stakeholder Issues Management Approach (5th Edition)*. Ohio, Cengage Learning.

Williams, B. (1985), *Ethics and the Limits of Philosophy*. Cambridge, Massachusetts, Harvard University Press.

4

Ethics of Care

Treasa Campbell

1. Introduction

Feminist ethics[1] has become a well-established sub-discipline within the broader field of moral philosophy. Feminist insights into ethics arise from and express the conditions of women's moral lives. At the heart of the feminist approach is the conviction that the lived experience of women is important and relevant to the development of moral theory. Ethics of care refers to a significant contemporary branch of feminist moral theory and is a relatively new way of thinking about ethics. Prior to 1982 the concept of care did not have a significant place in the discourse of mainstream Western ethics. It was not research in philosophy that generated the momentum to push the concept of care on to the ethical discussion table, but empirical work carried out in moral psychology. The findings of psychologist Carol Gilligan's investigation into women's moral development, set out in her 1982 publication *In a Different Voice*, ignited contemporary interest in care as a distinctive form of moral reasoning. Section 2 of this chapter sets out why her findings were so influential, while Section 3 examines how ethics of care can move beyond a strictly female morality.

The publication of Nel Noddings's *Caring* in 1984 was another significant origin of ethics of care. Noddings's work heralded the arrival of care ethics as a viable philosophical discourse. It provided important vocabulary which greatly advanced attempts to provide a description of ethics of care. While care ethics as a distinctive ethical approach was initiated by Gilligan and Noddings, others in the feminist tradition made contributions throughout the '80s, which significantly advanced its development[2]. This groundwork was greatly elaborated

---

[1] Feminist ethics are not a homogeneous set of ideas, there is no single feminist moral theory. See edited collections by Desautels and Waugh (2001) and Card (1991). Brennan (1999) surveys recent scholarship in feminist ethics which takes the discipline in different directions to ethics of care.

[2] See the research contained in edited collections by Brabeck (1989), Kittay and Meyers (1987) and Hanen and Nielsen (1987).

and extended upon by a host of advocates working from 1990 onwards[3]. These contributions have produced a series of independent models for an ethics of care and generated debates which have attracted the attention of moral philosophers of every persuasion. In Section 4 the central elements that give ethics of care its distinctive moral approach are discussed.

Ethics of care is a relationship-based approach to ethics, which offers an important alternative or corrective to more familiar principle-based approaches such as utilitarianism or Kantian ethics, as well as various types of contemporary liberalism such as that put forward by John Rawls. While consequentialist and deontological ethical theories are grounded in universal, abstract principles, the ethics of care emphasizes the importance of context, relationships, narrative and emotion. Section 5 looks at the difficulties care ethics faces in addressing the considerations of justice and impartiality. As the name suggests, at the foundations of ethics of care is the contention that care constitutes an essential element of morality. Through the work of its various proponents, ethics of care has developed and matured, increasing in theoretical sophistication. Today, we find that the moral theory set out in ethics of care is being applied to an ever-increasing array of issues of moral concern. Efforts to expand the moral significance of caring from the private sphere of domestic-familial relations into the public sphere of political and social policy will be explored in the final Section.

2. Tuning into the Voice of Care

The history of western philosophical thought is permeated with the belief that men and women not only think differently, but that women are less rational and therefore less morally developed than men. Key western thinkers such as Aristotle, Kant and Freud considered women morally and intellectually inferior to men. In the 1960's and '70s the women's movements vehemently rejected the idea that there existed psychological differences between women and men. It was argued that where differences occurred they were the result of conditioning by male patriarchal structures and not the manifestation of mental or moral differences between the sexes. However, the feminist thinking that gives rise to ethics of care is one that acknowledges and provides empirical evidence[4] for the view that women think differently to men. The female moral approach is

---

3   See edited collections by Larrabee (1993), Held (1995) and Cole and Coultrap-McQuin (1992) as well as individual contribution such as Bubeck (1995), Fisher and Tronto (1990), Hekman (1995), Held (1993), Jaggar (1995), Manning (1992), Ruddick (1995) and Tronto (1993).

4   Issues have been raised about the empirical correctness of Gilligan's test results as well as the inferences she draws from these findings. See for example Auerbach et al. (1985), Flanagan and Jackson (1987) and Nails (1983).

celebrated and held to yield crucial moral insights overlooked in male dominated approaches.

Carol Gilligan's empirical investigations charted how women conduct their moral reasoning on different premises from those of men. Earlier feminist work on mothering (Chodorow, 1978; Ruddick, 1980) emphasised the ethical relevance of maternal thinking beyond the practice itself. This work drew links between gender, the activity of caring and a distinctive moral outlook based on relationships and responsibilities. However, Gilligan's book *In a Different Voice* is widely considered to be the seminal text in the field of care ethics[5]. This work on women's moral development was a reaction to the research of her Harvard colleague Lawrence Kohlberg. Heavily influenced by Jean Piaget's theory of cognitive development, Kohlberg was a pioneer in the field of moral development. Kohlberg's research identified six stages of moral development. These stages can be grouped into three levels, each containing two stages.

Level I: Pre-conventional Morality

Stage 1 - Obedience and Punishment Orientation: At this stage the morally right action is conceived as the one that avoids punishment by obeying authority.

Stage 2 - Individualism and Exchange: At this stage the morally right action is conceived in terms of self interest.

Level II. Conventional Morality

Stage 3 – Interpersonal: At this stage the morally right action is the one that accords with the expectations of those we have relationships with such as family and community.

Stage 4. Maintaining the Social Order. At this stage the morally right action is seen as the one which upholds the laws and maintains the wider social order.

Level III. Postconventional Morality

Stage 5. Social Contract: At this stage the morally right action goes beyond laws to rights and attempts to promote general welfare.

Stage 6: Universal Principles: At this stage the morally right action is impartial and universal and is made with the knowledge of how justice is achieved.

Kohlberg's stages were derived exclusively from the interview responses of male children of various ages presented with abstract cases of moral dilemmas.

---

5   For useful discussions of Gilligan's work see collections of articles in Kittay and Meyers (1987), Brabeck (1989), Cole-Browning and Coultrap-McQuin (1992), Larrabee (1993) and Puka (1994) as well as books such as Okin (1989), Tronto (1993) and Young (1990).

Once presented with a dilemma the interviewee was then asked questions designed to elicit their moral judgments and to track the reasoning process by which they arrived at their judgements. Kohlberg identified each stage as morally more advanced than that which preceded it. Having established these stages as a gauge of moral development Kohlberg's test results found that men and women frequently scored at different stages on the scale. Women typically place at Stage 3 (Interpersonal) whereas men more commonly place at Stages 4 and 5. This carries with it the implication that women are not as morally developed as men. But it has been argued that Kohlberg, in excluding girls and women from his study of moral development, ignored and trivialized the moral orientation of women. Gilligan criticizes Kohlberg for basing his conception of moral maturity solely on observations of men. The moral orientation reflected in the responses of Kohlberg's male interviewees is one of formal justice in which moral reasoning appeals to rules, rights and abstract principles. Gilligan rejects Kohlberg's conception of moral maturity. Through her observations of women's moral reasoning, Gilligan develops an ethical framework that challenges the dominant justice based notion of moral maturity reflected in the Kohlberg stages.

Unlike the male respondents of Kolhberg's study who were presented with abstract cases of moral dilemmas, Gilligan's female respondents were faced with real moral dilemmas as opposed to merely hypothetical ones. What Gilligan found in her female respondents was a different moral orientation. In contrasting the primary moral orientation of boys and men with the primary orientation of girls and women her research confirms that men and women use fundamentally different approaches in ethical deliberations. They apply a different logic. Gilligan compares the different responses of two eleven year olds, Jake and Amy, when presented with the problem which is known as the Heinz's Dilemma[6]. Heinz's wife is critically ill and needs life saving drugs but the couple can not afford the price the druggist is charging for the medicine. The children are asked if Heinz should steal the drug. Jake is clear from the outset that Heinz should steal the drug. He reasons as follows:

> For one thing, a human life is worth more than money, and if the druggist only

---

6   The original dilemma is as follows: "A woman was near death from a special kind of cancer. There was one drug that the doctors thought might save her. It was a form of radium that a druggist in the same town had recently discovered. The drug was expensive to make, but the druggist was charging ten times what the drug cost him to produce. He paid $200 for the radium and charged $2,000 for a small dose of the drug. The sick woman's husband, Heinz, went to everyone he knew to borrow the money, but he could only get together about $1,000 which is half of what it cost. He told the druggist that his wife was dying and asked him to sell it cheaper or let him pay later. But the druggist said: "No, I discovered the drug and I'm going to make money from it." So Heinz got desperate and broke into the man's store to steal the drug for his wife. Should Heinz have broken into the laboratory to steal the drug for his wife? Why or why not?" (Kohlberg, 1969, 379)

makes $1,000, he is still going to live, but if Heinz doesn't steal the drug, his wife is going to die (Why is life worth more than money?). Because the druggist can get a thousand dollars later from rich people with cancer, but Heinz can't get his wife again (Why not?). Because people are all different and so you couldn't get Heinz's wife again (Gilligan, 1982, 26-28).

Jake sees the dilemma as a conflict between the wife's right to live and the druggist's property rights. In his reasoning he prioritises the value of life and justifies his recommended action (steal the drugs) on this basis. By contrast Amy's response, though hesitant and evasive, indicates that Heinz should not steal the drug.

> Well, I don't think so. I think there might be other ways besides stealing it, like if he could borrow the money or make a loan or something, but he really shouldn't steal the drug--but his wife shouldn't die either... If he stole the drug, he might save his wife then, but if he did, he might have to go to jail, and then his wife might get sicker again, and he couldn't get more of the drug, and it might not be good. So, they should really just talk it out and find some other way to make the money (Gilligan, 1982, 26-28).

Amy sees the dilemmas in terms of a conflict between the druggist and Heinz. As such, the resolution lies in further discussions and not in the identification of which rights trump others. The wider context such as the effect the theft could have on the relationship between Heinz and his wife is also central to her reasoning. What we see in Amy's reasoning is recognition of people's connections with others and a moral recognition that we need to care for those connections in our actions. She acknowledges that every person has a voice that deserves to be heard. As a result, she does not retreat into abstract logical deliberation but examines a narrative of relationships that extends over time. According to the Kohlberg stages of moral development, Jake's reasoning is much more advanced then Amy's. In prioritising personal relationships Amy places at Stage 3 whereas Jake's appeal to impersonal principles elevates him to level 4 or 5.

Gilligan rejects the suggestion that the female approach to moral reasoning reflected in Amy's response is in any way less developed. What emerges from her work is empirical support for the existence of two distinct moral voices[7]. These two different kinds of moral voices, the voice of justice and the voice of care, represent two ways of approaching moral problems. The voice of justice, represented in Kohlberg's stages and throughout the male dominated tradition of western moral theory, speaks of impartiality, impersonality, justice, formal rationality, equality and universal principles. Well-known ethical views such as utilitarianism and deontology come under this 'justice view' of morality, a conception of morality which, according to Gilligan, fails to capture a distinctly female voice on moral matters.

The women in Gilligan's interviews act on a very different moral voice, one

---

7   Flanagan (1991) goes further in arguing for a plurality of moral personality.

which spoke of personal attachment and the importance of sustaining personal relationships. In placing the focus on interpersonal relationships, rather than rights and universal principles, women tend to frame moral issues in terms of a responsibility to care. In their moral reasoning Gilligan's female interviewees did not focus on a series of moral decisions abstracted away from the details of each situation, but concentrated on narratives, contexts, and relationships of care. These women tended to recognize a plurality of moral interests and attempted to accommodate these diverse interests in their own moral reasoning. For those listening to the voice of care Gilligan describes how moral problems arise from "conflicting responsibilities rather than from competing rights" (Gilligan, 1982, 19). In order to resolve such problems what is required is "a mode of thinking that is contextual and narrative rather than formal and abstract" (1982, 19). In emphasizing solidarity, community and care within relationships, ethics of care leads to actions that seek to strengthen and protect attachments between persons. Moral development then is measured not upon one's understanding of rights and rules, but one's understanding of responsibility and relationships.

Ethics of care is a normative ethical theory. As such, it sets out to determine what makes actions right or wrong. Gilligan tunes into the voice of care using the descriptive empirical methods of moral psychology. However, she argues not only that the psychological reality of the voice of care has been ignored but that its normative significance has also been overlooked. She rejects the assumption that principle based ethics, called for by the voice of justice, is superior to an ethic that emphasizes intimacy, caring, and personal relationships. Gilligan's research led to widespread efforts to develop a systematic philosophical ethics of care. The insight driving such efforts remains a commitment to placing care at the very center of ethics. Before providing a more detailed description of the moral approach envisaged by ethics of care's adherents, let us first establish if, given its origins in female moral psychology, it is possible for the ethics of care to move beyond an exclusively female form of moral reasoning[8].

3. Beyond a Gendered Morality

One of the central feminist criticisms levelled at ethics of care is that it reinforces and perpetuates traditional female stereotypes. Such critics[9] hold that emphasizing caring as a virtuous feminine quality generates the expectation that a woman's job

---

8   Work which highlights the difficulties of demonstrating gender-relatedness in moral theory includes Walker (1995) and Skoe (1998). Aspects of gender-relatedness in moral theory have received considerable attention. For debate concerning the gender aspect of Gilligan's work see for example Tronto (1994) and Broughton (1983).
9   For feminist criticisms of ethics of care see Auerbach, et al. (1985), Card (1990), Greeno (1993), Hoagland (1991), Houston, (1987 and 1990) and Willett (1995).

is to care, an expectation which contributes to the subordination of women. It is argued that to attribute ethics of care exclusively to women is both inaccurate and dangerous (Card, 1990; Groenhout, 2004; Hekman, 1995; Koehn, 1998; Okin, 1994). However, many care advocates want to deny that care is an ethic that only women articulate, or an ethic that is valid only within the moral experience of women. The ethics of care is about more than highlighting issues of gender difference in morality. In arguing for the moral relevance of care, advocates contend that caring is an important ingredient within all human morality. Indeed many of its proponents are keen to reject any gender essentialism, arguing that men as well as women can learn from the testimony of women's experiences. Noddings argues that an ethical orientation that arises in female experience need not be confined to women (Noddings, 1990). Her expectation is that all people, not just women, should act as carers.

While Gilligan reported that women are generally more likely to emphasize care while men generally emphasize justice, she also noted that most men and women can reason in accordance with both care and justice. Gilligan warns that the voice of care should be characterized "not by gender, but by theme" (Gilligan, 1982, 2). Tronto (1993) argues that care cannot be a useful moral and political concept until its traditional and ideological associations as a 'women's morality' are challenged. For this reason the debate surrounding the viability of ethics of care is better served by framing it in terms of the adequacy of competing views of morality, 'care' and 'justice,' rather then in gender terms. There are people who are more inclined to adopt a caring perspective and there are those more inclined to think in terms of principles. Neither of these approaches is exclusively male or female.

Many researchers argue that an individual's preference for the use of a care over a justice ethic is not gender related. Instead they point to various other factors which they believe play a far greater role in shaping one's moral tendencies. In place of gender, factors such as economic class, education (Landau, 2006; Lykes, 1989) or culture (Vikana et al, 2005) have all been postulated as better guides in determining the likelihood that one will operate on an ethic of care. Indeed, studies have shown that there is a much greater employment of care ethics among men and women in non-Western cultures such as traditional African societies (Harding, 1987) and among minority groups such as African Americans (Stack, 1986). Having established that both men and women have the capacity to opt for a care based approach in moral reasoning, let us now take a detailed look at what such an approach entails.

4. Features of Ethics of Care

Like many ethical approaches, the proponents of care ethics do not form a homogenous, unified collective. It is a complex field within which contemporary care theorists differ about how to formulate their shared doctrine. However, despite these debates, there is enough communality to differentiate ethics of care from other ethical traditions and to sketch out the shape of its distinctive moral approach. Within ethics of care the fact that we care about things and about other people is a fundamental factor in how we resolve moral problems. Fisher and Tronto define "care" as:

> A species activity that includes everything that we do to maintain, continue, and repair our 'world' so that we can live in it as well as possible. That world includes our bodies, our selves, and our environment, a species of which we seek to interweave in a complex, life-sustaining web (1990, 40).

On this view not only is caring for others an integral part of living in social groups, it is what makes people human. Importantly, care is defined as an activity, an action and not as a set rules. Ethics of care incorporates the universal experience of caring into moral theory. Tronto maintains that even though the meaning of care may vary from one society to another, and from one group to another, care is nonetheless a universal aspect of human life (1993, 110). Conceptually, care is both particular (care differs depending on context) and universal (care is fundamentally human). Care is both a practical activity and an ethical framework. The activity of "good caring" is a complex process[10] involving attentiveness, responsibility, competence and responsiveness. Fisher and Tronto (1990) identified four phases of care which corresponded to these essential aspects of the caring process. To summarise, attentiveness is captured in the first phase "caring about", which involves becoming aware of and paying attention to the need for caring. Heinz's difficulty arose from the druggist's failure to respond to the need for care. It is not enough to simply see a need for care, we must then move to the "caring for" stage. In this second stage one assumes a responsibility to meet the needs that have been identified. It is then that the "care giving" phase takes place. Competence in meeting caring needs is an essential stage in good caring. Finally, the "care receiving" stage involves the response of the thing, person, or group that is the recipient of caregiving to the care received.

Caring is not seen as a less developed, primitive step to moral maturity. Each stage in the caring activity requires a complicated process of judgment. The complexities of this process have led Owen Flanagan and Kathryn Jackson to describe the justice approach's advantage over care as one of "cognitive economy" (1987, 626). The identification of individual needs is a time-consuming activity. Taylor captures the time-intensive aspect of ethics of care in the simple example of the division of a pie. The application of a justice ethic might lead to the swift implementation of some rule, such as equal division. Ethics of care, however, would "require more time-intensive communication among the participants in order to reveal individual needs and tailor the allocation to meet those needs" (Taylor, 1998, 478).

---

10 Tronto acknowledges that in reality the ideal process of care rarely occurs.

The fact that ethics of care is a practice rather than a set of rules or principles can lead to a certain level of ambiguity when it comes to describing exactly what is meant by an ethics of care. Generally, explanations invoke contrasts with the ethics of justice. We can delineate the shape of ethics of care by setting out its departures from the more familiar elements of a justice-based approach. Gilligan differentiated these contrasting approaches by stating that a conception of morality which is concerned with the activity of care "centers moral development around the understanding of responsibility and relationships". However, a "conception of morality as fairness ties moral development to the understanding of rights and rules"(1982, 19).

Bentham and Mill, as social reformers, extolled the abstract nature of utilitarian ethics. In seeking the greatest good at a nation-wide level, they are specifically geared to a quantitative justice that abstracts from individuality. In positing a justice based ethic as the dominant force of historical morality, care ethics is rejecting not only the language of Kantian rights and utilitarianism but also any morality grounded in such abstractions as a universal good or a social contract. The diversity of such ethical theories dissipates once all are viewed as reasoning their way to ethical conclusions in an abstract fashion. These ethics of justice focus on questions of fairness, equality and individual rights through the impartial application of universal moral principles. They conceive moral conflicts as arising from a clash between the opposing rights and duties of individuals. This conception results in a particularly adversarial understanding of moral discourse. On the relational view taken by ethics of care, moral problems arise from tensions or ruptures in relationships. Hence, moral inquiry is guided by a desire to maintain relationships through responding compassionately to the needs, feelings and desires of others. On this view, the primary focus of moral deliberation is placed on creating and sustaining caring relations. Consequently, ethics of care seeks to foster social bonds and cooperation rather then equality and freedom. If we recall Amy's request for Heinz and the druggist to reach a mutually acceptable arrangement we see how, in attempting to maintain relationships, ethics of care favours conflict resolution and dispute mediation in addressing ethical conflict. Amy's response tries to sustain rather than sever connection. The creation and maintenance of relationships is achieved not by concentrating on establishing and upholding equality and rights but by meeting the needs of those to whom we are connected. A moral solution to an ethical dilemma will be one that clarifies mutual responsibilities and maintains social coherence. In prioritising caring relations in moral inquiry, attentiveness, trust,[11] responsiveness to need and narrative nuance come to play an important part in ethical decision making. The differences between the principle based approach found in ethics of justice and the relationship based approach found in ethics

---

11   The element of 'appropriate trust' is emphasized by the work of Annette Baier (1985 and 1994).

of care can be drawn out further by focusing on four distinct points of division, namely: the value of impartiality, the importance of contextual sensitivity, the nature of the moral self and the role of emotion in moral deliberation.

4.1 The Rejection of Impartiality

On the justice approach it is the application of universal principles to ethical decisions that ensures fairness. Fairness and equity, on this view, are regarded as the key hallmarks of ethical reasoning. Consequently, impartiality forms a necessary bedrock for the justice approach to moral reasoning. To establish a breach of impartiality is tantamount to demonstrating a flawed ethical deliberation. We can think of how traditional liberal theory emphasises impartiality, universality and the standpoint of detached fairness. One of the central reasons why Gilligan's research in moral psychology made such an impact on moral philosophy is because it revealed the existence of a legitimate moral outlook which was not impartial. The starting point of the care view is not an impartial standpoint but rather a position which recognises how people are embedded within a web of ongoing relationships. The key criteria of morality shift from justice and fairness to care and sympathy.

Under the care approach we should not be abstracting away from these relationships but attending to, understanding and emotionally responding to the individuals with whom we stand in these relationships. On the care view then we are entitled to place the interests of those close to us above the interests of strangers. We have a stronger obligation to those nearby, those to whom we stand in close relationships. This is in stark contrast to the impartialist and consequentialist view according to which each person counts as one. Ethics of care recognizes the natural bonds of affection which exist between those with whom we stand in close relationships. An impartial ethic is seen to neglect the special responsibilities incurred by these bonds. In stressing equality, care theorists (Heldke, 1988; McLaughlin, 2003) argue that the justice approach imposes a universal and uniform model of personhood and in so doing strips moral agents of their differentiating characteristics. The worry is that "such a push towards universal inclusiveness marginalizes those who cannot be homogenized into this dominant 'inclusiveness'" (Cockburn, 2005, 83). Morally appropriate decisions are not made by abstracting from personal characteristics but by embracing differences.[12] This sensitivity to issues of difference and bonds of relationships ensures that ethics of care does not rest easily with the language of impartiality and individual rights.

---

12 It is not only in ethics of care that we find such concerns about the possible oppression generated by a failure to recognize difference. See Taylor (1992).

4.2 Context Sensitive

It will be recalled that the male respondents of Kolhberg's study were presented with abstract cases of moral dilemmas while Gilligan's female respondents were confronted with real and immediate moral dilemmas. The voice of care resisted any move to abstract from the particularities of the given situation. Patricia Benner and Judith Wrubel maintain that there exist no "context-free lists of advice" on how to care (1989, 3). In order to provide care, one must "identify the particular needs of concrete individuals", as caring requires "not an abstraction from the concrete case to a universal principle, but an explication of the 'full story'" (Tronto, 1998, 17). Care based moral reasoning remains concrete and contextual, refusing to generalize. In her moral reasoning, we saw how Amy was aware of and influenced by the personal aspect and particularities of Heinz's situation. From the perspective of care ethics, understanding the concrete context of a moral problem is necessary for the formation of appropriate moral judgments. As Gilligan states "morality from the perspective of an ethic of care shows up the limitedness of each solution to its specific context" (1982, 33). The contextual decision making demanded in ethics of care has little use for the obedient adherence to formalistic decision procedures.

Susan Glaspell's 1916 short story *Jury of Her Peers* tells the story of an oppressed wifre, Minnie Foster (Wright) who strangles her cruel husband (Mr. Wright). The sheriff's wife, Mrs. Peters, along with Mrs. Hale visit the house to collect some clothes for the imprisoned Minnie. Through careful observation they piece together Minnie's narrative from the smallest details of items in her home. While convinced of her guilt, they believe it to be morally appropriate to dismiss the charges in light of the context in which the action took place. However, the characters investigating Minnie Foster's case are blind to the tragic circumstances of her life. Their reasoning process is based on an official determination of the facts of the case. The attitudes of the investigators reflect the justice approaches to ethics, remaining neutral with respect to context. In contrast, care ethics is immersed in the details of relationships and narratives. This focus on the concrete and the contextual marks a distinct shift in method away from the abstract, principled approach. In the application of formal principles, one generally identifies only a few key features of any situation as relevant. We need only recall Rawl's famous 'veil of ignorance' to put in mind the great lengths justice theorists go to in order to formulate their rules in a way that excludes the complexities of context. Far from regarding the contextual nature of ethics of care as a sign of weakness or a deficiency, care theorists describe contextual reasoning as "a manifestation of moral maturity" (Benhabib, 1992, 149). Different groups have diverse levels of dependence, vulnerability and need. Noting this multiplicity of varying standpoints enables ethics of care to demonstrate how the affective relations between people are relevant to the resolution of ethical dilemmas.

This contextual sensitivity does not carry with it any implication of relativism. Ethics of care proponents reject subjective standards and hold that care reasoning provides:

> A standard that allows one to say that a certain thing was the appropriate action for a particular individual to take but not necessarily the right action for anyone in that situation (Blum, 1988, 52).

Gilligan emphasized that while a particular moral decision may not be appropriate for other scenarios, the care based process of moral decision-making can be applied to all moral conflicts. In each situation what is called for is a set of responses which fall outside any generalization. Remaining sensitive to the particularities of persons and situations enables needs and narratives to be located, interpreted and judged in specific contexts. Jagger describes such an approach as a "distinctively human way of engaging with others that leads to morally appropriate actions (1995, 181).

4.3 Interdependent Moral Agents

On a traditional justice based ethical approach the moral agent is an independent, autonomous, rational individual. Mill's utilitarianism for example, is founded on individual autonomy and neutrality. The independent self-sufficient decider conducts moral reasoning via the application of abstract general principles. Noninterference, self-determination, fairness and rights are given priority. As Robinson highlights, there is a "systematic devaluing of notions of interdependence, relatedness, and positive involvement in the lives of others" (1999, 10). It is not independence but rather the reality of human dependence that shapes the care view of the moral agent. Hankivsky locates the beginnings of care ethics in "the assumption that it is morally relevant to acknowledge that all human beings are specific, concrete individuals rather than abstract, generic beings" (2004, 32). Ethics of care takes shape around the practical acknowledgment of dependence (Meyers, 1998, 144), portraying individuals as uniquely constituted by their connections to others. Consequently, it adopts a relational view of self. This radically situated and particularised moral self leaves no room for an impersonal stand in moral reasoning. As we cannot abstract away from the particulars of the agent, the other[13] and the situation, these details become

---

13 The other is defined as the person toward whom one is acting and with whom one stands in some relationship. The role of the care giver has received the bulk of the attention in discussions of care ethics. Feminist models of disability (Lloyd, 2001; Morris, 1996) have provided a valuable corrective to the trend by promoting the voice of the 'cared for'.

relevant to morality itself. It is argued that the abstract model of human beings is disconnected from the reality that our lives are characterized by relationships with others. When considering Heinz's dilemma, Amy not only takes account of the value of the wife's life in a context of relationships, she linkd his wife's survival to the preservation of those relationships. Sevenhuijsen notes that:

> The ideal of abstract autonomy in fact overlooks what it is that makes care an element of the human condition, i.e., the recognition that all people are vulnerable, dependent and finite, and that we all have to find ways of dealing with this in our daily existence and in the values which guide our individual and collective behavior (1998, 28).

The idea of the isolated independent individual is rejected as a myth. We are not isolated individuals by nature but social beings. Held explains that:

> Every person starts out as a child dependent on those providing us care, and we remain interdependent with others in thoroughly fundamental ways throughout our lives. That we can think and act as if we were independent depends on a network of social relations making it possible for us to do so (2006, 13).

From a care perspective, the moral agent is interdependent with others and always already embedded in networks and relationships of care. The care view regards human beings as always and necessarily bound together. It is upon this mutual interdependence, not independence, autonomy, and individual rights, that ethics of care builds its morality. The care view describes the moral agent as "approaching the world of action bound by ties and relationships (friend, colleague, parent, child) which confront one, as at least to some extent given" (Blum, 1988, 52). The individualistic disregard for relationships is rejected and the interests of carers and cared-for are seen as intertwined rather than as competing individual interests. We come to see our interests as interconnected with those of others. Relationships, on this view, form us as ethical persons.

Benhabib (1987) contrasts the concept of the 'generalized other', separated from the day-to-day world of relationships and devoid of specific characteristics, with the 'concrete other', a unique individual, with his or her own life history, dispositions, needs and limitations. It is this 'concrete other,' firmly located within the context of relationships to others, who is the focus of ethics of care. In shifting our understanding of the moral agent to a relational rather than an individualistic conception of the self, care ethics sees moral responsibilities and obligations as flowing from interdependence and relationships. Human interdependency is regarded as morally more basic than autonomy or self sufficiency. The relational view of the self contributes to the widely held conviction in care ethics that the unifying goal of moral deliberation is the maintenance and fostering of caring relationships.

4.4 Value of Emotion

Justice-based approaches have traditionally shunned the involvement of emotion in moral reasoning, as it threatens the impartiality that it holds to be a fundamental component of morality. On this view emotion may play some role in motivating action but it has no part in the process of determining the moral status of that action. This moral determination is to be made on formal rationality alone. In attempting to decide an appropriate response to a given moral dilemma, ethics of care does not encourage emotional detachment and disengagement. Care proponents reject a dispassionate approach and regard emotions as a necessary component of an adequate morality. The care perspective regards emotions as having "an important function in developing moral understanding itself, in helping us decide what the recommendations of morality themselves ought to be" (Held, 1993, 30). Noddings states that, "to care is to act not by fixed rule but by affection and regard" (1984, 24). Adherents to ethics of care argue that empathy, compassion and feeling with others may often be better guides to morally appropriate actions then abstract rules and dispassionate rational calculations. Emotion is given a positive role in the job of determining what we ought to do. Caring, as Held argues, "involves feelings and requires high degrees of empathy to enable us to discern what morality recommends in our caring activities" (1993, 30).

It is envisaged that raw emotion would be educated and reflected upon. If we are to arrive at moral actions we need to cultivate moral emotions such as sympathy, empathy, sensitivity, and responsiveness. However, Held notes that:

> Even anger may be a component of the moral indignation that should be felt when people are treated inhumanely, and it may contribute to (rather than interfere with) an appropriate interpretation of the moral wrong (2006, 10).

It is argued that knowing what to do in a particular situation requires empathetic projection into another's life. In Minnie Foster's case the women acted on compassion and empathized with the humiliation, hardship, isolation and frustration of her existence. This ethos of compassion and care enables the women to understand and judge Minnie's violent act in the full context of her chronic and prolonged victimization. They then implement their own justice by withholding evidence of Minnie's guilt. Sensitivity and emotional response to particular situations provides a vital guide to morally acceptable actions. It is through compassion, concern and kindness that we can best meet our caring responsibilities. In this context emotions can motivate us to make the right choices by generating sympathy for the plight of others and solidarity with their feelings.

The differences discussed in this section point to clear incompatibilities between the care and justice approaches. In the following section various attempts to clarify the problematic nature of relationship between care and justice will be considered.

5. The Relationship Between Justice and Care

Feminist thinkers have been reluctant to fully break away from a justice ethic. This is reflected in the various attempts to address feminist moral concerns by extending rather than abandoning traditional ethical theories.[14] Even among many who recognize the moral significance of care, there remains a commitment to the view that an adequate ethics needs the impartiality of justice as well as care. Care is regarded as only one component of morality (Bebeau and Brabeck, 1987, Okin, 1989). For many ethicists, what is required is a theory of morality that integrates care and justice (Brabeck, 1993; Dillon, 1992). Contemporary feminist ethical theorists have devoted much of their attention to analyzing the possible integration of care and justice within moral theory. Among the different independent models of ethics of care we find that the deepest divisions and fractures relate to differing positions on this possible merger. While few care theorists argue that considerations of justice have no place at all in a care morality, the form of any possible hybridization of care and justice is an issue of considerable debate.

There have always been those who attribute no moral significance to care and remain fully committed to the traditional tenets of an impartial morality. As Warren Thomas Reich noted in 1995, care by itself can be easily manipulated, and does not offer tools for analyzing the moral importance of what we care about. Amongst those for whom the concerns of care remain a valuable corrective rather then an alternative to an ethics of justice we find the feminist neo-Kantian positions.[15] These positions allow care considerations to guide conduct. However, in the event of a conflict, considerations of impartiality trump those of care. Still, stronger positions are given to care in which care concerns might, in some circumstances, legitimately outweigh the considerations of impartiality. But even on this view it is only from an impartial perspective that we can determine when the claims of care are stronger.

Given the difficulties of combining the concerns of justice with the concerns of care it is not surprising that some believe that ethics of care should be subsumed into a contemporary version of Aristotelian virtue ethics.[16] The kind

---

14 Examples include Kantian moral theory - Baron (1995) and Herman (1993); utilitarianism - Purdy (1996) and contractualism - Hampton (1993).
15 Blum (1993) provides a categorization of such responses into eight separate positions.
16 Virtue ethics places developing one's moral character at the centre of its moral theory. See Groenhout (1998), Halwani (2003), McLaren (2001) and Widdershoven and

of character based ethics offered by virtue theorists such as Alasdair MacIntyre and Martha Nussbaum also stand in opposition to various forms of principle based approaches. However, the emphasis in virtue theory is on care as a quality of character, a fact at odds with the conception of care as grounded in relationships. Ethics of care regards care as an attribute of relations and strives to develop caring relationships rather than promote care as a character trait (Nodding, 2002, 20). The emphasis is not on the attitude of care but on care as a social practice. As Widdershoven and Huijer describes it "care is embedded in social practices and traditions rather than being just an individual response towards the needs of somebody else" (Widdershoven and Huijer, 2001, 307). Similar attempts have been made to strengthen care ethics by blending it with contemporary ethical thinking such as Heideggerian notions of care[17] (Benner and Wrubel, 1989) and Habermasian Discourse ethics (Benhabib, 1992; Fraser, 1986). We can also find many efforts to expand the ethics of care gene pool. This is done by examining resemblances and overlaps with earlier ethical systems such as Humean ethics[18] (Baier, 1994), Confucian ethics (Li, 1994) and Judeo-Christian ethics (Groenhout, 2004).

In addition to external critiques, there has also been internal feminist criticism of care ethicists for setting up what is regarded to be an artificial distinction between justice and care. The concern is that caring cannot function as an ethic that is complete unto itself because it can be exploited. These critics acknowledge that care ethics draws our attention to important aspects of morality which are often lacking in traditional ethical theories. However, they question whether ethics of care is sufficient to offer a complete account of ethics. Care is seen as a necessary but not a sufficient condition for ethical action. While recognizing the moral significance of care they remain committed to the view that an adequate ethics needs both the impartiality of justice as well as care. In disputing the dichotomy between conceptions of justice and care, such thinkers argue that justice and care are compatible forms of moral reasoning (Jecker, 2002; Okin, 1989). Gilligan, together with many others, argues that a complete morality would include both justice and care perspectives (Gilligan and Attanucci, 1988; Mendus, 1995; Manning, 1992). Mendus describes them as "complementary facets of any realistic account of morality" (Mendus, 1993,18). Card also rejects the idea that care approaches and justice approaches are mutually exclusive, insisting on the need to balance caring with justice and other values (Card, 1990, 106). Joy Kroeger-Mappes (1994) argues that the two ethics are part of one overall system, the ethics of care functioning as a necessary base for the ethics of rights. Baier, (1986) argued that a moral theory which places its emphasis on the concept of

---

Huijer (2001) for discussions of possible links between ethics of care and virtue theory.
17   It is Heidegger's understanding of care as the very being or ultimate reality of human life that is being appealed to.
18   The idea that fundamental moral distinctions arise, as Hume argues, from sentiment rather than from reason is the basis for this model.

trust can integrate justice and care. In arguing that ethics of care and justice are not mutually exclusive these thinkers do not hold that justice and care are reducible to each other but that they are mutually intertwined (Hekman, 1995).

Rather then seeking to find a place for care concerns within other more established ethical frames, many care proponents have attempted to place justice concerns into ethics of care. In this way they retain an ethical role for justice while still maintaining ethics of care to be an independent ethical alternative. For example, Bubeck argues that "considerations of justice arise from within the practice of care itself and therefore are an important part of the ethics of care, properly understood" (Bubeck, 1995, 206). Noddings (2002) also suggests that in linking justice and care we must come to see rights, duties and moral calculations as comprising an extension of caring. Nevertheless, working out the relationship between care and justice is an area that requires further study. As Held states, "how care and justice are to be meshed without losing sight of the differing priorities is a task still being worked on" (2006, 17). We must not forget that the discourse surrounding ethics of care is less then three decades old.

6. Moving Beyond the Private Realm

The distinction between the public and private spheres of life is one we find prevalent in political theory and one that finds ethical expression in the view that the public and private spheres are separate moral domains. One of the central concerns facing care ethics is its ability to function outside of the private sphere of domestic-familial relations. Those who relegate care ethics to the private realm believe that it is unworkable at a social or institutional level, dismissing it as irrelevant to broader moral and political concerns. Without recourse to general rights and principles how can we design public policies?

Over the last few decades there have been great efforts to bring care out of the private realm, stressing its radical social and political implications[19]. These proponents argue that ethics of care forms a radical ethic which calls for a profound restructuring of society. In resisting attempts to limit ethics of care to the private sphere of family and personal relations, these theorists recognise that such confinement opens the door to abusing care. They see a need to expand care ethics into the public sphere in order to create a context in which the practice of caring is not exploited[20]. It is argued that a fully functioning care

---

19 Examples of such efforts include Bubeck (1995), DiQuinzio and Young (1997), Folbre (2001), Hankivsky (2004), Harrington (1999), Held (2006), Kittay (1999), Nodding (2002), Sevenhuijsen (1998), Tronto (1993) and Young (1997).
20 As was noted in Section 3 (Beyond a Gendered Morality) there are concerns that care ethics might reinforce and perpetuate the oppression of women. On a more general level there are similar worries about the possibility that care might degenerate into

morality cannot be insular. Ethics of care must acknowledge the political reality, material conditions, and social structure of the world (Hoagland, 1991). In fully embracing the contextual nature of care ethics, there is a need to look at the political and economic context within which people make their moral decisions. The Heinz dilemma, for example, should be seen as arising from a corporate controlled health care system. As Friedman noted, ethical consideration of Heinz's situation needs a political analysis of a system which "allows most health care resources to be privately owned, privately sold for profit in the market place, and privately withheld from people who cannot afford the market price." (Friedman, 1987, 202) In recognising the contextual details of economics and politics as well as those of social and domestic life ethics of care is intent on motivating actions which effect change at the system level. As a result, much of the research in ethics of care attempts to reconceptualise traditional notions about the public and private spheres. For many the goal is not simply to make a private ethic public but to collapse the very notion of the public/private distinction. The personal and the interpersonal are shown to be publicly and politically significant. Tronto for example insists that we think of care as a public virtue as opposed to just a private relationship. Care is to be seen as a collective social responsibility to be shared evenly between government, community and family. The role of relationships is then placed at the heart of social and political theory.

It is in developing this political agenda that care ethics attempts to include those outside the already established circle of caring. The contextual and particularized nature of care ethics has been cited as a reason for its unsuitability for the public realm. On that view, ethics of care is regarded as too partial and parochial to fully ensure the interests of those outside specific relationships. How can ethics of care function in the public sphere without losing its distinctive contextual character? While ethics of care locates our primary ethical responsibilities within relationships that are already established, its proponents maintain that the effect of adopting an ethics of care would radiate beyond our immediate relationships, serving as a foundation for a more egalitarian and peaceful world. But how is this circle of care to be widened out beyond our most intimate relationships? In sanctioning the prioritizing of close relationships there is the worry that ethics of care allows "blindness to the needs of those who are at a distance from oneself, socially, physically, or culturally (Groenhout, 1998, 185). Care ethics claims that a person of normally developed empathic capacity would care more about the immediate than the distant needy person. However, care advocates maintain that this is not to deny some obligations toward the distant needy (Stole, 2007).

Many care theorists refer to the distinction between 'caring about' and 'caring for.' This distinction may help clarify the mechanism by which caring can be expanded. Humans "care about" many people in their personal and professional

---

the oppression and exploitation of either the 'cared for' of the carer. See Card (1990), Friedman (1987) and Narayan (1995) for discussion of these concerns.

lives. "Caring about" is a generalized form of care the direct relatedness to specific others is missing. I may 'care about' earthquake victims even if I have not experienced the particular conditions of a particular person living in a specific village in a specific country affected by a specific earthquake. According to Noddings, in 'Caring about' there is always an element of "benign neglect," a distance, an ability to put the issue away (1984, 112). As care becomes diffused we find that our responsibilities become less urgent. However, it is envisaged that such generalized 'caring about' could lead me to take the kinds of actions that would bring me to 'caring for' particular persons in the context of their particular histories. The strongest voices for social or political change are seen to be those who have entered the lived reality of the person for whom they are caring. We should, Held advocates, be attempting to extend an ethic of care into our relations with strangers instead of trying to extend an ethic best suited for strangers into our personal relationships. The justice thought possible only through the impartial application of abstract rules is now achieved but via a very different process. As Nodding notes, "justice itself is dependent on caring-about, and caring-about is in turn dependent on caring-for" (2002, 6). It is in this way that, "the caring response in moral reasoning is capable of becoming universal, including the self, those who are close to us, and those who lie outside of our circle of personal relationships" (Leffers, 1993, 74).

The success of attempts at establishing care's viability in the public realm is reflected in a wide variety of literature which applies ethics of care to specific areas in the public realms, such as medicine, law, politics, social policy, etc. Any glance through the applied literature will quickly reveal that ethics of care has not been confined to the realm of personal morality and relationships (Baines et al., 1991). Care theorists address a wide variety of contentious social and political issues. This is most evident in healthcare, in particular nursing ethics. Here we find calls to dispense with the idealized conception of moral action in favour of a relational and contextual moral view.[21] But it is not only in the caring profession that ethics of care is being applied. Recent literature shows that ethics of care can be used as a theoretical basis to add a new and important dimension to issues in many diverse public domains e.g. citizenship, social work, children's place in society, media ethics, bioethics, business ethics etc.[22] Ethics of care is also applied to global issues in international relations such as global poverty, humanitarian intervention and peace building (Robinson, 1999; Porter, 2007). In the field of animal and environmental ethics, the fact that ethics of care does not rely on

---

21 For examples of this work see Allmark (1995), Bradshaw (1996), Bowden (1997), Fry (1989), Hanford (1994), Kuhse (1997) and Waston (1989).
22 Examples include Sevenhuijsen (1998) on citizenship; Clifford (2002), Lloyd (2006), Orme (2002) and Parton (2003) on social work; Cockburn (2005) and Barnes (2007) on children's rights; Chakraborti (2006), Kane et al. (2008) and Tong (1997) on bioethics; Pech (2006) on media ethics; Liedtka (1996) and Machold et al. (2008) on business ethics.

the language of rights enables it to bypass debates which revolve around the attribution of rights to both nonhuman animals and the environment. Regardless of whether or not nonhuman animals have rights, we can and do care for them. In this way, ethics of care can be extended to include the natural world (Orr, 1992). As a result, the discourse of care may be more appropriate and fruitful than that of rights (Curtin, 1991; King, 1991).

What emerges from the research taking place in the applied field is that the adoption of an ethics of care has implications for the kinds of moral judgements we generate. Significantly, in changing from a justice based moral orientation to a care based moral orientation we find that not only has the process of moral thinking changed, but so too has our assessments of various moral actions. Take for example the case of allowing a neo-Nazi March to pass through a predominantly Jewish neighbourhood. The liberal right to free speech is tightly bound to autonomy which is a key value for this approach. However, under the relationship model envisaged by ethics of care hate speech and the harm it does to others in the name of free speech would not be permitted. Any act, including the banning of hate speech, would be deemed right or wrong depending on whether it exhibited a caring or uncaring attitude/motivation on the part of the agent (Stole, 2007). The justice system need not be guided by impartial rules and procedures. As Stole argues, we can speak of institutions and laws as caring or exhibiting empathy. In our moral assessment of laws, as well as social customs and practices, we can say that they are just if they reflect or express "empathically caring motivation towards their compatriots on the part of the legislative group that is responsible for passing it" (Stole, 2007, 95). We find then that in both the private and public realms ethics of care assess judgment in terms of empathic caring. Similarly, in stressing human dependence through a relational view of the self, the concept of citizen utilized in social policy is transformed. To be regarded as a good citizen on a care framework, we must place mutual obligations and relations of trust above self-reliance and autonomy.

6. Conclusion

Ethics of care now forms an independent moral alternative to the traditional ethical theories of rights and justice. It has moved far beyond a critique of mainstream moral philosophy and has established itself as a moral theory in its own right. Interconnections between individuals are at the center of this ethical system for it is these relationships which form the basis for assuming moral obligation. In focusing on close, intimate relationships involving particularity, ethics of care challenges the classical impartial conceptions of morality. It is a moral theory that captures the realities of lived experience. In real-life moral situations, ethics of care holds that concepts of abstract rules and rights are inadequate. What is needed is a moral approach that takes on board the complexities and moral salience of caring relationships. When we look at moral issues through this new lens the implications for moral judgment are profound.

BIBLIOGRAPHY

Allmark, P. (1995). Can There Be an Ethics of Care? *Journal of Medical Ethics*, 21, 19–24.

Auerbach, J., Blum, L., Smith, V., and Williams, C. (1985). Commentary on Gilligan's In a Different Voice. *Feminist Studies*, 11(1), 149-61.

Baier, A. (1985). What Do Women Want in a Moral Theory? *Nous*, 19, 53-63.

_____ (1986). Trust and Anti-Trust. *Ethics*, 96, 231–260.

_____ (1994). *Moral Prejudices*. Cambridge, Harvard University Press.

Baines, C. Evans, P. and Neysmith, S. (eds.) (1991). *Women's Caring: Feminist Perspectives on Social Welfare*. Toronto, McClelland and Stewart.

Barnes, V. (2007). Young People's Views of Children's Rights and Advocacy Services: A Case for "Caring" Advocacy? *Child Abuse Review*, 16,140–52.

Baron, M. (1995). *Kantian Ethics Almost without Apology*. Ithaca, Cornell University Press.

Bebeau, M. and Brabeck M. (1989). Ethical Sensitivity and Moral Reasoning Among Men and Women in the Professions. In Brabeck, M. (ed.). *Who Cares? Theory, Research, and Educational Implications of the Ethic of Care*. New York, Praeger, 144-163.

Benhabib, S. (1987). The Generalized and The Concrete Other: The Kohlberg-Gilligan Controversy and Moral Theory. In Feder Kittay, E. and Meyers D. (eds.). *Women and Moral Theory*. Lanham, Rowman and Littlefield, 154 – 178.

_____ (1992). *Situating the Self: Gender, Community and Postmodernism in Contemporary Ethics*. London, Routledge.

Benner, P. and Wrubel, J. (1989). *The Primacy of Caring: Stress and Coping in Health and Illness*. California, Addison-Wesley.

Blum, L. (1988). Gilligan and Kohlberg: Implications for Moral Theory. *Ethics*, 98, 472-491. Reprinted in Larrabee, M. (ed.) (1993). *An Ethic of Care: Feminist and Interdisciplinary Perspectives*. New York, Routledge, 49-68.

Bowden, P. (1997). *Caring: Gender-Sensitive Ethics*. Routledge, London.

Brabeck, M. (ed.) (1989). *Who Cares?: Theory, Research, and Educational Implications of the Ethic of Care*. New York, Praegar.

_____ (1993). Recommendations for Re-examining Women's Ways of Knowing. *New Ideas in Psychology*, 11(2), 253-258.

_____ Bradshaw, A. (1996). Yes! There is an Ethics of Care: An Answer for Peter Allmark. *Journal of Medical Ethics*, 22, 8-15.

Brennan, S. (1999). Recent Work in Feminist Ethics. *Ethics*, 109(4), 858-893.

Broughton, J. (1983). Women's Rationality and Men's Virtues: A Critique of Gender Dualism in Gilligan's Theory of Moral Development. *Social Research*, 50, 597-642.

Bubeck, D. (1995). *Care, Gender, and Justice*. Oxford, Clarendon Press.

Caputo, G. (2000). The Voice of Justice vs. the Voice of Care: The assignment of criminal sanctions. *Current Psychology*, 19(1), 70-82.

_____ (2002). Social justice, the ethics of care, and market economies. *Families in Society*, 83, 355-364.

Card, C. (1990). Caring and Evil. *Hypatia*, 5(2), 101-8.

_____ (ed.) (1991). *Feminist Ethics*. Lawrence, University Press of Kansas.

Chakraborti, C. (2006). Ethics of Care and HIV: A Case for Rural Women In India. *Developing World Bioethics*, 6(2), 89–94.

Chodorow, N. (1978). *The Reproduction of Mothering: Psychoanalysis and the Sociology of Gender*. Berkeley, University of California Press.

Clement, G. (1996). *Care, Autonomy, and Justice: Feminism and the Ethic of Care*. Boulder, Westview Press.

Clifford, D. (2002). Resolving Uncertainties? The Contribution of Some Recent Feminist Ethical Theory to the Social Professions. *European Journal of Social Work*, 5(1), 31–41.

Cockburn, T. (2005). Children and the Feminist Ethic of Care. *Childhood: A Global Journal of Child Research*, 12(1), 71-89.

Cole, Browning E. and Coultrap-McQuin, S. (eds.) (1992). *Explorations in Feminist Ethics: Theory and Practice*. Bloomington, Indiana University Press.

Curtin, D. (1991). Toward an Ecological Ethic of Care. *Hypatia*, 6(1), 60–74.

DesAutels, P. and Waugh, J. (eds.) (2001). *Feminists Doing Ethics*. Lanham, Rowman and Littlefield.

Dillon, R. (1992). Care and respect. In Cole, E. and Coultrap-McQuin, S. (eds.) (1992). *Explorations in Feminist Ethics*. Bloomington, Indiana University Press, 69–81.

DiQuinzio, P. and Young, I. (eds.) (1997). *Feminist Ethics and Social Policy*. Bloomington, Indiana University Press.

Fisher, B. and Tronto, J. (1990). Toward a Feminist Theory of Caring. In Abel, E. and Nelson, M. (eds.). *Circles of Care*. Albany, State University of New York Press, 35–62.

Flanagan, O. (1991). *Varieties of Moral Personality: Ethics and Psychological Realism*. Cambridge, Harvard University.

Flanagan, O. and Jackson, K. (1987). Justice, Care, and Gender: The Kohlberg-Gilligan Debate Revisited. *Ethics*, 97, 622-637.

Folbre, N. (2001). *The Invisible Heart: Economics and Family Values*. New York, New Press.

Fraser, N. (1986). Toward a Discourse Ethic of Solidarity. *Praxis International* 5.4, 425-429.

Friedman, M. (1987). Care and Context in Moral Reasoning. In Kittay, E. and Meyers, D. (eds.). *Women and Moral Theory*. Totowa, Rowman and Littlefield,190-204.

Fry, S. (1989). Role of Caring in a Theory of Nursing Ethics. *Hypatia*, 4, 88-103.

Gilligan, C. (1982). *In a Different Voice: Psychological Theory and Women's Development*. Cambridge, Harvard University Press.

Gilligan, C. and Attanucci, J. (1988). Two moral orientations. In Gilligan, J. Ward, V. and McLean, Taylor J. (eds). *Mapping the Moral Domain*. Cambridge, Harvard University Press.

Greeno, C. and Maccoby, E. (1993). How Different Is the 'Different Voice'? In Larrabee, M. (ed.). *An Ethic of Care: Feminist and Interdisciplinary Perspectives*. New York, Routledge, 193-198.

Groenhout, R. (1998). The Virtue of Care: Aristotelian Ethics and Contemporary Ethics of Care. In Freeland C. (ed.). *Feminist interpretations of Aristotle*. Pennsylvania, Pennsylvania State University Press, 171-200.

_____ (2004). Theological Echoes in an Ethic of Care. Occasional paper published of the Erasmus Institute, Notre Dame: University of Notre Dame.

_____ (2004). *Connected Lives: Human Nature and an Ethic of Care.* Lanham, Rowman and Littlefield.

Habermas, J. (1995). *Moral Consciousness and Communicative Action* (trans. Lenhardt, C.). Cambridge, MIT Press.

Halwani, R. (2003). Care Ethics and Virtue Ethics. *Hypatia*, 18(3), 161-192.

Hampton, J. (1993). Feminist Contractarianism. In Antony, L. and Witt, C. (eds.) (1993). *A Mind Of One's Own: Feminist Essays On Reason And Objectivity.* Boulder, Westview Press, 227–255.

Hanen, M. and Nielsen, K. (eds.) (1987). *Science, Morality and Feminist Theory.* Calgary, University of Calgary Press.

Hanford, L. (1994). Nursing and the Concept of Care: An Appraisal of Noddings' Theory. In Hunt, G. (ed.). *Ethical Issues in Nursing.* London, Routledge, 181-94.

Hankivsky, O. (2004). *Social Policy and the Ethic of Care.* Vancouver, University of British Columbia Press.

Harding, S. (1987). The Curious Coincidence of Feminine and African Moralities. In, Kittay, Feder E. and Meyers D. (eds.) (1987). *Women and Moral Theory.* Lanham, Rowman and Littlefield, 296–315.

Harrington, M. (2000). *Care and Equality: Inventing a New Family Politics.* London, New York, Routledge.

Hekman, S. (1995). *Moral Voices, Moral Selves: Carol Gilligan and Feminist Moral Theory.* Oxford, Polity Press.

Held, V. (1993). *Feminist Morality: Transforming Culture, Society, and Politics.* Chicago, University of Chicago Press.

_____ (2006). *The Ethics of Care: Personal, Political and Global.* Oxford, Oxford University Press.

Held, V. (ed.) (1995). *Justice and Care: Essential Readings in Feminist Ethics.* Boulder, Westview Press.

Heldke, L. (1988). Recipes for Theory Making. *Hypatia* 3(2), 15–29.

Herman, B. (1993). *The Practice of Moral Judgment.* Cambridge, Harvard University Press.

Hoagland, S. (1991). Some Thoughts About Caring. In Card, C. (ed.) (1991). *Feminist Ethics.* Lawrence, University Press of Kansas, 246-263.

Houston, B. (1987). Rescuing Womanly Virtues: Some Dangers of Moral

Reclamation. In Hanen, M. and Nielsen, K. (eds.). *Science, Morality and Feminist Theory*. Calgary, University of Calgary Press, 237-262.

_____ (1990). Caring and Exploitation. *Hypatia*, 5, 115-119.

Jagger, A. (1995). Caring as a Feminist Practice of Moral Reason. In Held, V. (ed.) (1995). *Justice and Care: Essential Readings in Feminist Ethics*. Boulder, Westview Press, 179-202.

Jecker, N. (2002). Taking Care of One's Own: Justice and Family Caregiving. *Theoretical Medicine and Bioethics*, 23, 117-133.

Kane, F., Clement, G. and Kane, M. (2008). Live Kidney Donations and the Ethic of Care. *Journal of Medical Humanity*, 29,173–188.

King, R. Caring About Nature-Feminist Ethics and the Environment. *Hypatia*, 6, 75-89.

Kittay, E. (1999). *Love's Labor: Essays on Women, Equality, and Dependency*. New York, Routledge.

Kittay,E., Feder E. and Meyers D. (eds.) (1987). *Women and Moral Theory*. Lanham, Rowman and Littlefield, 296–315.

Koehn, D. (1998). *Rethinking Feminist Ethics: Care, Trust and Empathy*. London, Routledge.

Kohlberg, L. (1969). Stages and Sequence: The Cognitive-Developmental Approach to Socialization. In Goslin, D. (ed.) (1969). *Handbook of Socialization Theory and Research*. Chicago, Rand McNally.

Kohlberg, L. (1981). *The Philosophy of Moral Development*. San Francisco, Harper and Row.

Kroeger-Mappes, J. (1994). The Ethic of Care vis-a-vis the Ethic of Rights: A Problem for Contemporary Moral Theory. *Hypatia*, 9(3), 108-131.

Kuhse, H. (1997). *Caring: Nurses, Women and Ethics*. Oxford, Blackwell.

Landau, I. (2006). *Is Philosophy Androcentric?* Pennsylvania, Pennsylvania State University Press.

Larrabee, M. (ed.) (1993). *An Ethic of Care: Feminist and Interdisciplinary Perspectives*. New York, Routledge.

Leffers, M. (1993). Pragmatists Jane Addams and John Dewey Inform the Ethic of Care. *Hypatia*, 8, 64-77.

Li, Chenyang. (1994). The Confucian Concept of Jen and the Feminist Ethics of

Care: A Comparative Study. *Hypatia*, 9(1), 70-89.

Liedtka, J. (1996). Feminist morality and competitive reality: a role for an ethic of care? *Business Ethics Quarterly*, 6 (2), 179-200.

Lloyd, L. (2006). A Caring Profession? The Ethics of Care and Social Work with Older People. *British Journal of Social Work*, 36,1171–85.

Lloyd, M. (2001). The Politics of Disability and Feminism: Discord or Synthesis? *Sociology*, 35(3), 715–28.

Lykes, M. (1989). The Caring Self: Social Experiences of Power and Powerlessness. In Brabeck, M. (ed.). *Who Cares?: Theory, Research, and Educational Implications of the Ethic of Care*. New York, Praegar,164-179.

Machold, S. Ahmed, P. Farquhar, S. (2008). Corporate Governance and Ethics: A Feminist Perspective. *Journal of Business Ethics*, 81(3), 665-678.

MacIntyre, A. (1981). *After Virtue: A Study in Moral Theory*. Notre Dame, University of Notre Dame Press.

_____ (1988). *Whose Justice? Which Rationality?* Notre Dame, University of Notre Dame Press.

Manning, R. (1992). *Speaking From the Heart: A Feminist Perspective on Ethics*. Lanham, Rowman and Littlefield.

McLaren, M. (2001). Feminist Ethics: Care as a Virtue. In DesAutels, P. and Waugh, J. (eds.). *Feminists Doing Ethics*. Lanham, Rowman and Littlefield,101-118.

McLaughlin, J. (2003). *Feminist Social and Political Theory*. Basingstoke, Palgrave Macmillan.

Mendus, S. (1993). Different Voices, Still Lives: Problems in the Ethics of Care. *Journal of Applied Philosophy*, 10(1), 17-27.

_____ (1995). Human Rights in Political Theory. *Political Studies*, 43, 10–24.

Meyers, P. (1998). The "Ethic of Care" and the Problem of Power. *The Journal of Political Philosophy*, 6 (2), 142-170.

Morris, J. (ed.) (1996). *Encounters with Strangers: Feminism and Disability*. London, The Women's Press.

Nails, D. (1983). Social-scientific Sexism: Gilligan's Mismeasure of Man. *Social Research*, 50(3), 643-64.

Narayan, U. (1995). Colonialism and its Others: Considerations on Rights and Care Discourses. *Hypatia*, 10(2), 133–40.

Noddings, N. (1984). *Caring: A Feminine Approach to Ethics and Moral Education*. Berkeley, University of California Press.

_____ (1990). Ethic from the Stand Point of Women. In Pearsall, M. (ed.). *Women and Values: Readings in Recent Feminist Philosophy*. California, Wadsworth Publishing Company.

_____ (2002). *Starting at Home: Caring and Social Policy*. Berkeley, University of California Press.

Nussbaum, M. (1999). *Sex and Social Justice*. New York, Oxford University Press.

Okin, Moller S. (1989). Reason and Feeling in Thinking about Justice. *Ethics*, 99(1), 229–49.

Orme, J. (2002). Social Work: Gender, Care and Justice. *British Journal of Social Work*, 32(6), 799–814.

Orr, D. (1992). *Ecological literacy*. New York, SUNY Press.

Parton, N. (2003). Rethinking Professional Practice: The Contributions of Social Constructionism and the Feminist "Ethics of Care". *British Journal of Social Work*, 2003, 33(1), 1–16.

Pech, G. (2006). Writing in Solidarity: Steps Toward an Ethic of Care for Journalism, *Journal of Mass Media Ethics*, 21, 141–155.

Piaget, J. (1965). *The Moral Judgment of the Child*. New York, The Free Press.

Porter, E. (2007). *Peacebuilding: Women in International Perspective*. London. Routledge.

Puka, B. (ed.) (1994). *Caring Voices and Women's Moral Frames: Gilligan's View*. New York and London, Garland Publishing.

Purdy, Laura M. (1996). *Reproducing Persons: Issues in Feminist Bioethics*. Ithaca, Cornell University Press.

Rawls, J. (1971). *A Theory of Justice*. Cambridge, Harvard University Press.

Robinson, F. (1999). *Globalising Care: Feminist Theory, Ethics and International Relations*. Boulder, Westview Press.

Ruddick, S. (1980). Maternal Thinking. *Feminist Studies*, 6, 342–367.

_____ (1995). *Maternal Thinking: Toward a Politics of Peace*. Boston, Beacon Press.

Sevenhuijsen, S. (1998). *Citizenship and the Ethics of Care*. New York, Routledge.

Skoe, E. (1998). The Ethic of Care: Issues in Moral Development. In von der Lippe, A. and Skoe, E. (eds.). *Personality Development in Adolescence: A Cross National and Life Span Perspective*. London, Routledge, 143–171.

Stack, C. (1986). The Culture of Gender: Women and Men of Color. *Signs: Journal of Women in Culture and Society*, 11, 321-324.

Stole, M. (2007). *The Ethics of Care and Empathy*. London, Routledge.

Sunstein, C. (ed.) (1990). *Feminism and Political Theory*. Chicago, University of Chicago Press.

Taylor, C. (1992). *Multiculturalism and "The Politics of Recognition"*. Princeton, Princeton University Press.

Taylor, R. (1998). The Ethic of Care Versus the Ethic of Justice: An Economic Analysis. *Journal of Socio-Economics*, 27, 479–494.

Tong, R. (1997). *Feminist Approaches to Bioethics: Theoretical Reflections and Practical Applications*. Boulder, Westview Press.

Tronto, J. (1993). *Moral Boundaries: A Political Argument for an Ethic of Care*. New York, Routledge.

_____ (1994). Beyond Gender Difference to a Theory of Care. In Puka, B. (ed.) *Caring Voices and Women's Moral Frames: Gilligan's View*. New York and London, Garland Publishing, 504-524.

_____ (1994). *Caring Voices and Women's Moral Frames: Gilligan's View*. New York, Garland Publishing, 504-524.

_____ (1998). An Ethic of Care. *Generations*, 22,15-20.

Vikana, A. Caminob, C. and Biaggio, A. (2005). Note on a Cross-Cultural Test of Gilligan's Ethic of Care. *Journal of Moral Education*, 34(1),107-111.

Walker, L. (1995). Sexism in Kohlberg's moral psychology? In Kurtines, W. and Gewirtz, J. (eds.). *Moral Development: An Introduction*. Boston, Allyn and Bacon, 83–107.

Walker, Urban M. (1998). *Moral Understandings: A Feminist Study in Ethics*. New York, Routledge.

Warren, Reich T. (1995). Care: III. Contemporary Ethics of Care. In Warren, Reich T. (ed.). *Encyclopedia of Bioethics. (2nd Edition)*. New York, Simon and Schuster Macmillan, 336-344.

Watson, J. (1989). Watson's Philosophy and Theory of Human Caring in Nursing. In Riehl-Sisca J. (ed.). *Conceptual Models for Nursing Practice*. Norwalk, Appleton and Lange, 219-236.

Widdershoven, G. and Huijer, M. (2001). The Fragility of Care: An Encounter Between Nussbaum's Aristotelian Ethic and Ethic of Care. *International Journal in Philosophy and Theology*, 62, 304-316.

Willett, C. (1995). *Maternal Ethics and Other Slave Moralities*. New York, Routledge.

Young, I. (1990). *Justice and the Politics of Difference*. Princeton, Princeton University Press.

5

Contractualism: History, Theories and Critiques

Sebastian Schleidgen

1. Introduction

Most contractualist theories are concerned with the questions of why humans would/should submit to the coercive power of states as well as what legitimate states look like, i.e. what rights and duties a state has in relation to its citizens, and/or what civil rights citizens have in relation to a state. Contractualist theories date back to the 17th century and are - in most cases - closely connected to the social and political situation in which they were developed. Particularly, this holds for classical theories, such as that of Thomas Hobbes. Hobbes began to work on political philosophy in the 1640s, which resulted in his famous book *Leviathan* being published in 1651 where he argues - against the background of the English civil war - that a state primarily has the task of keeping peace.

John Locke in his 1689 published *Two Treatises of Government* turned against this doctrine, which at that time also was endorsed by the Church of England. Locke had close connections to the Whigs, a party which stood in opposition to absolute monarchy. Accordingly, he held the view that governments are legitimate exclusively through the peoples' consent. Consequently, in his theory several rights of liberty, as well as rights vis-à-vis a state are assigned to the citizens. Furthermore, citizens are obliged to participate in revolutionary acts in cases where a state violates their rights.

Jean-Jacques Rousseau's *The Social Contract, Or Principles of Political Right* (1762) also has to be understood with reference to the political background of heated debates on civil rights in the years preceding the French Revolution. Rousseau (similarly to Locke) puts the focus on individual rights vis-à-vis a state and furthermore adopts the term sovereignty of the people, which is considered to be the basis of modern elections. This also is the reason why Rousseau often is referred to as one of the pioneers of the French Revolution alongside, for instance, Voltaire.

After Rousseau, contractualist theories were not en vogue in political philosophy until John Rawls published his canonical book *A Theory of Justice* in 1971. In this work, Rawls - standing in the tradition of Hobbes - extends the contractualist focus by dealing with the question of how an extensively just societal system could develop and what it would look like. In addressing these questions, Rawls develops a liberal theory of distributive justice with an emphasis on individual liberty and equal opportunities for all members of a society.

Subsequently, in 1974, Robert Nozick became one of the most important opponents of Rawls' theory when he published *Anarchy, State, and Utopia*, in which - by referring to Locke - he argues against any theory of distributive justice and for a maximum of individual liberties and property rights. As a consequence, for several years Nozick became one of the most important representatives of libertarian theories.

Somewhat different from the theories mentioned so far is Thomas Scanlon's account, which he presents in *What We Owe to Each Other* (1988). Although Scanlon sees himself in the tradition of Rousseau, he is not interested in the question of establishing legitimate states, but rather focuses on the justification of moral principles. Therefore, his pattern of argumentation also differs decisively from earlier contractualist works: Scanlon's theory does not include any hypothetical contract for establishing a state, but rather is concerned with the hypothetical justification of one's actions and their impact on others as a criterion for morally right actions.

The remainder of this chapter presents the work of the aforementioned theoreticians in chronological order of their appearance. First, the classical theories of Thomas Hobbes, John Locke and Jean-Jacques Rousseau are presented, followed by a description of the modern theories of John Rawls, Robert Nozick and Thomas Scanlon. Included are overviews of their respective traditions, as well as their most important critiques.

2. Classical Theories

2.1. Thomas Hobbes: *Leviathan* (1651)

The starting point of Thomas Hobbes' contractualist considerations in *Leviathan* ([1651] 2008) is the thesis that all humans in principle are alike with regard to their physical and mental abilities. Thereby, he does not understand all humans actually having identical abilities, but rather that any differences in physical and/or mental abilities may be compensated for (Hobbes 2008, 81). For instance, it is possible to compensate for physical inferiority by developing particular aptitudes. As a consequence, every individual is a potential source of danger for any other individual - a physically weaker individual, for example, may poison a stronger one, kill him by using a weapon etc.

From this potential equality Hobbes concludes that all humans have the same hope for achieving their respective individual goals. This fact, however, inevitably results in competitive situations - for instance, if several individuals strive for (material or immaterial) goods, which are not equally available to all of them. As humans become aware of possible ramifications of equality of possibilities (i.e. personal endangerment from others), general distrust will evolve and subsequently everyone will take precautionary measures to ensure self-preservation, that is "to use force or wiles to master the person of all other men [...] until he sees no other power great enough to endanger himself" (2008, 82). Hobbes additionally points out that self-preservation in this sense is also necessary for persons who actually strive for a peaceful life.[1]

From this Hobbes concludes that "[o]*ut of civil states, there is always war of every one against every one*" (2008, 82).[2] This state of anarchy, which has to be understood hypothetically, not historically, constitutes the so-called *state of nature*,[3] which forms the argumentative basis of almost every contractualist theory. Hobbes describes the state of nature as a situation in which individuals live without any social relations, industry or the like. In the state of nature, only the so-called *right* of nature (*jus naturale*) is prevalent, which "is the liberty each man has to use his own power as he wills himself, for the preservation of [...] his life" (2008, 86). However, since humans are guided by reason, they also are subject to the *laws* of nature (*leges naturalia*), which Hobbes defines as "precept[s] or general rule[s], found out by reason, by which a man is forbidden to do what is destructive to his life, or takes away the means of preserving it, or to omit that by which he thinks his life may be best preserved" (2008, 86). In the anarchic state of nature, according to Hobbes, the fundamental law of nature states: "*Naturally every man has the right to every thing*" (2008, 86).

It follows that in the state of nature there is no safety for the individual: everyone has to fear being attacked, killed, manipulated or robbed by others. Since this situation endangers the self-preservation of each and every person, Hobbes concludes that human reason would formulate a first law of nature: "*every man, ought to endeavor for peace as far as he has hope of obtaining it, and when he cannot obtain it, he may seek and use all helps and advantages of war*"

---

1   Thus, Hobbes does not - as often stated - consider humans to be purely evil by nature. Rather, his thesis is that even peaceful individuals have to submit to general and violent competition in order to survive.
2   In this context, Hobbes for the first time indicates that he is primarily interested in the peace-keeping function of a state: "All other time [than the state of nature] is PEACE" (2008, 83). In the course of the history of contractualist theories, this focus changes considerably, as will be shown.
3   Hobbes himself points out that he understands the state of nature hypothetically rather than historically (2008, 84, 136 et seqq.). As such, the construct explains patterns of behavior embodied in human nature (2008, 86 et seq., 113).

(2008, 87). Thus, what ultimately requires the individuals to think of their self-preservation in terms of peace is their reason.

From this, Hobbes concludes, without further explanation, the second law: "It is, *that a man be willing as he shall think necessary to lay down the right to all things when others are too, as far as they are, for peace and the defense of himself, and be contended with as much liberty against other men as he would allow other men against himself*" (2008, 87). Thus, the second law of nature states that every individual ought to refrain from exercising his right to everything voluntarily, if others do the likewise in order to achieve peace and self-defense. It therefore contains the means of overcoming the state of nature, namely the mutual restriction of everyone's right to everything. According to Hobbes, such a restriction is called a *contract* (2008, 89). However, it is not possible to overcome the state of nature by one or more single contracts between individuals: as long as no controlling power exists, which supervises the observance of contracts, any such contract between individuals is a classical prisoner's dilemma: If one party fulfills the contract, the fulfillment by the other is no longer guaranteed, because her gain would be greater by not fulfilling the contract. Thus, according to Hobbes, "[t]he one who performs first in the condition of mere nature just betrays himself to his enemy" (2008, 91).

Therefore, establishing an entity which has the right and power to supervise and enforce contracts is a necessary condition for overcoming the state of nature. The individuals' reason thus demands a contract, which is enforced by such an entity. According to Hobbes, a satisfactory contract can only be achieved, if all individuals yield their right to everything as well as their power to enforce this right in any particular instance:

> There is only one way to erect such a common power [...]. This way is to confer all of their power and strength upon one man, or upon assembly of men, that will reduce all of their wills, from a plurality of voices into one will (Hobbes, 2008, 116).

Such a transmission of the individual's rights and liberties is, according to Hobbes, a contract of everyone with everyone, which unites them to a state, "who can act for the ends of using his strength and any means he thinks is expedient for the multitude's peace and common defense" (2008, 116).[4]

In Hobbes' opinion, the so-established state requires great powers in order to be able to fulfil the tasks of securing internal peace as well as protecting its citizens against external enemies (2008, 118 et seqq.): for instance, the contract in Hobbes' opinion must be established and enforced in such a fashion that neither changes nor withdrawals by any individual are allowed. Furthermore, an existing

---

4   Here again, it becomes clear that Hobbes is primarily interested in the peace-keeping function of a state.

dominion in principle may not be changed. Moreover, the state exclusively has legislative and jurisprudential authority. Such a sovereign, according to Hobbes, is the crucial political quality of a state and independent of the concrete system of government, although Hobbes himself explicitly argues against the separation of powers (Hobbes 2008, 127). However, one should keep in mind that Hobbes is not interested in debating the separation of powers, but in accounting for (modern) statehood as such.

To summarize: based on anthropological premises, which are reflected by a hypothetical state of nature, Hobbes argues that humans submit to a sovereign by reason. This sovereign then has the exclusive power for legislation, supervision and jurisdiction. It is rational for them to submit themselves to a state, because living in an anarchic state would endanger their self-preservation permanently. Giving up their right on everything, however, promises peace and safety. Thus, according to Hobbes, a non-anarchic state effectively is more pleasant and beneficial than an anarchic one.

2.2. John Locke: *Two Treatises of Government* (1689)

In *Two Treatises of Government* ([1689]1969) John Locke goes far beyond the question of governmental peacekeeping. In the first Treatise he primarily argues against the writings of Sir Robert Filmers, who was emphatic on the thesis of the divine origin of absolute monarchy. In the second Treatise he concerns himself with the questions of why individuals submit to a state and what rights they would have vis-à-vis a legitimate state. Especially the answer to the latter question leads his theory beyond Hobbes' claims, since Locke establishes a legitimate state as one that acts "only for the Publick Good" (Locke, 1993, 268).

Locke, too, starts by characterizing a state of nature, in which the individuals are absolutely free "to order their Actions and dispose of their Possessions" (1993, 269), whereby humans have the natural right to three fundamental possessions: their life, liberty and possessions acquired by work. The formulation "absolutely free" does not imply, however, that the state of nature is a state of pure arbitrariness. Rather, what prevails here is the law of nature, which obligates the individuals to self-preservation - to defend their life, liberty and possessions. Furthermore, and here Locke goes beyond Hobbes, it requires the individuals not to endanger anybody's life, liberty or possessions. Finally, the law of nature implies the right of every person to punish offences by others: the state of nature entails a right of private justice (1993, 270 et seqq.).

Accordingly, war breaks out if a person tries to violate the natural rights of another. In such a case, the attacked person, in accordance with the law of nature, is obliged to defend his rights - even by force (1993, 279 et seq.). However, Locke - in contrast to Hobbes - does not understand the state of nature as a permanent state of war. Rather, he explicitly distinguishes the state of nature from a state of war:

> Men living together according to reason, without a common Superior on Earth, with Authority to judge between them, is properly the State of Nature. But force, or a declared design of force upon the Person of another, where there is no common Superior on Earth to appeal to for relief, is the State of War (1993, 289).

The fact that Locke's state of nature is not a permanent state of war, however, does not make it considerably more pleasant than Hobbes' state of nature: on the contrary, Locke is of the opinion that war is very likely in the state of nature. First, he states that not all individuals abide the law of nature which requires one not to endanger anybody's life, liberty or possessions. Any violation, in accordance to the duty of self-defense, however, leads to measures of retaliation, counter-retaliations and so forth. Thus, the individuals' life, liberty and possessions, at the very least, often are endangered in the state of nature (1993, 280 et seq.).

Similar to Hobbes, Locke believes that the individuals' interest of avoiding war ultimately is the most important reason to overcome the state of nature and establish a civil society: "[f]or where there is an Authority [...] from which relief can be had by *appeal*, there the continuance of the State of War is excluded" (1993, 282). Thus, humans overcome the state of nature by constituting a state and submitting to it, because they hope to gain more safety than they have by practicing private justice.

The constitution of a state is thereby carried out by concluding a social contract, according to which individuals dispense with their natural right of private justice in favor of a common instance (a state) to which they may appeal in cases of conflict (1993, 324). Contrary to Hobbes, Locke does not understand such a contract as hypothetical, but as an historical event (1993, 334 et seq.). As plausible as this view may be, Locke sees the practical problems of agreeing on a contract: in contrast to Hobbes he states that in the course of contractual agreements between large numbers of individuals almost never, if ever, do all individuals share one opinion (1993, 332 et seq.). Therefore, according to Locke, the process of concluding a social contract has to permit majority decisions, to which representatives of minority opinions would have to submit (1993, 332).

Once such a contract is concluded, it is solely the state that is allowed to enact laws and/or punish violations of the law (1993, 324). The nature of the concrete governmental system (in Locke's view, democratic, oligarchic or monarchic system are eligible) also depends on a majority decision (1993, 354). Although, in Locke's opinion, monarchy is a particularly suitable system of government with regard to a peaceful beginning of civil societies (1993, 337 et seqq.), absolute monarchy would contradict the idea of civil society: as absolute monarchy does not offer an instance to which all citizens may equally appeal in cases of conflict, it is incapable of overcoming the state of nature: "whereever any persons are, who have not such an Authority to Appeal to, for the decision of any difference between them, there those persons are still *in the state of Nature*" (1993, 326). This shows another important difference to Hobbes: whereas the latter thoroughly regards absolute monarchy as a suitable system of government concerning peacekeeping measures, Locke introduces equal rights for all citizens as additional criterion for a legitimate statehood.

According to Locke, independent of its concrete governmental system, a legitimate state has to meet further fundamental principles. For example, it would be bound to the duty of protecting the natural rights of its citizens (1993, 356). As natural rights primarily are liberty rights, it follows that laws must not be enacted arbitrarily, but must take into account the interests of all citizens (1993, 357 et seqq.). In order to avoid violations of these fundamental principles, Locke - in contrast to Hobbes - first proposes to introduce a separation of powers (1993, 364 et seq.). Second, he awards fundamental rights of defense vis-à-vis the state. Whereas Hobbes spoke of the established governmental authority as being unchangeable, Locke is of the opinion that it is a right, if not a duty, to overthrow a state which permanently violates the citizens' civil rights and liberties and/or arbitrarily enacts laws (1993, 409 et seqq.).

To summarize: Locke - similar to Hobbes - puts forward the argument that humans unite in civil societies in order to escape the uncertainties of the state of nature. However, contrary to Hobbes, he is of the opinion that humans possess naturally given rights and liberties, which remain within a state.[5] Therefore, in Locke's theory, a state is clearly limited regarding what it is, and is not, legitimately allowed to do. Its citizens even have the right, if not the duty, to overthrow and replace an existing state, if it violates its legitimate competences. Due to his focus on civil rights, Locke is often referred to as being the founder of the idea of civil liberty.

2.3. Jean-Jacques Rousseau: *The Social Contract, Or Principles of Political Right* (1762)

About 75 years after Locke's *Two Treatises of Government*, in 1762 Jean-Jacques Rousseau entered the debate on individual rights and liberties in relation to the state, asking "whether, taking men as they are and laws as they can be made to be, it is possible to establish some just and reliable rule of administration in civil affairs" (Rousseau, [1762] 2002, 155). Moreover, he was concerned with the question of the nature of a legitimate state, which acts in favor of its citizens.

---

5   Thus, Locke often is interpreted as being an opponent of Hobbes. However, Locke never intended to argue for or against Hobbes.

He starts by assuming that no naturally given relationships of power exist, and concludes that agreements can be the only basis of legitimate authorities (2002, 158). As did Locke, Rousseau considers absolute forms of dominion as illegitimate, since they imply a complete abandonment of individual freedom. However, such abandonment would contradict human nature from which Rousseau concludes that absolute forms of dominion are not legitimate (2002, 159).

Rousseau, too, approaches the question of how justified authorities may be established by first designing a hypothetical state of nature.[6] However, in contrast to Hobbes and Locke, he is of the opinion that the state of nature is neither a permanent state of war nor implies the permanent danger of war, since humans on the one hand would not be enemies by nature and wars, on the other hand, (formally) could only be carried out between states (2002, 160). The state of nature outlined by Rousseau is characterized by the fact that individuals are driven solely by their instincts and appetites (2002, 166 et seq.). However, even if individuals in the state of nature are not in permanent war against each other, they nevertheless are exposed to certain risks: as soon as individuals with conflicting interests confront each other, the stronger succeeds over the weaker and thus the individual's lives and possessions are always potentially endangered. Therefore, individuals at a certain point come to recognize substantial advantages in leaving the state of nature and uniting in a community, namely improved personal security (2002, 163). In order to satisfy human nature and its substantial aspects of *self-preservation* and *liberty*, forming such a community, according to Rousseau, has to follow the principle: "[t]o find a form of association that may defend and protect with the whole force of the community the person and property of every associate, and by means of which each, joining together with all, may nevertheless obey only himself, and remain as free as before" (2002, 163). Such a formation of an association (i.e. a society) has to be carried out by concluding a social contract, whereby Rousseau - similar to Locke - at first considers the problem that different individuals usually have different points of view. He is also of the opinion that majority decisions are the only solution to this problem. However, majority decisions would have to be legitimized by an initial agreement, so that a unanimous decision is required at least on one occasion for majority decisions to be legitimate (2002, 162).

After legitimizing majority decisions, establishing the actual social contract is possible, which consists in "[e]ach of us put[ting] in common his person and all his power under the supreme direction of the general will; and in return each member becom[ing] an invisible part of the whole" (2002, 164). The social contract thus constitutes, in a manner of speaking, a collective body (i.e. a

---

6 In *The Social Contract*, Rousseau does not explicitly mention his understanding of the state of nature as a hypothetical situation. However, one finds such specifications in Rousseau (1992).

society), driven by the general will, which results from the individuals' voices. The individuals are therefore at the same time active citizens who form the general will, and passive citizens who are subjected to it. Thus, every individual at the same time is sovereign and governed (2002, 164).

According to Rousseau, after constituting such a state, the individuals have doubled obligations - towards themselves as well as towards the community, which they constitute. The protection of every individual follows from the obligation towards the community: since each individual is obligated towards the community, it contributes to protecting each member of the community and is at the same time protected by the contribution of all other members. Thereby, security - which was the sole motivation for leaving the state of nature - is ensured (2002, 165 et seq.).

Besides the establishment of a protective function, the transition to societal community leads to further serious changes. According to Rousseau, instinct and appetite as incitements of human action are replaced by justice and reason. Moreover, human abilities, concepts and convictions develop. Although the individuals lose their natural liberty - i.e. the right to everything that was only limited by their respective individual strength - they gain civil liberty, which is limited by the general will, but in exchange contains, for instance, property rights. Thus, according to Rousseau, the individuals reach true liberty by overcoming the state of nature, which stands in opposition to the slavery of instinct and appetite (2002, 166 et seq.).

Civil liberty, however, does not rule out a certain sovereign who specifies the general will. Rather, such a sovereign is legitimate as long as his decisions are not opposed by the citizens. Such opposition - as with Locke - however, is an explicit right (2002, 179 et seq.), if the sovereign acts contrary to the actual general will. However, in contrast to Locke, Rousseau argues against introducing a separation of powers: in his opinion, legislation, executive and jurisdiction are all components of sovereignty and therefore must be submitted to the sovereign. A separation of powers, in contrast, would render the idea of a ruling general will ad absurdum (2002, 171).

Concerning principles of legislation, Rousseau at first makes similar points to Locke: enacting specific laws has to respect the liberty and equality of the citizens (2002, 189). Thus, for Rousseau, the naturally given rights of liberty and equality are important values that are to be secured by a state. However, as he argues against the separation of powers, an alternative account of controlling governmental institutions is in need to that of Locke. Rousseau solves the problem by stating an even more radical claim than Locke's: in his opinion the only legitimate government is one which is submitted to the laws enacted by the general will, i.e. by the citizens (2002, 179). Thereby, Rousseau again strengthens individual rights within the state and introduces the concept of the people's sovereignty.

Rousseau approaches the question of suitable governmental systems similarly to Locke: the question of which system of government is eligible strongly depends on the context of establishing a state, for instance on state size and number of citizens. As a consequence, aristocracy, democracy or monarchy may be most suitable (2002, 200).

To summarize, what stands at the center of Rousseau's considerations is, as was the case with Locke, the naturally given rights of human individuals. From this, Rousseau ultimately concludes certain rights of the individual in and vis-à-vis a state. Beyond that, his theory of the general will particularly is to be understood as an attempt to undermine the basis of the feudalistic dominion prevalent at his time and to introduce the concept of people's sovereignty.

3. Modern Theories

3.1. John Rawls: *A Theory of Justice* (1971)

3.1.1. The Theory

Only in 1971, when John Rawls published his *Theory of Justice*, was the contractualist project revitalised and extended in terms of its focus. Rawls dedicated himself to the question of the ordinal principles of a well-arranged society, in which all individuals share a common conception of justice that is implemented by societal institutions (Rawls, 1999, 6 et seqq.). By implementing justice Rawls means "the way in which the major social institutions distribute fundamental rights and duties and determine the division of advantages from social cooperation" (1999, 6). Accordingly, Rawls takes justice defined "by the role of its principles in assigning rights and duties and in defining the appropriate division of social advantages" (1999, 9).

Thus, a common conception of justice within a society consists of those principles on which its members agree. The question arises of how such an agreement may be understood. In order to answer this question, Rawls resorts to a hypothetical situation - which he calls the *original position* - in which individuals establish their common principles of justice by contractual agreement (1999, 11). Contrary to the classical theories, Rawls' original position, however, is not to be understood as an anarchic state of nature, in which the individuals lead war against each other for their respective benefit. The reason is as follows: when Rawls speaks of principles of justice as principles which "determine the division of advantages from social cooperation", he already presupposes a social formation with a certain degree of cooperative discipline. Otherwise, no such social advantages would be at hand, whose distribution raises a problem of justice.

Rawls' original position is thus a *social* condition, which is not characterized by anarchic violence, but rather by distributional conflicts within a cooperative society.

It is these distributional conflicts which nevertheless specify Rawls' original position as similarly unstructured and unregulated as for instance Hobbes' state of nature: the economic, legal, political and ecological conditions of coexistence are not regulated. Therefore the individuals' contractual agreement must refer to all kinds of societal produced goods. Such a conception of the original state as universally unstructured situation is necessary in order to be able to develop principles of justice whose claims apply to all domains of society.

At first, however, Rawls has to explain what formal criteria have to be met in order to establish acceptable principles of justice. Therefore, he identifies such principles as justified and generally binding which "free and rational persons concerned to further their interests would accept in an initial position of equality as defining the fundamental terms of their association" (1999, 10). Thus, justified principles of justice result from an agreement between rational utility maximizers under fair conditions. In order to ensure such conditions, individuals in the original position are bargaining behind the so-called *veil of the ignorance* (1999, 11), which means that they do not have any information about, for instance, the social conditions in which they will stand after establishing the principles of justice. Therefore, the individuals may only vote for such principles, which are favorable due to general and formal interests, which every person has.

Furthermore, the veil of ignorance crucially affects the decisional behavior of the individuals. Rawls concludes that all individuals choose a strategy of risk minimizing and therefore decide according to the maximin rule (1999, 130 et seqq.).[7] They do so, because it is impossible for them to accurately predict objective probabilities for being in certain social positions after raising the veil of ignorance. Therefore, as Rawls states, it is rational for them to minimize their risk by not voting for principles of justice which, for instance, assign advantages only to individuals in certain social positions. In his opinion, this means that it is in their best interests to decide according to the maximin rule.

In addition, the original position is characterized by the fact that choosing principles of justice is both unique and final, i.e. no repetitions of the procedure of agreement are allowed.[8] Here again, Rawls' account is similar to Hobbes'.

---

7 The maximin rule is a decision-theoretical rule, which prescribes 1) to arrange the alternative options according to their worst possible outcomes 2) opt for the alternative, whose worst possible outcome in comparison with the worst possible outcomes of all other options is the best.
8 Of course, the original position contains several other assumptions. For an extensive list cf. Rawls (1999, 126 et seq).

According to this specification of the original position, the individuals agree on two principles for organizing a society, which concretize the maximin rule with regard to basic social goods:

> First: each person is to have an equal right to the most extensive scheme of equal basic liberties with a similar scheme of liberties for others (Rawls, 1999, 53).
>
> [Second] Social and economic inequalities are to be arranged so that they are both (a) to the greatest expected benefit of the least advantaged and (b) attached to offices and positions open to all under conditions of fair equality of opportunity (1999, 72).[9]

The first principle refers to immaterial social goods and specifies the egalitarian distribution of basic liberties and political rights as well as the maximization of individual freedom. The second principle - the so-called *difference principle* - refers to material social goods and claims that improvements of the situation of certain members of a society are only allowed if the worst-off individuals gain advantages from their promotion. It is especially this principle that implements the maximin rule in distributional manners.[10]

In order to avoid conflicts between the two principles, Rawls further assumes that individuals in the original position agree on a lexical order, which gives priority to the first principle over the second. Thus, if certain basic liberties and rights are not ensured, a society is not just even if it distributes material goods in accordance to the difference principle (1999, 53 et seq.).

In consequence, according to Rawls, three societal conditions may be distinguished: first, the *perfectly just scheme*, "in which the expectations of the least advantaged are indeed maximized [...]. No changes in the expectations of those better off can improve the situation of those worst off". Second, the *just throughout* scheme, "in which the expectations of all those better off at least contribute to the welfare of the more unfortunate. That is, if their expectations were decreased, the prospects of the least advantaged would likewise fall. Yet the maximum is not achieved. Even higher expectations for the more advantaged would raise the expectations of those in the lowest position". And third, the *unjust scheme*, in which "the higher expectations, one or more of them, are excessive. If these expectations were decreased, the situation of the least favored would be improved" (1999, 68).

To summarize: Rawls exceeds the focus of classical contractualism by far, as he is not only concerned with the question of legitimately established and working states, but is also interested in what constitutes a just society. Furthermore,

---

9 The second principle presented here is not Rawls' original formulation (1999, 53), however, according to him, a simpler, but equivalent one (1999, 72).
10 For an example of a justified improvement for some members of society cf. Rawls (1999, 98 et seq.).

the original position serves quite a different task for Rawls' argument than the classical state of nature did. Whereas the latter clarifies why humans with certain properties and/or rights decide to establish and submit to states, the former primarily constitutes a fair basis for agreeing on principles of justice by taking certain information as being inaccessible to the individuals concerned.[11] Nevertheless, Rawls' theory is to be interpreted as standing in the tradition of Hobbes, because he only attaches certain properties to humans, e.g. them being rational utility maximizers. Thus, Rawls - as Hobbes - only assumes anthropological premises when looking at the individuals reaching an agreement. Moreover, he describes the conclusion of an agreement on principles of justice as a unique event.

3.1.2. Critiques

Rawls' theory mainly has been criticized through two lines of thinking: on the one hand one finds libertarian theoreticians such as Robert Nozick, on the other communitarians like Charles Taylor, Michael Walzer or Michael Sandel.[12]

Nozick puts forward several points of criticism against Rawls of which three are to be highlighted (Nozick 1974, 183 et seqq.). First, he criticizes Rawls for characterizing his prinicples of justice as final and unchangeable. This, Nozick states, contradicts Rawls' procedural account: "If processes are so great, Rawls' theory is defective because it is incapable of yielding process principles of justice" (1974, 208). Second, Nozick contests the fact that, according to Rawls, certain distributional patterns are morally preferable to others. This would entail limiting the options for acting of those who are better off, which in Nozick's view cannot be justified - as cannot any restriction on the options for individual action (219 et seq.). This critique - as we will see - is rooted in Nozick's opinion that any redistributional action per se is morally wrong. It is furthermore connected with his view that the natural lottery of personal talents is *not* unfair (225 et seq.). Therefore, Rawls' veil of ignorance, which masks - amongst other things - these naturally given talents, would not result in a fair situation for agreement, but rather illegitimately veil certain properties and knowledge of the individuals. Nozick concludes that because the agreement on principles of justice is grounded in this account, only unfair principles of justice can be established (which, in turn, results in morally wrong patterns of distribution). Ultimately, Nozick criticizes Rawls' principles of justice as actually being unjust becuase they are based on the account of the veil of ignorance.

Communitarians, too, mainly criticize Rawls regarding his theoretical

---

11   This is why Rawls speaks of "justice as fairness" (1999, 11).
12   Of course, a large number of other criticisms do exist (e.g. Dworkin, 2000; Nagel 2000), which will not be dealt with here.

preconditions. In this context, the two most famous critics are Charles Tayler and Michael Walzer.[13] Taylor basically argues that Rawls does not give sufficient attention to the fact that modern societies including their goods and values, are grounded in historical and cultural processes. Therefore, his nonhistorical deduction of principles of justice would miss social reality and fail to stress any normative commitment (Taylor 1988, 173). Taylor thus criticizes the original position as standing in no connection with social reality. As a consequence, principles of justice which are deduced from it are generally incapable of meeting the requirements of modern societies. Consequently, Taylor argues against any universal principles of justice and in favour of contextual ones (1988, 179). In the context of western societies what would be just is not the difference principle, but rather a principle of contribution, by which the members of a society receive certain amounts of social goods in relation to their contribution to social utility (170).

Walzer takes the same line of criticism when he states that justice cannot be defined without looking at the respective form of societal coexistence. Therefore, the inhabitants of the original state only conclude temporary agreements, which they would adapt to the actual social conditions after raising the veil of ignorance (Walzer, 1987, 13 et seqq.).[14] Thus, Walzer also holds that it is impossible to establish universal principles of justice, as suggested by Rawls. However, in contrast to Taylor, he suggests no single alternative principle which holds for the whole of society, but rather states that modern societies have to be interpreted as pluralistic entities consisting of different spheres, which all imply respective distributional patterns (1983, 11 et seq.). As a consequene, one may only state a single universal meta-principle of justice, according to which every societal good is to be distributed in view of a principle that holds in the respective sphere in which the good is produced (1983, 11 et seq.).

3.2. Robert Nozick: *Anarchy, State, and Utopia* (1974)

3.2.1. The Theory

Whereas Rawls is interested in a contractualist development of distributional principles of justice, Robert Nozick in *Anarchy, State, and Utopia* (1974) primarily focuses on the questions of whether - in the light of naturally given rights of liberty - establishing a state would be morally permissible at all, and if so, which tasks a state could legitimately undertake: "Individuals have rights […] so strong and far-reaching […] that they raise the question of what, if anything, the state

---

13   Thereby, Michael Sandel is not to be forgotten. However, currently his critique (1982) is for the most part considered invalid.
14   Ronald Dworkin stated a similar argument (Dworkin, 1977, 152).

and its officials may do" (Nozick, 1974, ix). In order to answer these questions, Nozick starts at a stateless condition, in which the individuals "generally satisfy moral constraints and act exactly as they should" (5).[15] According to Nozick, this would be the best anarchic condition that one may reasonably assume. If, in this condition, serious problems for human coexistence appeared, one would have crucial reasons for legitimizing a state (5). Hence, for Nozick it is not a priori evident that a state is morally permissible at all. Therefore, he asks how an anarchic state of human coexistence can be transformed into a situation which improves human coexistence through the establishment of a state. Individual rights of liberty form the only normative premise, with regard to which a state is to be evaluated concerning its moral permissibility and hence its legitimacy.

The reference to individual rights of liberty already suggests that Nozick chooses Locke's state of nature as the starting point for his considerations. As already shown, in this state the individuals have naturally given rights to their life, liberty and possessions, and are obligated not to violate the rights of others. Furthermore, individuals in this state of nature have a right to private justice in cases where others violate their natural rights.[16] Locke assumed that the fundamental problems of such a state of nature provide sufficient reasons for justifying the establishment of a state. Nozick, however, does not agree. In his opinion, these problems are not a sufficient basis for justifying a state as long as it remains unclarified as to whether there are alternative possibilities to overcome the disadvantages of the state of nature *within* the state of nature (10 et seq.). Nozick continues by stating that individuals in the state of nature at first react to their permanent endangerment by uniting in groups in order to form so-called *protective associations*. Since Nozick assumes that persons in the state of nature act in accordance to the law of nature, he concludes that they actually protect each other after unification (12). However, two substantial problems arise: first, it is impossible for the individuals to be always ready to protect others. And second, it is impossible to solve conflicts between members of one protective association (12 et seq.). With regard to the second problem, Nozick states that the protective associations develop certain procedures in order to be capable of determining the permissibility and validity of complaints by members. In order to address the first problem, Nozick introduces the principles of division of labor and exchange: "Some people will be *hired* to perform protective functions, and some entrepreneurs will go into the business of selling protective services" (13). Thus, the protective associations begin to develop internal structures, and which is necessary for its members to abandon their right to private justice: "Such [private] retaliation may well lead to counterretaliation by another agency or individual, and a protective agency would not wish *at that late stage* to get drawn

---

15 What Nozick means by "moral constraints" is, of course, to be clarified (fn 16).
16 It becomes clear what Nozick means when he states that the anarchic living individuals "generally satisfy moral constraints and act exactly as they should": they act in accordance to the law of nature and usually do not violate other's natural rights.

into the messy affair by having to defend its client against the counterretaliation" (15). What underlies the prohibition of private justice is an idea of efficiency: private justice leads to counter-measures, which again provoke counter-measures and so forth. This - in the worst case - leads to a never ending chain of counter-measures. The protective associations, however, would have to protect their members from every single measure, if private justice was not abandoned. This would be ineffective, which makes it necessary to prohibit private justice.

Nevertheless, problems arise if two or more protective associations exist in the same spatial territory. Nozick mentions three possible consequences of such situations, of which two are of special importance. First, it is possible that one of the associations wins in every case of conflict; in consequence, the members of the (always) loosing association(s) feel poorly protected and move into the (always) winning association. In the long run, this constitutes a situation in which only one protective association exists in a given spatial territory. Second, a situation may be hypothesised, in which two or more associations of roughly equal strength fight against each other frequently. In such cases, the associations appoint an independent party to settle conflicts in order to avoid expensive and unproductive conflicts. As a consequence, nearly all individuals - namely the members of the aforementioned fighting associations - living in a certain territory are subject to a common system, according to whose rules conflicts are solved. Thereby, the so-called *dominant protective association* is established (16 et seq.).

Such a construction - one might think - appears to be a state: within a certain territory a system exists, which protects its members against assaults and settles conflicts between them according to certain rules. However, as Nozick holds, a state is defined by the fact that it:

> [...] claims a monopoly on deciding who may use force when; it says that only it may decide who may use force and under what conditions; it reserves to itself the sole right to pass on the legitimacy and permissibility of any use of force within its boundaries; furthermore it claims the right to punish all those who violate its claimed monopoly (1974, 23).

Thus, one substantial task of a state consists in offering protection to *all* individuals living in its territory. The dominant protective association developed so far, however, offers protection only to its members and furthermore cannot force non-members to abandon the practice of private justice, i.e. the criterion of a state to claim a monopoly of force within its boundaries is not fulfilled. Therefore, according to Nozick, dominant protective associations are *ultraminimal states* (1974, 26).

It is noticeable that so far Nozick has not spoken of a contractual agreement between individuals.[17] A central feature of Nozick's account is that the unification

---

17 On the contrary, in the course of his explanations on prohibiting private justice for members of a protective association Nozick holds that contracts are not necessary

of individuals is not based on an explicit social contract, but rather on an implicit, tacit contract. This model has its origins in idea of the 'invisible hand' proposed by Adam Smith (1937, 423) and is, according to Nozick, attractive, because it shows how processes of unification take place without being intended (1974, 18 et seq.): although all individuals in the state of nature solely act for their respective own sake and reasons, an ultraminimal state is developed. Thus, in Nozick's opinion, the individuals reach an end (the ultraminimal state), which they neither had prior knowledge of, nor intentionally pursued (1974, 21 et seq.). This also is the reason why the transition from the state of nature to the ultraminimal state is morally permissible: the ultraminimal state developed on the basis of the individuals' free decisions and actions and hence does not violate their natural rights of liberty.

On the other side, however, the ultraminimal state, as Nozick argues, is morally inadmissible with reference to the *universal* non-violation of natural rights, since the rights of non-members are not protected (1974, 27 et seq.). Thus, the necessity arises of overcoming the ultraminimal state by establishing a minimal state, which leads to two questions that must be answered. First, is the dominant protective association allowed to prohibit non-members practicing private justice and if so, why? Second, is the claim of states to offer universal protection morally permissible, given the natural rights of individuals? The first question is answered by Nozick as follows: it is *rational* for the dominant protective association to prohibit practicing private justice for non-members, if such practice bore a certain amount of risk for its members (1974, 88 et seq.). However, the protective association has the *right* to prohibit practicing private justice for non-members only, if non-members are compensated in the sense that their utility after compensation is at least as high as it had been for practicing private justice after compensation (Nozick 1974, 57). The motivation for prohibiting private justice for non-members thus lies in the member's wish to eliminate the risk resulting from non-members practicing private justice. Consequently, they prohibit private justice for non-members within their territory. This, however, would be an illegitimate violation of the non-members' natural rights, which is why the non-members have to be compensated for being not allowed to practice private justice (1974, 81). The question is what form such compensation may have. What Nozick has in mind is that non-members get a free membership in the protective association, paid for by its members and hence are themselves protected by the association.

From this also follows the answer to the question of the legitimacy of universal protection by states: since general prohibition of private justice is legitimate - even for non-members if they are compensated - the dominant protective association now legitimately offers universal protection to all individuals within its territory (91 et seqq.). Nozick calls the so developed "stateslike entity" (118) a *minimal*

(1974,15).

state. In his view, it was developed in morally permissible steps, as in the course of its establishment the individuals' natural rights were not violated. However, such a state, according to Nozick, is legitimate only if it is "limited to the narrow functions of protection against force, theft, fraud, [and the] enforcement of contracts [...]" (1974, xi). State activities which go beyond these tasks, on the other hand, are not legitimate, because they violate the individuals' rights. In particular, any kind of distributional measures would be unfair, which is why Nozick states that any theory of distributive justice is morally inadmissible.[18] This thesis is rooted in Nozicks entitlement theory of justice, in which he argues that:

> [...] holdings of a person are just if he is entitled to them by the principles of justice in acquisition and transfer, or by the principle of rectification of injustice [...]. If each person's holdings are just, then the total set (distribution) of holdings is just (153).

What Nozick means by the principle of justice in acquisition is the right of everyone to acquire unowned goods; by the principle of transfer he understands the legitimate exchange of goods by donation or trade. These principles in his opinion are the only legitimate possibilities of appropriating holdings. Since, however, illegitimate appropriation of holdings factually does happen, Nozick introduces the "principle of rectification of justice", which claims to balance any illegitimate acquisition of possessions (151 et seqq.).[19] Thus, justice consists in the possibility of trading with legitimately acquired holdings freely and/or the rectification of illegitimately acquired holdings. Accordingly, it becomes clear why Nozick considers any state activity which interferes with free trading as unjustified: such activities simply do not correspond to the entitlement theory, since certain holdings are distributed according to principles other than those of acquisition and transfer.

To summarize: Nozick holds that the only legitimate states are those which guarantee security for their citizens without, however, interfering with their natural rights, in particular their right of free trading. Contrary to Rawls, Nozick holds that theories of distributive justice are in principle morally inadmissible. The reason for the difference between Rawls' and Nozick's opinions mainly lies in them being connected to different contractualist traditions: where Rawls' thought is in line with Hobbes' account, Nozick's stands in Locke's tradition. Like Hobbes, Rawls assigns greater powers to social institutions than Nozick, who proposes and defends the premise of naturally given rights and - similar to Locke - primarily justifies individual rights vis-à-vis the state, and limits the state in its powers as far as possible.

---

18 Here the reason for Nozick's vehement critique on Rawls becomes clear: Nozick regards any distributive account - like the one of Rawls - as an inadmissible interference with individuals' rights.

19 However, Nozick does not specify this principle.

3.2.2. Critiques

Nozick's theory has been criticized from many angles. One important critic is Thomas Nagel who, in his review "Libertarianism without Foundations" (1975), presents several points of objection. I will mention three of them. First, Nagel criticizes the inductive approach Nozick takes in deriving the rights and obligations of a state. In Nagel's opinion, it is not admissible "to determine what governments may and should do by first asking what individuals, taken a few at a time in isolation from large-scale society may do, and then applying the resultant principles to all possible circumstances, including those which involve billions of people, complicated political and economic institutions, and thousands of years of history" (Nagel, 1975, 140). Principles, for which universal validity is claimed, would have to be, contrary to Nozick's procedure, examined with regard to the consequences of their universal validity from the beginning. Second, Nagel holds that Nozick's moral intuitions concerning the status of individual liberties and possessions are implausible: even individual rights - as with almost every right - are not absolute, but rather *prima facie* rights, which may be overridden in certain situations, for instance in order to avoid negative outcomes (140 et seq.). According to Nagel, to completely leave aside consequentialist considerations, as Nozick does, is simply not plausible. Third, he states that Nozick deals with the basis of his libertarian rights in insufficient ways. Instead of solely basing individual rights on the value of forming one's own life in accordance with one's will, Nozick would have had "to concentrate on the actor and his relation to the person he is constrained not to treat in certain ways, even to achieve very desirable ends" (144). What Nagel is criticizing here is the fact that Nozick does not deal with individual obligations towards others, and thus does not (sufficiently) justify the individual rights he claims. A sufficient justification, in Nagel's opinion, would have to consider individual obligations, and he understands Nozick's rights as "rights not to be deliberately treated or used in certain ways, and not to be deliberately interfered with in certain activities" (143). Thus, Nagel states, Nozick's rights primarily are rights towards *others* which conversely results in certain obligations.

Furthermore, Nozick - similar to Rawls - has been criticized by communitarianists, in particular by Charles Taylor who primarily argues against Nozick's set of premises. Taylor, in principle, holds that humans are social beings, and therefore rejects any theory which is based on the assumption of humans as isolated beings with rights vis-à-vis the community. According to Taylor, such an "atomistic" idea of man (Taylor, 1985, 187 et seqq.), which is the basis of Nozick's theory, is simply implausible. Furthermore, he holds that any conception of naturally given rights - like Nozick's - is also implausible. In Taylor's opinion, human rights are acquired by mutual acknowledgment and based on the affiliation to a community (198). Accordingly, natural rights do not exist; rather, rights can only be established within a society.

Yet another critic of Nozick is Amartya Sen, who concentrates his criticism on the practical consequences of Nozick's theory. Sen argues that Nozick completely ignores the consequences of his libertarian philosophy, which ultimately characterizes his theory as unacceptable in normative terms. In Sen's opinion, the nonobservance of possible consequences may - while staying in complete accordance with Nozick's libertarian rights - lead to catastrophic extremes such as severe famines (Sen, 1999, 66; 1981, 45 et seqq.).[20] This however would prove the absolute priority of individual property rights "lead[ing] to the violation of the substantive freedom of individuals to achieve those things to which they have reason to attach great importance, including escaping avoidable mortality [...]" (1999, 66), which, in Sen's opinion, is morally inadmissible.

3.3. Thomas M. Scanlon: *What We Owe to Each Other* (1998)

3.3.1. The Theory

Thomas Scanlon's *What We Owe to Each Other* (1998) differs fundamentally from all theories presented so far. Although Scanlon sees himself rooted in the tradition of Rousseau, he states:

> What distinguishes my view from other accounts involving ideas of agreement is its conception of the motivational basis of this agreement. The parties whose agreement is in question are assumed not merely to be seeking some kind of advantage but also to be moved by the aim of finding principles that others, similarly motivated, could not reasonably reject (Scanlon 1998, 5).

Thus, Scanlon does not proceed by assuming that humans are purely egoistic utility maximizers, who agree on a certain kind of coexistence. Rather, he assumes the possibility of altruistic characteristics in individual actions. A further difference consists in the fact that Scanlon's contractualism is not directly connected to the domain of political philosophy: he is uninterested in the question of establishing states and their legitimacy, focussing instead on the justification of moral principles. In addition, Scanlon wants to show why individuals are motivated to act morally at all.

The starting point of his project is the assumption that human life is of intrinsic value (1998, 103 et seqq.). Since it is constitutive of being human to act in accordance with one's own evaluations and reasons, a morally appropriate

---

20   Since Nozick rejects any kind of redistribution, in Sen's view it follows no moral obligation to help individuals who are not able to ensure their subsistence even if in consequence they starve. Nozick, however, seems to see and accept this problem (1974, xi).

way to interact with others would be to treat them "in a way that recognizes the capacity of human beings [...] to assess reasons and to govern their lives according to this assessment" (106). This, in Scanlon's opinion, is possible only if one acts according to the formula that "an act is wrong if its performance under the circumstances would be disallowed by any set of principles for the general regulation of behavior that no one could reasonably reject as a basis for informed, unforced general agreement" (153). The crucial point is: if we have good reasons to reject an action then we will reasonably likewise reject any principles, which would permit such an action. Similarly, such principles are (morally) wrong which others could reasonably reject. Ultimately, this means that we are morally obligated to justify our actions towards others - in the sense that our actions should not be reasonably rejected by others. So, what do we owe to each other? We owe to each other to refrain from actions that others could reasonably reject and to act only according to principles which others cannot reasonably reject.

The question of moral motivation is answered as follows. According to Scanlon, such motivation simply arises from acknowledging the intrinsic value of humans. In Scanlon's opinion, the contractualist formula is the only adequate answer to such an acknowledgment. Thus, moral motivation directly follows from factual acknowledgment (1998, 153 et seq.). If one factually recognizes the intrinsic value of humans, it firstly follows that one has reasons to find out "what would be allowed by principles that others could not reasonably reject" and secondly that one has reason "to govern [...] our conduct in the ways that these principles require" (1998, 154). Furthermore, we are morally motivated because we want to stand in a certain relation to our fellow men: "Contractualism [...] locates the source of the reason-giving force of judgments of right and wrong in the importance of standing in a certain relation to others" (177 et seq.). What Scanlon means by certain relation is "us [...] being 'in unity with our fellow creatures'" (163). Although Scanlon does not explain more precisely what he means by being in unity, he holds it to be a historically proven fact that it is important for us to stand in such a relation to our fellow men (163). Standing in good relation to our fellow men, however, again is only possible by acting in accordance with the contractualist formula. Therefore we are - if interested in having certain relations with our fellow men - motivated to act morally in Scanlon's sense.

So far, Scanlon has explained what we owe to each other in moral terms and under which conditions we are motivated to act accordingly. However, as Scanlon speaks of an act being wrong if it would be disallowed by any principle that no one could reasonably reject, the question remains as to how to derive such principles. Generally, Scanlon notes that:

> [...] an assessment of the rejectability of a principle must take into account the consequences of its acceptance in general, not merely in a particular case that we may be concerned with. Since we cannot know, when we are making this assessment, which particular individuals will be affected by it in which ways

[…], our assessment cannot be based on the particular aim, preferences, and other characteristics of specific individuals. We must rely instead on commonly available information about what people have reason to want (1998, 204).

As the principles in question are to be examined universally, such examination, must not be carried out on the basis of certain individuals' preferences, but rather on commonly available information about what people have reason to want "in virtue of their situation, characterised in general terms" (204). Therefore, no reasons may enter the decision about a principle, which are specific to certain individuals, as only such reasons are permitted that we can assume any individual has.

Yet, the reference to *individuals'* reasons is still of particular importance, because - as Scanlon states - the only reasons that are eligible for judging whether or not a principle can be reasonably rejected are "various individuals' reasons for objecting to that principle and alternatives to it" (1998, 229). By referring to generic reasons of (potential) *individuals*, Scanlon wants to exclude any aggregation of objections to principles: any (potential) individual who has reason to reject a principle cannot be overruled by any number of individuals who do not have reason to reject that principle. Hence, a principle can be reasonably rejected if any (potential) individual who may be affected by the principle has generic reasons to reject the principle. Thereby, a central feature of contractualism has been taken into account: "its insistence that the justifiability of a moral principle depends only on various *individuals'* reasons for objecting that principle" (229).

However, the question of how to determine principles that can be reasonably rejected is still unsolved. For it is difficult to determine any principle that cannot be reasonably rejected - hence any moral principle - according to this criterion. In order to solve this problem, Scanlon additionally links the rejectability of a principle to the question of whether other individuals have better reasons for rejecting alternatives to the principle in question, than the reasons of those individual(s) who want to reject it. Conversely, this means that an individual can reasonably reject a principle, if he is able to suggest an alternative principle, which cannot be reasonably rejected by at least equally strong reasons by any other individual. The strength of a reason to reject a principle thereby depends on the expected effect that the principle will have on the well-being of an individual. Although Scanlon states that individual well-being is not the sole basis for rejecting principles, he argues: "In many cases, gains and losses in well-being (relief from suffering, for example) are clearly the most relevant factors in determining whether a principle could or could not be reasonably rejected" (1998, 215). Thus, what primarily counts when assessing a principle is its effects on the well-being of those individuals that may be governed by it.

To summarize: in contrast to Rawls, Nozick and the classical contractualists, Scanlon's theory is not concerned with the question of establishing and legitimizing states. Rather it is concerned with a person's moral obligations towards others, as well as their motivation to act according to these obligations. In principle, Scanlon is of the opinion that we have a moral obligation to respect the reasons of others for wanting something, which ultimately underlies their actions. This, however, is only possible by (hypothetically) justifying our actions towards others and acting solely on basis of such principles, which others (hypothetically) could not reasonably reject. Good reasons for rejecting a principle are reasons which we can assume are common to everyone and which usually refer to the well-being of individuals. The motivation for acting in accordance with our obligations originates, in Scanlon's view, in the acknowledgment of human life and its inherent value, and also in the fact that we want to stand in good relations with our fellow men.

3.3.2. Critiques

Authors like Philip Pettit criticize Scanlon's ethical ideal of referring only to what can be justified to others, stating that the moral rightness of an action does not only result purely from the fact that it is justifiable to others:

> [H]e [Scanlon] neglects the fact that when we try to justify certain actions to others we do not try to establish that they are [...] well, actions that we can justify to others. We try to establish that the actions are right in some independent sense of right and that, for precisely that reason, they are justifiable. Specifically, we try to establish that they are right by showing that they are fair or kind or for the general good, or whatever. The very linkage between justifiability and rightness suggests [...] that rightness must be characterized in a justifiability-independent manner (Pettit, 1999, 8).

Thus, according to Pettit, the moral rightness of an action is in fact tied to its justifiability. However, it is not sufficiently justified - as Scanlon states - by the fact that it cannot be reasonably rejected by others, but rather on the basis of other independent considerations. In Pettit's opinion, we justify actions against the background of different values - for instance, the values of fairness or justice.

Other authors, such as Gerald Dworkin, object that morally uninterested individuals may not be bound to the principles established in accordance with Scanlon's account:

> By hypothesis, the correct principles are ones that nobody (similarly motivated) could reasonably reject. Why those? Because standing in such a relationship with our fellow creatures is recognized as an ideal of human relationship that is worth seeking for its own sake (Dworkin, 2002, 477).

This, according to Dworkin, raises the question, "why [...] such principles are binding upon those who are not similarly motivated" to stand in a certain relationship to their fellow creatures (478). He concludes:

> Remember that *the* reason that the fact that an action is wrong provides me

with reason not to do it *is* just the fact that the action cannot be justified to others on grounds I could expect them to accept. But this is exactly the reason that the disaffected cannot see the force of, because they cannot see the value of being in unity with their fellow creatures. The very thing which explains our motivation to act rightly has no motivational force with them, and cannot, given their (defective) appreciation of the value of being in a certain relationship with others (481).

What is criticized here is Scanlon's account of moral motivation. In Dworkin's opinion, what follows from Scanlon's account is that only individuals who factually are motivated to stand in a good relation to their fellow men are bound to justifiable principles. Thus, Scanlon's theory of moral motivation does not have universal validity..

4. Conclusion

Based on the foregoing discussion, contractualist theories may be categorized according to their respective fundamental premises. On one side theories are rooted in Hobbes' tradition - like that of Rawls - and start by ascribing certain *features* to human nature, due to which humans (under certain circumstances) decide to establish certain forms of states and/or societies. These theories base their arguments on anthropological premises, for instance, assuming humans to be purely rational utility maximizers. On the other side, one finds theories like Nozick's which stand in the tradition of Locke, which go beyond characterizing human features, and ascribe certain *natural rights* to humans. These theories are primarily interested in the legitimacy of states, given the natural rights ascribed to individuals.

Finally, theories like Scanlon's open up a third category which must be distinguished from both of these approaches. Such accounts are based on the assumption that humans have an intrinsic *value* and as a consequence ask how such value is to be handled appropriately.

Despite these differences, however, all contractualist theories ultimately share one fundamental interest - the shape that human coexistence should ultimately take.

BIBLIOGRAPHY

Dworkin, G. (2002). Contractualism and the Normativity of Principles. *Ethics*, 112, 471-482.

Dworkin, R. (1977). *Taking Rights Seriously*. Cambridge (Mass), Harvard University Press.

_____ (2000). Justice and Hypothetical Agreements. From: The Original Position. In Solomon, R.C. and Murphy, M.C. (eds.) (2000). *What is Justice? Classic and Contemporary Readings*. New York, Oxford University Press, 288-294.

Hobbes, T. (2008). *Leviathan*. New York, Longman.

Kamm, F.M. (2002). Owing, Justifying, and Rejecting. *Mind*, 111, 323-354.

Locke, J. (1993). *Two Treatises of Government*. Cambridge, Cambridge University Press.

Nagel, T. (1975). Libertarianism without Foundations. *The Yale Law Journal*, 85, 136-149.

Nagel, T. (2000). "Internal Difficulties with Justice as Fairness", from "Rawls on Justice". In Solomon, R.C. and Murphy, M.C. (eds.) (2000). *What is Justice? Classic and Contemporary Readings*. New York, Oxford University Press, 295-300.

Nozick, R. (1974). *Anarchy, State, and Utopia*. New York, Basic Books.

Pettit, P. (1999). Doing unto Others. *The Times Literary Supplement*, June 25th, 7-8.

Pogge, T. (2001). What We Can Reasonably Reject? *Noûs Supplement*, 11, 118-147.

Rawls, J. (1999). *A Theory of Justice*. Cambridge (Mass), Harvard University Press.

Rousseau, J.J. (1992). *Discourse on the Origin of Inequality*. Indianapolis, Hackett.

_____(2002). T*he Social Contract and The First and Second Discourses*. New Haven, Yale University Press.

Sandel, M.J. (1982). *Liberalism and the Limits of Justice*. Cambridge, Cambridge University Press.

Scanlon, T.M. (1998). *What We Owe to Each Other*. Cambridge (Mass), Harvard University Press.

Sen, A. (1981). *Poverty and Famines: an Essay on Entitlement and Deprivation*. New York, Oxford University Press.

_____ (1999). *Development as Freedom*. New York, Knopf.

Smith, A. (1937). *An Inquiry into the Nature and Causes of the Wealth of Nations*.

New York, Modern Library.

Taylor, C. (1985). Philosophy and the Human Sciences. *Philosophical Papers 2*. Cambridge, Cambridge University Press.

Taylor, C. (1988). Negative Freiheit. *Zur Kritik des neuzeitlichen Individuums*. Frankfurt a. Main, Suhrkamp.

Walzer, M. (1987). *Interpretation and Social Criticism*. Cambridge, Harvard University Press.

Walzer, M. (1983). *Spheres of Justice: A Defense of Pluralism and Equality*. New York, Basic Books.

6

Egoism and Ethics

Andy Cochrane

1. Introduction

All varieties of philosophical egoism hold that there is a systematic relation between human action and self-interest, but this doctrine has been developed in a variety of different ways. Egoism can be a descriptive position (i.e. one about how agents *do*, as a matter of fact, act, cf. psychological egoism); a normative position (i.e. one about how agents *ought* to act, c.f. ethical egoism and rational egoism); or an explanatory position (i.e. one about *why* we act as we do, c.f. Hobbesian ethical egoism)[1]. The relation between the different varieties of egoism is complicated, and disputed, but this chapter will aim to draw out these relationships, as well as considering the arguments for and against these different varieties of egoism.

Both the normative and descriptive varieties of egoism come in weaker and stronger versions. Historically, the stronger versions have been propounded first, and these have come down to us from the likes of Thomas Hobbes (1651), Jeremy Bentham (1789), John Stuart Mill (1861),[2] and Ayn Rand (1964). The critical attention of this chapter will be given over to the stronger versions of egoism. However, I will discuss some of the weaker or more 'moderate' versions of egoism that have been developed along the way.

---

1   Many people have read Hobbes as a psychological, ethical and explanatory egoist in Leviathan (1651). But others (e.g. Gert, 1967) argue that it is a mistake to derive psychological egoism from Hobbes' mechanistic account of human behaviour and motivation, and that Hobbes' political theory is, in fact, incompatible with psychological egoism. Whether or not Gert is correct, Hobbes certainly had a strong influence in popularising psychological egoism.

2   There is also some debate as to whether Mill endorsed a form of psychological egoism or not. Although some philosophers have interpreted Mill as supporting such a doctrine (see, e.g. Sidgwick, 1874), others (see, e.g. Brink, 2007) argue that this is a mistake.

2. The Relationship Between the Varieties of Egoism

Psychological egoism holds that all intentional action is fundamentally motivated by perceived self-interest. The earliest rigorous defence of this position is usually attributed to Hobbes in *Leviathan*. Some utilitarians have also been powerful advocates of a version of psychological egoism, known as psychological egoistic hedonism (I will refer to this thesis as 'psychological hedonism' henceforth). Psychological hedonists, such as Bentham, argue that every agent is, as a matter of fact, set up as to pursue their own pleasure or happiness, and thus that all intentional action aims at securing one's perceived happiness[3].

Psychological egoism (PE) comes in a stronger and a weaker form, which can be captured roughly as follows:

Strong PE: All intentional actions are performed with the sole aim of securing benefits for oneself.

Weak PE: All intentional actions are performed with the expectation that one will achieve at least one of one's own self-regarding ends by so acting.[4]

Strong psychological egoism is often taken to form the crux of the egoist's position. Rational egoism holds that an agent always has most reason to perform the act that will best promote his self-interest, whilst ethical egoism holds that an agent is morally required to perform an action if and only if it maximises his own best interests. Some egoist's consider ethical and rational egoism to be entailed by the truth of psychological egoism, together with the premise that 'ought implies can'. They reason roughly as follows. If all intentional actions aim at securing what we believe to be in our best interests, and we can only be morally or rationally required to perform an act if we have the ability and opportunity to perform that act, then we can only be morally or rationally required to perform those acts that maximise our own best interests.

I will have more to say about this argument, and the relationships between the different varieties of egoism as the chapter proceeds. However, given that psychological egoism is often taken to provide the foundation of the egoist's position, this is the natural form of egoism to consider the merits of first.

---

3   See Bentham (1789), Chapter 1, paragraph 1. Bentham says that: "It is for them [pain and pleasure] alone to point out what we ought to do, as well as to determine what we shall do". Bentham is not an ethical or a rational egoist, however, since he holds that the pleasure and pain of others, as well as our own, is also a factor in determining what we ought to do. In holding this, he combines his psychological hedonism with Utilitarianism rather than ethical egoism.

4   See Mercer (2001) for a defence of such a position, and LaFollette (1988) for a defence of a similarly weakened version of psychological egoism. LaFollette's and Mercer's positions are considered at the end of section 3, below.

3. Psychological Egoism

An initial attraction of strong PE comes simply from the observation of people's motivations in performing their actions, and reflection about one's own motivations for acting. Such reflection yields the fact that people are often motivated by perceived self-interest or personal gain, and human beings are frequently concerned by how they are perceived in the eyes of others. So one simple attraction behind strong PE is the thought that, given that agents are known to be *very frequently* motivated by perceived self-interest, then it is more reasonable to explain away the few cases of *apparent* altruistic motivation under a unified theory of motivation (that grounds all intentional action in self-interest), than it is to propose a theory of motivation that holds that, on a few rare occasions, we are fundamentally motivated by a completely different sort of consideration (i.e. non-self-interested concerns) than we are in the vast majority of other situations.

However, this line of reasoning only provides us with any motivation to accept strong PE if it really is the case that strongly altruistic motivations are, or appear to be, few and far between. And this just doesn't seem to be the case. Many people frequently appear to make sacrifices for their friends, family, or even for faraway strangers (for example, through making charitable donations). Even if many of these actions are not *purely* altruistic, they still seem to be largely or significantly motivated by altruistic concerns. Human motives are often complex, and it seems quite reasonable to believe that we can have both altruistic and self-interested motives for performing many acts, where sometimes the former types of motive are primary, and at other times the latter ones are.

Moreover, even if most people, most of the time, are motivated by perceived self-interest, this does nothing to show that, as a matter of fact, all intentional actions primarily aim at securing some personal advantage. It may be that we are often motivated by perceived self-interest *so frequently* because of capitalist market forces, for instance. Perhaps different social, economic and political organisations could cause us to be motivated by perceived-self-interest much less frequently.[5]

The psychological egoist insists on construing *every* actual, or even possible, instance of seemingly altruistic action as merely appearing to be altruistic or primarily other-regarding, so he incurs a heavy burden of proof. This is because he insists on a narrower range of plausible explanations of human motivation than the non-egoist does. The psychological egoist thus needs a compelling argument to move us away from the commonsense assumption that some people,

---

[5] See, for instance, Rousseau (1754), and Macpherson (1968), for such lines of argument.

some of the time, perform actions that are not *primarily* aimed at securing their own advantage.

3.1 Two Arguments for Strong Psychological Egoism

One egoist argument to show that all intentional actions, as a matter of *logical necessity*, are motivated by self-interest, runs as follows:

1. We always perform the act that we most desire (all-things-considered) to perform.

2. So, we always act to satisfy our own desires.

3. Hence, we always act self-interestedly.

However, this argument is not valid. It conflates the fact that our desires our always our own, with the thesis that our desires are always self-regarding. Even if we are always motivated by our own desires, those desires are not necessarily self-directed. Assuming that our desires are always self-directed simply assumes the truth of psychological egoism. Thus, this argument either assumes that strong PE is true, in which case it fails to provide any support for strong PE, or else it conflates 'desiring' with 'desiring-for-ourselves', and is thus invalid.

The psychological egoist's other main strategy for arguing against the commonsense assumption that some people, some of the time, are not fundamentally motivated to act from perceived self-interest, is to argue that whenever an agent performs the act that she most desires to perform, that person experiences pleasure from performing that act (or else avoids negative feelings, such as guilt). For example, if I offer to help my friend move house, or I donate money to charity, the psychological egoist will point out that I will expect to feel good about myself through performing such acts. The egoist may also point out that I will benefit from acting in such ways in the long-term. If I aid my friend now, I will increase the chances that my friend will help me out if I am in need in the future. If I give to charity, others may have more favourable attitudes towards me, and this may also benefit me in the long-term.

However, it does not follow from the mere fact that I will get pleasure from aiding others that this is the consideration that is the sole or strongest motive for any helpful act that I perform. It may be that getting pleasure from performing certain acts is sometimes a by-product of successfully achieving what one aims to accomplish. Successfully realising those ends that one attaches most value to, and most strongly identifies with, is always likely to bring a feeling of pleasure or satisfaction, simply because one is successfully bringing about the states of affairs that one believes to be most valuable. Intentional actions often produce unintended consequences as by-products, even when we know or expect these outcomes to occur. For instance, if one drinks a lot of beer, one expects to need to make more trips to the toilet than if one doesn't drink a lot of beer, but that does not mean that numerous visits to the toilet is any part of my motivation for drinking lots of beer on any occasion.

Moreover, we must be careful to distinguish between actions that are in accordance with our interests, and acting to promote our perceived self-interest. This is a distinction that the psychological egoist sometimes blurs[6]. It is clearly false that every agent always performs actions that, as a matter of fact, *best promote* their own self-interest. People often fail to do what is in their best interests, as a result of, for instance, a lack of relevant knowledge about what is good for them, poor judgment, or a lack of control over their actions.

The psychological egoist's thesis is that all intentional action is motivated by *perceived* self-gain, whish means that every agent always performs the act that he *believes* will best promote his self-interest, and acts for this reason. But suppose that I am deliberating about what to do with some money that I have been given for my birthday. I really want to buy a new bike. I believe that buying the bike will better promote my self-interest than donating the money to some charitable organisation would do, although I believe that doing both will promote my self-interest to some degree.

The psychological egoist must hold that, since self-interest is the only motive that directs my action, then given that I believe that buying the bike will better promote my self-interest than donating the money to charity will, I could not even seriously consider the idea of giving the money to charity. If I do seriously consider this option, then the egoist must hold that what I am doing is considering whether my belief that buying the bike will promote my self-interest much better than donating the money to charity will is in fact mistaken (perhaps because I expect that giving the money to charity would benefit me much more as a person in the long-run). However, deliberating in such a way seems rather unlikely to be in one's interests, or something that one would perceive to be in one's interests.

The problem that is lurking here can be seen if we consider an argument that was originally brought against Bentham's psychological hedonism. Bentham's psychological hedonism holds that all intentional actions are performed in the belief that they will best promote our pleasure or happiness. However, this leads us straight into what has been called the 'paradox of hedonism'. If one pursues nothing but pleasure or happiness, then one will find that 'it vanishes utterly from sight and cannot be captured' (Feinberg 2007, 187). We do not attain happiness or pleasure, when we do, from actively seeking or pursuing them, but from immersing or involving ourselves in projects and activities that we take

---

6 For more on this, see McConnell (1978); LaFollette (1988).

to be valuable (and which are, in fact, valuable or rewarding for us). Happiness and pleasure often result from immersing oneself in desirable and worthwhile activities, rather from actively pursuing them.

Similarly, if we chose what acts to perform purely on the basis of what we believed would best promote our self-interest, then it is unclear that we would see the value in any particular activity. It is also unclear just why we would believe that certain acts would benefit us. For instance, why would I believe that giving money to provide life-saving treatment for starving children would benefit me more (in the long-term) than buying a bike, if I didn't believe that this is an act that it is desirable *in-itself* to perform? If donating the money to charity makes me feel better about myself, then I must think that this is because it is something worthwhile or important to do: that it is an action supported by non-self-interested reasons. If I do not think that it is an important thing to do, I will not get satisfaction from doing it. One does not get satisfaction simply because one satisfies one's desires. What those desires are desires for, and how one evaluates and associates with the objects of those desires, also matters to the satisfaction one gets in satisfying a desire.

The psychological egoist can reply to these criticisms, however, by rejecting *ethical* and *rational* egoism. By doing so, he can hold that there are non-self-interested reasons to perform actions, so we can believe that these actions are important or worthwhile. However, if he does this, then he must hold that although there are non-self-interested reasons to act, one can never actually act *for* these reasons, but only in accordance with them. So, although this sort of egoist can say that there are acts that are worthwhile to perform, regardless of whether one stands to benefit from them personally, this still leaves him unable to explain why he feels good about himself through making his charitable donations. Since he believes that he can't act for the right reasons, in such cases, his egoistic motivations should be a form of terrible frustration for him. Only if he really believes that he can be motivated to give to charity out of a direct concern for those that he is giving to, will he be able to derive any pleasure from performing such an act.

Strong PE thus faces a number of problems, many of which have not been considered here[7]. Its central problem is that it strongly diverges from our commonsense account of human motivation, without actually having strong arguments to support it. The argument for psychological egoism as a *necessary* truth is fallacious. Strong PE is usually presented as an empirical doctrine, but the psychological egoist does not provide any empirical evidence to support it. Rather, he relies on people's worries about their own motives. But this, too, seems

---

7   For further arguments against strong PE see, for instance, Feinberg (2007), for an interesting argument that any attempted explication of psychological egoism leads to an infinite (and vicious) regress.

to undermine his position. Only those with a strong desire to act unselfishly will be concerned with the idea that they may be much more selfish than they believe themselves to be. One worry that people have is whether they are ever motivated *purely* by altruistic concerns. But even if we are not, this does not force us to accept strong PE, and if other-regarding concerns are not something that we ever take to provide us with *more* reason to act than self-interested concerns do, it is unclear why we would be worried by the *possibility* that we never act purely from altruism.

3.2 Weak Psychological Egoism

Some authors have sought to account for the appeal that Strong PE has had for some philosophers, and for many non-philosophers, whilst rejecting its uncompromising claim that every act-token that an agent performs is motivated by perceived self-interest. They have done so by arguing that a more modest version of PE is true. For instance, Hugh LaFollette (1988) argues for a position that I will call 'pattern-based egoism'. According to this:

> **Pattern-based egoism**: A person will *continually engage* in an activity only if it has the effect of satisfying what she perceives to be in her self-interest (LaFollette 1988, 503 [my emphasis]).

LaFollette calls this the 'truth in egoism'. His position entails that, although agents can act on desires whose object is to bring about states of affairs that are good-for-others *on specific occasions,* any agent will refrain from acting on such desires if bringing about states of affairs that are good for others *systematically fails* to satisfy his or her own self-interest. For instance, if I continually help out a friend, but never get any favours returned, I will eventually stop helping that friend out, even though I may have been motivated to help that friend on the occasions that I did out of my concern for his well-being. On this view, if I do not receive some benefit from a *pattern* of altruistic behaviour, my altruistic behaviour will fail to get the reinforcement it needs to endure. Mark Mercer also argues for a form of weak psychological egoism, according to which:

> **Weak PE**: Behind any action whatever that an agent performs intentionally, ultimately there lies the agent's expectation of realizing one or more of her self-regarding ends, an expectation without which the agent would not have performed the action (Mercer, 2001, 221).

Both Mercer and LaFollette's weakened versions of egoism explain why agents are often satisfied when they do not maximise their own self-interest on a particular occasion, whilst nonetheless retaining egoist positions. Moreover, both positions hold that we are not always motivated primarily by self-interest, and thus attempt to accommodate, rather than revise, our commonsense understanding of human motivation. Mercer (2001) has argued that LaFollette's version of weak PE is unstable, however. As Mercer says, it is hard to see how "failing to realise a self-regarding end on some occasion could weaken an agent's general desire to perform actions of some type, when that agent had no expectation of realising a self-regarding end on that occasion" (2001, 227). Mercer's own position does not suffer from such problems. Like LaFollette, he allows that our desires for acting can be purely other-regarding in certain circumstances, since we need not *intend* to realise a self-regarding end through our actions. However, he holds that we always *expect* to realise a self-regarding end when we perform any intentional action, and that, without this expectation, we would not act (2001, 222-23).

However, Mercer's account may suffer from the following worry. On his account, an agent cannot be motivated to act unless he expects to satisfy one of his self-regarding ends. So, it may be that the self-regarding end that an agent expects to promote on some given occasion is a very weak one. Say, for instance, that somebody regularly gives to charity, and that his motivation is beneficent on many of the particular occasions that he donates. The question we then need to ask is why, on a particular occasion, does he expect that donating money to Oxfam, say, will promote one of his self-regarding ends? It may be that he *believes* that living a good life involves, amongst other things, striking a reasonable balance between self-interested and altruistic actions and activities. If he then believes that making this donation *now* is compatible with leading a good life in which he strikes a good balance between various kinds of activities, then he may well believe that donating to Oxfam is compatible with promoting a self-regarding end of his: leading a good, worthwhile life. However, this does not mean that he expects to promote a self-regarding end *on this occasion*. Rather, he may *believe* that this donation is part of a choice-worthy pattern of actions, and he expects to realise his self-regarding ends *through* engaging in such a *pattern* of actions.

Moreover, Mercer's account seems odd when we consider expectations with reference to relatively simple other-regarding motivations for actions. For example, say that it is dark, and I see my wife approaching our house. I turn on the outside light so that she can see a bit better. What self-regarding end can I plausibly expect to realise by doing this? My action of turning on the light is intentional, even though it is also largely habitual: I act with the expectation that in performing this act, my wife will be able to see more easily. But it seems odd to say that I should have any expectations regarding my own life when I perform such actions, or that I wouldn't perform this intentional action unless I did have such expectations. That seems to attribute too high a degree of expectation and planning to simple actions: it fetishes self-regarding ends. Of course, it is always possible to attribute self-regarding expectations to such actions. The question is whether it is always more plausible to do so than not to do so.

4. Rational and Ethical Egoism

Rational egoism (RE) is the view that, for any action f, and any agent A, f-ing is in accordance with reason (i.e. it is *'rationally'* permitted) if and only if it best promotes A's own self-interest. Ethical egoism (EE) is the view that an agent is *morally* permitted to perform an act if and only if it best promotes his own self-interest.

Unless one held that a version of RE is correct, there would be little motivation to accept any version of EE. Ethical egoism, that is, is unmotivated unless one accepts the truth of rational egoism. This is because it would be very odd to advance a position under which one would be morally required to promote one's self-interest, but could act in accordance with reason in sacrificing one's self-interest in order to promote the interests of others. If one held that strong EE was true, but strong RE is false, for example, then one would hold that it is morally *im*permissible for some agents to make charitable donations, but rationally permissible (i.e. in accordance with reason) for them to do so. This would involve holding that such agents act in accordance with nonmoral reasons when they make charitable donations, but act against moral reasons in doing so. Such a position would commit one to a very implausible conception of what morality is.

One can, however, accept rational egoism without accepting ethical egoism. It is plausible to hold that one is rationally required to promote one's own self-interest, but not morally required to do so. It doesn't *obviously* flout our understanding of morality to hold that one is morally required to donate money to charity, but rationally permitted to refrain from doing so. Moral requirements, according to such a position, simply are not requirements of reason. Thus, if one accepts rational egoism, but rejects ethical egoism, then one must reject moral rationalism:

> **Moral Rationalism**: A is morally required to f only if A has most reason, overall, to f.

Many philosophers have sought to defend moral rationalism[8]. To deny it involves denying that moral requirements are requirements of reason. This is not to say that some do not reject moral rationalism. Moral error theorists, for example, think that moral rationalism is true as a conceptual claim, but false as a substantive one. That is, they hold that moral requirements have the form of non-self-interested requirements of reason, but they hold that there are no such requirements. Thus they hold that nobody is ever under a moral obligation, and

---

8   Although some defend weaker versions of it than the one presented here. For instance, some defend the view that if an agent is morally required to perform an action, then he has a defeasible rather than a decisive reason to do it (see, e.g. Shafer-Landau, 2003).

that moral claims, strictly speaking, are all false (or untrue)[9].

Some moral realists[10] also reject moral rationalism. They hold that moral facts are not facts about reasons for action, but earn their right to a realist construal by pulling their weight in the best explanation of features of our experience[11]. They hold that this is the criterion under which any discourse earns its right to a realist construal, and so morality earns its realism in the same way as claims about the existence of chairs or electrons do: by having causal or explanatory potency.

However, for many moral philosophers, the consequences of rejecting moral rationalism have seemed too problematic. Either one accepts that there are no moral requirements, or one holds that a moral requirement only provides an agent with any reason to act if he has the appropriate contingent desires or ends. Under the former account, we are misguided in our very practice of making moral judgments. Under the latter account, agents may act morally wrongly in failing to perform certain acts, but these are nonetheless not acts that they can be *criticised* for failing to perform, as such agents act perfectly in accordance with reason when they act immorally. If this is the case, one can intentionally act morally badly, violating all sorts of moral requirements, without being the appropriate target for moral criticism or blame. Under this account, then, it may be true that an agent morally ought not to have acted in a certain way, but the judgment that he morally ought not to have acted as he did amounts to no criticism of the agent's actions, but rather simply an observation that he has not acted in accordance with what morality requires.[12] Thus, if one accepts rational egoism, the appeal of moral rationalism provides good reason to accept ethical egoism as well.

4.1 Arguments for Rational and Ethical Egoism

Rational egoism is a theory of *objective* rationality. Objective rationality is concerned with what acts agents ought or ought not to perform in the most fundamental sense. An act is objectively rationally permissible if and only if it there is more *overall* reason to perform that act than to perform any other available act-alternative, regardless of what an agent believes to be the case. By contrast, an act is *subjectively* rationally permissible if and only if it is supported by the reasons that an agent (justifiably) believes there to be for performing the act in question.

---

9   See, for instance, Mackie (1977); Joyce (2001).
10   Moral realists hold that there are objective or mind-independent moral facts.
11   See, for instance, Brink (1988); Boyd (1986); Railton (1988).
12   See Morgan (2006), for an in-depth criticism of this variety of naturalism.

4.1.1 Presumptive arguments for Rational Egoism

Rational egoism often appears to be motivated by intuitive appeals to what is 'rational' and 'irrational'. If I frustrate or fail to promote my own ends, this seems to be a clear case of irrational action, whereas if I frustrate or fail to promote the ends of others, this is clearly a case of acting morally badly, but, it has often been suggested, this is not clearly a case of acting 'irrationally'. The rational egoist may also hold that he can account for the existence of rational *immoral* actions, and that this is an advantage of his position, since holding that immoral actions are necessarily irrational is just hopelessly wishful thinking. There are some agents, the egoist will suggest, whose ends are well served through acting in a morally bad way. And the rational egoist may argue that it is simply commonsense to hold that it would be rational for many agents to act immorally if they knew they could get away with doing so. For example, if we could accrue massive personal wealth and prosperity by stealing, and we knew for certain that we could get away with it, then there would be very good reasons to do so. Moreover, she may argue that it is clearly irrational to fail to perform actions that would seriously benefit ourselves, but it is not irrational to refrain from performing actions that would seriously benefit others. There doesn't seem anything 'irrational' about refraining from donating money to charity, for instance. There are three things to note about this general line of argument.

Firstly, if a rational egoist offers such an argument, then he must either reject ethical egoism, or else hold that certain agents are morally *required* to perform those acts that we would intuitively judge to be seriously morally wrong (such as killing for financial gain).

Secondly, such an argument is question begging with the anti-egoist, who occupies the *default* position concerning objective rationality. Both egoists and anti-egoists typically hold that reasons are considerations that count in favour of or against actions. For instance, the fact that it will prevent dehydration is a consideration that counts in favour of my drinking some water on a hot day. However, the anti-egoist will hold that the fact that it will prevent dehydration is a consideration that counts in favour of giving some of my water to others who require it, whereas the egoist will hold that this is not the case. The egoist will hold that the only reasons that exist are self-interested reasons – other-regarding considerations only *derivatively* provide us with reasons for action. I only have a reason to give a badly dehydrated person a swig of my water if it happens to promote my self-interest to do so, on the egoist's account. The egoist needs a strong argument to convince us that this is the case: that self-interested reasons are the only type of reasons that exist. This is why the anti-egoist occupies the default position regarding objective rationality.

Lastly, such lines of argument gain their appeal through a conflation of different uses of 'rational'. Few people would argue that every instance of immoral action is performed on the basis of *reasoning* or *deliberating* badly, and this is one sense in which we use the term 'rational'. However, the sense of rationality relevant to the egoist's position is the sense in which an action is *in accordance with* the reasons that there are for and against performing it. There may be very strong reasons against performing certain actions, even if one has very good reasons to believe they are the best ones to perform on the basis of good processes of reasoning from the motives and values one contingently holds. Objective rationality is concerned with actions, however, not agent's mental states. Thus, it is only implausible to say that all morally required action is rationally required *if* one is talking about the sort of rationality associated with deliberating well, and that is not the sort of rationality with which the rational egoist is concerned.

4.1.2 Rand's Argument for Ethical Egoism

Ayn Rand (1964) argues for the truth of EE by contrasting morality with self-interest. Rand sees morality and self-interest as being fundamentally opposed. She takes morality to be purely and excessively other-regarding[13] and, as such, she thinks that morality requires us to sacrifice everything that is valuable in our individual lives. To see why Rand may think this to be the case, let us look at altruistic and self-interested reasons. Morality, many are inclined to think, is a matter of what we have most reason to do from the moral point of view[14]. Now, the following assumptions seem pretty uncontroversial. It is good, from the moral point of view, to aid those in desperate need by giving away small proportions of our disposable income and spare time to charity. But it is better, from the moral point of view, to give away much more of our disposable income and spare time to aid others who are in desperate need of that aid. There is more reason to do the latter, from the moral point of view, than the former. Now, if we add the premise that what an agent ought, morally, to do, is what it is morally best to do, this seems to lead us to the conclusion that agents are morally required to give up most of their disposable income and spare time to aiding others. This leads to what Rand refers to as 'The Ethics of Altruism', or what I will call 'Ethical Impartialism':

> **Ethical Impartialism**: An agent, A, is morally permitted to f if and only if f-ing best promotes the impartial good (i.e. if and only if f-ing promotes the impartial good better than any other available act-alternative).

This is almost directly[15] opposed to ethical egoism, which holds that:

---

13   I borrow the phrase 'purely and excessively other-regarding' from Stephen Finlay (2006).
14   See, for example, Zimmerman (1993); Dreier (2004).
15   It doesn't completely contradict ethical egoism, as the impartial good includes

Ethical Egoism: An agent, A, is morally permitted to f if and only if f-ing best promotes A's self-interest (i.e. if and only if f-ing promotes A's self-interest better than any other available act-alternative).

However, both ethical impartialism and ethical egoism diverge considerably from 'commonsense morality'. Neither accommodates for the distinction between the obligatory and the supererogatory. Commonsense morality holds that there are certain actions that are 'beyond the call of duty' – those that it is morally good to perform, but which are not morally required – such as sacrificing one's life to save the lives of others in certain circumstances. Many moral theorists attempt to defend this commonsense position by trying to show how our close ties and relationships to our friends and families give us specific duties to ensure their well-being, and weaker duties to aid strangers, for instance[16]; or by attempting to account for the commonsense assumption that we are also permitted to engage in a whole range of non-moral activities that we value, so long as we strike a reasonable balance between acting altruistically and self-interestedly over the courses of our lives[17]. Thus, holding that ethical impartialism and ethical egoism are the only two available options to choose between ignores the prospects that commonsense morality can be vindicated, and this seems to force us very hastily into choosing between two alternatives that are both unattractive in many ways.

4.2 Problems for Rational Egoism and Ethical Egoism

4.2.1 Ethical Egoism

Let us continue to leave PE to one side, for the time being, and look at RE and EE as *independent* theses. A commonly discussed problem surrounding ethical egoism is whether the egoist can formulate an internally consistent moral theory. This problem arises for the following reason. Say that a certain action is morally required – e.g. my taking the last piece of cake on the table – because doing so will best promote my self-interest. However, taking the last piece of cake on the table will also best promote your self-interest, so that action – you taking the last piece of cake – is also morally required. So you have a moral obligation to take the last piece of cake, but you also lack a moral obligation to take the piece of cake (or perhaps have an obligation to refrain from performing this action), as morality requires me to perform this action. If ethical egoism is presented as an account of universal obligation – an action is morally required if and only if it best promotes an agent's self-interest – then it appears to yield contradictory obligations.[18] However, Rachels argues that this line of argument only works if

---

one's own good.
16   See, e.g. Parfit (2008), Ch. 2.
17   See Portmore (2008 and 2010).
18   See Baier(1958) for this objection to ethical egoism; and Taylor (1975) for a good

we suppose that the egoist is committed to the premise that every agent ought not to prevent any other agent from doing her duty (2007, 219). This is not a premise that an ethical egoist would want to accept, however, since whether or not one ought to prevent others from doing their duty depends on whether it is in one's self-interest to do so (219). Since the egoist has good reason to reject this premise, it does not seem that there is any logical inconsistency in her position. However, even if there is no logical inconsistency in the ethical egoist's position, many have found the fact that egoism yields such contradictory obligations problematic for other reasons. Baier, for example, also argues that since one of the essential functions of morality is conflict resolution, ethical egoism fails to provide a plausible account of how we ought to act (1958, 189-90).

Moreover, the ethical egoist's position is deeply counter-intuitive for other reasons. The ethical egoist holds that an agent is morally required to perform some act if and only if performing that act best promotes his own self-interest. This means that, if staying in bed late this Saturday better promotes my self-interest than keeping my promise to go and help my friend to move house (or performing any other available act-alternative) does, then I will be *morally required* to stay in bed, since all other available act-alternatives will be morally *im*permissible. Thus, in such a scenario, the ethical egoist's account implies that I will not be morally blameworthy if I make a promise to aid a friend, and then don't keep this promise because of sheer laziness. However, I will be morally blameworthy if I don't stay in bed, as staying in bed best promotes my self-interest.

Take another example. Say that toothpaste A is vastly superior to toothpaste B in terms of cleaning power, but identical in terms of every other consideration (e.g. price, availability, ethical production etc.). Given that using toothpaste B would fail to best promote my self-interest, it is morally impermissible for me to use it according to the ethical egoist. Ethical egoism holds that morality requires me to use toothpaste A. And this is just implausible as an account of moral requirement.

So if ethical egoism cannot be formulated in terms of necessary *and* sufficient conditions, one may wish to try formulating it as follows:

Weak Ethical Egoism: An agent, A, is morally required to f *only if* f-ing best promotes A's self-interest.

This position avoids the previous worries. However, it suffers from the following problem. Either unfair acts always go against our own self-interest or they do not. If they do not, then we will not be morally required to refrain from performing certain acts that are clearly unfair, such as taking advantage of vulnerable people for our own advantage. If this is the case, then the weak ethical egoist must hold

---

discussion of the objection.

that it is sometimes morally permissible to take advantage of vulnerable people for our own advantage. If, on the other hand, immoral actions never best promote our self-interest, then we need to give an explanation for *why* this is the case.

Say the explanation is something like this. In order to best promote our own self-interest, we need to adopt the happiness or welfare of others as a 'serious, major, continually relevant, life-shaping end' (Hill, 2002, 206). Perhaps we *need* to do this simply in virtue of the fact that we flourish through a mixture of social and independent activity. And perhaps consistent moral action is also in our long-term best interests, because acting morally is the best way to *ensure* that we are not on the receiving end of punishments or sanctions for moral defections.

This is the version of *explanatory* ethical egoism that Hobbes defends. Hobbes holds that *commonsense* morality is derivable from rational egoism, and thus ethical egoism is not a radical doctrine at all. However, although these sorts of response may save weak ethical egoism from refutation, they do nothing to support ethical egoism over *other* moral theories. The explanatory ethical egoist needs to hold that an agent is morally required to perform some action *when and because* it best promotes his own self-interest. Even if it is true that self-interest requires us to adopt the happiness or welfare of others as an ultimate end, or requires us to consistently follow certain moral rules or norms, there may be more *basic* reasons that explain why we are morally required to aid others: for instance, the fact that they are beings just like us, and no less important than us from an unbiased perspective. Explanatory ethical egoists must show why self-interest is the *only* grounds for acting morally, rather than one *common* ground. They must also show why there are not certain occasions in which it is in certain agents' self-interest to cheat or deceive when they can easily get away with doing so, and accrue massive personal gains in the process.

4.2.2 Rational Egoism

The main problem for RE is that, in stipulating that only an agent's own best interests provide him with reasons for action, RE holds that we never have the rational option of making any form of sacrifice of our own good. If we are only rationally permitted to perform those actions that maximise our own self-interest, it is implausible to hold that I am permitted, right now, to either spend some money on a new pair of shoes, or donate that money to Oxfam instead, for instance. These two actions will not be on a par in terms of how they best promote my self-interest. If buying a new pair of shoes best promotes my self-interest, then it will be rationally impermissible for me to donate the money that it would cost to buy these shoes to Oxfam instead. If rational egoism is true, I never have the rational option to benefit others over myself. There may be cases in which benefiting others *does* best promote my own self-interest, and in these cases, I will be rationally *required* to do so, but I will never have the option of sacrificing my own interests for the good of others.

Another way to see this problem for strong RE is to bring in the notion of preferences. Strong RE is an agent-centred theory of objective rationality, but it gives agent's preferences no weight or relevance in determining the rational status of actions. Consider the following example.

Suppose that you have a very strong non-self-interested preference for others to be benefited by some money that you have inherited, so you give it away to a good charity. Giving the money away best promotes your interests, but not your self-interest, since doing what is in your interests doesn't always involve doing what is in your self-interest. Had your preferences been for *you* to be benefited by the money, your interests would have lain in promoting your self-interest, but they weren't. The rational egoist must hold that a preference is only a rational one if it is self-directed. In the above example it would be irrational for you to give the money away, whether you wanted to or not. However, it seems much more plausible to think that there are occasions in which one's actual preferences can be a rationally decisive factor. The above sort of case (in which one can choose to perform an act that one is not morally required to perform) seems to be one plausible case. So by not allowing actual preferences to have *any* weight in themselves, strong RE seems to needlessly constrain our rational options.

Of course, rational and ethical impartialism fare no better than rational and ethical egoism here. Rational impartialism will hold that agents are only ever rationally permitted to perform acts that bring about the most impartial value. And this claim is just as extreme as ethical egoism's claim that we are never morally permitted to sacrifice our own self-interest in order to aid others. One solution to these problems is to simply hold that impartialism and egoism are both true, in the sense that one is always permitted to perform actions that best promote either the impartial good or one's self-interest. This is the position that Henry Sidgwick adopts. Sidgwick (1874) holds that there are two equally valid but competing conceptions of objective rationality.[19] According to the first conception, one acts rationally if and only if one best promotes one's own self-interest, and according to the second, one acts rationally if and only if one best promotes the general or impartial good. Thus, Sidgwick holds that one only acts rationally if one maximises either the general good or one's own good, and acting in either way is always supported by reason. According to Sidgwick, this is because self-interested and altruistic reasons both exist, but are *wholly* incomparable: one is always permitted to act either in accordance with the best self-interested reasons or the best impartial reasons.

Sidgwick's position also faces problems, however. According to Sidgwick's

---

19 See also Parfit (2008), Ch. 2, for a defence of such a position.

account, an act is only ever rationally permitted if it maximises either the impartial good, or one's own self-interest. However, there seem to be many actions that we are morally and rationally permitted to perform that do not maximise the impartial good. For instance, it seems implausible to hold that one is always forced to make the choice between maximising the impartial good *or* maximising one's self-interest, as opposed to striking a balance between the two. Say, for instance, that one has a choice between the following three options.

Option 1: To save many lives, at a very high risk to one's own.

Option 2: To save a few lives, at a low to moderate risk to one's own.

Option 3: To save no lives, with no risk to one's own.

Option 1 is rationally permissible under Sidgwick's account, since this best promotes the impartial good. Best promoting one's own self-interest supports choosing option 3, so this is also rationally optional here. However, since option 2 does not *best* promote either the impartial good or one's self-interest, this makes it rationally impermissible under Sidgwick's account of objective rationality. This is a deeply counter-intuitive result, since saving some lives at low risk to one's own appears to be both morally admirable and well supported by the balance of relevant reasons. However, the Sidgwickian approach at least shows one possible route for providing an alternative to impartialism and egoism that gets close to accommodating for commonsense morality and rational options. The rational egoist holds that an action is only in accordance with reason if it maximises an agent's own good. Sidgwick argues that an action is only in accordance with reason if it maximises either the overall good, or an agent's own good. A third alternative is to hold that an action is only in accordance with reason if it is part of a series of actions that strikes a choice-worthy balance between maximising an agent's own good, and maximising the overall good, over the course of the agent's life.[20]

In considering rational and ethical egoism, like any other philosophical theory, it is important to look at whether alternative theories capture many of the intuitions behind egoism, whilst lacking its core weaknesses. Sidgwick's dualism

---

20 This is, very roughly, the route that Douglas Portmore (2010) takes. However, Portmore's account does not directly appeal to the agent's own good and the overall good. Rather he argues that the rational permissibility of an action depends on whether it is part of any of the possible future series or sets of actions available to an agent, at that time, which the agent in question has most reason to desire to obtain. For Portmore, any agent has most reason to desire to live out the rest of his life by striking a reasonably choice-worthy balance between various kinds of pursuits and activities: relaxing, aiding others, having culturally enriching experiences etc., and the balance between these activities or pursuits will vary depending on other facts about agents, (such as their financial status, their interests and preferences, the type of work they do, their familial responsibilities).

about practical reason, in allowing that we are always permitted to maximise either our own good or the overall good, doesn't say that there are always reasons against performing altruistic actions, as the egoist does, but it doesn't hold that we are ever required to perform altruistic actions over self-interested ones. And this is what attracts many people to rational egoism: the idea that benefitting others cannot *require* us to sacrifice what is in our interests.

5. The Relationship between Psychological, Rational and Ethical Egoism

We assumed during the above discussion of EE and RE that strong PE is false (or, at least, we did not assume that strong PE is true). What the above considerations show is that both rational egoism and ethical egoism are not independently attractive positions. At the start of section 4, we saw that the motivation for accepting EE rests on the truth of RE. And now we can also see that, unless we accept strong PE, RE and EE are left unmotivated. Nonetheless, the committed egoist may insist that all of these arguments against strong RE miss the mark because strong PE is true. Since strong PE is true, she will hold that we are, as a matter of fact, all out to optimise our own self-interest. And since we are all out to do so, she will hold that the correct moral theory must be one that tells us to maximise our own self-interest. She will point out that a moral theory that tells us that we ought to do what we cannot do fails to meet the practicality requirements for a moral theory.

However, a number of authors have argued that strong PE is in fact *in*compatible with RE and EE. If these arguments are successful, then EE and RE will be left on very shaky ground. Terrence McConnell (1978) provides the following argument for the incompatibility of psychological and ethical egoism:

> 1) Strong PE holds that it is impossible for an agent to perform an act that he believes is contrary to his own best interests.
>
> 2) If strong PE is true, and ought implies can, then agents can't be morally required to perform acts that they believe are contrary to their own best interests.
>
> 3) However, agents sometimes have mistaken beliefs about what it is in their best interests to do.
>
> 4) Ethical egoism holds that agents are morally required to perform those acts that do, *in fact*, promote their best interests.
>
> 5) Thus, ethical egoism implies that agents will sometimes be morally required to perform acts that are contrary to what they believe to be in their best interests.
>
> 6) Since the combination of PE and ought implies can entails that agents can't

be morally required to perform acts that they believe to be contrary to their best interests, but ethical egoism does imply that agents will sometimes be morally required to perform acts that they believe are contrary to their best interests, ethical egoism is incompatible with the truth of both strong PE and ought implies can (McConnell 1978, 45-7).[21]

Thus the egoist faces a dilemma if McConnell's argument is successful. If psychological egoism is true, and ought implies can, then ethical and rational egoism are false. However, if the analysis of this chapter has been correct, and the plausibility of rational and ethical egoism do ultimately rely on the truth of strong psychological egoism, then even if strong psychological egoism is true, but ought does not imply can, ethical and rational egoism are left unmotivated. Thus the rational or ethical egoist needs a direct reply to McConnell's argument.

6. Conclusion

Psychological egoism is a doctrine that has very wide appeal to non-philosophers, and its tantalising simplicity is likely to endure even though its proponents never actually manage to provide, or to attempt to provide, the empirical backing that the theory requires. On the other hand, weaker versions of psychological egoism have considerable theoretical appeal, and are not obviously in tension with commonsense theories of human motivation. Without strong psychological egoism, however, rational and ethical egoism are left unmotivated. Moreover, even if strong psychological egoism is true, then there are forceful arguments for believing that ethical and rational egoism cannot follow from the truth of strong psychological egoism at best, and that ethical and rational egoism are incompatible with it at worst (if ought *does* imply can). Many philosophers have, however, sought to show that there is some truth in different versions of egoism, and so research into egoism may still prove to be fruitful.

BIBLIOGRAPHY

Baier, K. (1958). *The Moral Point of View*. Ithaca, Cornell University Press.

Bentham, J. (1970 [1789]). *Introduction to the Principals of Morals and Legislation*. Burns, J. H. and Hart, H. L. A. (eds.). London, The Athlone Press.

Boyd, R. (1988). How To Be A Moral Realist. In Sayre McCord, G. (ed.). *Essays*

---

21   For a reply to McConnell's argument, see Simpson (1978); and for a reply to Simpson, see Russell (1982).

in Moral Realism,

Brink, D. (1988). *Moral Realism and the Foundations of Ethics.* Cambridge, Cambridge University press.

_____ (2007). Mill's Moral and Political Philosophy. *Stanford Encylopedia of Philosophy.* http://plato.stanford.edu/entries/mill-moral-political.

Dreier, J. (2004). Why ethical satisficing makes sense and rational satisficing doesn't. In Byron, M. (ed.). *Satisficing and Maximizing.* Cambridge, Cambridge University Press, 131-154.

Feinberg, J. (2004). Psychological Egoism. In Shafer-Landau, R. (ed.) (2007). *Ethical Theory, An Anthology.* Oxford, Blackwell.

Finlay, S. (2007). Too Much Morality. In Bloomfield, P. (ed.). *Morality and Self-Interest.* Oxford, Oxford University Press.

Gert, B. (1967). Hobbes and Psychological Egoism. *Journal of the History of Ideas,* 28 (4), 503-20.

Hill, Jr., T. E. (2002). *Human Welfare and Moral Worth.* Oxford, Oxford University Press.

Hobbes, T. (1968 [1651]). *Leviathan.* Macpherson, C. B. (ed.). London, Penguin.

Joyce, R. (2001). *The Myth of Morality.* Cambridge, Cambridge University Press.

LaFollette, H. (1988). The Truth in Psychological Egoism. In Feinberg, J. (ed.) (2004). *Reason and Responsibility (7th Edition).* Belmont, CA, Wadsworth.

Mackie, J. (1977). *Ethics, Inventing Right and Wrong.* London, Penguin.

Macpherson, C. B. (1962). *The Political Theory of Possessive Individualism, Hobbes to Locke.* Oxford, Oxford University Press.

Mercer, M. (2001). In Defence of Weak Psychological Egoism. *Erkenntnis,* 55 (2), 217-37.

McConnell, T. (1978). The Argument from Psychological Egoism to Ethical Egoism. *Australasian Journal of Philosophy,* 56 (1), 41-7.

Mill. J. S. (1979 [1861]). *Utilitarianism.* Sher, G. (ed.). Indianapolis, Hackett.

Morgan, S. (2006). Naturalism and Normativity. *Philosophy and Phenomenological Research,* 72 (2), 319-45.

Parfit, D. (2008). *Climbing The Mountain.* http://individual.utoronto.ca/stafforini/

parfit/parfit_-_climbing_the_mountain.pdf .

Portmore, D. (2008). Are Moral Reasons Morally Overriding? *Ethical Theory and Moral Practice,* 11 (4), 369-88.

_____ (2010). Imperfect Reasons and Rational Options. Forthcoming in *Nous.*

Rachels, J. (1986). Ethical Egoism. In Shafer-Landau, R. (ed.) (2007). *Ethical Theory, An Anthology.* Oxford, Blackwell.

Rand, A. (1964). *The Virtue of Selfishness.* New York, Signet.

Rousseau, J-J. (1987 [1754]). *Discourse on the Origin of Inequality.* Cress, D. A. (trans.). London, Hackett.

Russell, B. (1982). On the Relation between Psychological and Ethical Egoism. *Australasian Journal of Philosophy,* 42 (1), 91-9.

Railton, P. (1986). Moral Realism. *Philosophical Review,* 95, 163-207.

Sidgwick, H. (1874). *The Methods of Ethics (7th Edition).* London, Macmillan. http://www.henrysidgwick.com/themethodsofethi00sidguoft.pdf.

Simpson, P. (1979). A vanishing "can". *Australasian Journal of Philosophy,* 57, 76-78.

Shafer-Landau, R. (2003). *Moral Realism, A Defence.* Oxford, Oxford University Press.

Taylor, P. (1975). *Principles of Ethics, An Introduction.* Encino, CA, Dickenson.

Zimmerman, M. (1993). Supererogation and doing the best one can. *American Philosophical Quarterly,* 30, 373-80.

7

Environmental Ethics

Steven Bond

1. Introduction: The Scope of Environmental Ethics

Of all the fields of applied ethics, environmental ethics is surely the broadest in scope. Consider the deep historical, political, scientific and ethical relevance of a major environmental issue such as global warming and this is readily evident. It is difficult to draw a clear line around environmental ethics. Is it concerned with textbooks only or does tying oneself to a condemned tree constitute environmental ethics also? There is no easy answer to this question, and the varied emphases the relevant textbooks place on theory or activism are proof positive of the difficulty. Environmental Ethics sprawls in all directions. This brief chapter considers historical progress and its chemical consequences spanning from the earliest agricultural civilisations to the latest technological developments. It is concerned with traditional ethical theory, with environmental ethics more specifically, and makes occasional forays into the realms of theology, economics and politics, as well as various other unavoidable philosophical sub-disciplines. To a lesser degree it is concerned with practice, both with public policy and ecological activism. To detail such a sprawling field in one short chapter can't but treat of a myriad of themes in all too succinct a fashion. We look firstly to the distant historical roots of this applied field (2), define some of the traditional philosophical terminology it borrows (3), outline the central tenets of some of its key proponents (4), and examine the core case study of Global Warming as a means of illustrating the practical implications of their theories (5). Giving but a brief sketch of this vast field, we have endeavoured also to include a comprehensive bibliography that will enable the interested student to more easily navigate the seemingly boundless terrain that is touched upon here.

2. The Historical Roots of Environmental Ethics

What are the historical roots of environmental ethics?

The above question is too broad, is more than a single question, and the attempt to answer it engages one in (at least) four distinct endeavours:

- seeking the cultural roots of anthropocentrism (human-centeredness)
- delineating the scientific roots of the current environmental crisis
- seeking the cultural roots of the moral consideration of nature
- outlining the twentieth century rise of environmental ethics

This section confines itself to no single alternative for answering this question, but rather details the central responses to the question as recast under the various subheadings above.

2.1. Cultural Roots of Anthropocentrism

Firstly, taking an environmental ethic to be first and foremost a cure for an anthropocentric (human-centred) cultural mindset, we may seek the historical source of that mindset in Biblical, early agricultural or some alternative tradition. The attempt to present the archaeology of man's conception of man as somehow of more moral worth than other life forms might take one in many directions. As far as the philosophical underpinnings of this mindset go, one could look to Descartes' reduction of animals to mere beast-machines, soulless automatons, "furry robots" if you will. That the father of modern philosophy was a keen practitioner of vivisection is no small fact. Nor can one overlook Aristotle's hierarchical appraisal of nature in which man featured somewhere between animals and angels. It is not so much what these thinkers said, for many thinkers said such things, but the reach of their influence that condemns them. But if a text's influence is to be taken as paramount here, then we need not look beyond the Bible: "have dominion over the fish of the sea, and over the fowl of the air, and over every living thing that moveth upon the earth." (Genesis, 1:28)

Medievalist Lynn White published an article in *Science* (1967) which awakened many to his contention that "Christian arrogance towards nature" (Pojman and Pojman, 2008, 21) lies at the root of our detrimental attitude towards the environment. Created in God's image, the Christian feels him/herself entitled to treat all other living things without so much as a modicum of respect. The stated purpose of nature is to serve man, who stands apart from and above it. White is quick to add that Christians could not be blamed wholesale for humanity's sense of entitlement. St. Francis of Assisi already provided us the ideal example of how to live in accordance with nature in the early thirteenth century.

2.2. Scientific Roots of the Environmental Crisis

Secondly, we may wish to answer that the roots of environmental ethics are as one with the roots of the current environmental crises, citing the Industrial Revolution of the 18th century as a key turning point. It is notable, for instance, that 50% of the CFCs released into the air since the beginning of the Industrial Revolution are still there, and that the resulting Global Warming is the foremost environmental crisis of our age.

Lewis Moncrief went further in placing the aforementioned Christian influence in perspective, not exonerating the religion of its negative role, but viewing that limited role in the context of other political, technological and cultural developments. On this view, we can say that the Bible is itself the product of its historical setting; and the fundamental shift in attitude that permits destroying one's environment has more to do with technological advances in land cultivation. The industrial revolution plays its role, but just as important are pre-Biblical developments such as the plough. It is difficult to determine whether ideological or materialist factors were paramount in creating our current arrogance towards nature, or even whether primacy in this instance is stable or alternating throughout history.

2.3. Cultural Roots of the Moral Consideration of Nature

Thirdly, we may turn to the roots of the cultural mindset that first rejected anthropocentrism for the moral consideration of nature, citing perhaps the Romantic poets of the nineteenth century, or the increased understanding of nature derived from contemporaneous developments in the sciences of geology and evolution. British utilitarian philosophers Jeremy Bentham and John Stuart Mill (See 3.1) both extended ethical value beyond humanity. "The question," Bentham remarks, "is not, Can they reason? nor, Can they talk? but, Can they suffer?" (2005, 311). Animals do, and so are deserving of moral consideration. Mill adds that "The reasons for legal intervention in favour of children apply not less strongly to the case of those unfortunate slaves and victims of the most brutal part of mankind - the lower animals." (1998, 344) Mill was under direct influence of not only Bentham but also British Romantic poetry, William Wordsworth being a favourite lover of nature. On the other side of the Atlantic, American Romantic Ralph Waldo Emerson chimes, "You have just dined, and however scrupulously the slaughterhouse is concealed in the graceful distance of miles, there is complicity" (2004, 3).

Beyond poetry, one might look to science. Just as the twentieth century saw environmental ethics grounded in a unitary conception of nature derived from the recent science of ecology, so the unity perceived by the Romantics also had its scientific counterpart. For as the 17th century witnessed William Harvey's discovery of the circulation of the blood in man, so the latter 18th century saw James Hutton, father of geology, proclaim that the same circularity was apparent in the water cycle of earth. There is unlikely a more critical leap forward in the scientific understanding of the harmonious balance of earth, in the appraisal of earth as a self-contained, self-regulating entity. Not until the public was exposed to photographs of earthrise from the moon (1969) was our planet's unitary nature again given such clear expression. The proposed unity is central to environmental philosophies, particularly those of the last half century.

2.4. The Twentieth Century Rise of Environmental Ethics

Lastly, in determining the historical roots of environmental ethics, we may suppose these roots to lay in the emergence of environmental ethics as an ethical sub-discipline in the last century or so. This may refer to the period of the early twentieth century, with those first few pioneers who might be retrospectively labelled as precursors of the environmental movement, though who were unaware of their status as such (Aldo Leopold, Albert Schweitzer, John Muir, Gifford Pinchot).[1] Or we may wish to confine ourselves to the latter half of the twentieth century, whence individual nature lovers united in global consensus to fashion Environmental Ethics as a definite, self-conscious philosophical discipline and social movement (J. Baird Callicott, Dale Jamieson, Arne Naess, Homes Rolston III, Paul Taylor).[2]

---

1   For Schweitzer (4.2) and Leopold (4.3), see section 4 below. Scottish-American Muir was founding president of the Sierra Club, a 1,000,000 strong worldwide conservationist organisation that through Muir became strongly linked with the National Park Service in the United States. Muir was central in forming the American concept of the National Park, campaigning for Yosemite Park specifically. He was effectively introducing ecology into nature writing, before the term or concept was in wide use. While he did not have a systematic philosophy like Schweitzer would after him, Muir did extend moral consideration to all living things – an advance for which Schweitzer is often given credit. Pinchot was the first chief of the U.S. Forest Service, and with Muir was already fighting for American conservation in the 1800's. Pinchot's strongly utilitarian (See 3.1) conservationist approach brought him into conflict with former friend Muir, who argued for the complete protection of wild areas like Yosemite National Park, "the greatest happiness of the greatest number" notwithstanding.

2   For Arne Naess, see section 4.4. J. Baird Callicott was central to the development of Environmental Ethics as an academic discipline. His philosophy defends and extends the Land Ethics of Aldo Leopold (See 4.3). Dale Jamieson is a consequentialist, who uses a utilitarian ethics to argue against the poor treatment of nonhuman animals as well as contributing to recent work on climate change and other environmental issues. Holmes Rolston III was another pioneer of academic environmental ethics, founding

3. Some Fundamental Ethical Distinctions

Environmental Ethics is firmly grounded in the terminology of traditional ethical theory and in the dichotomies of traditional philosophy in the broadest sense. Before delving into environmental theory itself, we will thus need to clarify the fundamental philosophical distinctions that a comprehensive understanding of environmental ethics presupposes. 'Deontology contra utilitarianism' and 'individualism contra holism' have here been selected as providing an indispensable backdrop to the latter.

3.1. Deontology versus Utilitarianism

The deontology of Immanuel Kant, supposing as it does that ethical decision making consists in following rules for their own sake, stands in direct opposition to the utilitarianism of Jeremy Bentham and John Stuart Mill, which instead grounds the ethical good firmly in best consequences. Deontology is rule based, on this account one will not commit murder because murder is inherently or intrinsically wrong. The utilitarian, on the contrary, is not concerned with impure motives for action, and is thus free to take the life of another if it will have good consequences for society as a whole. This distinction between Kant's intrinsic good (good in itself) and the extrinsic, consequential good of utilitarianism is fundamental to the ethics of both animal rights and the environment.

It is of note, however, that Kant's application of deontological ethics extends only to the realm of the rational human subject. While he remains the classic deontological ethicist, his morality dissipates into utilitarianism once he is faced with animal or environmental issues. Kant says of man that "he must practice kindness towards animals, for he who is cruel to animals becomes hard also in his dealings with men." (Kant, 1930, 240) In the realm of the rational human subject then, "thou shall not kill" under any circumstances because it is inherently wrong. But in so far as the animal kingdom goes, it is only the possible knock-on effect upon mankind that incites Kant's sympathy. If that were not complication enough, it is equally true that Bentham and Mill, the classic utilitarian philosophers, both argue conversely (though not exclusively) for the *intrinsic* worth of animals. Broaching environmental concerns, in sum, has long led philosophers into head on collisions with their own core doctrines. Little has changed, with Peter Singer, a modern utilitarian, perhaps more responsible than any other for couching animal ethics in the Kantian language of 'rights'. Former president of Animal Rights International, Singer published *Animal Liberation* in

---

the first journal in the field, Environmental Ethics. Paul Taylor's Respect for Nature (1986) offers a biocentric (life-centred) ethics which can be said to continue the work of Albert Schweitzer (See 4.2).

1975, which more than any other text took the animal rights movement beyond the marginalised doctrine of a few free thinking hippies.

The animal rights movement, whose most prominent spokespeople are Singer and Tom Regan, extends ethical consideration to some non-human animals. For Singer specifically, in direct inheritance of Jeremy Bentham's utilitarianism, only those animals that are sentient are deserving of moral consideration. In equating animal liberation with the black liberation movement (he coins 'speciesism' as a term which should be loathed as much as 'racism'), Singer is borrowing an analogy invoked by Bentham as early as the 18th century. Despite the turn to the 'rights' of animals, Singer's argument is consequentialist, couched in terms of the benefits of vegetarianism for mankind. That is, he remains utilitarian, with consequences as opposed to motive being his major concern. Tom Regan argues instead from within a Kantian, deontological framework towards the immorality of treating animals with intrinsic worth for utilitarian, means-to-end purposes. That the utilitarian and deontologist nevertheless comply in this instance on the extension of moral concern to sentient creatures only, is a fitting illustration of the malleability of theoretical frameworks. Opposing theories may give rise to similar conclusions in practical application, or conversely, similar theories to opposing conclusions. This malleability can be sought out in all fields of applied ethics. It is relatively easy to agree with Regan's proposed ban on sports and entertainments that are needlessly exploitative of animals, more difficult to condone the proposed ban on *all* animal testing for medical science. Mary Anne Warren, for one, rejects this "strong animal rights position" (Pojman and Pojman, 2008, 91) for a "weak" alternative that is not so stringent in its policies.

3.2. Individualism versus Holism

Another fundamental distinction to be considered here is that between individualism and holism. An individualistic or atomist account of reality views it as composed of many separate individuals. Holism on the other hand stresses the interconnectedness, even the unity of all things. It is no coincidence that many environmental ethicists, the more radical of which are often holists, have been influenced by Eastern philosophy (See 4.4). Ethical extensionism beyond the individual ego is often equated with a realisation of the truth of holism, of the interconnectedness of self with others, of self with world. The different roots of holism – philosophical in Spinoza or Eastern thought, scientific in Hutton's geology or twentieth century ecology, religious in descriptions of the world as God's unified creation – are all influential in the field of environmental ethics.

The general trend within environmental ethics is the chronological expansion of self into the world, a gradually progressive equation of self with environment; although this expansion does typically involve a return to older cultures and modes of thought. Arne Naess (4.4) and James Lovelock (4.5) offer two recent examples. Naess illustrates by way of a young Sámi taking part in "a direct action in favour of the river that should not be used for hydroelectric dams." When asked by the police "Why do you stay here?," the young man replied "Well, this here, is part of myself." (Boeckel, 1995, 16) He had identified with the reindeer river crossing since childhood to such a degree that the boundaries between them had dissolved. An injury to the river was an injury to his self. This way of thinking is typical of more holistic approaches such as 'Deep Ecology' (4.4) or 'the Gaia Hypothesis' (4.5).

But holistic appraisals of earth and man's place within it do not necessarily give rise to complete reverence for all things natural. Aldo Leopold (4.3), for example, turns to holism as a means of supporting his passion for hunting and eating animals. For Leopold, what is paramount is the maintenance of the land, species diversity, and the cultivation of renewable resources. But beyond the need to uphold the environment considered as a whole, the killing of individual animals is considered fair game. As with deontology and utilitarianism, holism must be understood not in terms of a restrictive ideology but one of varying influences, with an accompanying amenability to alternate uses.

4. Some Key Theorists and their Theories

In considering some of the major theories and theorists that comprise the field of environmental ethics, we will follow the following schema. We take the German Enlightenment philosopher, Immanuel Kant, for whom rational mankind alone is deserving of moral consideration, as our fixed starting point. From this central point, the various environmental philosophies may be conceived of as the ever expanding boundary of that which is deserving of moral consideration. Firstly we look to Rachel Carson's *Silent Spring* as influential in defining the terrain of environmental ethics (4.1). We have seen Singer and Regan extend ethics to some non-human animals. Now, we look to Albert Schweitzer and his doctrine of 'reverence for life,' a standard by which the ethical boundary drawn up by Singer, though a vast expansion upon that of Kant, is conceived of as yet too narrow (4.2). For Schweitzer, an oyster, sentient or not, is no less deserving of moral treatment than a chimpanzee. We will then consider the Land Ethic of Aldo Leopold, which extends ethics beyond the domain of individual living organisms, into a consideration of the land itself (4.3). On this account, soil falls within the domain of the ethical, and as such is demanding of ethical treatment, though a mountain yet stands beyond this boundary. Ethical extensionism increases its vast reach yet further in the Deep Ecology of the Norwegian philosopher Arne Naess. Naess, a keen mountain climber, felt a kinship to the Sherpa culture of the Himalayas, which held that certain mountains were sacred and beyond the remit of sports enthusiasts. The inherent value of the mountain, as distinct from its utility to humans, became an integral element of Naess' Deep Ecology (4.4). Alongside Naess, and arguably extending the boundaries of ethics still further, we place the Gaia hypothesis of James Lovelock (4.5).[3]

The schema we are here following of the ever expanding boundary of moral consideration does not permit a strictly chronological presentation of the theories. St. Francis of Assisi extended intrinsic value into nature long before Immanuel Kant explicitly confined it to mankind. Notwithstanding this fact, we can yet pinpoint ethical extensionism in general as a chronological, one-way process, from an Enlightenment concern with man, through the Romantic turn to the inherent value of the wilderness, to the more recent discourse of the inherently valuable biosphere.

4.1. A Very Loud *Silent Spring*

One of the single most important treatises in the field of environmental ethics is Rachel Carson's *Silent Spring*. The significance of this 1962 text is partly grounded in the fact that it instigated the move away from environmentalism as a specialised, scientific discipline towards environmentalism as a core ethical concern in the popular consciousness. Environmental ethics, consequentially, was poised to make the further transition from a rather loose conglomerate of disparate texts and opinions into a social movement with a fixed philosophy, and a set agenda for action. Carson encapsulates many of the traits that typify the environmental ideal, and notwithstanding the fact that broad generalisations are often eliminative of individual cases; the following observations on Carson may be deemed relevant to the vast majority of environmental ethicists. Firstly, she lived what she preached, spending much of her non-writing adult life working for the U.S. Fish and Wildlife Service. That the philosophical biography should second motion the accompanying philosophy is an ideal which the history of ideas all too frequently falls short of. The 19th century German idealist, Arthur Schopenhauer, preached an Eastern ethic of eternal justice and unity, yet was faced with the prospect of a law suit for allegedly pushing an aging landlady down the stairs. Such incommensurability of theory and biography does not typically feature in the field of environmental ethics, whose most prominent spokespeople,

---

3   It is noteworthy that even these broad categories fall hopelessly short of an exhaustive analysis of the field. Further to this, any attempt to provide an overview of this vast and sprawling discipline by means of reference to a handful of key practitioners can't but be selective. As such, it ought to be made explicit that despite attempts to circumnavigate the unavoidable, what follows owes something to personal inclination. Ecofeminism, for example, a large field in its own right, is omitted entirely, for no other reason than that space permits only a personal, as opposed to an exhaustive selection. No bias is intended against those omitted.

Carson included, are moreover keen practitioners of the way of life they advocate. Carson further anticipates the general trend of the environmental ethicist in that she was, in addition to being a practitioner of her own theory, a keen activist, who until her death in 1964 petitioned against the unchecked use of chemical pesticides – which she called "elixirs of death" (Des Jardins, 2001, 3) – such as DDT. Like many to follow in the discipline that she helped to define, Carson emphasised the aesthetic appreciation of nature above the intricacies of logical argument, appealing to the sentiment of the reader to follow her own example. We are asked to "turn again to the earth and in the contemplation of her beauties to know of wonder and humility." (Jamieson, 2001, 91) Carson's transgression of the boundaries between ethics, aesthetics, politics, biology and ecology among various other philosophical and scientific sub disciplines helped to define the terrain within which environmental ethics continues to unfold. In the all too brief account of key theorists outlined below, we find that theoretical leanings, practical implications and a keen sense for activism are inextricably linked with a degree of consistency unmatched in other fields of applied ethics. Environmental ethics tends more towards an Eastern conception of philosophy as a way of life, as opposed to an abstract set of principles. Here, the painstaking refinement of definitions that characterises analytic philosophy, and the convoluted academic terminology which precludes the masses from engaging with philosophy of most any orientation, is subordinated to the contribution to public awareness and immediate, direct action.

4.2. Reverence for Life

"Reverence for life means to be in the grasp of the infinite, inexplicable, forward-urging will in which all Being is grounded" (Schweitzer, 1987, 283). This does not sound immediately like environmental ethics, and strictly speaking it isn't. Schweitzer's philosophy of "reverence for life," for *all* life and not just Singer's sentient life forms, is heavily influenced by the early existentialism of Nietzsche. As far as his ethics is concerned, it is typically invoked in the context of animal rights exclusively. It does, however, mark that move away from sentience towards the moral consideration of non-sentient plant life that might be deemed a necessary precondition of the environmental ethics proper which was to follow. "Ethics is responsibility without limit towards all that lives" (311) is Schweitzer's self-consciously revolutionary central philosophy. Even Jeremy Bentham, Schweitzer claims "defends kindness to animals chiefly as a means of preventing the growth of heartless relations with other men" (297). In turning to the inherent value of *all* life forms, Schweitzer lays a groundwork for overcoming the problem of speciesism to a degree that Singer cannot, confined as he is to the sphere of sentience.

Another notable development of Schweitzer was in the rejection of ethics as an abstract system of values. Though Kant and Bentham, for example, were arguing converse ethical viewpoints, they are both seeking a foolproof test for all ethical actions, applicable to all people. Their ethic is primarily conceptual, an attempt to grasp the abstract rules of how we ought to behave. Schweitzer breaks from this, exemplifying the move towards later environmentalists in presenting an ethics of action, a practical and concrete attempt to attain ethical enlightenment through an engagement with the world's many life forms. Reverence for Life is alive and well, though one may miss the fact given its modern designations as "biocentrism" or "biocentric egalitarianism". They denote the same central premises, life (bio) is central and all life is equal. Perhaps the greatest danger for Schweitzer, as for any ethical theory that does not begin with the search for abstract principles, is the slippery slope of relativism. By Schweitzer's admission, one man's sense of "reverence" may not equate to another's, and it is by no means clear how to resolve such conflicts.

The problem we wish to look at is easier to solve. It is the problem of "biocentrism" being yet too narrow. Though Darwin, amidst others, had long posited the interconnectedness of living things and their environments, it wasn't until the ecological developments of the 1930's that the complex harmony of various ecosystems was unfolding. It made little sense anymore to posit reverence for all life forms without reverence for the natural habitats of rock, sand, water and soil that allowed them to flourish. The scene was set for an even more encompassing ethics, and it would be known as the Land Ethic.

4.3. The Land Ethic

American Aldo Leopold is a hero to environmentalists, and rightly so. Decades working for the U.S. Forest Service, the first written text on *Game Management*, founding member of the Wilderness Society, creator of the first designated wilderness area in the United States; the list goes on. But it was *A Sand County Almanac*, a short book published one year after Leopold's 1948 death, for which he is best remembered. The opening line lures one into a false sense of security, "when the tinkle of dripping water is heard in the land." (Leopold, 1949, 3) The introductory essays are works of pure naturalism, and belie the fact that by the final essay, 'The Land Ethic,' Leopold is rejecting "the belief that economics determines *all* land use." (225) The subordination of economic policy to an environmental philosophy is one of Leopold's notable achievements. His utilisation of then recent developments in ecology, such as the terminology of "energy circuits," allowed Leopold to develop the first holistic environmental ethic.

Between the poetic opening and the anti-economic close, Leopold argues convincingly for his theory that all aspects of the environment, both living and non-living, are deserving of moral consideration. One of his more illuminating developments is to posit an evolving ethics, one that will not be set in stone as, say, a Kantian categorical imperative, but which is fluid enough to adapt to our changing needs – "because nothing so important as an ethic is ever 'written.'" (225) In its most condensed form, Leopold's ethics states that "A thing is right when it tends to preserve the integrity, stability, and beauty of the biotic community. It is wrong when it tends otherwise." (224-225) As the first statement of a holistic environmental ethic, and one which furthermore transgressed the bounds between ethics, aesthetics, and economics, Leopold made a monumental leap towards the yet broader ethical considerations of the latter twentieth century.

4.4. Deep Ecology

Until his recent death in January, 2009, Arne Naess, then aged ninety six, was widely considered the single most significant living environmental philosopher. For Naess, humans must be an integral part of the ecosphere in order to attain self-realisation.[4] Self realisation in this instance amounts to the Eastern conception of dissipation of self, a loss of egoism which allows one to view themselves as being one with nature, an integral part of the biosphere as opposed to the detached 'man in the wilderness'. In extending ethics to all natural objects, animate and inanimate, Naess places himself at the opposing pole to Singer, whose utilitarian environmental ethics is classifiable as 'shallow ecology' on Naess' account. Deep Ecology strives for a radical shift in mindset, a change in attitude towards nature away from the human centred values of utilitarianism. An environmental ethics that does not dispense with the primacy of man and that proposes piecemeal reforms as the solution to our environmental crises is, by contrast, termed 'Shallow Ecology'.

Naess' commitment to environmentalism began, under influence of Carson's *Silent Spring*, during the revolutionary fervor of the nineteen sixties. Like Carson, Naess highlights the need to counter anthropocentrism as fundamental to solving the current environmental crisis. His founding of the respected

---

4   The Guardian obituary surmises his contribution as follows:

Næss taught that ecology should not be concerned with man's place in nature but with every part of nature on an equal basis, because the natural order has intrinsic value that transcends human values. Indeed, humans could only attain "realisation of the Self" as part of an entire ecosphere.

http://www.guardian.co.uk/environment/2009/jan/15/obituary-arne-naess.html.

interdisciplinary journal *Inquiry* in 1958 betrays his then radical willingness to transgress disciplinary boundaries, which prepared the way for a seamless transition into ecophilosophy, or 'ecosophy' as Naess prefers to term it. Naess also shares with Carson a turn to activism, his interest in the nonviolent non-cooperation of Gandhi leading him in the direction of the peaceful protest, rather than the ecological sabotage or 'monkeywrenching' that such activist movements as Earth First openly appraise. In 1970, along with 300 other activists, Naess famously chained himself to rocks below the waterfall of Mardalsfossen, in northern Norway, in protest against the impending construction of a damn. Notwithstanding this fact, it was the politicization of 'deep ecology' by Naess and George Sessions in an eight point manifesto which was eventually adopted as the bedrock of the more radical environmentalism of Earth First. A select summary of this "Deep Ecology platform" offers the clearest exposition of Naess' Deep Ecology.

> (1) The value of nonhuman life-forms is independent...(2) richness and diversity of life-forms are values in themselves...(3) Humans have no right to reduce this richness and diversity except to satisfy vital needs...(6) Significant change of life conditions for the better requires change in policies. These affect basic economic, technological, and ideological structures...(8) Those who subscribe to the foregoing points have an obligation directly or indirectly to participate in the attempt to implement the necessary changes (Des Jardins, 2001, 206-207).

Positing inherent value in nature and an obligation to implement policy changes are admirable but somewhat unspecific tenets. And herein lies what is perhaps the central problem of any discussion about Deep Ecology. A flexible, non-systematic philosophy, Deep Ecology has been adopted by such diverse thinkers, and adapted to such diverse purposes, that the question of precisely what Deep Ecology consists in becomes infuriatingly difficult to answer. Joseph DesJardins encapsulates a widely held attitude succinctly when he states that "In some ways, the claims of Deep Ecology are so sweeping and general as to become empty" (2001, 219) With influences in European and Eastern philosophies, both new and ancient, in romantic poetry, along with contemporary science and folk musicians, the attempt to criticise Deep Ecology can prove as infuriating as an attempt to criticise twentieth century Marxism, when one cannot even grasp hold of one central tenet that Marxists still share in common.[5]

But this fact itself remains open to criticism. And one might also criticise

---

[5] Earth First, for example, a movement entirely committed to the basic non-anthropocentric tenet of Deep Ecology, states that its own 'members' range "from animal rights vegans to wilderness hunting guides, from monkeywrenchers to careful followers of Gandhi, from whiskey-drinking backwoods riffraff to thoughtful philosophers." http://www.earthfirst.org/about.htm Deep Ecology itself exhibits this same inclusiveness of such diverse ideals that it is difficult to reduce it to a core philosophy.

Naess, as one might Marx, for a failure to be more specific regarding positive policy or suggested political action. It is easy to talk policy with a narrow focused object such as the rights of a particular endangered species, but when the question broadens to how we are to treat the biosphere as a whole, the correct policy is not so easily defined. Naess' personification of Norwegian mountains – a throwback to mediaeval animism – is easily disparaged from the perspective of contemporary science, but such criticism misses the point. Naess does not require definitive policies, nor is he bounded by modern science from turning to the Nature Gods of dead mythologies. Indeed, his sometimes infuriating refusal to argue with modern science and politics on its own terms is central to his philosophical method. This method is to shake his readers into older, holistic modes of thought, in which imbuing natural objects with souls is no less controversial than imbuing humans with same.

4.5. The Gaia Hypothesis

James Lovelock has done more than any other to imbue the popular consciousness with the contention that the earth is a single, harmoniously balanced, living organism. On the suggestion of friend and neighbour William Golding, author of *Lord of the Flies*, Lovelock adopted the Greek Earth Goddess, Gaia, as a suitable designation for the newly personified Earth. A pre-philosophical involvement with NASA's planet exploration programme allowed Lovelock to view the Earth from outer space, "from the top down," (Lovelock, 2000, xii) an experience which facilitated a shift in perspective from the apparent multiplicity of our terrestrial lives to the consideration of Earth as a living unity. The delicate chemical balance of this unity requires a similarly delicate ethics, which respects the Earth as a totality and endeavours at all times to promote the harmony which this Earth naturally strives for.

We have mentioned that Deep Ecology stands alongside the Gaia hypothesis of James Lovelock in bringing ethical extensionism to its logical conclusion in a holistic appraisal of the earth in its entirety. Lovelock's *Gaia: a New Look at Life on Earth*, published in 1979, popularized the notion "that the entire range of living matter on Earth…could be regarded as constituting a single living entity." (2000, 9) That this entity was moreover deemed capable of manipulating the earth's atmosphere to suit its own needs suggested to many not only a personified Earth but a self-conscious one, and this view was received with an accompanying backlash from scientists and philosophers alike. The distance that we have come from Peter Singer's more pragmatic utilitarianism is captured in Singer's comment that "Calling the global ecosystem by the name of a Greek goddess seems a nice idea, but it may not be the best way of helping us to think clearly about its nature" (Singer, 1993, 283).[6] Lovelock's dual tendencies to fashion claims of scientific certainty *and* to rely on the metaphorical power of poetry and myth are difficult to amalgamate. With the proviso that opinions are made to be challenged, this author opines that Naess' Deep Ecology supersedes Lovelock's Gaia hypothesis in this respect. Naess is free from the conceptual and linguistic constraints of modern science, and consistently writes and acts as such. Lovelock by contrast is trying to have his cake and eat it, holding fast to notions of Gaia's "revenge" but expressing these very non-scientific ideas in an unfitting scientific terminology.

5. A Case in Point: Global Warming

> Global warming is only one problem among many. It may not even count as the most serious problem (Sayre, 2007, Introductory Lecture).

In focusing so strongly upon the single environmental issue of Global Warming, we do not discount the opinion of University of Notre Dame's Kenneth Sayre, above. Certainly, media presentation of the current environmental crisis is imbalanced - weighted in favour of global warming above deforestation, the protection of wilderness, ensuring species diversity, or decreasing pollution in our rivers, oceans and air. Without denying that other such issues are central to environmental concerns, we hereby treat of global warming as *the* central issue of environmental ethics today. Our reasons for doing so are partly those of convenience.

The issue of global warming provides a means of illustrating many facts of environmental ethics in a single sweeping case study. It exhibits, most clearly, the trans-disciplinary nature of the subject, with economics, science, politics and public policy all unavoidable components of such a study. Furthermore, it is intricately bound with a whole host of other environmental issues, which – while not necessarily minor or lesser concerns – can be viewed as either dependant upon or contributory to the earth's changing climate. Increased CO_2 emissions, for example, lead to CO_2 absorption into increasingly acidified oceans, an acidity

---

6 It is perhaps unfair on Lovelock the extent to which criticism has focused upon this identification of Earth with a Greek Goddess. The term Gaia was adopted, after all, merely on the suggestion of a friend, and as Lovelock made explicit in the preface added to a new millennium reprint, "it is the story of a planet that is alive in the same way that a gene is selfish." (Lovelock, 2000, ix) That is to say, the earth is no more a self aware individual than a gene actually possesses the character trait of selfishness, but the adoption of the metaphor is deemed a fitting means of coaxing the reader into the required shift of perspective. Though Lovelock will at times refer to the Earth as 'she,' he is quick to add that "this is meant no more seriously than is the appellation 'she' when given to a ship." (x)

which in turn threatens the continued existence of shell forming marine plankton central to the ocean food chain. Similarly, the introduction of salt into coastal fresh waters that is to be the unavoidable consequence of rising sea levels is set to contaminate inland water supplies. Species diversity and water pollution are thus directly bound up with global warming, as are the further issues of deforestation and farming animals for food. Consider methane, which after CO2 is the second most abundant carbon compound in the atmosphere. Both the clearing of lands for agriculture and the ruminants (secondary stomachs) of cattle and sheep are major contributors to atmospheric methane levels. 20% of global production is accounted for by ruminants alone. One proposed solution of the Kyoto Protocol, genetically engineered cattle, illustrates how the reformist approach does not break with the fundamental problematic human premise that other life forms are to be our playthings. In turning to the question of methane production as an argument against the mass harvesting of animals for food, Peter Singer offers us another illustration of his utilitarianism. The 'rights' of animals is not Singer's primary concern here, but rather that their abuse contributes directly to the unmistakably human problem of global warming.[7]

Having briefly introduced the problem of global warming, we proceed to discuss it under three headings. Firstly, we consider how pinpointing the problem invokes questions in the philosophy of science. Turning towards proposed solutions to the problem, we look secondly at the question of technological advance and the stark methodological differences it highlights between the aforementioned 'shallow' and 'deep' ecologists. Lastly, continuing with proposed solutions, we look at how this same theoretical distinction (shallow v. deep) leads to alternate conceptions of right public policy.

To begin then, what is global warming? Global warming results from an imbalance in the earth's energy system caused primarily by the vast quantities of carbon dioxide that man has added to the earth's atmosphere since the industrial revolution. In 1700, CO2 levels in the earth's atmosphere were 280 parts per million. They have risen to about 380 ppm since this time. If we do not curtail our use of fossil fuels soon, CO2 levels are predicted to rise to 700 ppm in the coming century, figures unknown since the age of the dinosaurs.[8]

The effect of these increased CO2 levels is that the sunlight being allowed to

---

7   We can squeeze yet another general truth from the particular case of global warming. Its direct encroachment upon a whole host of other environmental issues concerning land and sea, plant and animal, is illustrative of that central monist tenet of many environmentalists. The earth's current crises cannot be understood as a series of minor and discreet problems to be solved in isolation. It is the malady of the biosphere taken in its totality that requires treatment. Global warming's infringement upon all of the earth's ecosystems offers a clear illustration of this fact.

8   This year (2009) the Zeppelin research station on Svalbard, Norway, recorded levels of 397 ppm, likely the highest figures of CO2 in the Arctic for 50 million years.

enter the atmosphere is not allowed to leave it, thus destroying the natural energy balance that allows earth's life forms to proliferate. Since 1900 alone, the earth's average temperature has risen by 0.6 °C, not a small increase considering that a few degrees above the average body temperature of 98 is fatal to a human. The earth is no less a single complex interdependent system, and the effect of such seemingly small increases are likewise catastrophic. More worrying than global averages, however, is the fact that the Arctic has warmed by 3 °C in this same time period. Since the 1980's it has become apparent that ozone (earth's protection from the sun's harmful UV rays) has begun to disappear over certain parts of the Antarctic. The first decade of the 21st century has witnessed extreme and unpredictable weather conditions. In France in 2003, 15,000 people were killed as a result of unprecedented heat waves. 2005 surprised us with the worst Hurricane season ever recorded, including Hurricane Katrina which devastated New Orleans. This catastrophe was tied directly to the fact that water temperatures in the Gulf of Mexico were then the highest ever recorded. This same year, 2005, saw Amazonian fish stocks decimated in droughts of such ferocity that scientists are now predicting an Amazonian desert beginning in this century. The happy influx of aesthetically pleasing Mediterranean species into the once colder climbs of Northern Europe is scant compensation for the worst forest fires on record in both South America and Australia's history. Every year, it seems, is fraught with catastrophes that supersede all predecessors. Given that all the evidence pinpoints humanity as the direct cause of crisis, and given also our continued refusal to do much about it; it is difficult to argue with Sayre's simple summation of current affairs: "We are in the process of suicide." (Sayre 2007, Introductory Lecture) Notwithstanding all this, there are yet vast proportions of the general public who view global warming as mere 'theory', as opposed to a proven fact. The establishment of global warming as a genuine threat *should* be decades behind us, but frustratingly remains our necessary starting point.

5.1. Science as Theory or Fact?

Since the development of ecology in the 1930's, Environmental Ethics has become increasingly dependent on advances in scientific knowledge to provide its food for thought. It was the ecologist's construction of complicated food chains as much as the monism of Eastern philosophy that first highlighted the interdependence in nature which has culminated in totalising modern terms such as the 'biosphere'. The fundamental issues of the philosophy of science are, consequentially, of utmost relevance. Environmental ethicists have been forced to join the science wars, most emphatically by a worldwide media presentation of global warming as a hypothetical creation of a group of theoretically minded scientists. It is, in fact, a universal scientific consensus. Dr. Naomi Oreskes of University of California at San Diego sampled almost 10% of all peer-reviewed science journal articles on global warming. Of the 928 articles sampled, not one was in any doubt as to the reality of global warming, nor to its human causes. Such consensus amidst the scientific community is itself what scientific 'truth' consists in. In fact, consensus upon the issue of global warming far surpasses the initial varied receptions of such current scientific mainstays as evolution in biology or relativity in physics. To continue to question global warming is thus tantamount to questioning the veracity of the scientific method, not unlike holding fast to Bishop James Usher's calculation that the earth was created in 4004 BC.

A comparative study of popular media articles in a select group of influential American newspapers uncovered a 53% uncertainty rate as to the causes of global warming. The American public have here been subjected to a deliberate fabrication, an economically driven push from oil and coal companies to "reposition global warming as theory, rather than fact" – in the words of one internal memo (Gore, 2006, 263). One tactic of those wishing to quash drastic environmental policies is to disparage the scientific methods that call for the drastic approach. Media reports thus exhibit a tendency to focus on what's separating scientific opinion than what's keeping scientists together. It is agreed, for example, that if we continue to burn fossil fuels as we have done in the past the earth's temperature is set to rise dramatically over the next century. Climate models predict anywhere from a 1.5 to 5 °C increase. To a public unclear as to what science consists in, this may seem to cast global warming as a dubitable hypothesis. If the scientists cannot agree upon the implications of their own data, we can hardly be expected to. But the fact remains that temperatures will rise. Upon this all scientists converge. That they disagree on the more precise details is not to say that the predicted rise is unscientific, for such disagreement is in fact central to the scientific method. Just as two scientists arguing over the evolution of one particular species do not cast doubt on the theory of Evolution as a whole, so the theory of Global Warming is upheld here, minor disagreements notwithstanding.

The twentieth century's most famous philosopher of science, Karl Popper, highlighted the open-ended nature of the discipline. Scientific 'truth' is always open to public scrutiny, to future modifications. Popper's theory of demarcation for scientific theories is that they are 'falsifiable' – possess the possibility of being proven false. Global warming *is* sufficiently 'falsifiable'. It posits a direct link between rising CO2 levels and rising temperatures which empirical evidence consistently verifies, but which it *could* negate.[9] For Popper, a theory qualifies

---

9   The neighbouring planet Venus possesses temperatures in excess of 500 °C. Whereas its proximity to the sun would lead to a predicted 55°C, this is magnified almost tenfold by an atmosphere that is 96% carbon dioxide. The predicted correlation is likewise confirmed by a look into earths distant past when warm climate dinosaurs roamed the arctic regions. CO2 levels were then in excess of 1000 ppm, levels we could reach in the next century.

as science only when put to the test, when making risky predictions about the world that can then be tested. Older climate models already passed their tests in predicting the exponential rise in CO2 levels and the climactic unpredictability that have characterised the last two decades. Worryingly, these same models predict that current temperatures (and catastrophes) will be dwarfed by the present century's developments unless environmental policies and individual action do not alter dramatically.

5.2. Technology as Problem or Solution?

Moving onto proposed solutions for this scientifically verified problem, one of the more illuminating questions to be posed in this connection is whether it is contradictory to pose a technological fix for a problem that has originated with technology itself? Deep Ecologists provide a negative answer here. What is required is a wholesale return to older ways of living, to bygone modes of thinking. Shallow or reformist policy, on the contrary, is more open to providing new technological solutions to counter specific environmental problems 'one solution at a time'.

Prior to the problem of Global Warming, environmental policy centred on the question of air pollution. As with Global Warming, this problem reached a critical historical pass in the 18th century, with the coal-fuelled Industrial Revolution. It was not until London's 'killer smog' of 1951 or, Stateside, the deaths of 19 people in Donora Valley (PA) three years previously, that the word 'smog' became part of the Western social vocabulary. Herein lies one potential problem of the reformist approach to ethics; it aims primarily at providing a cure rather than a preventative medicine. That is to say that it often engages with issues after they have reached a critical stage. Moreover, *if* this initial criticism is valid, we may add that the resulting solutions will be piecemeal and ultimately ineffective. The immediate solution to smog, for example, was to build industry with increasingly higher smokestacks, so that highly populated industrial urban centres would not be faced with the prospect of death inducing coughs. In so far as the problem in question was the sudden death of many individuals in one concentrated area, high smokestacks offered a viable solution. But in so far as the problem was pollution itself they offered no solution whatsoever, for it takes but a few days for those same pollutants to return in the form of acid rain, dispersed somewhere downwind, where they would not stare polite society so bluntly in the eye. The problem is not solved, but transferred in the form of toxic metals to the aquatic life of our rivers and oceans. The 'deep' solution in this instance would not be modification of the problematic smokestacks but disuse of them. Clearly the 'deep' solution is more effective but it likewise fails in achieving the desired energy supply.

Now, as the question of air pollution has become subsumed under the broader crises of Global Warming, we are faced again with a myriad of proposals for providing technological solutions to a technological problem. As a means of cutting down our use of fossil fuels, we are encouraged to improve the fuel efficiency of automobiles. Electric cars, or hybrid vehicles, which utilise a percentage of their gasoline intake to produce electricity, provide two alternatives. The 2006 documentary film *Who Killed the Electric Car?* incited much controversy in citing the law suits of automobile manufacturers and oil companies as the reason why the General Motors EV1 (Electric Vehicle 1) was removed from the market, having been introduced in the 1990's. With this possible detour into the economics of big business we find yet another example of the sprawling, undefined terrain of environmental ethics, which one cannot extricate from a broad array of other questions. Seeking further confirmation of this point, we might add that one cannot simply state that nuclear power does not contribute to CO_2 production by way of a fitting conclusion to the question of alternate energy sources. For the very availability of nuclear power, many deem to go hand in hand with the production of nuclear weapons, and so we are led inevitably into another difficult issue that we do not here have time to explore.[10]

Returning to the possibility of providing a technological solution to a technological problem, we can say that the single example of smokestacks is by no means the deciding issue. We can just as quickly cite examples of the positive use to which technology has here being put. When, for example, in 1958, scientists began to measure the atmosphere by direct sampling of air, it marked a technological advance. One of those locating new instrumentation in Hawaii and Antartica was Charles David Keeling, who hit upon the idea of monitoring changes in atmospheric CO_2 concentrations. That Keeling was the first person to confirm that CO_2 levels were rising, and that this has proven to be the ultimate cause of Global Warming, is clearly a fact of fundamental importance to shallow and deep ecologists alike. If it seems absurd to the 'deep' radical to utilise technology in order to solve a technological problem, the 'shallow' reformist may counter that it is doubly absurd to disparage the very technology you have used to pinpoint the problem in question. There is no easy solution to this paradox, and it will doubtless prove a core point of contention between reformist and radical environmentalists in the future.

Those who oppose the technological fix highlight that the consequences of technological advances are unpredictable. To use yet another example, CFC's were invented by chemists at General Motors back in the 1930's. They were almost indestructible, thought to be non-toxic, and these facts considered their primary benefits. But CFC's do decompose, releasing chlorine atoms that destroy the ozone. As such, we find a concrete example of good intentions gone awry,

---

10 Nuclear power is an under tapped alternative to fossil fuels but radioactive disasters in Chernobyl (1986) and Takaimura, Japan (1999) further complicate the issue.

due to technologies utilising the latest science, of which we only ever have an incomplete understanding. The scientist, like everyone else, learns from his/her mistakes. The question remains as to whether the stakes are becoming too high to allow the scientist to keep making them. The problem is becoming more acute, and the proposed solutions more ambitious (or desperate depending on your politics). Some of the more inventive solutions include the following:

- The reflection of sunlight away from earth either by placing mirrors in orbit or by the injection of sulphur particles into the upper atmosphere.

- Adding iron to the oceans, which would allow carbon soaking phytoplankton to proliferate.

- Carbon capture and sequestration: We keep burning fossil fuels but learn to effectively remove the carbon either after or (preferably) before burning fuel. These vast quantities of unburned carbon could then be stored somewhere such as the ocean depths, safely away from the atmosphere.

The obvious question here is what effect vast quantities of carbon will have on the ocean depths? And the equally obvious answer is that we will not know until we try it. Or likewise, what the effects of iron in the oceans or sulphur in the atmosphere? Given that scientific knowledge is always acquired via a two-way dialogue with experimental evidence, we must pose the question of whether the above 'experiments' are worth the risk? If we accept Popper's account of scientific advance as a series of 'yes' and 'no' answers to risky scientific predictions, then it is difficult to ignore the 'deep' conviction that the risk in this instance does not warrant the possibility of another failed experiment.

6. Conclusion

As we saw above, from the perspective of deep ecology, reformist approaches are seeking a quick fix to environmental problems, whereas any true solution to the current crises requires a more fundamental alteration of our philosophical assumptions. Public policy decisions surrounding the issue of Global Warming further illustrates the stark contrast in approach between deep and shallow reformists.

1958 saw the launch of the International Geophysical Year, the 1st global political commitment to understanding the earth. The Montreal Protocol of 1986 set itself the task of phasing out CFC's. On the plus side Montreal made the Global Environmental Fund available to developing countries. Nevertheless, the plight of developing countries was not the economic priority here. Developing nations were effectively forced to sign, for participating nations were not allowed to take CFC products from abstaining ones. Bowing to Western markets remains, for many countries, the only alternative to extreme poverty. But should such policy decisions be enforced upon developing nations? Should the world's developed nations not be leading by example here, as opposed to utilising its technology as a means to further imbalance the economies of undeveloped ones? They should be, of course, but they are not.[11] The introduction of genetically engineered crops into struggling nations has no doubt increased food production but the by-product is complete dependence upon technologies that these developing countries do not possess. Countries such as Bangladesh that are in immediate threat of widespread flooding have no control over their situation. They possess neither the technologies to contribute greatly to the problem, nor the political sway to affect the countries that do.

That Americans in particular have been the target of fuel company vendettas is not accidental. For the American contribution to global warming is three times that of the entire continents of South America and Africa, along with Central America, Australia and the Middle East combined. Even amidst the world's developed countries, America's per person carbon emissions are twice as high as its closest 'competitors'. That these trends seem set to continue is partly a consequence of the fossil fuel market's having succeeded in its vendetta to reduce global warming to a mere theory, as also upon a general misunderstanding as to what a 'scientific theory' consists in, but economic factors are also pivotal. Dealing with these public policy questions leads us inevitably into questions of economic justice. Take, for example, the fact that China, by virtue of its northern 'coal belt' is now believed to have surpassed the United States as the world's No. 1 culprit for CO_2 production. The quick ethical fix might suppose that this extent of industrial production must stop, period. But we are then led into the equally unethical predicament of having denied a developing nation its right to develop along the very same lines that has made the Western world so prosperous. Were every adult in India or China to drive an automobile, effects on the environment would be catastrophic. We cannot afford to allow these economies to develop to this degree. Yet an automobile each is acceptable in the Western world. One must conclude either that a car per person is acceptable, in which case CO_2 levels increase beyond even our worst predictions, or else that different rules apply to wealthy countries and those countries we must keep poor for the sake of the planet as a whole. Neither alternative is ethically justifiable but the Western world still works on fossil fuel and automobiles.

---

11   Peter Singer has been vocal on the fact that the United States is proving the most unethical country in the world in this regard. With 5% world population and 30% world CO_2 production, the U.S. nevertheless refused to commit to the Kyoto Protocol, a plan to address climate change. Singer argues correctly that developed nations should bear the initial brunt of forward looking plans, especially considering that developing nations are at least one century behind on CO_2 contributions.

Easter Island has been cast by more than one environmentalist as prophetic of the earth's current crisis, as a sort of earth in miniature. The island nation collapsed, having used up its natural resources when its population to land mass ratio equalled the earths at present. More recently, the tiny Pacific island nation of Tuvalu has become symbolic of the global crisis. Already, rising sea levels have flooded the country and led to mass evacuations. Unsurprisingly, Tuvalu is one nation leading the way in the fight against CO_2 levels. By 2020 it proposes to rely entirely upon renewable energy. Predicted expenditure of $20 million dollars began with the installation of a solar system on the roof of the capital's main soccer stadium. It makes for a nice image, but in reality its effect will be insignificant unless it can incite developed nations to similar action.

Questions of whether age old deforestation or the clearing of grasslands by tribesmen in Brazil and Indonesia should be stopped miss the point entirely. This is only a third world problem in the sense that the third world is first in line to suffer at the hands of flash floods, droughts and crop failures. Thousands of years of tribal culture, of small farming, has proven itself to be sustainable. Two and a half centuries of industrialisation leaves no doubt that the source of the problem, and so any possibility of solution, must come from America and Europe. Increasingly it seems that piecemeal technological and economic policies *alone* cannot solve this crisis. "Our environmental crisis can be alleviated only by a fundamental shift in the social values that govern our daily activities" (Sayre, 2007, Introductory Lecture).

BIBLIOGRAPHY

A Guide to the Bibliography

The International Society for Environmental Ethics (ISEE) have compiled a "master bibliography" of texts on environmental ethics, referenced below. Anyone delving deeply into this area will find that bibliography to be the best available. This bibliography attempts to guide less advanced students towards the most accessible web resources and textbooks available.

In the application of moral theory to concrete cases, environmental ethics avails of contemporary scientific and technological advances. Happily, the best sources for up to date scientific data are web based and cost free. Listed under 'Web Resources' below are some of the best maintained and user friendly websites for factual information on environmental issues. Where appropriate, a brief description of the site is given. Environmental groups listed range from major intergovernmental organisations (EEA, IPCC, UNEP) to non-governmental practitioners of "economic sabotage" (ELF, ALF). There are also cost free web based resources that deal with the more theoretical aspect of environmental ethics. When searching the web for free educational materials, a good place to start is the Open Courseware Consortium ://www.ocwconsortium.org/). The opening web resources listed in 6.2. below (those beginning 'http://ocw...') are all relevant open courseware courses. The best place to start is the video lectures series 'Environmental Philosophy' by Dr. Kenneth Sayre of University of Notre Dame. The other courses listed offer various reading materials on related issues. For more practical information on how to personally contribute to good environmental practice, see the World Resources Institute. There are also numerous organisations (World Wildlife Federation, Greenpeace) that provide information on what you can do to support good environmental practice – without breaking the law.

There are many good edited collections in which one can find a broad selection of readings in a single book. Which one to purchase depends on whether your interests are theoretical (Pojman and Pojman 2008), partly applied (List 1993), heavily applied (Gudorf and Huchingson 2003), trans-disciplinary (Jamieson 2001), or grounded in classic philosophical theory (Chappell 1997).

Web Resources

Please note that while all of these links were active at the time of publication, there is always the possibility that their addresses will change or the sites will cease to exist.

Anon (n.d.). http://www.animalliberationfront.com/

Anon (n.d.). http://www.cep.unt.edu/ISEE.html 'Master Bibliography' for Environmental Ethics

Anon (n.d.). http://www.ciesin.org/TG/AG/AG-home.html looks at livestock, agriculture and its effect on the environment e.g. methane issue.

Anon (n.d.). http://www.co2science.org/ Center for the Study of Carbon Dioxide and Global Change.

Anon (n.d.). http://www.earthfirst.org/ Earth First

Anon (n.d.). http://www.earthsystemgovernance.org/ Earth System Governance Project

Anon (n.d.). http://www.eco-forum.org/ European Eco Forum

Anon (n.d.). http://www.eea.europa.eu/ European Environmental Agency (EEA).

Anon (n.d.). http://www.elfpressoffice.org/ Earth Liberation Front News (ELF)

Anon (n.d.). http://www.energy.gov/ US department of energy on fossil fuel usage.

Anon (n.d.). http://www.enn.com/ - Environmental News Network.

Anon (n.d.). http://www.epa.gov/ United States Environmental Protection Agency.

Anon (n.d.). http://www.fws.gov/index.html U.S. Fish and Wildlife Service

Anon (n.d.). http://www.greenpeace.org/international/ Greenpeace International

Anon (n.d.). http://www.ipcc.ch/ Intergovernmental Panel on Climate Change official website (IPCC).

Anon (n.d.). http://www.millenniumassessment.org/en/index.aspx Millennium Ecosystem Assessment. 2005. Living Beyond Our Means, Natural Assets and Human Well-Being, Statement from the Board.

Anon (n.d.). http://www.nas.nasa.gov/About/Education/Ozone Nasa on the ozone Problem.

Anon (n.d.). http://www.panda.org – World Wildlife Federation Homepage.

Anon (n.d.). http://www.pewclimate.org/ Pew Center on Global Climate Change.

Anon (n.d.). http://www.realclimate.org RealClimate, an up to date, accurate scientist run discussion forum.

Anon (n.d.). http://www.unep.org/ United Nations Environment Programme (UNEP).

Anon (n.d.). http://www.unfccc.int/2860.php The United Nations Framework Convention on Climate Change; including detailed discussion of Kyoto Protocol.

Anon (n.d.). http://www.wri.org/ World Resources Institute, with many practical suggestions on protecting the earth.

Carmin, J. (n.d.). Environmental Justice. http://ocw.mit.edu/OcwWeb/Urban-Studies-and-Planning/11-368Fall-2004/CourseHome/index.htm.

Fleming, M. (n.d.) Environmental Ethics. http://ocw.capcollege.bc.ca/philosophy/phil-208-environmental-ethics.

Greenstone, M. (n.d.). Environmental Policy and Economics. http://ocw.mit.edu/

OcwWeb/Economics/14-42Spring-2004/CourseHome/index.htm.

Karl, H. (n.d.). Role of Science and Scientists in Collaborative Approaches to Environmental Policymaking. http://ocw.mit.edu/OcwWeb/Urban-Studies-and-Planning/11-375Spring-2006/CourseHome/index.htm.

Kibel, A. (n.d.). End of Nature. http://ocw.mit.edu/OcwWeb/Literature/21L-449End-of-NatureSpring2002/CourseHome/index.htm.

Rutvo, H. (n.d.) Introduction to Environmental History. http://ocw.mit.edu/OcwWeb/History/21H-421Spring2004/CourseHome/index.htm.

Sayre, K. (2007). Environmental Philosophy. http://ocw.nd.edu/philosophy/environmental-philosophy. Susskid, L. (n.d.). Introduction to Environmental Policy and Planning. http://ocw.mit.edu/OcwWeb/Urban-Studies-and-Planning/11-601Fall-2005/CourseHome/index.htm.

Books

Benson, J. (ed.) (2000). *Environmental Ethics: An introduction with readings.* London, Routledge.

Bentham, J. (2005). *An Introduction to the Principles of Morals and Legislation.* New York, Adamant Media Corporation.

Berinstein, P. (2001). *Alternative Energy: Facts, Statistics and Issues.* New York, Oryx Press.

Bocknek, J. (2003). *Antartica the Last Wilderness: Understanding Global Issues.* New York, Smart Apple Media.

Boeckel, J. V. (1995). *Interview with Arne Naess.* Rerun Prducties.

Callicott, J. B. (1989). *In Defense of the Land Ethic: Essays in Environmental Philosophy.* Albany, NY, SUNY Press.

Callicott, J. B., and C. Palmer (eds.). (2005). *Environmental Philosophy: Critical Concepts in the Environment.* London/New York, Routledge.

Carson, R. (2000). *Silent Spring.* London, Penguin Books.

Chappell, T. D. J. (ed.) (1997). *Respecting Nature: Environmental Thinking in the Light of Philosophical Theory.* New York, Columbia University Press.

Derr, P. G. and E. M. McNamara. (2003). *Case Studies in Environmental Ethics.* Lanham, MD, Rowman and Littlefield.

Des Jardins, J. R. (2001). *Environmental Ethics: An Introduction to Environmental Philosophy (3rd Edition)*. Belmont, CA, Wadsworth/Thomson Learning.

Devall, B., and G. Sessions. (1985). *Deep Ecology: Living as if Nature Mattered*. Salt Lake City, UT, Peregrine Smith.

Elliot, R. (ed.) (1995). *Environmental Ethics*. New York, Oxford University Press.

Emerson, R. W. (2004). *The Conduct of Life*. Montana, Kessinger Publishing.

Engel, J. R. and J. G. Engel (eds.) (1990). *Ethics of Environment and Development*. Tucson; London, The University of Arizona Press.

Frodeman, R. (ed.) (2000). *Earth Matters: The Earth Sciences, Philosophy, and the Claims of Community*. Upper Saddle River, NJ, Prentice-Hall.

Gore, A. (2006). *An Inconvenient Truth*. Emmaus, PA, Rodale.

Gottinger, H. (1998). *Global Environmental Economics*. New York, Kluwer Academic Publishers.

Gudorf, C. E. and James E. Huchingson (eds.) (2003). *Boundaries: A Casebook in Environmental Ethics*. Washington, DC: Georgetown University Press.

Hargrove, E. C. (1996). *Foundations of Environmental Ethics*. Denton, TX, Environmental Ethics Books.

Houghton, J. (2004). *Global Warming: The Complete Briefing (3rd Edition)*. Cambridge, Cambridge University Press.

Jamieson, D. (ed.) (2001). *A Companion to Environmental Philosophy*. Malden, MA, Blackwell.

Kant, I. (1930 [1775/80]). *Lectures on Ethics* (Infield, L. trans). London, Methuen.

Leopold, A. (1949). *A Sand County Almanac*. New York, Oxford University Press.

Light, A. and H. Rolston III (eds.) (2003). *Environmental Ethics: An Anthology*. Oxford, Blackwell.

List, P. C. (ed.) (1993). *Radical Environmentalism: Philosophy and Tactics*. Belmont, CA, Wadsworth.

Lovelock, J. (2000). *Gaia: A New Look at Life on Earth*. Oxford, Oxford University Press.

Mill, J. S. (1998). *Principles of Political Economy*. Oxford, Oxford University

Press.

Moroto-Valer, M. M., Fauthb, D. J., Kuchtaa, M. E., Zhanga, Y, and Andre´sen, J. M. (2002). *Environmental Challenges and Greenhouse Gas Control for Fossil Fuel Utilization in the 21st Century*. New York, Plenum Publishing Co.

Naess, A. (1973). The Shallow and the Deep, Long-Range Ecology Movements: A Summary. *Inquiry*, 16, 95–100.

Naess, A. (1989). *Ecology, Community, and Lifestyle: Outline of an Ecosophy*. New York, Cambridge University Press.

Ouderkirk, W. and Hill, J. (2002). *Land, Value, Community: Callicott and Environmental Philosophy*. Albany, NY, SUNY Press.

Pojman, L. P. and Pojman, P. (eds.) (2008). *Environmental Ethics: Readings in Theory and Application (5th Edition)*. Belmont, CA, Thomson/Wadsworth.

Regan, T. (2004). *The Case for Animal Rights*. Berkeley, University of California Press.

Rolston III, H. (1986). *Philosophy Gone Wild*. Buffalo, NY, Prometheus Books.

Rolston III, H. (1988). *Environmental Ethics: Duties to and Values in the Natural World*. Philadelphia, Temple University Press.

Schneider, S., A. Rosencranz, and J. O. Niles (eds.) (2002). *Climate Change Policy: A Survey*. Washington, DC, Island Press.

Schweitzer, A. (1987). *The Philosophy of Civilization* (trans. Campion, C. T.). Buffalo, NY, Prometheus Books.

Singer, P. (1993). *Practical Ethics (2nd Edition)*. Cambridge, Cambridge University Press.

_____ (2002). *Animal Liberation (2nd Edition)*. New York, Ecco (Harper Collins).

Taylor, P. (1986). *Respect for Nature: A Theory of Environmental Ethics*. Princeton, Princeton University Press.

Traer, R. (2009). *Doing Environmental Ethics*. United States of America, Westview Press.

Van DeVeer, D. and C. Pierce (eds.) (2003). *The Environmental Ethics and Policy Book: Philosophy, Ecology, Economics (3rd Edition)*. Belmont, CA, Thomson/Wadsworth.

Wenz, P. S. (2001). *Environmental Ethics Today*. New York, Oxford University

Press.

8

Global Ethics

Sylvie Loriaux

1. Introduction

Global (or world) ethics can roughly be defined as the philosophical inquiry into the content and justification of values and principles that are to inform human interactions and institutional design at the world level. As such, this subdiscipline of ethics is not a new phenomenon: philosophers have long been debating about the ethical standards that should guide the conduct of individuals and groups in their mutual relationships throughout the world. The idea that all human beings belong to a global moral community, or that war should be restrained by ethical considerations, has indeed a long history.

However, this does not mean that the idea of global ethics is an obvious matter. Not everyone agrees that the same ethical values and principles can apply to the world at large. Some might believe that the very criteria of right and wrong vary from culture to culture and that this fact seriously compromises the plausibility of a global ethical theory. Others might believe that moral relationships are wholly constituted by the community life and doubt the existence of a global community susceptible to generating global moral duties. And still others might believe that, given the absence of a world authority endowed with the power to enforce rules and agreements at the world level, global agents should not be moved by considerations other than the promotion of their own interest. The latter view has chiefly been advanced with respect to states, the point being that since their very survival is at stake, states simply cannot afford paying attention to ethics in their mutual conduct; and where there is no real choice between ethical and non-ethical courses of action, it makes no sense to talk about ethics either.

These worries are certainly not unfounded; yet, they fail to appreciate some other realities of world affairs. One of them is that, ethical considerations often *do* affect the conduct of global agents, including that of states (Cohen, 1984). States are most of the time respectful of one another, prepared to honour agreements, and using moral language in their mutual relationships (even if they do not always mean what they say). These facts, in themselves, show that ethical behaviour *does* make some difference at the global level and is thus held to be of value by key global actors (in particular, the public opinion and electorates represented by states). There also seems to be broad agreement across the world that all human beings have a moral status and that this status generates some fundamental moral duties (e.g., duties to not kill or harm others unduly, to provide them assistance when they are in need or not to deceive them), even though these status and duties may be interpreted differently from society to society. Another point concerns the depiction of international politics as the realm of necessity as opposed to choice: the actions that a state takes vis-à-vis other states are most often the result of a political decision-making process; they are debated and thus treated as matters of choice to which ethical considerations can properly be applied (Walzer, 1977, 3-20).

There is also some sense in which the growing interdependence of states can be said to involve the progressive development of a 'world community' - that is, to make membership of mankind a significant locus of identity and loyalty - and to reinforce the need for a sustained global ethical reflection. Not only have scientific and technological progress, the tremendous increase in wealth in some parts of the world, and the emergence of intergovernmental or nongovernmental organisations increased the capacity to address foreign issues in a way never seen before (e.g., world poverty, natural disasters, genocides); our rapidly globalising world has also given rise to a certain number of global issues whose settlement requires international decision-making and cooperation (e.g., terrorism, pandemics, migration). New global normative challenges are to be addressed, and it is not sure that the prevailing ethical approach to world affairs can address them properly. Global ethics has long been dominated by a focus on states' rights to political sovereignty and territorial integrity. Yet, in such an interdependent world as ours, agents other than states (e.g., transnational companies, financial institutions, NGO's) can interfere with states' internal affairs and impact on individual life prospects in many different ways. In addition, an increasing number of individuals are moving from one country to another - be it for professional or leisure reasons, or to escape a politically and/or economically difficult situation - which suggests "a need for principles that track individuals across borders - principles that specify the rights that individuals have irrespective of which society they happen to belong to" (Buchanan, 2000, 698). Viewed from this perspective, a chief challenge of global ethics will be to reconcile the rights of states with ethical demands made in the name of individuals.

This chapter will be divided into three parts. The first part will consider two distinctive normative approaches to world affairs, namely: cosmopolitanism and communitarianism. Section 1 will start by showing how the currently in vogue concept of 'cosmopolitanism' arose in classical Greek thought and was rediscovered during the Enlightenment by philosophers of very diverse persuasions. It will then stress the importance of distinguishing between 'moral' and 'institutional' cosmopolitanism, on the one hand, and between 'extreme' and 'moderate' cosmopolitanism, on the other hand. Section 2 will present the main alternative to cosmopolitanism: 'communitarianism'. Again, it will start by providing a brief overview of the history of this concept. The focus will then be on how membership of different kinds of community can generate different kinds of ethical demands and on how these demands are to be balanced against each other. The second part will deal with the ethics of war. It will start by outlining the central tenets of the three main ethical traditions with respect to war issues: realism, pacifism, and just war theory. Equipped with this theoretical background, it will then pay some attention to humanitarian intervention. Part three will address the issue of world poverty and inequality. It will consider whether our social and economic responsibilities toward the global poor entail 'only' that we work toward the satisfaction of their basic needs, or whether they also entail that we work toward the elimination of world inequalities.

2. Cosmopolitanism - Communitarianism

The debate between cosmopolitanism and communitarianism brings into relief a central issue in global ethics: the significance of individual human beings as such against the significance of certain types of communities (Brown, 1992; Caney, 2005; Dower, 1998; Thompson, 1992). While cosmopolitanism focuses on some morally relevant and independent characteristics of those individual human beings to whom one might relate (e.g., their autonomy, their needs or their happiness), communitarianism stresses the relationships in which one already stands. More particularly, cosmopolitan theories tend to agree on the following three claims (Pogge, 2002, 169). First, the ultimate units of moral concern are *individual* human beings, not collective bodies like families, tribes, nations or states. Second, human beings are *all equally* ultimate units of moral concern, whatever their race, gender, class, age, nationality, etc. And third, *everyone is under a duty* to show consideration for human beings as equal ultimate units of moral concern. In its most general terms, cosmopolitanism entails that our personal conduct, as well as the design of institutional structures, are to be assessed in terms of how they affect individual human beings considered as such (Beitz, 1994, 124; and 1999b, 519). Now, it is precisely the adequacy of such an external individualistic standpoint that communitarians will bring into question, arguing that individuals (including their ethical judgments) are fundamentally constituted by their community life. In their view, value stems primarily from the community, not from some independent characteristic(s) of the person, and the scope of one's primary duties is restricted to those with whom one already stands in some 'special' relationship, be it through shared understandings or through common social and political institutions.

2.1. Cosmopolitanism

Traces of cosmopolitanism are already found in classical Greece, with Diogenes the Cynic (fourth century BC) who famously described himself as a 'citizen of the world' and thereby seemed to deny that he owed special allegiance to his city of origin and to its members. It was later affirmed by the Stoics of the third century BC (e.g., Chrysippus) who liked to compare the cosmos to a *polis* governed by the universal reason of nature and the cosmopolitan to a citizen of the cosmos, observing the divine law of nature and acknowledging the common reason and equal worth of all human beings. The whole point of being a cosmopolitan entailed a commitment to serving the universal human community as best as one could and thus a readiness to also help people living outside of the city (which needed not mean that local attachments were devoid of moral significance) (Kleingeld and Brown, 2006).

The idea that all human beings everywhere form a single moral community enjoyed a marked resurgence of interest in the Enlightenment. So, in spite of their different philosophical persuasions, Immanuel Kant and Jeremy Bentham both shared the cosmopolitan attitude that regards individual human beings as the ultimate units of moral concern, places all human beings in a fundamental moral relationship with one another, and makes the moral legitimacy of institutional structures conditional on how they affect individual human beings as such.

Thus, in Kant's view, each person has an absolute worth in virtue of her humanity or rational nature (i.e., her general capacity to set ends and to pursue them by selecting appropriate means) and this standing imposes moral constraints on what all other persons are permitted to do. Acting morally is not a matter of bringing about valuable states of affairs, but is a matter of showing unconditional respect for the absolute worth of humanity. This requirement is expressed in the so-called Formula of Humanity: "*So act that you use humanity, whether in your own person or in the person of any other, always at the same time as an end, never merely as a means*" (Kant, 1996 [1785], 80; 4:429). In Kant, one also finds the idea that all human beings have equal rights to freedom and property, and that securing these rights requires that all individuals who can physically affect one another enter a civil constitution with coercive public laws, and more specifically, a 'republican' state. But this is not all, for Kant also insists that a state will not be able to secure the rights of its individual members as long as its own independence and territorial possessions are threatened by the existence of other states. Therefore, the same reason that enjoins the establishment of republican states also requires the establishment of an interstate rightful condition - with the crucial difference that Kant does not support the idea of a world state, which he deems conducive to tyranny, but that of a "*permanent congress of states*" understood as a "voluntary coalition of different states which can be *dissolved* at any time, not a federation (like that of the American states) which is based on a constitution and can therefore not be dissolved" (Kant, 1996 [1797], 487-8; 6:350-1).

Like all utilitarian theories, Bentham's theory is deeply cosmopolitan too. It might be viewed as resting on two basic claims: the first is that happiness (which Bentham scarcely distinguishes from pleasure) is the only thing that is absolutely valuable or good in itself, the second is that the morally right action is the action that most promotes the good (Ellis, 1992, Brown, 1992, 41-3). Taken together, these two claims entail that our basic duty is to promote the greatest happiness of the greatest number. When deliberating about how to act, 'each counts for one and no one for more than one': the happiness of each must be given equal weight, that is, no discrimination is allowed between one's own happiness, that of one's near and dear, that of one's compatriots, and that of distant strangers. Favouring the happiness of particular persons is authorised only if and insofar as doing so maximises the happiness of mankind as a whole. And what holds for personal conduct also holds for the conduct of states: their basic duty is to mankind as a whole - they may favour the well-being of their own members only if and insofar as they thereby best promote the well-being of the greatest number. This explains why Bentham can write that it is criminal if a "nation should refuse to render positive services to a foreign nation, when the rendering of them would produce more good to the last-mentioned nation, than it would produce evil to itself" (Bentham, 2001 [1843], 538).

As we can see, a commitment to the cosmopolitan ideal of world citizenship has implications for the kind of political institutions that can claim moral legitimacy. But a further question is whether the realisation of this ideal also requires the establishment of specific supra-state legal and political arrangements. Contemporary cosmopolitan thinkers frequently distinguish between what they call 'moral' and 'institutional' (or 'legal') cosmopolitanism, and deny that endorsement of the former, which consists in the affirmation of a set of moral claims, *logically* entails endorsement of the latter, that is, the affirmation of specific global political institutions - like a centralised world state or a network of looser regional political bodies (Beitz, 1999, 286-7; Caney 2005, 5, 152; Pogge 2002, 169). The kind of political structures recommended by moral cosmopolitanism at the world level will be a function of the empirical circumstances. If the existing states system happens to provide an adequate protection of individual rights or interests, then its acceptance is wholly compatible with an adherence to moral cosmopolitanism. Under present circumstances, however, a considerable number of cosmopolitans do argue for the need of deep global institutional reforms. Few of them have gone so far as to advocate the establishment of a world state endowed with the power to make and to enforce world laws and policies (Cabrera, 2004; Höffe, 2007; Nielsen, 1988; Tannsjo, 2008; Wendt, 2003). For the majority, cosmopolitan duties could be adequately discharged through the implementation of more modest forms of 'global governance' like a multi-level system of governance (Pogge, 2002, 168-95; Tan, 2000, 101), a global parliament

(Held, 1995) or 'global governance through government networks' (Slaughter, 2004).

Cosmopolitan theories can be further divided into 'moderate' and 'extreme' cosmopolitan theories (Scheffler, 2002, 111-30). 'Moderate' cosmopolitanism acknowledges that world citizenship is an important form of membership, but adds that it is not the only one: besides our moral relationship to mankind as a whole, we are also engaged in morally significant relationships with particular persons, relationships that generate obligations toward them that we do not have toward everyone. A 'moderate' cosmopolitan is someone who is prepared to constrain his local commitments by a commitment to taking into account the interests of human beings everywhere. 'Extreme' cosmopolitanism, by contrast, conceives of world citizenship as the ultimate source of duties: special relationships provide no independent reasons for action; special treatment and special obligations are justified on exclusively instrumental grounds, by reference to the interests of all individual human beings considered as equals (Goodin, 1988; Nussbaum, 1996; Singer, 2002, Ch. 5).

'Extreme' cosmopolitanism has been the subject of sharp criticism, especially from moderate cosmopolitans. Many have questioned its denial of 'non-instrumental' special obligations, arguing that the recognition and fulfilment of such obligations are constitutive of numerous valuable relationships (Miller, 2007, 34-6; Scheffler, 2002, 121-4). Friendship or parenthood *means* doing for certain persons things that we do not do for everyone - such relationships cannot exist between persons who do not regard them as providing legitimate reasons for preferential treatment. Those who reject special obligations on the ground that they do not maximise the general happiness overlook the intrinsic value that people attach to their relationships in their daily life. Viewed from the perspective of global ethics, the central question will be to determine whether membership of a political community - in particular, a state or a nation - can be seen as justifying special obligations between fellow members, and if so, to determine how these special obligations are to be balanced against global duties owed to mankind in general. It is with these questions in mind that we now turn to the main alternative to cosmopolitanism: communitarianism.

2.2. Communitarianism

Communitarian theories have in common an emphasis on the ethical life of the community. At their core is the idea that persons are constituted and find meaning in life by virtue of their membership of a particular community, and that they are therefore permitted, or even required, to show partiality toward their fellow members. Communitarians need not deny the existence of global duties: it is perfectly possible for them to acknowledge that all human beings are part of a same 'world community', however minimal, in virtue of their sharing a common humanity and a single Earth, and to accommodate (at least some) global duties (Miller, 1995, 53). Yet, they will generally consider these duties less demanding and less weighty than the obligations generated by more local communities.

Plato and Aristotle's political writings already offer some important contributions to the communitarian tradition. Man is depicted primarily as a citizen of a *polis*, not of the *cosmos*: his identity is forged by his belonging to a particular city, which is the primary source of meaning in life. Correlatively, living a good human life requires first and foremost protecting the life of the *polis* and helping its members, not serving the universal community of human beings (which does not mean that outsiders are owed no moral consideration at all).

Jean-Jacques Rousseau's interpretation of the social contract and his insistence on the ties that it creates makes it reasonable to regard him as a communitarian too. Rousseau's main concern is to find a form of political association that would enable individuals to unite while at the same time remaining free, and he believes this can be achieved if they contract to put themselves under the direction of what he calls the 'general will'. The 'general will', whose decisions are by definition just, comes to expression when individuals pursue the interests of the community as a whole, and not only their own particular interests. A political association reflecting the general will is therefore more than a collection of individuals: by acquiring a political interest in the common good, individuals identify with their community and regard the general will as their own will. This, Rousseau specifies, presupposes however that individuals are capable of exercising rational judgment, have the possibility of directly participating in decision-making, and are already united by some pre-existing social ties - the underlying idea being that they will be more able and willing to legislate for the good of all if they understand each others' needs, interests and values. The fact that the state, by protecting what individuals come to define as their own will, enables them to fully express themselves provides, in turn, a justification for its ethical primacy: it puts individuals under an obligation to protect the integrity of their state and to promote the freedom and well-being of their fellow citizens.

The communitarian idea that individuals truly find themselves by identifying with a political community is also supported by Hegel. He too conceives of the state as that community which provides a people unity, and thereby allows its individual members to fully realise their freedom. However, he locates the source of this unity not in the general will but in the constitution and in the institutions that define and permit the pursuit of the interests of the state as a whole. So Hegel is not a supporter of constitutional democracy, which he regards as reflecting and reinforcing division, but of constitutional monarchy, where individuals' wills are unified through the will of the monarch. In Hegel, one also finds the idea that the state cannot provide a satisfactorily ethical life unless it has other states to oppose itself to: it is when they experience external resistance that individuals reveal the distinct values that the state has inculcated in them and recognise the state as the very source of their individuality, thereby reinforcing its individuality and unity. It is therefore ethically important for individuals that the existence of both their state and the states system be preserved: insofar as the state constitutes them in their individuality, their primary commitment is loyalty to their state; and insofar as the individuality of their state is itself conditional on the individuality of other states, it is also imperative that other states be maintained in existence.

Nationalism represents a distinct communitarian position. For nationalists, like Mazzini, Herder, Tamir or Miller, it is not so much the state itself but rather the nation - understood chiefly in terms of a shared culture, history or language - which provides the proper foundation for a sense of collective political identity and allows political values like social justice and democracy to flourish. Unity does not flow from political relationships (like the general will or the acceptance of a common sovereign power) or from confrontation with outsiders, but from the assertion of the values, beliefs and practices embodied in the nation. Like friendship and parenthood, nationhood is also held to involve intrinsically valuable relationships which could not exist if special obligations between co-nationals were not acknowledged and acted upon. The nation not only shapes individuals' ways of living and thinking; by allowing them to locate their lives within a collective intergenerational project, it also enriches their lives (Miller, 2005, 39). It is therefore good for individuals to value their nation, that is, to preserve and develop their national identity and to pay special attention to the interests of their co-nationals.

It is important to distinguish between nations and states. Since nations are defined in terms of a common culture, history or language rather than in terms of a common political authority over a territorially defined group of people, their borders need not coincide with the borders of states. Members of a nation may live in different states and, conversely, a state may include different national groups as witnessed by the existence of multinational states. Now, like cosmopolitans, nationalists regard the moral legitimacy of the state as conditional. But whereas cosmopolitans base this legitimacy on individual rights or interests, nationalists bring into relief the right of nations to determine their own fate - states that undermine the ethical life of the nation do not deserve the loyalty of their members. Put more positively, the commitment to national self-determination translates into a demand to give nations statehood, or at least some form of self-government, and might therefore involve considerable reform of the existing states system. But in spite of these differences, nationalist and statist approaches all share a fundamentally community-centric perspective: whereas cosmopolitan approaches are primarily committed to individual human beings and to whatever political institutions best serve their interests, nationalist and statist approaches aim, as a matter of fundamental principle, at an ideal of equal and free political communities respecting each other's independence and observing a norm of non-intervention.

How are special obligations between members of a political community to be balanced against global duties between members of the human community? For radical communitarians, communitarian commitments cannot be reconciled with cosmopolitan commitments (MacIntyre, 1984). Some of them will simply deny that there are any duties outside the sphere of the 'relevant' political community; others, while acknowledging that there may be duties to benefit mankind as a whole, will argue that these duties are, as a matter of fact, always overridden by special obligations owed to fellow citizens or fellow nationals. Moderate communitarians, by contrast, will leave room for duties owed to all human beings in addition to special obligations owed to those with whom one stands in some particular relationship. So, most of them will agree on a minimal list of basic rights that ought to be respected everywhere and by everyone, especially negative rights not to be killed, attacked, coerced, deceived or stolen from. Nationalists will also typically emphasise the right of all human beings to live the ethical life of their nation and endorse a universal right to national self-determination. But as a matter of principle, moderate communitarians will at the same time insist on the unavailability of any overarching perspective from which global and local demands could be weighed against each other, and on the limits that individuals' involvement in morally significant particular relationships places on the content and extent of their global duties.

From the foregoing, it appears that disagreements between cosmopolitans and communitarians are in most cases a matter of degree rather than of kind. As long as they are not taken in too strong a form, cosmopolitan and communitarian insights and commitments are in large part mutually consistent. One could imagine a continuum with at the one end extreme cosmopolitanism, which assigns to all human beings the same moral weight, and at the other end radical communitarianism, which denies outsiders any moral weight. Between these two extremes, a multitude of more moderate positions are conceivable depending on the relative weight that is assigned to membership of the universal community of human beings and to membership of a local political community, and on the content that is given to their respective ethical demands. It what follows, we will have a look at how these two tendencies manifest themselves in specific fields of application of global ethics, and more particularly, when issues of war and world poverty are at stake.

3. War

Wars can be defined as *actual, deliberate* and *widespread* armed conflicts between political communities - be it states or communities intending to become states - aiming at resolving governance disputes and determining who gets authority within a given territory (Orend, 2006, 2-3). Wars are brutal and deadly events; yet, they have always been part of human life and the questions they raise are quite familiar: Can wars ever be (morally, legally or prudentially) justified? Is it not paradoxical to speak of an ethical way to launch or to conduct war? Is the ethics of war exclusively aimed at protecting the rights of political communities, or should it also take into consideration the rights of individuals? Over the years, reflection on the role that ethics has to play in issues of war has given rise to three broad traditions of thought: realism, pacifism and just war theory.

Realists are generally suspicious of the application of moral concepts to the conduct of world affairs (e.g., Hobbes, Machiavelli, Morgenthau, Thucydides, Waltz). States ought to respect the alleged rights of other states and of their individual members only if it is in their interest to do so; established rules concerning the waging and conduct of war may or even should be disregarded if adhering to them impedes the promotion of the state's interest. One of the underlying assumptions is that it would be irrational for a state to comply with rules of war if it cannot expect its opponents to reciprocate, which is likely to be the case in the absence of a supra-state authority capable of enforcing compliance with such rules.

Unlike realists, *pacifists* believe not only that wars can be subject to moral assessment, but also that wars are always wrong and therefore illegitimate (e.g., Holmes, Norman, Teichman). Some of them adopt a consequentialist approach and derive the unavoidable wrongness of wars from the unavoidable badness of their overall consequences - the benefits resulting from a war can never outweigh the costs incurred by fighting it. This conclusion could potentially be undermined by two lines of counter-argument: first, by questioning the way in which the costs and benefits of a war are measured and compared to each other, second by identifying some situation in which a war would produce more good than harm and would therefore be permitted, indeed required (on consequentialist grounds). Other pacifists take a different track and understand the wrongness of wars as an intrinsic wrongness: the reason wars are always wrong is that they always and necessarily involve violating basic moral duties, most notably the duty not to harm or kill other human beings. Some pacifists like Robert L. Holmes have qualified this claim and have located the intrinsic wrongness of wars not in the killing of other human beings as such, but in the killing of innocents (defined by Holmes as those persons who have done no wrong relative to the war) (1989, 186). By this qualification, they can accommodate the widespread belief that it is permitted to kill other human beings in cases of legitimate self-defense (on the ground that the commission of aggression causes the aggressor to forfeit his own right not to be aggressed). But their moral condemnation of war remains unaffected: since no single war can avoid killing innocents and since the killing of innocents is presumptively wrong, all wars (even self-defensive wars) are presumptively morally illegitimate.

Proponents of *just war theory* have a more nuanced appreciation of war: they typically hold that wars can sometimes be morally justified, namely, when they satisfy certain ethical requirements regarding the resort to war (*jus ad bellum*) and the conduct of war (*jus in bello*) (e.g., Aquinas, Augustine, Grotius, Vattel, Walzer):

a. Jus ad Bellum. It is broadly admitted that for any resort to war to be morally justified, a political community must satisfy the following six principles:

1) Just Cause:

A political community may wage war only for the right reason, and most notably, to defend itself when it is subject to an external attack and to defend other political communities when they are subject to an external attack. The just cause condition sounds relatively simple; yet, it contains several subtleties that invite dispute. A first question is whether war may be waged in order to punish a political community for its wrongdoing (e.g., Grotius, Orend) or not (e.g., Kant, Pufendorf). A second question is whether political communities must wait until they have been actually attacked before responding (e.g., Vitoria) or whether they may launch strikes pre-emptively when the threat of external attack is clear and imminent (e.g., Orend, Walzer). A third question is whether third parties have only a *right* or may also have a moral *duty* to wage war in defense of an attacked political community (e.g., Caney). Even the rightness of defensive wars is not unproblematic. Whereas modern just war theorists tend to grant all states a right to defend themselves against external attack, some thinkers reserve this right only to what they consider to be 'legitimate' states (Barry, 1999; Beitz, 1999, 71-83; Caney, 2005, 203; Luban, 1980, 167-70; Orend, 2006, 33-7; Teson 1998, Ch. 2). In their view, states have no intrinsic value: those that fail to satisfy certain independent criteria of moral legitimacy - those that fail, for instance, to respect the rights of their individual members or of other legitimate political communities, those that are not recognised by their people or by the international community - have no moral right to political sovereignty and territorial integrity, and therefore no moral right to defend themselves. Finally, it is worth noting that there is also some resistance against the just cause condition itself: some thinkers indeed contend that there is more to fear from a war waged for moral aims than from a war waged for purely self-interested reasons, because the conviction that one is fighting for the 'good' can lead to hatred and to a violence devoid of ethical restraints (e.g., Schmitt, Vitoria).

2) Right Intention:

A political community must enter a war with the intention to fight only for the sake of its just cause, not for the sake of other ends like revenge, occupation of territory, oil grab, etc. Although this condition has a long history, it has not always been accorded significant weight. The problem lies not only in the difficulty of identifying what a political community's true intentions are before it actually wages a war. Some thinkers have also doubted whether the goodness of one's intentions is of great relevance for judging the moral legitimacy of resorting to war. According to them, what matters is that war results in a better protection of rights, not that it is fought with the right intentions (Moellendorf, 2002, 122).

3) Legitimate Authority:

Given the likelihood of disagreements as to whether a particular war is to be fought or not, it is important that decisions be made by a legitimate authority, in accordance with a proper process.

4) Last Resort:

War is authorised only if all other plausible peaceful alternatives to resolving the conflict have been considered.

5) Probability of Success:

The war must have reasonable chance of reaching its objective.

6) Proportionality:

The costs expected to result from the war must not be exaggeratedly high compared with the expected benefits. This, again, raises the issue of how the costs and benefits of a war are to be measured and compared to each other. On the one hand, it may not be possible to tell in advance how long a war will last and thus what costs will be involved. And on the other hand, the question arises of whether the death of one's own soldiers should be treated on a par with that of enemy soldiers or whether a certain degree of partiality toward the members of one's community is morally permissible.

b. Jus in Bello. Standard accounts of the ethical standards that should govern the conduct of war focus on the following two rules: *a) Proportionality between the end sought and the means used:* the means used to wage war should not involve disproportionate casualties or unnecessary suffering; *b) Non-combatant immunity:* deliberate attack on individuals who do not participate in the military effort is wrong. It is important to notice that this rule prohibits not all, but only intentional attacks on non-combatants. Unlike pacifists, just war theorists indeed concede that some acts of war leading to the death of non-combatants may be morally permissible, provided at least that they satisfy a certain set of conditions (the so-called 'doctrine of double effect'): *1)* they are otherwise permissible acts; *2)* those performing them, while they foresee that they will result in the death of non-combatants, do not intend their death; *3)* the death of non-combatants is not a means to the end that these acts aims at achieving; and *4)* the goodness of the end is proportionately greater than the badness of the non-combatants' death. As may be expected, this doctrine has stirred much controversy: the moral significance of the distinction between 'intending harm' and 'merely foreseeing harm' is contested by many authors; so too is the idea that some end might ever be worth the foreseeable killing of innocents. Another line of questioning concerns the moral foundation of the 'non-combatant immunity' rule: given its fundamentally individualistic character, it might be wondered whether endorsing it does not commit us to endorsing a cosmopolitan approach to the ethics of war. How could a prohibition on the deliberate killing of innocent persons spring from community-centric arguments, concerned primarily with the rights of states or nations? It could be pointed out that such killing is likely to encourage similar conduct on the part of enemies, to raise new enemies, and to make a peaceful termination of war more difficult to attain. But it is important to see that these reasons, however sound they may be, are merely prudential, not moral: the deliberate killing of innocents is inadvisable, but not morally prohibited; and situations are conceivable in which it would, on balance, promote the interest of its perpetrators and thus be justified. A moral alternative account of the 'non-combatant immunity' rule rests on the cosmopolitan idea that persons have an unconditional worth that in a certain way transcends their concrete connections to the war effort (e.g., their membership of an enemy political community, their political convictions or economic role) and which must be protected during war, at least if they do not pose serious threats to the lives of other persons (Slim, 2003).

The tension between the rights of individuals and the rights of political communities is also at the core of the ongoing debate on humanitarian intervention. Humanitarian intervention can be defined as the use of force by a state or group of states within the jurisdiction of another state, without its permission, and with the aim of protecting its population from violence committed or permitted by its government. In order to maintain certain continuity with the preceding section, I will here work with a narrow definition of humanitarian intervention, according to which interventions necessarily involve the use of armed force. But it should be kept in mind that several thinkers extend their definition to cover non-military uses of force too (like economic sanctions).

At first glance, humanitarian interventions look like ordinary acts of aggression: they involve the use of armed force, but not for the sake of self-defense, and thus in apparent violation of a state's rights to political sovereignty and territorial integrity. Their only distinctive feature is that they are intended to address grave wrongs perpetrated by a state against its own population (e.g., genocides, ethnic cleansing). The point will be to determine whether this feature can make a cross-border use of armed force morally permissible or not.

Insofar as pacifists believe that, as a matter of fact, no use of armed force can avoid killing innocents or doing more harm than good, they will be prone to condemn all acts of humanitarian intervention (Bittner, 2005, 207-13). Realists, for their part, while they need not disapprove humanitarian interventions as such, will insist that states should be concerned with another state's internal affairs only if it is in their own interest to do so. There is no point in protecting the basic rights or interests of foreigners for their own sake. From the perspective of just war theory, the central question posed by humanitarian intervention will be to determine whether the protection of innocents from domestic oppression or internal wrongs can constitute a 'just cause' for war.

A standard argument against humanitarian intervention invokes the communitarian claim that some communities are of primary ethical significance and have therefore the right to govern themselves without interference from outsiders. In its harsh form, it pictures humanitarian intervention as being nothing but a covert totalitarian imposition of Western individualistic values on all communities (Zolo, 2002). This should not be taken to mean that a communitarian defense of humanitarian intervention could not be provided. According to the communitarian Michael Walzer, humanitarian interventions can come to be viewed as morally legitimate in extreme circumstances, where there is obviously no 'fit' between a given community and its state (e.g., massacre, enslavement) (Walzer, 1977: 90, 101-8). His approach to humanitarian intervention hinges on the notion of 'communal integrity', which, he says, "derives its moral and political force from the rights of contemporary men and women to live as members of a historic community and to express their inherited culture through political forms worked out among themselves" (Walzer, 1980, 211). He agrees with cosmopolitans that states have no independent moral value and that the offensive use of force against them is not necessarily unjustified, but depends on the moral quality of their domestic institutions and practices. Yet, he departs from them by making the moral legitimacy of states conditional not on their respecting the rights of their individual members considered as such, but rather on their 'fitting' with the norms of the communities they represent. He also believes that, most of the time, outsiders can hardly make out whether there is a 'fit' between a particular community and its state, and should therefore presume that there is one and avoid intervening. As a result, Walzer's position may come down to according sovereignty rights to states which cosmopolitans would judge morally illegitimate because of their lack of concern for (what they consider to be) basic individual rights.

Before closing this section, it is worth noting that humanitarian intervention might also be taken to contradict conditions other than that of the just cause. So, those who regard the protection of innocent victims of internal grave wrongs as constituting a just cause for war might nevertheless oppose acts of humanitarian intervention on the grounds that they are unlikely to succeed or that they would undermine the stability of the international order and thus incur costs that are disproportionate to their expected benefits.

4. World Poverty And Inequality

Can the 'fact' of globalisation have an impact on the nature of our social and economic responsibilities toward the poor? More precisely: Can "the growing integration of economies and societies around the world", as the World Bank defines it (Collier, Dollar and The World Bank, 2002, ix), give a new foundation to our duty to help those in need, wherever they reside? Few thinkers have denied that the global rich have a moral duty to help the global poor satisfy their basic needs. Yet, far more numerous are those who have contested that this duty could be understood in terms of justice and have preferred to talk of beneficence or of humanity. The underlying idea is that the imperative of justice presupposes certain conditions which are not met at the global level and that, for this reason, world poverty, however morally objectionable it may be, cannot be characterised as unjust.

Against this view, certain contemporary philosophers have argued that in virtue of the profound changes that have occurred in the world over the last decades, we have not only duties of beneficence or of humanity, but also duties of justice toward those who, in the world, suffer absolute poverty. Some have even gone so far as to affirm the relevance of principles of egalitarian distributive justice - and thus the moral necessity to reduce relative poverty - on a global scale. From their point of view, the current process of globalisation presents itself an occasion to rethink the nature of our social and economic responsibilities, and to critically reassess existing poverty relief initiatives.

In order to make a decision about the *scope* of egalitarian distributive justice, it is necessary to first elucidate its *grounds*, that is, to determine what could legitimate or even require the equalisation of social and economic resources. On this point, the distinction between cosmopolitan and communitarian approaches proves once again to be particularly helpful.

Proponents of strong cosmopolitanism argue that the content and justification of principles of distributive justice depend exclusively on morally relevant aspects of the person (Beitz, 1983, 595; Beitz, 1999, 203-4; Caney, 2005, 107, 110-2; Richards, 1982). As a general rule, they base their arguments on two kinds of moral premises. In a first stage, they put forth a certain conception of the equal worth of all human beings (e.g., the capacity to have plans, the possession of rational capacities, the possession of an effective sense of justice, the capacity to experience pleasure or pain, etc.) and which give them the right to be treated 'as equals' - that is, to be treated equally if they are equal in the relevant respect(s) and to be treated unequally if they are unequal in the relevant respect(s). In a second stage, they provide a specification of the appropriate distributive criteria, and more particularly, they specify which characteristic(s) of the person is (are) to be deemed relevant from the point of view of distributive justice. For some, it will be important that social and economic resource be distributed 'to each according to his needs'; for others, it will be 'to each according to his desert' or 'to each according to his contribution'. For 'luck egalitarians', the point will be to see to it that persons are not socially (dis)advantaged because of factors they are not responsible for (such as their social class, their race, their religion, their gender, their place of birth or their place of residence, etc.)

But if these are the sole considerations underlying the relevance of principles of egalitarian distributive justice, then the scope of these principles can only be global. If the imperative of distributive equality is grounded exclusively in certain universal and morally pertinent aspects of the person, then it must in principle extend to all human beings - independently of the particular relationships in which they stand and thus of their national, state or institutional affiliations - provided only that, through their actions, they can have an impact on one another.

Proponents of communitarian approaches, by contrast, contest that principles of justice could be formulated and justified without consideration of the nature of the relationships they are intended to regulate. According to them, the fact that human beings all possess a moral personality generates principles of egalitarian distributive justice only in appropriate empirical social circumstances. Unlike strong cosmopolitans, communitarians do not necessarily extend the principles of egalitarian distributive justice to all inhabitants of the world: the scope of these principles will depend on *1)* the kind of relationships which is said to generate requirements of distributive equality and on *2)* the existence or not of this kind of relationships at the world level. In fact, all communitarian approaches to the question of global egalitarian distributive justice present the same structure:

(a) Normative premise which explains why a certain type of relationships, and only this one, imposes requirements of egalitarian distributive justice:

--- *Relationships of the type R are a necessary and sufficient condition for the activation of principles of egalitarian distributive justice*

(b) Empirical premise which establishes whether this type of relationships does or does not exist at the world level:

--- *Relationships of the type R do not exist at the world level* versus *Relationships of the type R exist at the world level*

(c) Consequence:

--- *The scope of egalitarian distributive justice is not global* versus *The scope of egalitarian distributive justice is global*

The emphasis will sometimes be placed on the idea that distributive equality can make sense only between agents who sufficiently agree on the meaning and relative significance of particular social goods. From this point of view, egalitarian distributive justice presupposes a community of persons united by 'shared understandings' allowing the comparison and equalisation of their social and economic resources or opportunities (Boxill, 1987, 148; Miller, 2007, 62-8; Walzer, 1983, 9; Walzer, 1995, 292-3). But, most often, it is the sharing of certain social and political institutions which, for some reason, will be considered necessary and sufficient for the activation of egalitarian distributive requirements (Beitz, 1999, 127-76; Blake, 2001; Buchanan, 2000; Freeman, 2007, Ch. 8 and 9; Nagel, 2005; Sangiovanni, 2007). A distinction can be made between three kinds of institutional approaches to egalitarian distributive justice, and correlatively, three kinds of reasons for supporting or rejecting the idea of 'global egalitarian distributive justice':

1. Impact-Based Approaches:

Hold that the reason why certain institutions are the primary subject of egalitarian distributive justice is that they have a deep and pervasive impact on the life prospects of individuals. Now, given the undeniable impact that existing international institutions (such as the WTO, IMF, the World Bank, etc.) have on the distribution of social and economic resources within and between states, proponents of such approaches are also likely to be proponents of global egalitarian distributive justice. As Allen Buchanan has observed, such institutions can affect both a state's capacity to produce what its members need to lead a decent life and its capacity to decide how resources will be distributed among them; therefore, they should directly and systematically be subject to egalitarian distributive principles.

2. Cooperation-Based Approaches:

Hold that the reason why certain institutions call for the implementation of principles of egalitarian distributive justice is not only that they have deep and pervasive distributive effects, but also and more fundamentally, that they constitute systems of social cooperation. Principles of egalitarian distributive justice are aimed at defining and regulating the fundamental terms of social cooperation. On this account, a central question will be to determine whether a 'global system of social cooperation' can already be said to exist. For some, the answer is affirmative: they point to the existence of a network of global interactions organised by a global institutional structure and producing advantages that would not exist if states were self-sufficient, and conclude on this basis that state boundaries no longer delimit the scope of social cooperation and thus the scope of egalitarian distributive justice (Beitz, 1999, 129-53). Others, however, deny that the kind of cooperation found at the world level could properly be regarded as a 'system of social cooperation'. According to Samuel Freeman, for instance, social cooperation presupposes 'political cooperation' in accordance with the terms of a political constitution; and since there is no 'world political society' endowed with original political power, there is no global system of social cooperation that would require the implementation of global principles of egalitarian distributive justice either (Freeman, 2007, Ch. 8 and 9).

3. Coercion-Based Approaches:

Hold that the reason why certain institutions call for the implementation of principles of egalitarian distributive justice is not only that they have a deep and pervasive impact on individuals' life prospects, but also, and more fundamentally, that they involve a specific way of interacting with the will of individuals. The implementation of principles of egalitarian distributive justice is needed to justify certain forms of coercion to those on whom they are imposed. The two most prominent advocates of this approach, Michael Blake and Thomas Nagel, are critical of the idea of global egalitarian distributive justice: they acknowledge that existing international institutions are coercive, but they believe that the kind of coercion they involve is fundamentally different from that which characterises states (Blake, 2001; Nagel, 2005). So on the one side, Blake underlines the fact that it does not directly bear on individuals' lives, that it is not necessary to the protection of their autonomy and that it is not of the same kind as that involved in domestic private and tax law; and on the other side, Nagel stresses the fact that existing international institutions are not imposed coercively in the name of all those individuals whose life they affect, but act in the name of those states that established them voluntarily through negotiation. In both cases, the conclusion is the same: only state coercion against citizens needs to be justified in terms of egalitarian distributive justice.

It is worth noting that in spite of their divergences, institutional approaches to egalitarian distributive justice are all vulnerable to the same line of criticism. It might indeed be objected that the inexistence today of the 'relevant' global institutions in no way rules out that their development could itself be a requirement of justice. Making the activation of principles of egalitarian distributive justice conditional on the existence of certain institutional relationships can amount to arbitrarily favouring the status quo, especially when the reasons for their inexistence remain unaddressed (Abizadeh, 2007; Pevnick, 2008). Assuming that the inexistence of certain global institutional relationships is a political creation and depends as such (at least in part) on the interests and relative power of the parties concerned, it might indeed seem misplaced to take it as a reason for denying the applicability of global egalitarian distributive duties. It might instead be wondered whether the existence of certain forms of individual interactions - especially those that are likely to have a considerable impact on the life prospects of individuals - does not already call for the implementation of institutions governed by principles of egalitarian distributive justice in order to coordinate them in a way that is fair. If so, one could be heading toward a strong cosmopolitan conception of egalitarian distributive justice: the establishment of the 'relevant' global institutions would no longer be a precondition of the applicability of egalitarian distributive justice, but a means to achieve its demands.

A major contribution of the debate on global distributive justice has been to trigger a sustained reflection on the nature of the ties that unite us to the members of our political community and to the rest of mankind, as well as on their implications in terms of social and economic responsibilities. Because of their open character, duties of egalitarian distributive justice are undoubtedly more demanding than duties of beneficence or humanity. And insofar as they define that which belongs to each - and which each can use as he pleases, including in order to perform acts of beneficence or of humanity - they also seem to enjoy a certain priority. Yet, these two observations should not blind us to the fact that even if the inapplicability of duties of egalitarian distributive justice proves to be justified at the world level, meeting the demands emanating from principles of beneficence or humanity - such as the duty to respect basic human rights or to provide assistance to those who are in danger or in need - remains decisive for the survival of millions of persons.

BIBLIOGRAPHY

Abizadeh, A. (2007). Cooperation, Pervasive Impact, and Coercion: On the Scope (not Site) of Distributive Justice. *Philosophy and Public Affairs*, 35, 4, 318-58.

Barry, B. (1999). Statism and Nationalism: a Cosmopolitan Critique. In: I. Shapiro and L. Brilmayer (eds.) *Global Justice*. New York, New York University Press, 12-66.

Beitz, C. R. (1983). Cosmopolitan Ideals and National Sentiment. *The Journal of Philosophy*, 80, 10, 591-600.

_____ (1999) *Political Theory and International Relations (Revised Edition)*. Princeton, Princeton University Press.

Bentham, J. (2001). *The Works of Jeremy Bentham: Published under the Superintendence of His Executor, John Bowring*. Vol. II. Boston, Adamant Media Corporation.

Bittner, R. (2005). Humanitarian Interventions are Wrong. In G. Meggle (ed.) *Ethics of Humanitarian Interventions*. Ontos, Verlag.

Blake, M. (2001). Distributive Justice, State Coercion, and Autonomy. *Philosophy and Public Affairs*, 30, 3, 257-96.

Boxill, B. (1987). Global Equality of Opportunity and National Integrity. *Social Philosophy and Policy*, 5, 1, 143-68.

Brown, C. (1992). *International Relations Theory. New Normative Approaches*. New York, Columbia University Press.

Buchanan, A. (2000). Rawls's Law of Peoples: Rules for a Vanished Westphalian World. *Ethics*, 110, 4, 697-721.

Cabrera, L. (2004). *Political Theory of Global Justice: A Cosmopolitan Case for the World State*. London, Routledge.

Cohen, M. (1984). Moral Skepticism and International Relations. *Philosophy and Public Affairs*, 13, 4, 299-346.

Collier, P., Dollar, D. and The World Bank (2002). *Globalization, Growth, and Poverty: Building an Inclusive World Economy*. Oxford, Oxford University Press.

Dower, N. (1998). *World Ethics: the New Agenda*. Edinburgh, Edinburgh University Press.

Ellis, A. (1992). Utilitarianism and International Ethics. In T. Nardin and D.R. Mapel (eds.). *Traditions of International Ethics*. Cambridge, Cambridge University Press, 158-79.

Freeman, S. (2007). *Justice and the Social Contract. Essays on Rawlsian Political Philosophy*. Oxford, Oxford University Press.

Goodin, R. (1988). What is so Special about our Fellow Countrymen? *Ethics*, 98, 4, 663-86.

Held, D. (1995). *Democracy and the Global Order: From the Modern State to Cosmopolitan Governance*. Stanford, Stanford University Press.

Höffe, O. (2007). *Democracy in an Age of Globalisation*. Dordrecht, Springer.

Holmes R. L. (1989). *On War and Morality*. Princeton, Princeton University Press.

Kant, I. (1996). *Practical Philosophy*. Gregor M. J. (transl. and ed.). Cambridge, Cambridge University Press.

Kleingeld, P. and Brown, E. (2006). Cosmopolitanism. In E. N. Zalta (ed.). *The Stanford Encyclopedia of Philosophy*. http://plato.stanford.edu/archives/fall2002/entries/cosmopolitanism.

Macintyre, A. (1984). Is Patriotism a Virtue?. *The Lindley Lecture*. Lawrence, University of Kansas.

Miller, D. (2007). *National Responsibility and Global Justice*. Oxford, Oxford University Press.

Nagel, T. (2005). The Problem of Global Justice. *Philosophy and Public Affairs*, 33, 2, 113-47.

Nielsen, K. (1988) .World Government, Security, and Global Justice. In Luper-Foy, S. *Problems of International Justice*. Boulder, Westview Press.

Nussbaum, M. (1996). Patriotism and Cosmopolitanism. In J. Cohen (ed.). *For Love of Country: Debating the Limits of Patriotism*. Boston, Beacon Press, 2-17.

Orend, B. (2006). *The Morality of War*. Peterborough, ON, Broadview Press.

Pevnick, R. (2008). Political Coercion and the Scope of Distributive Justice. *Political Studies*, 56, 2, 399-413.

Pogge, T. (2002). *World Poverty and Human Rights*. Cambridge, Polity Press Cambridge.

Richards, D. (1982). International Distributive Justice. In J. R. Pennock and J. W. Chapman (eds.). *Ethics, Economics, and the Law*. New York, New York University Press.

Sangiovanni, A. (2007). Global Justice, Reciprocity, and the State. *Philosophy and Public Affairs*, 35, 1, 319-44.

Scheffler, S. (2002). *Boundaries and Allegiances*. New York, Oxford University Press.

Singer, P. (2002). *One World: The Ethics of Globalization*. New Haven, CT and London, Yale University Press.

Slaughter, A. M. (2004). *A New World Order*. Princeton, Princeton University Press.

Slim, H. (2003). Why Protect Civilians? Innocence, Immunity and Enmity in War. *International Affairs*, 79, 3, 481-501.

Tan, K. C. (2000). *Toleration, Diversity, and Global Justice*, Pennsylvania, The Pennsylvania State University Press.

Tannsjo, T. (2008). *Global Democracy: The Case for a World Government*, Edinburgh, Edinburgh University Press.

Teson, F. (1998). *A Philosophy of International Law*. Boulder, Westview Press.

Thompson, J. (1992). *Justice and World Order: A Philosophical Inquiry*. London, Routledge.

Walzer, M. (1977). *Just and Unjust Wars: A Moral Argument with Historical Illustrations*. New York, Basic Books.

_____ (1980). The Moral Standing of States: A Response to Four Critics. *Philosophy and Public Affairs*, 9, 3, 209-29.

_____ (1983). *Spheres of Justice*. New York, Basic Books.

_____ (1995). Response. In D. Miller and M. Walzer (eds.). *Pluralism, Justice, and Equality*. Oxford, Oxford University Press, 281-97.

Wendt, A. (2003). Why a World State is Inevitable. *European Journal of International Relations*, 9, 4, 491-542.

Zolo, D. (2002). *Invoking Humanity: War, Law and Global Order*. London, Continuum.

9

Kantian Ethics

Joyce Lazier

"Two things fill me with constantly increasing admiration and awe, the longer and more earnestly I reflect on them: the starry heavens without and the moral law within." - Immanuel Kant

1. Introduction

We've all experienced situations where a friend will ask us a question that we really don't want to answer, whether it be "do I look fat in these pants?" or "do you think my husband is cheating on me?" Figuring out how to answer these types of questions can be tricky. If you say "yes, you look fat" and tell the truth, your friend will be hurt. If you lie and say "no, you don't look fat" then you have breached the trust that you have built with your friend. The issue at hand with these types of situations is, "what ought you to do?" This issue is at the heart of ethics. Some ethical theories look to the consequences of your action to determine what you ought to do, and some look solely to what you personally will gain from the action. In this chapter, we will focus on an ethical theory that focuses neither on consequences nor on personal gain, but instead focuses on duty. This type of ethical theory is called a deontological moral theory.

2. Kantian Deontology

The word "deontology" comes from the Greek "deon" which roughly means "obligation." Deontological ethics is a moral theory based around obligation and not the consequences of your actions. If something is right to do, it is right to do regardless of the outcome. For example, if telling the truth turns out to be the right thing to do, then it doesn't matter if it will hurt someone's feelings. Never ask a deontological ethicist if you look fat in your pants if you don't want to hear the truth! The best example of a deontological moral theory is provided by the 18th century German philosopher, Immanuel Kant. Since Kant was the founder of this theory, the terms "Kantian ethics" and "deontological ethics" are often used interchangeably. The starting point for an ethical theory rooted in obligation, or a deontological moral theory, is how to figure out the right thing to do if the consequences of our action are irrelevant to the action's moral worth.

Kant begins his construction of a deontological moral theory by investigating what is meant by "morality." Three main points emerge from this investigation. First, Kant argues that morality must be a standard that all people adhere to. If some people follow a different moral standard than us, then those people cannot be held responsible when they act differently. If lying is not wrong for everyone, then we cannot condemn those who choose to lie since perhaps they merely adhere to a different standard. But this seems counter intuitive to "morality." What we want from a moral standard is some guide point about how all people ought to act, not just some people. We want morality to have legislative authority. Legislative authority can only happen if we all buy into the same standard. Imagine a court system where a defendant's own legal standard were as legitimate as the court's – the lack of a universal standard would remove the court's authority to claim what the defendant did was wrong. What good is a moral standard if we can't hold people accountable for immoral action? So since we need morality to have legislative force, it must be a universal standard.

The second point emerging from Kant's investigation is that morality is opposed to inclination or feeling. Sometimes what is moral to do is actually opposed to your personal feelings. You may really be attracted to your co-worker and want to cheat on your spouse, but cheating is wrong. Hence, you must not cheat on your spouse even though inclination is telling you quite the opposite.

Combining these two previous ideas, Kant's third point involves finding the source of this universal moral standard that does not stem from feeling or inclination. He concludes that the source of morality is reason. Kant argues that it is reason, not experience that discovers the moral standard. According to Kant, experience can teach us advantages that we might gain if we act or don't act in a certain way. Reason uses experiential knowledge as a background to make sure that we are not acting according to inclination or want but according to duty (or what the moral law commands). For example experience informs us that our best friend is a sensitive person when it comes to their weight and that it is to our advantage not to bring that subject up with that person. When our best friend, therefore, asks us if they look fat in their new jeans, experience would guide us to lie. However, our reason should take over here by correctly identifying this outcome as knowledge by experience and therefore making us well aware that lying is merely ensuring our advantage in the situation, it is not necessarily the right thing to do. Reason discovers the right thing to do by steering us away from inclination. It does this by utilizing what Kant calls "the categorical imperative." The categorical imperative will be discussed in more detail below, but briefly it is considering what would happen if the action you are thinking about doing were something that everyone did. What would happen if lying became the universal standard? Imagine yourself getting on a loudspeaker and announcing to everyone that lying is perfectly fine to do now.

It is okey dokey to lie away with no restraint or repercussions. So now everyone knows it is ok to lie and will do so whenever they want. What would be the result of such a universal declaration? The result would be catastrophic! We would not be able to trust anyone, nor would people trust us when we needed them to. What if later I fully intend to pay someone back if they loan me money but now they don't believe me when I say, "I'll pay you back?" By making lying a universal standard to justify lying in one situation, I've shot myself in the foot in the other. Given this catastrophic result, we cannot make lying a universal standard. Since we are amongst the "all" in that universal standard, we cannot lie in our situation. To put this scenario in Kantian terms, we must "act in such a way that we can will the maxim of our action as a universal law" (Kant, 1991, section 225). Acting in such a way that you can will the maxim of your action as a universal law is what Kant famously calls the categorical imperative. The maxim of our action is "I will lie." Can we will that maxim into a universal law? No, for the reasons cited above.

3. The Categorical Imperative

Kant's "categorical imperative" is the solution to finding a universal moral standard that stems from reason and not experience. The term "categorical" simply means all inclusive. That Kant uses this term should come as no surprise since it reiterates his thought discussed above that "morality is for everyone." Kant defines the term "imperative" as a law that represents an action as necessary. And, when you think of what you mean when you use the word, "imperative," Kant's definition doesn't seem too far off the mark. If something is imperative to do, then it is necessary. In order to follow the categorical imperative, you use your reason to think of what you want to do, exclude what experience tells you you might gain, and make the maxim of your action. Using our example, I use reason to discover that I want to lie, I use reason to exclude any personal gain that I might get from that lie, which in turn erases the details of my specific situation and helps make the maxim more all inclusive or universal, and then I formulate the maxim, "I will lie." It is important to contrast this with a maxim that did not exclude personal gain from our consideration. If we included personal gain in our consideration, the maxim would be quite different. It would read, "I will lie to avoid hurting my friend's feelings which will also help me." This maxim, however, is far from universal. Not everyone who lies is doing so to avoid hurting a friend's feelings and my gain in a situation is certainly not universally held – it is mine. So personal gain must be excluded from the formulation of our maxim.

Now that all personal details have been removed from the formulation of our maxim, we can apply the categorical imperative and figure out how we ought to act. Once we have our maxim, we universalize it, or see what happens if everyone were to adopt that maxim. You can imagine it as building a world just like this one except that in this world, your new maxim has forever been a part of everyday life. Using reason, you can discover what that world would be like. In the lying example, in a world just like this one but where no stigma is attached to lying, where everyone would lie and everyone would know that people lie, there would be no trust. Since trust is essential to our dealings with other people, we cannot will that this maxim become a universal law. Living in such a world would be maddening! Furthermore, it is inconsistent. In order for a lie to be successful, it requires an assumption of truth. You would not believe my lie that you look great in your new jeans unless you assumed I was telling the truth. What the categorical imperative brings into focus is that by universalizing lying, you make it impossible to lie since the assumption of truth is eradicated. The maxim collapses on itself and is inconsistent. A rational agent would not will such an inconsistency. Furthermore, you would be confounding your own interests. In passing such a maxim, no one would believe that you were telling them the truth even when you were and when you needed them to. No rational agent would freely choose to confound their interests in such a way. So, since your lying maxim does not pass the categorical imperative, you cannot do it. It is immoral to lie. This is Kant's solution to how to figure out what is moral to do without considering what the consequences of your action will be for other people.

It is important to note that the categorical imperative is a negative test. Maxims that do not pass the categorical imperative are immoral to do, but maxims that do pass it are merely permissible but not therefore the moral thing to do. For example, I want to add milk to my coffee and I ask myself if I can universally will that maxim of my action. So, I imagine a world just like this one where it is ok for everyone to add milk to their coffee. Well, the law does not collapse on itself (adding milk to coffee does not negate coffee drinking), nor do I confound my interests by making it universal (I will still be able to add milk to my coffee when I need to even if everyone else is doing so). So, adding milk to my coffee passes the categorical imperative. But, it would be ridiculous to then state that it is a moral imperative that I add milk to my coffee. Lots of things pass the categorical imperative: showering, eating, writing e-mail. But this just shows that the action is permissible. However, when a maxim does not pass through the categorical imperative, it is immoral. It is a negative test. Murder, for instance, does not pass. If I universalize the maxim to murder, I am essentially sanctioning my own murder if someone else wants to kill me. No rational agent would confound their interests in such a way, so murder is immoral.

4. Criticisms

The universal nature of the categorical imperative also means that once you figure out what is moral to do, it holds for all cases at all times. If you figure out that lying is wrong, then it is always wrong. Many critics of Kant's theory find this to be too rigid. Certainly, they protest, lying must be justified in some cases. A famous example supposes that Hitler is at your door in Germany during World War II. He asks you if you are hiding any Jewish friends. You are. Surely, the critics argue, it is morally justified to lie in this case. Hitler is evil, you know he will kill and possibly torture your friends if you tell him the truth. Certainly your duty to your friends outweighs telling the truth to Hitler. As a Kantian it is tempting to rebut this criticism by trying to tweak the maxim somehow, changing it from, "I will lie" to, "I will lie to Hitler," or, "I will lie to evil people." Imagining worlds with the second two maxims does not create inconsistency since the practice of truth telling does not collapse on itself since only evil people (and not all people) are being lied to, nor do I confound my own interests since I am not evil and people will therefore not lie to me. However, the second two maxims rely too heavily on experiential knowledge – the kind Kant rules out as the source for morality. How do you know who Hitler is and what kind of a person he is? Through experience. How do you know what an evil person is or how they would act? Through experience. Experience can only tell you what advantages you can gain by acting in a situation, but personal gain is not morality. Experience tells me that I should lie to Hitler because my friends will be saved and I will be happy because of it. However, this is not to be confused with what is moral to do. What is moral to do is universal and therefore impersonal. My maxim, therefore, cannot contain any experiential elements. It must be universal. So, tweaking the maxim will not be consistent with the foundations of Kant's moral theory. However, the Kantian has another available reply.

The Hitler objection is a cleverly disguised moral conundrum. Looking at the Hitler objection, it is easy to see that the morality of lying is at stake. Looking more closely brings to light that there is another moral issue at stake. This moral issue is aiding in a murder. In telling Hitler the truth, I am in essence aiding in my friends' murder. The question then becomes, does aiding in a murder pass the categorical imperative? The answer is no, for reasons similar to why murder is immoral. You would ultimately be sanctioning someone else to aid in your murder, which would confound your interests and no rational agent could will such a thing. So, what we actually have with the Hitler objection is an example of a moral conundrum. Either way you act, you are acting immorally. If you lie, you are acting immorally. If you tell the truth and aid in murder, you are acting immorally. In this situation, there is no way that you can act and act morally. Since you cannot possibly make a moral decision in this situation as a Kantian, then some other standard can be used to make the decision. Since you like your friends more than Hitler, you decide to help them and to lie. This decision, however, was not made using the categorical imperative. The categorical imperative instructs you not to lie. This decision was made on personal grounds since you had no moral recourse available to you (either way you acted, you were going to be immoral). Deciding in this situation to lie does not make it moral to lie – you have still acted immorally. It is like being presented with two bad apples and having to choose one. One is green and one is red but both are equally bruised. You choose the green one because you prefer green apples, but in so choosing you have not therefore made it less bruised. It is still just as bad as the red one. So, as a Kantian you can lie to Hitler (and most probably would), but in so doing you are not therefore indicating that lying is moral. It is still just as immoral as aiding in a murder, you just prefer your friends to Hitler.

Some might still object that it seems wrong to call lying in that example immoral since it seems like the right thing to do. However, this is merely semantics. Lying is, in one sense, the right thing to do, it's just not the morally right thing to do. In fact, getting a person to recognize that lying is still technically the immoral thing to do (while still choosing to do so) in the Hitler example is exactly what deontology strives for. Lying is never morally justified no matter how compelling the particular instances of a situation may be. This is success and not failure to a Kantian.

Remaining now are three aspects to Kant's moral theory that bear explanation: The motive of duty; obligatory ends; and respect for persons. The first aspect is the motive of duty. Kant insists that when you act morally, you must always be acting solely from duty and for no other reason. Kant argues:

> For what is distinctive of ethical lawgivng is that one is to perform actions just because they are duties and to make the principle of duty itself, wherever the duty comes from, the sufficient incentive for choice (Kant, 1991, section 221).

Acting ethically means acting from the motive of duty, not from the motive of inclination or want. Your reason to not tell a lie for example, is not because you want to do the right thing. This would be acting from inclination or want and therefore uses experience and not reason to determine your action. Instead, you do not tell a lie because you recognize that duty requires it. You know what your duty is by using the categorical imperative. Maxims that do not pass the categorical imperative imply a duty to not do that action contained in the maxim. Once your reason sees that telling a lie does not pass the categorical imperative, you then do not tell a lie because duty requires it.

There are a couple of objections that flow from the requirement that you must act solely from the motive of duty. The first one is how would you ever know if someone was acting from the motive or duty or some other motive? You could ask them, but they may be lying. You can never really know anyone's motives but your own. So, judging other people's actions as moral or not becomes difficult since according to Kant, in order to be acting morally you must be acting from the motive of duty. However, a large aspect of Kant's moral theory is maintaining one's own moral perfection, which will be discussed in more detail below. What you can know is whether or not you are acting from the motive of duty and therefore if you are truly maintaining your own moral perfection. Maintaining your own moral perfection is a vital aspect of Kant's theory and so making sure that you are acting only from the motive of duty is what is at stake here (and not whether other people are acting from the motive of duty).

This brings us to another objection about Kant's requirement to act only from the motive of duty: It seems harsh. It seems to require a pleasure-less existence. Who wants that? Surely it is ok to derive some pleasure from acting morally. Why is it so awful if I feel good when I don't tell lies? This kind of objection, however, misrepresents Kant's theory. It is not that you absolutely cannot feel any pleasure. Pleasure of all kinds is available in the sensory world and the world of experience, but this is outside the world of morality since morality should be derived from reason and not experience. So, in following a Kantian moral theory, you are not therefore committing yourself to some kind of robotic, pleasureless life. You can have all sorts of experiential pleasures, you just can't make moral decisions based on the fact that it will bring you pleasure. Furthermore, you can derive pleasure from acting morally, you just can't act morally because of pleasure. If you act from the motive of duty, you have acted morally. If afterwards you derive some pleasure from acting from duty, that pleasure comes from the experience of acting rightly and belongs to the world of experience and not the world of reason and morality. Kant merely cautions you not to let that pleasure you feel be the driving force in your moral actions. Sometimes, as Kant points out, it feels absolutely rotten to do the right thing, but you still must do it if it is what duty requires. Similarly, sometimes it will feel good to do the right thing but you can still do it and do it solely from the motive of duty. So, you don't have to become some sort of emotionless automaton in order to be a Kantian ethicist. The requirement is simply that you constantly check that your motives for action in ethics are only derived from duty.

5. Obligatory Ends

The second aspect of Kant's theory that bears explanation are the "obligatory ends," which involves the notion mentioned above of maintaining one's own moral perfection. Maintaining one's own moral perfection is is one of Kant's two "obligatory ends" coupled with the happiness of others. What this means is that according to Kant, maintaining your own moral perfection and seeing to the happiness of others are two things worth striving for. Not only are they worth striving for, they are the ends of all moral action. Kant claims that all action is for some end. I get up to get a drink water because I am thirsty. Quenching my thirst is the end of that action. I watch very bad reality TV shows because I need to turn my brain off. Getting pleasure at the end of a long day is the end of that action. These are two examples of non-moral action. Quenching my thirst and getting pleasure are ends derived from experience. Since the end of a moral action cannot be derived from experience, what could the end of moral action be if all action is for some end? Kant's answer to this are the two obligatory ends: one's own moral perfection and the happiness of others. What is the end of my not telling a lie – especially if it results in my friend not being happy? The end of that action is my own moral perfection. In acting according to the categorical imperative from the duty motive and not from inclination I have further guaranteed my moral health. That is a good thing according to Kant. What is the end of the moral action of giving to charity? The happiness of others. All moral action is aimed at one of these two obligatory ends.

6. Respect for Persons

The third aspect of Kant's moral theory that bears explanation is his notion of respect for persons. Kant argues that you must never treat another person merely as a means to your ends. In plain speak this simply means that you cannot treat other people as objects to manipulate in order to get what you want. If I lie to you because I don't want to deal with the hassle of how you will handle the truth, I am not respecting you as a rational human being and am merely using you to get what I want – a hassle free afternoon. All people because they are rational human beings require that you treat them with respect. This means that you cannot turn them into objects for your manipulation, or that you cannot treat them merely as means to your ends. Kant's defense of this notion is easy – using the categorical imperative, you cannot universalize the maxim of using someone merely as a means to your end. That maxim does not pass the categorical imperative since through universalization it would ultimately sanction your being so treated. No rational agent would will that their interests be confounded in such a way. So, you cannot treat others as merely a means to your ends.

An objection that arises about using people as a means to your end involves situations where a person is doing their job. For example, when I go to the cashier to pay for my groceries, am I not using them as a means to my end? I want to pay for my groceries and get home to make dinner. I use the cashier to get what I want, or as a means to that end. Am I therefore acting immorally when I pay her for my kumquats? No, and here's where a small word solves the problem. Kant states that you cannot use others "merely" as a means to your ends. Part of using the cashier is recognizing that it is her job to collect money for the groceries (which is why I go to her and not some random person in the store!). I am not turning her into an object for my manipulation, I am recognizing that she is paid for helping me and that she is required to do so. Yes, she is a means to my end, but she is not "merely" a means. I have not objectified her while paying for my groceries.

Kant's deontological theory is quite simple. Based on the two assumptions that morality must hold for everyone and therefore be a universal rule, and that the source of morality must be reason and not experience, Kant arrives at the categorial imperative. The categorical imperative states that you should act in such a way that your maxim of action could be a universal law. This is a negative test and is quite simple to use. For example, I have some extra money and I'm wondering if I should spend it on myself or give it to charity. Can I universalize the rule to not give to charity? If the world were exactly like this one where people did not give to charity when they could, what would happen? Well, I might need help someday and if I universalize the rule not to give to charity I would ultimately be shooting myself in the foot. So, I should give to charity. The maxim of not giving to charity does not pass the through the categorical imperative.

7. Kant and Other Ethical Theories

Besides being simple, Kant's theory also retains the positive aspects of other ethical theories while eradicating their respective negative aspects. Let's take Utilitarianism first. The great thing about Utilitarianism is that it is founded on a consideration of other people. After all, Utilitarianism basically instructs us to act in such a way that our actions will maximize pleasure and reduce pain for the most people. In following this instruction, you must consider the pain and pleasure of others. This empathetic nature of Utilitarianism seems like a fine way to start a moral theory. However, one of the main flaws of utilitarianism is that you cannot accurately calculate how your actions will affect other people. Utilitarianism states that you must act in such a way that ensures the greatest good for the greatest number. Or, that you should maximize happiness and reduce pain for the greatest number. On an utilitarian scheme, if I'm wondering if I should lie, I consider how my lie will affect all involved. This includes consideration of my interests as well as the person I'm lying to and any repercussions to anyone who knows us. In one situation for a utilitarian, lying is the morally right thing to do if it maximizes happiness and reduces pain. For example, I need to borrow money but know I can never pay you back, so I lie to you that I'll pay the money back so that I can feed my family of six. By telling the lie and getting the money, my family of seven people are made better off and one person, you, is not. Given that calculation, lying is the moral thing to do according to utilitarianism: there are seven goodies and one baddie. However, in another situation for the utilitarian, lying is the wrong thing to do. For example I lie to you that I'll pay the money back and then go and buy some cigarettes. I'm made better off momentarily but am causing harm to myself which will ultimately hurt my family and you are made worse off by not getting your money back. Given this calculation, lying is wrong for the utilitarian since there are eight baddies and no goodies. So using utilitarianism, lying is both morally wrong and not wrong depending on the circumstances. Obviously Kant disagreed with this principle. If lying is wrong, then it is wrong for everyone in all cases. But, utilitarianism has the following difficulty: how can you know for certain that your action will affect someone in a certain way? It is possible in the first scenario where I lie to feed my family that I justify it on utilitarian grounds – seven people made better off - but then the food I buy is poisonous and we all die. My calculations of happiness turned out to be way off base! Seven people were actually worse, not better off due to the lie. If I could've foreseen those circumstances, the calculations would've shown that it was immoral to lie, not moral! Or, in the second example with the cigarettes (I decide not to go buy them based on utilitarian reasoning because we were all made worse off), the person who purchases the pack of cigarettes that I would've bought wins a contest by the manufacturer and wins $100,000. I could've paid off my debt and put money in my kid's college fund with that cash. Seven people were actually better off due to the lie. If I could've foreseen those results, the calculations would've indicated that lying was moral, not immoral. Simply put, you cannot accurately know the future. You cannot, therefore, accurately know how your actions will affect other people. At best, you are making a guess. Basing a moral theory on such tenuous grounds seems irresponsible. However, other people certainly are affected by our actions and a moral theory should not dismiss this fact. So, how can a moral theory take into consideration the fact that our actions do not stand alone, that they will affect others, without trying to predict how particular people will be affected by our action? Enter Kant's theory.

Kant's theory retains Utilitarianism's notion that an ethical theory must consider other people's happiness but does so without requiring that people perform the impossible task of predicting the future. When you use your reason to consider how the world would be if your maxim of action were universally adopted, you are, in essence, imagining consequences of your action. But, unlike Utilitarianism, this consideration of consequences is abstract. You imagine people in general acting in such a way and imagining how the world would be with such a maxim in place. This does not involve accurately predicting the behavior of specific people, which is impossible. With Kant's theory, therefore, I can therefore consider my action and the affect it would have on others without having to be a fortune teller. Kant's theory therefore retains the positive aspect central to utilitarianism, which is consideration of other people, without having the problem that it is impossible to predict what the outcomes of your action will be on particular individuals.

Kant's theory also retains the positive aspects of egoism without committing to the negative aspects. According to egoism, you should always act in your best self interest. The basic tenant behind this theory is that one thing that you can know for certain is what is in your own best self interest. You cannot know for certain what someone else's best interest is and other people cannot know for certain what is best for you. Again, you could guess about others' best interest and you might get it right, but you could also be ignorant of some important details that would change your evaluation. For example, assume that I ask you if

I look fat in my new jeans. You think that I'll be hurt if you say "yes," so you lie and say that I look amazing. However, what you don't know about me is that I value truth over anything and would not be hurt by you're telling the truth – I'd just change my pants! You can never fully know what is in someone else's best interest. Therefore, by focusing only on the self, egoism has psychological force. It seems true that you can know, and that you should be concerned with, your own self interest. However, egoism seems to ignore the fact that your actions do affect other people. If acting in your own self interest ends up really hurting those you love and others, is it really a moral thing to do? Egoism appears to be incredibly devoid of empathy. Central to Kant's theory is the notion that a rational agent would not act in such a way that would confound her interests. This is very similar to the egoist's idea that you can only know for certain what is in your own best self interest. Is Kant's theory therefore devoid of empathy? No, because Kant's notion of "confounding your interests" arises after consideration of how your action would affect others if your maxim were adopted as a universal rule. I do not, under Kant's theory, consider only what is in my own self interest. Instead, I first consider how my action would affect others if my maxim were universally adopted and then I see if if it would confound my own interest as a rational agent. Therefore, Kant's theory incorporates consideration of others while also utilizing the strong psychological force of egoism that you can only know for certain what is in your own best self interest.

Finally, Kant's theory retains virtue ethics' idea that you must act in order to be virtuous, but avoids the criticism that virtue ethics does not give you a reliable guideline about which virtues to act upon. According to virtue ethics, in order to be moral, one must act like the virtuous man. It is not enough to know what is virtuous, in order to truly be moral, you must act. However, how do you know how to act? The theory states that you must act like the virtuous man. How do you find him and how would you know when you find him? You must have some standard of virtue in place in order to pick one man from another and say, "he is the virtuous one, I will act like him!" But, what is that standard? Aristotle, the founder of virtue ethics, suggests that the right action is the one that is the mean between the extremes. The virtue "courage" falls between the lowly "coward" and the lofty "fool-heartedly." Therefore one ought to consider courage as a virtue and attempt to act courageously and not cowardly or fool-heartedly. But this standard, once you really try to use it, seems ad hoc. Let's go back to the lying promise example. As a virtue ethicist, should I tell the lying promise to get the money I need when I don't intend on paying it back? We could assume that the virtue in question here is "honesty." To determine whether "honesty" is a true virtue we need to see if it is the mean between extremes. What would be the lofty extreme? Perhaps "cruelty?" And the lowly extreme could be "liar?" Maybe you came up with different ones? If you did, then there is no standard available to us to determine whose extremes are the right ones. Maybe it doesn't matter because we still have extremes and "honesty" lies between them.

However, the bigger problem with virtue ethics is that it seems like some of the extremes could also be the mean in other cases. For example "cruelty," our lofty extreme from above, could also be the mean between the lowly "dispassionate" and the lofty "sadistic" (sometimes you have to be cruel to be kind). This is problematic because "cruelty" is now both a virtue because it is the mean, but it is also not a virtue because it is an extreme. The fact that "cruelty," and others can both be the mean and extreme indicates virtue ethics' failure to provide a reliable guideline. Kant's theory, however, provides a reliable guideline with the categorical imperative. As stated earlier, it is a pretty simple technique that yields concrete results. Kant's theory also incorporates the message that one must act in order to be moral. It is not enough to figure out that lying is wrong. In order to be moral according to Kant you must then act in the way that the categorical imperative instructs. You must be motivated only by the motive of duty. You must not lie. Ever. Therefore, Kant's theory incorporates virtue ethics' notion that action is necessary for morality while avoiding the objection that it doesn't provide a clear standard of action. Kant's theory, therefore, is simple to use, withstands any serious objections, and incorporates the benefits of three major ethical theories while avoiding those theory's downfalls. However, it is a theory that is 260 years old. Can such an old theory be relevant today?

8. Conclusion

Today, more than ever, we are aware of a global community and a deontological moral standard is exactly what is required to help us sort out all of the difficulties presented by such a large community of people. Thanks to the internet and a wide variety of cheap, accessible information, we are more aware than ever that the global community is not homogenous. It is a mix of people of different cultures, religions, and races. We are also, therefore, more aware of the atrocities that occur on other parts of the globe: young girls having their genitalia mutilated, genocide and systematic rape of certain people, politicians from all over who lie and cheat. How do we make sense of all of these horrors? Relativism tells us that what their culture believes is right is right for them so we must let those people be raped (it's just not what we do here). Egoism instructs us to act in my own self interest but this seems to ignore the needs of those being raped or killed merely because of their race – especially if I am not of that race. Utilitarianism tells us that sometimes such atrocities are actually moral depending on whether there is an increased amount of happiness for more people. Virtue ethics doesn't really instruct us at all but calls us to action. Kant's theory, however, does give us hope. Using deontological ethics, we can accurately judge other people's actions as immoral and therefore hold them accountable. We can do so by utilizing the categorical imperative. Clearly no rational agent would universalize the maxim to mutilate female genitalia, or the maxim to perform genocide (that would justify you being killed by genocide if people decided that your race had to go), or to lie and cheat. These things are wrong to do. With a sturdy standard in place we can better advance the argument that these things must be stopped. How we do so is a difficult matter, but according to Kant's theory your own moral health is equally as important as the happiness of others. So even if you cannot stop these atrocities, you can in your daily life improve upon your own moral health and be an example to others. You can speak out against wrong action (as well as not participate in wrong action) and in so acting you are improving your moral health. At the very least, you have become a more moral person and are achieving one of Kant's obligatory ends, your own moral perfection. At the very most, if you are successful in stopping immoral behavior, you are helping achieve the other obligatory end which is the happiness of others. The objection that it might be impossible to get everyone to come to agreement about what is wrong is not an argument that we therefore should not try and stop particular wrong things from occurring. This is the perfectionist fallacy. It is true that not every teenager will follow the rule to abstain from alcohol, but this is not an argument to therefore not stop individual teenagers from drinking. If it is the right or good thing to do, then it must be done whether or not the ultimate standard can be achieved or if no one else gets on board. In conclusion, Kant's theory, which is often over complicated, is actually quite simple to use and provides a reliable standard for moral action which is more relevant than ever in today's growing global community.

BIBLIOGRAPHY

Aristotle. (1987 [350 B.C.]). *The Nichomachean Ethics* (Welldon, J.E.C. trans.). New York, Prometheus Books.

Caygill, H. (1995). *A Kant Dictionary*. Cambridge, Blackwell.

Gulyga, A., and Despalatovic, M. (1987). *Immanuel Kant: His Life and Thought*. Boston, Birkhauser.

Harper, A. W. J. (1988). *Notes on Kant's Theory of Morals*. London, Phelps.

Kant, Immanuel. (1991 [1797]). *The Metaphysics of Morals* (Gregor, M. trans.). New York, Cambridge University Press.

Kuehn, M. (2001). *Kant: A Biography*. Cambridge, Cambridge University Press.

Louden, R. B. (2002). *Kant's Impure Ethics: From Rational Beings to Human*

Beings. Oxford, Oxford University Press.

Melnick, A. (2004). *Themes in Kant's Metaphysics and Ethics (Studies in Philosophy and the History of Philosophy, Volume 40)*. Washington, Catholic University of America Press.

Pasternack, L. (ed.) (2002). *Immanuel Kant: Groundwork of the Metaphysic of Morals in Focus*. London, Routledge/Kegan Paul.

Sedgwick, S. (2008). *Kant's Groundwork of the Metaphysics of Morals: An Introduction*. Cambridge, Cambridge University Press.

Seung, T. K. (2007). *Kant: A Guide for the Perplexed*. London, Continuum.

Stratton-Lake, P. (2000). *Kant, Duty and Moral Worth*. New York, Routledge.

Sullivan, R. J. (1994). *An introduction to Kant's Ehics*. New York, Cambridge University Press.

Timmons, M. (ed.) (2002). *Kant's Metaphysics of Morals: Interpretative Essays*. Oxford, Oxford University Press.

Ward, K. (1972). *The Development of Kant's View of Ethics*. Oxford, Blackwell.

Wood, A. (2005). *Kant*. Malden MA, Blackwell Publishing.

10

Law and Rights

Claudio Corradetti

1. Introduction

The Legal, Moral and Political Dimensions of Rights

When reflecting upon rights, the first and often easily overlooked question to address regards the very dimension in which rights are placed. One initial distinction consists in separating three possible domains of rights, that is the legal (also defined as the positive), the moral and the political dimension. While these three domains are deeply interconnected, it is relevant to isolate each and to evaluate the problems and issues that they raise separately.

Suppose that the government of a fictional democratic state is ready to approve a new electoral procedure, according to which only those who raise a gross salary in excess of $50,000 a year are allowed to vote in national elections. Suppose also that this new law replaces an older one, which was inclusive of all national citizens of adult age devoid of a criminal record. As soon as the parliament approves the new law, groups of citizens gather together in public and start protesting for what they claim to be a profoundly unfair decision. One group, in particular, claims that the new law runs against the constitutional right of the equal participation of citizens to political self-determination. Another group claims that no political consultation has been carried out with the opposition before deciding upon the implementation of the new procedure. Due to the increasing protests and strikes, the Constitutional Court finally meets and proclaims the following verdict:

> Due to our constitutional principles, we have come to recognize that a certain number of fundamental rights must be respected by any legislative act of the government. These principles are indeed what we take to be our inviolable rights. Any derogation from them, unless a state of emergency is declared, constitutes an illegitimate restriction of the liberties of the constituent body, the people, who are the only legitimate source of the validity of our constitution. In the specific case, the parliament has limited one of our most precious rights, the right to political participation and democratic self-determination. This right also touches upon the right of dignity, which is one of the major sources of validity of our constitutional principles.

In a subsequent passage, the Court adds the following qualification:

> A legitimately elected government can modify some parts of the constitution, as long as these do not involve the limitation of any recognized fundamental liberties, as in the case of a modernization of the division of powers between the central state and its regions/counties. In these cases though, the government has to obtain a minimum consent from the opposing parties, a consent which is specifically determined in the number of two thirds of the members of parliament.

This fictional case (which does not take into consideration a specific constitutional setting, but rather concentrates on some of the features that different democratic constitutional systems might have) is instructive for understanding how rights can be claimed and enforced at different levels. The constitutional revision of a legislative body, the parliament, is clearly an example of the political dimension of rights. In a democratic system, the political exercise of rights is always counterbalanced by the constitutional check of the Constitutional Court with respect to proposed legislative acts. In this case, there is a truly legal enterprise, which, while often accompanied by moral considerations, has the primary objective of providing a reliable interpretation of what is allowed by the legal constitutional system. Finally, the moral status of constitutionally recognized fundamental rights is not only a matter of past discussions by the constitutional fathers, but also the central core of ongoing debates in possible specifications, extensions and applications of our existing rights to new ethical challenges.

Rights not only belong to different dimensions of exercise and speculation, but also fall within different categories defined by the content they protect: the right to have one's private sphere of action protected would fall within the category of civil rights, the right to vote within the category of political rights, and the right to freely access the job market could be defined as an economic right. Rights, be they moral or legal, also exhibit a structure and generate intersubjective connections by allocating subjects a set of rights-duties assignments. For instance, let us suppose that I want to purchase a car from you, and that we agree upon a certain amount for the purchase. While you have a right to receive the agreed amount, I hold the duty to pay you as established. This relation between rights and duties has been often defined in terms of "correlativity". Correlativity means that rights and duties are two sides of the same coin, which means that whenever one asserts a right, one can be sure that there is *at least one* corresponding duty. As explained below, the correlativity thesis works in all cases with the exception of the so called "imperfect duties". In these cases, as will be clarified, duties are not paralled by rights.

The basic correlative structure of rights becomes even more complicated in relation to the specific typologies of rights under consideration. Hohfeld (1919), for instance, has claimed that while the correlativity of rights and duties defines rights in the strictest sense, it is still possible to describe other sorts of interrelations to which rights give rise. Furthermore, the asymmetry between rights and duties is clearly represented by the so called "supererogatory" category, or that of imperfect duties. Take for instance the case of the duty to be charitable. While it might be morally relevant to be charitable, it is not a duty which follows from someone else's right. To refuse to be charitable is something that can be judged as morally deficient, but not as something violating someone else's rights.

This incomplete correlation of rights and duties, might become even more instructive if considered within a legal system where, under a certain interpretation, a space of free choice (autonomy) is granted by a system of recognized rights. Let us once again consider the case of being charitable. Not being charitable does not violate a legal right, but instead a moral imperative which is not paralled by a right. Therefore, it falls within the sphere of a protected choice, which nevertheless appears morally reprehensible. For some, including Waldron (1993), rights grant a certain number of open choices, and to have such choices reduced would consequently reduce our capacity for autonomy itself. One might disapprove of certain behaviour, but as long as one's actions fall within the boundary of recognized rights, we must allow that one can do as one wishes.

Traditionally, legal or moral rights are said to fall within the two main categories of *positive* or *negative* rights. Here the term "positive" does not refer to the legal status of the right considered, but rather to the active role that the state or citizens are called to perform. Conversely, the term "negative" refers to the passive role, the act of non-interference, that everyone is called to endorse in order to allow someone else to enjoy his recognized right. Due to the implicit reference to the duty bearer's behaviours, it would appear more appropriate to speak of "positive" or "negative" duties rather than rights. But perhaps we need to think whether this classification is satisfactory at all. Consider, for instance, the right to freedom of movement, which is normally taken as a negative right requiring no interference by third parties. Would it be at all possible to fully exercise this right if no positive duty was fulfilled by the state? What about if no infrastructural connections were established among cities, or no system of transportation was in place? It seems that the right to free movement, while not completely waived, would be severely limited. The overly simplistic understanding of the correlation between a right and either a negative or a positive duty needs to be integrated into a more complex picture, as the following scheme shows:

S having a right to φ implies S^1, S^2, S^n to be under correlative negative and positive duties (D- and D+)

This means that the enjoyment of a right to φ is possible due to the fulfilment of multiple negative and positive duties. The encroachment of such structural elements introduces us to a further kind of interconnection – the one between individual and group rights, which once again reveals how things are more complex than they may initially appear.

Kymlicka (1999), has tried to develop a liberal approach to group rights and the rights of minorities in general. He has insisted on the relevance of a diversification of rights, which has been obscured by a persistent model of idealized society inspired by the cultural uniformity of the ancient *polis*. The unified model of rights has often led to forced expulsions, segregation and violence against minority groups, calling for a reformulation of the theory itself. Following Kymlicka (1999), it is important to first distinguish between multicultural and multiethnic states at the theoretical level. Such a distinction amounts to the following: a multicultural state is characterized by cultural diversity due to once independent cultures being placed within a single state community, whereas the diversity of a multi-ethnic state is based upon the phenomenon of migration. In the first case, one has minorities that want to maintain their autonomy within a major cultural framework, whereas in the second case one has flexible groups desiring to be integrated within the dominant culture.

These claims are generally defined in the context of collective rights, but according to Kymlicka, they should not be seen as being in competition with individual rights. For Kymlicka, the very wording "collective rights" is ambiguous since, among other things, it suggests that collective rights are to be understood in opposition to individual rights. The solution to this *prima facie* opposition consists for Kymlicka in considering collective rights as the rights of individuals enjoyed within groups. This formulation saves both the collective value for the enjoyment of these rights as well as the ultimate source of individual validity of collective rights as such. How can one "have her cake and eat it too" ? Let's take the case of the collective right of the protection of language x of ethnic minority y. The protection of this right is very important for the survival of that ethnic group, as it ensures that certain traditions and inherited knowledge are transmitted to the following generations. It is really a key point for the survival of a minority culture and of a culture in general. But let's suppose that a community member, precisely in view of the internal protection of this right, is prevented from learning and speaking the national language. Would the strict compliance to a collective right infringe in this case upon the full exercise of an individual right? It seems, indeed, that when the individual is prevented from exercising freedom of expression and thought, collective rights clash with individual rights. Even though this is something likely to happen, according to Kymlicka's view, it is not the case that it must necessarily happen. Indeed, the perspective he defends believes that the final ground on which any collective right relies is the individual, and that even though such rights are finally rooted in the individual they can only be exercised collectively.

Kymlicka's move is indicative of yet another extremely important character of rights in context, that is, the profoundly conflicting dimensions in which rights happen to be claimed and enforced. Were social contexts such that only the violation of one right per instance was occurring, then there would be no problem in maximizing the enforcement of just one dimension over the others and coming up with an easy solution to the problem in question. Unfortunately, conflicting situations very often imply a conflict of rights, and this latter requires a *balancing* among the rights at stake in order to achieve a just conclusion.

From these initial distinctions, it is quite clear that there are two fundamental aspects one must separate when analyzing rights. The first concerns the possible theoretical subdivision of categories, functions, and justifications of rights, whereas the second regards the way in which rights are implemented. As far as the second aspect is concerned, a full exercise of rights is dependent on a system of justice, which is the precondition for what is traditionally defined as a "rule of law". The rule of law is a situation in which decisions are taken in accordance with a legitimate system of law production. This process not only has to respect a fair process of decision making, but it has also to comply with general substantive conditions of equality. Systems of representative democracies as we know them, even with their imperfections, are the most advanced political forms we have for the guarantee of a system of rights.

From the nineteenth century onwards, it has been the State, together with its institutional apparatus, that has acted as the exclusive agent for the enforcement of the law. Nevertheless, nowadays, we are subject to an ever growing number of systems and subsystems of international and regional institutions, which are actually endowed with the power to legislate either on specific international issues (as for instance in the case of the United Nations) or on competences that were once part of the activity of national Parliaments (as in the case of the European Union). Also, the relevance that the international order as a system of law is now assuming is strictly interconnected with the ever growing functions of international and regional courts. Some examples in this sense are the *European Court of Human Rights* and the *ad hoc* Tribunals for Rwanda and the Former Yugoslavia. These institutions are all empowered with legal sanctioning (the definition of *ad hoc* Tribunals is due to their specific and limited competence in time and space). The internationalization of the rule of law, as well as the internationalization of competences once in the hands of national states, is one of the most intriguing challenges that modernity is facing today. It is not by chance that academic scholarship and university curricula are orienting themselves more and more towards the so called "cosmopolitan studies".

2. The Legal Dimension of Rights

Hohfeld on Claims, Privileges, Powers and Immunities

One of the most traditional distinctions of categories of rights is Hohfeld's (1919) division of rights into the categories of claims, privileges/liberties, powers and immunities. Rights are classified in accordance with such categories according to the structure they exhibit. For instance, when I stipulate a contract for the rent of a house, I commit myself to pay a monthly sum to the owner and he commits himself to leave the house at my disposal. This contractual relationship, following Hohfeld, falls within the category of claims: A has a claim-right to φ against B and B is under a correlative duty to not prevent A from φing. Things are complicated when further scenarios are considered as, for instance, when a claim-right is defended against a potentially indeterminate number of people, and when such a right is not a result of an intentional action such as signing a contract. Hohfeld's analysis of claim-rights also takes such cases into account, since the correlative relation of rights and duties is only minimally connected to just two people, and they involve subjects (like children) who are unable to actively claim for their own rights. This shows that Hohfeld was well acquainted with another kind of distinction, that of rights *in personam* (a right keeping under correlative duty to just one other person) and that of rights *in rem* (a right raising correlative duties to a potentially infinite number of people), and that he regarded claim-rights as also including the latter notion.

A second category of rights is that defined in terms of privileges/liberties. A has the privilege/liberty to φ if and only if he has no duty not to φ. This means that whenever there are no laws forbidding or requiring A to φ, then he is free to φ. Whereas in the case of claim-rights, my right to φ gave place to a logical correlation to someone else's duty not to prevent me from φing, in this second case there is no correlation to someone else's duties, since my being at liberty to φ implies a logical absence of a duty not to φ.

Finally, the third and fourth categories include, respectively, rights as powers and rights as immunities. In the case of powers, the capacity to modify a legal scenario is dealt with and, finally, in the case of immunities, a legal dispensation from being under someone else's power is covered. It is important to refer to the legal dimension of recognized powers since it is the only case of recognized powers that gives place to an opposing relationship of disability.

Take for instance the right to vote, to stipulate a contract, or to start a business. These rights fall within the class of *powers*. Whenever a power is recognized, as in the case of the power of law production to members of parliament, it follows that a correlative relation of compliance and liability is placed to all those falling within the sphere of exercise of that power. The intersubjective dynamics of power entitlement foresees that for A to have a power to φ with respect to B implies B being under a relation of liability to φ with respect to A. Further, power entitlements introduce new abilities in the socio-legal interplay, and therefore they allow for the possibility to alter a legal status.

Whenever a certain power is lacking, it is possible to talk about someone's immunity from a legal power, so that B has immunity whenever A lacks the ability to modify B's legal status. Such a relation can be described in terms of the following formula: *A* has immunity towards *B* with respect to φ, which implies that *B* has no power to φ with respect to *A*.

Take for instance the case of any legislative body within a liberal democracy being prevented from legislating against certain freedoms. In this case, it might be said that citizens have certain immunities which cannot be overcome, even by any legitimately elected government. The following scheme summarizes the relations presented so far:

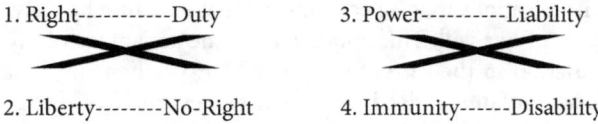

1. Right-----------Duty   3. Power----------Liability

2. Liberty--------No-Right   4. Immunity------Disability

Hohfeld's distinctions are based on analytical implications, that is, they are true by definition. It is analytically true, for Hohfeld, that there is a necessary correlation between rights and duties. This means that any attempt to criticize these correlations on the basis of empirical evidences is unjustified. McCormick (1977 and 1982), for instance, has claimed that Hohfeld's correlative axiom between rights and duties is liable to criticism in virtue of the fact that a right is not simply a notion generated from the idea of duties, but rather a concept which confers subjects certain benefits. This means that rights do not exist simply on the basis of the prior existence of duties (McCormick 1977, 199). On the contrary, they provide necessary reasons for the conferral of certain duties. If this is the case, then the hierarchical relation between rights and duties is reversed, since it is on the basis of the reasons provided by rights that it is possible to correlate a certain number of duties.

This final point, which highlights the different possible interpretations one can grant to the spheres protected by rights, leads to the consideration of two interpretatively adversarial positions in legal theory: Will Theory and Interest Theory.

2.1 The Functions of Rights: Will Theory *Versus* Interest Theory

Hohfeld believed that the four typologies of rights could all be conceived as protecting a certain number of fundamental interests or benefits. Were one of the legally recognized rights not beneficial to anyone, then it would be meaningless to consider it a right.

One fundamental issue that has inflamed contemporary debate in legal theory is that pertaining to the specific functions of rights. There are two main trends at stake, the so called 'Will Theory' and the 'Interest Theory', each claiming to be an exhaustive explanation of the function of rights. Where the Will Theory defends a view in which rights protect a power of the subject to control and waive the fulfilment of someone else's duty, the Interest Theory claims that rights protect interests whose relevance is independent from the power control of the subject of those rights. In the first case, to have rights is to be empowered with the capacity to determine which duties bearers must follow, or abstain from following. In the second case, the protection of an interest is independent from the will of a right holder, that is, the protection of an interest is due to the cogency of the interest itself. That an interest is recognized as relevant on the basis of the moral implications that it bears, means that it cannot be waived by a subject on the basis of her will. This approach has the advantage of offering a satisfactory explanation in the case of temporarily or permanently disabled people, or in the case of infants. Indeed, in such instances, one faces the case of defective or absent wills incapable of claiming or waiving a right so that it seems relevant to recognize interests independently from the actual subjects' capacities to exercise their will. This point represents an advantage of the Interest Theory over the Will Theory, since this latter is not capable of providing an explanation for such difficult cases. However, the Interest Theory also encounters some problems. For instance, some have noted that there might be interests that do not represent rights, and there might be rights whose motivations do not consist in the protection of interests. Take, for example, the case of third party beneficiaries, as famously stated by Hart: "if I promise someone I will take care of her mother, I generate a situation where it is the promisee who holds the right, whereas her mother is the beneficiary of my promise" (Hart, 1982, 187ff). Here it seems that right and interest are disjoined, and thus incapable of providing a satisfactory explanation of the function performed by rights. A different case is represented by those scenarios in which a public officer, such as a judge, has the right to send someone to prison without having a specific interest in doing so. While such cases might represent controversial instances, they nevertheless need further explanation (on this point see Jones, 1994, 31-32).

3. The Moral Justification of Rights and the Case of Human Rights

So far, I have principally presented the case of legal rights, which are the kind of rights that one can find in law documents such as Acts, Codes, Constitutions etc. A different, and much discussed case in the literature, is that of moral rights. A distinction to be made when addressing the issue of moral rights is the separation of positive moralities from critical moralities. In the first case, the reference is simply to factually existing moralities of a culture, whereas in the second case the reference is to normatively required rights. Whereas the first meaning of morality is based upon a *de facto* observation of what is actually believed, the second meaning refers to which moral rights would be agreed to, were we to decide freely on what should govern us. In this second sense what is deployed is a very common philosophical strategy, that of *counterfactuality*, where a hypothetical scenario is imagined in order to decide what rights would be agreed upon.

Moral rights, while they may be thought of as exhibiting a similar function to that of legal rights, do not rely on the authority that courts and legislatures might have on the basis of powers conferred by further legal rights, but on the philosophical understanding of the ethical concepts that are the basis of the legitimacy of the state itself. Indeed, it seems that even the same conferral of authority to a parliamentary body by the constituent power (the People) implies that certain moral constraints are respected by the former, such as certain ethical requirements definable in terms of human rights. Many philosophers, such as Hobbes' in his *Leviathan*, have thought that a sovereign can legitimately promulgate laws, as long as he does not arbitrarily violate the life and the security of his citizens. Very concisely, this means that the legitimacy of power is dependent upon the fulfilment of certain conditions that are defined in moral terms. These moral constraints have traditionally been defined in terms of "natural law" principles. Natural law principles consist in a set of unavoidable constraints valid by nature, that is, independently from any deliberative agreement upon them, and as principles whose disruption would make illegitimate any enacted law (a more detailed account of this notion will be provided in the following paragraph).

Possible philosophical strategies pursued for the justification of natural law not only affect the extent to which natural law principles may be applied, but also the same normative status of the principles involved. Indeed, the same notion of natural law has been regarded by modern philosophers as an untenable position for the defence of the moral determinants of law and different forms of justifications. Some contemporary philosophy has reacted against traditional natural law doctrines by proposing "post-metaphysical" theories for rights and human rights. To assert a post-metaphysical theory means to attempt at a justificatory strategy that refuses any first principles upon which a system must rely. Post-metaphysical views are those which do not admit "foundations" in the traditional sense, but which rather prefer speaking of validation procedures and anti-foundational explanations. An intuitive image explaining the perspective adopted by post-metaphysical theories is that adopted by Quine's example of Neurath's boat. This is a boat floating in a landless sea which can be repaired only from within the boat itself and through the same material available on board. As an image, it represents the epistemological status of science as well as its non transcendent foundation. If translated into the recent reflection upon human rights moral status, the Neurath's boat can become instructive in the understanding of Habermas' notion of "co-implication between popular sovereignty and human rights" (1998a). Habermas describes this co-implication in the following terms:

> The desired internal relation between human rights and popular sovereignty consists in this: human rights institutionalize the communicative conditions for a reasonable political will-formation. Rights, which make the exercise of popular sovereignty *possible*, cannot be imposed on this practice like external constraints. To be sure, this claim is *immediately* plausible only for political rights, that is, the rights of communication and participation; it is not so obvious for the classical human rights that guarantee the citizen's private autonomy (Habermas, 1998b, 160).

As is made clear here, the justification of human rights does not rely on a divine source of natural law, nor in any metaphysical view of the "inherent dignity" of man, as stated in several declarations based upon natural law perspectives, such as the *Universal Declaration of Human Rights* (1948). Instead, human rights are viewed as necessary conditions for the discursive participation in the formation of a political decision whose structural property resides in being as rational as possible. If human rights are conceived as an "institutionalization" of the discursive practice, then the plurality of agents' views must respect certain constraints. To respect certain constraints means to satisfy certain conditions of non-contradiction or non-infringement of the rights of the others. Only those speeches which fulfil such conditions can be admitted within a democratic public sphere, where "reasonability" (that is, openness to others' views and perspective), constitutes an essential requisite. Habermas' position, though, is more subtle than this. He claims that human rights show both the property of being *pragmatic* and *transcendental* in their status. They are pragmatic, in as much as they are embedded in discourses themselves, whereas they show a character of transcendentality due to the fact that they stand as prerequisites for the validation of any discourse aimed at achieving social coordination. This is a crucial point for the understanding of the contemporary philosophical debate in human rights and its full elucidation deserves more consideration. In order to understand the multiplicity of the sources of validity for legal rights, it is necessary to make an enquiry into the possible determinants of law. In the following section I will propose a classification of the most relevant determinants of law. From this it will become clear how systems of rights can be classified according to different criteria of validity.

4. The validity of Rights: Inclusive/Exclusive Positivism, Critical Moralities and Natural Law Theories

The previous section introduced the idea according to which rights, and human rights in particular, should comply with some moral standard in order to claim validity. Further, it also introduced a distinction between those moralities based upon natural law moral constraints and those based upon post-modern approaches to ethics (i.e. Habermas' theory on human rights). While such distinctions quite distinctly depict the current debate on the justification of rights, they are not exhaustive of the spectrum of the possible strands of justification that have gained resonance in legal and philosophical debate. One of the main consequences of choosing one justificatory strategy over another consists in the political understanding of the role that rights bear in society. For instance, to claim, as Habermas does, that there is a strict interconnection between rights and democracy, has the consequence of constructing a political institutional framework where democratic communicative interplay has a central role. This is not the case for other kinds of justificatory strands. Indeed, in the instance of the already referred to case of Hobbes' Leviathan, the fulfilment by the king of a certain number of human rights prerequisites is sufficient for the exercise of power. The Leviathan, as long as it respects a certain number of inviolable principles, can legitimately exercise its power towards the citizens. As is clear from such example, there is no necessary correlation between human rights understood in terms of natural law principles and the democratic exercise of power. The natural law model of human rights justification does not require the development of a democratic institutional framework. This cannot be the case with the Habermasian model for human rights. In the latter, rights, and human rights in particular, are inherently intertwined with the exercise of popular sovereignty.

In the following paragraphs, the main focus of attention will be switched to the understanding of the different typologies of justification of rights in general. This will complete the overall framework required for the underpinning of the different levels of analysis on the basis of which rights can be analysed. When attempting an introductory classification of the determinants of rights' legal validity, one initial distinction can be drawn between those theories referring to the validity of law *according to its source* (also defined as the "pedigree" of law), and those referring to the validity of law *according to its substantive moral merits*. Whereas the first kinds of doctrines propose that there is a *conventional* relation between law and morality, it is still possible to further distinguish between those who place the determinant of law externally, and those who place it internally, that is, within a legal system of law production.

Doctrines following the first line of argument are *positive* law doctrines, whereas those following the second line are *natural*, or *critical morality*, law doctrines.

The following scheme provides an overall picture of the main determinants of law. While not being exhaustive of all possible models that might be provided, it classifies theories in accordance with four mutually exclusive criteria:

Let's start from the upper right subdivision. There, H.L.A. Hart's inclusive legal positivism claims that although there is no necessary implication between law and substantive moral claims, it is still possible for a system to introduce, *conventionally*, moral criteria for establishing conditions of validity within the specific legal system itself. The conventional relation between law and morality is dependent upon the *rule of recognition*, which consists in the social capacity to recognize something as being a binding rule. The rule of recognition operates within the social space, and it allows for *internal* acceptance by officials (that is, judges) of further new rules. The validity of rules is thus subordinated to their acceptance by a social body which, on the basis of the rule of recognition, transfers authority to new rules. This is what is known as the *separability thesis*, which claims that moral principles *can* be admitted as parts of the validity conditions for a legal system without being *necessary* conditions for defining something as being law.

Differently from inclusive legal positivism, which allows for a contingent relation between law and morality, exclusive legal positivism claims that morality is *necessarily* unconnected to law. Exclusive legal positivism, therefore, defends a strong version of the separability thesis, according to which there are neither necessary nor sufficient implications between law and morality. Law is a purely social and conventional fact whose validity turns on the role of the authority which provides reasons for action to the governed (Raz, 1985).

If one moves to the upper left section, then she can see that instances of the combination of an internal and a conventional criterion for the underpinning of a specific model of law theory might be found in Aristotle. In the *Nichomachean Ethics* (book 5 para. 7) Aristotle claims that natural law is an essential part of political justice, which is to be understood as something fixed and given once and for all.

It might seem that this position reduces the external character of natural law to the internal-conventional process of law production arising from political deliberation. However, such a reading is precluded by Aristotle's recognition that there is a distinction between, on the one hand, conventional laws arising from popular deliberation and binding only the deliberative body from whence they spring and, on the other hand, natural law relations among individuals that are not part of the same *polis*. Hence, it seems that the problem becomes that of finding a balance between the internal character of natural law and the conventionality and mutability of political law. The problem for Aristotle, however, is that he admits that natural law itself is mutable, thus introducing further complication into the understanding of its meaning. Here, an interesting interpretation can be found in Marsilius of Padua, who states that, for Aristotle, natural law is to be taken as grounded upon human conventions, but distinguishes itself from mere positive law because it relies on conventions that are universally valid. It differs from pure natural law because there can be specific political instances in which it is necessary to contravene such laws, as for instance when the survival of that same political society is at risk. Thus, under this interpretation, Aristotle's natural law is a conventional notion. As suggested by Strauss (1957, 161), one could even interpret the Aristotelian notion of natural law as not referring primarily to general principles of law, but rather to concrete decisions, so that natural law does not reside in general principles, but in specific deliberations. Generality can prevent the possibility of taking a just decision in a specific instance and natural law, so understood, requires the examination of all empirical evidence and circumstances in order to indicate what is just. If natural law is apprehended in this way, generality is implied within concrete judgments, and a degree of conventionality and mutability can be admitted within natural law theory, as a form of justified exception to what Aristotle believes to be the general aim characterizing justice: the determination of the common good.

Non-conventional natural law theories address precisely the point of convergence between law and morality, and the idea of a *necessary* interlinking between law and morality, which implies that wherever law fails to meet a moral standard it can be considered either as defective law (weak-naturalist thesis) or as not law at all (strong naturalist thesis). If natural law positions were all reducible to the strong naturalist thesis, there would be no scope for their compatibility with inclusive positivism. However, as already mentioned, there is another version of naturalism which does not consider legal codes completely conditional upon morality. This is the view advanced by weak naturalists. According to weak naturalism, a legal code failing to comply with moral principles can still be defined as law, albeit in an imperfect way. Therefore weak naturalism does allow an interesting connection with the form of revised inclusive positivism presented above.

Following from the distinctions between internal-external and conventional-normative theories, one can distinguish theories that view the normativity of law as springing from an external source and those that instead conceive of it as springing from an internal source. In the first case, one is committed to a metaphysical view which conceives of a specific ontological being as the source of legitimacy of morality and of law, whereas in the second, one may justify the morality of law on the basis of procedural principles, or alternatively on the basis of substantive principles.

Fuller (1969) can be seen as the most interesting representative of natural-internal proceduralism. Central to his view is the assertion that law is a "purposive activity", where to him natural laws "have nothing to do with any "brooding omnipresence in the skies" [...] They remain entirely terrestrial in origin and application". The natural morality of law is thus internal and procedural, the latter meaning that "a system of rules for governing human conduct must be constructed and administered if it is to be efficacious and at the same time remain what it purports to be". Procedurality means that law, in order to advance moral claims, must conform to certain standards, or "ways in which a system of rules for governing human conduct must be constructed and administered if it is to be efficacious and at the same time remain what it purports to be" (Fuller, 1969,

96-97). Law as a "purposive activity" can thus be conceived as achieving its functionalist goal only if positive standards guiding the production of law are respected. Fuller considers eight procedural pitfalls that, if avoided, guarantee the success of the law production enterprise[1]. He introduces such constraints by narrating a fictional story where a king, Rex, attempting to behave wisely by introducing reforms, completely fails to create a system of law. A system of law can be so defined only if all such conditions are respected, whereas a system ceases to be a system of law if only one principle is omitted. This does not prevent a system of law from conforming 'more or less well' to a standard of well-formedness; there might, indeed, be degrees of well-formedness to a supposedly perfect legal enterprise respecting all eight criteria.

A line of attack against Fuller's internal proceduralism is the one pursued by Hart, which claims that if law validity is simply depending on law as purposive activity, then: "Poisoning is no doubt a purposive activity, and reflections on its purpose may show that it has its internal principles" (Hart 1965, 1285-86). This seems to confirm that Fuller's internal procedural principles, while necessary conditions of the morality of law, cannot yet be taken as sufficient conditions. The morality of law, for Fuller, rests only on such constraints while aiming to remain neutral between the different goals each moral view might pursue. Even with the introduction of the concepts of reciprocity and self-determination, two unfortunate conclusions can be drawn: first, the validity of the theory cannot be accepted as remaining on a purely formal level; second, admitting the hypothetical case of a malign charismatic ruler, the eight principles do not suffice to guarantee morally constrained purposive activity.

Within what I have defined as the internal-normative naturalist paradigm, a substantive view of the morality of law is taken by Finnis (1980). According to Finnis, inquiry into the necessary and sufficient conditions for what counts as law is not relevant; more fruitful is establishing paradigmatic cases of what defines law as morally justified. Substantive natural law principles explain "the obligatory force (in the fullest sense of "obligation") of positive laws, even when those laws cannot be deduced from those principles" (1980, 23-24). This means that, in the case where a law disrespects such principles, it can still be considered

---

1   "The first and most obvious lies in a failure to achieve rules at all, so that every issue must be decided on ad hoc basis. The other routes are: (1) a failure to publicize, or at least to make available to the affected party, the rules he is expected to observe; (2) the abuse of retroactive legislation, which not only cannot itself guide action, but undercuts the integrity of rules prospective in effect, since it puts them under the threat of retrospective change; (3) a failure to make rules understandable; (4) the enactment of contradictory rules or (5) rules that require conduct beyond the powers of the affected party; (6) introducing such frequent changes in the rules that the subject cannot orient his action by them; and, finally, (7) a failure of congruence between the rules as announced and their actual administration" (Fuller, 1969, 39).

a valid law, but as long as it fails to be law in its fullest sense, it can neither ground individual moral obligation nor justify enforcement by the state.

Let us try to disentangle this view by reconsidering definitions. One can distinguish between strong and weak criteria of natural law with reference to two different interpretations of the following statement: "Necessarily, law is a rational standard for conduct". This claim can be interpreted either as meaning "necessarily, two plus two equals four", or as "necessarily, cars have four wheels"[2]. If the first interpretation refers to an all or nothing fulfillment of the definitional criterion, the second interpretation can admit the existence of imperfect cars which, while not being four-wheeled still fall, nonetheless, within the category of cars. Finnis' view of law falls within this second reading. He sees law as a multi-property category, whose validity is detached from substantive motivating reasons law might provide to agents. Once the paradigmatic case of law as endowed with morally convincing reasons is underpinned, imperfect law can be still thought of as valid, even if not as an adequate motivating standard for action. In order for law to be an adequate motivating standard for action, it has to be adequate in the eyes of a hypothetical fully reasonable citizen. A completely different route of justification is advanced by what I have called external naturalism. Several varieties of this theory can be identified, some of which extend beyond the strictly philosophical domain to occupy also the religious and theological domains.

Within the classical philosophical tradition, the most interesting instances are those represented by Cicero, Aquinas and Locke. This represents only a small indicative option for the many scholars who have advanced a theory of obligation on the basis of a classical theory of natural law. According to Cicero, for instance, an enquiry into the significance of natural law is strictly entrenched in an understanding of the significance of justice (Cicero, 2001, 35). By starting from the assumption that reason is the most "superior attribute" present both in men and God and that there is no people so savage not to be acquainted with the law of God, then, reason as a rule of the celestial body is the normative source of natural law. But once such an argumentative pattern is reconstructed through inferential reasoning, then the relation between natural reason and its attainment through the cultivation of men's virtues can be reverted, so to state that: "[…] Nature created all mankind to share and enjoy the same sense of right of which I may speak is derived from Nature […] if wise men, prompted by Nature, would agree with the poets that whatever touches humanity concerns them too, then everyone would cultivate justice. For all to whom Nature gave the power of reasoning have received from her also the ability to reason correctly. Thus has arisen law, which is right reason as expressed in commands and prohibitions; and from law has come justice" (Cicero, 2001, 38). There are at least three distinct definitions of natural law springing from this passage: (a)

---

2   On this point see Murphy (2005), 21.

natural law as just or 'right' reason; (b) natural law as an essence of things; (c) natural law as a law of God.

While under (a), a state of affairs can be assessed as 'right' if it is in accordance with nature, the law of nature, in turn, is the product of God's will, so that agreement with natural essences *a fortiori* constitutes concordance with the law of God. Compliance with law is compliance with the law of God and not with the written law of nations very often based upon a criterion of utility. Were utility to be the criterion for the production of laws, then, according to Cicero, not only would instability result due to ever changing perspectives on the maximization of utility but, most importantly, compliance to law as utility would not lead to the fulfillment of the criteria of justice.

Similarly, for Aquinas, the conception of natural law theory is constructed around two basic properties: God as the source of natural law, and natural law as an evaluative standard for assessing the reasonableness of human action (Aquinas, 1991, *Question 94 Prima Secundae*). From these two premises, it follows that compliance with natural law draws human beings into participation in God's eternal law (Aquinas, 1991, IaIIae 91, 2), that is, into the rational plan God has foreseen for his creatures as a design of providence to which men can freely adhere. Natural law principles, springing from the benevolence of God, are both universally binding (IaIIae 94, 4) and universally knowable by nature (IaIIae 94, 4). Upon rational reflection over what is good to do they are freed from evil sentiment and desires (IaIIae 94, 6). In these two authors it is possible to find the central elements that mark the focus of the classical paradigm for natural law, as developed from the Stoic-Scholastic tradition onward, and grounded upon the notion of *partecipatio* (participation) of human reason into the divine *lex aeterna*. The Stoic notion of *logos* as a cosmic form of rationality is thus reinterpreted in terms of the *lex aeterna* (eternal law) by the medieval tradition and part of the divine reason (*ratio divina*). As defined by Aquinas, the elements of the *lex aeterna* regarding men are then properly defined in terms of natural law (Aquinas, 1991, Chap.3 n.1, Ia IIae, quaest.91, art.2).

Generally, external naturalism promotes an ordered view of beings, placing the source of truth at the top of the hypothetical hierarchy. And even when not committed to a metaphysical-ontological ordering of beings, external naturalism maintains a metaphysical view according to which "truth is something out there", waiting to be apprehended by the individual subject; in other words, it is something objectively and realistically knowable. But the problem with objectivism and realism is precisely that they mistake an *epistemological* problem for an *ontological* one. Let us suppose that realism and objectivism are correct that there are "true facts out there". Does this compel each and every one of us to reach a precise, unanimous conclusion once our judgment is exercised? One might claim that this would indeed be so, "if rational moral judgment were exercised in the right way". But how do we assess which way is the correct way, if not through an argumentative discussion in which the best and most convincing explanation prevails? So, if the problem becomes that of making the best argumentative presentation of our thesis, in order to convince our counterparts of its plausibility, the fact that there is an objective truth out there, to be grasped, becomes irrelevant. The confrontation remains one between different opinions, tested in terms of which best explains the matter in question. If this is so, then the argument remains within the confines of moral and semantic epistemology, and does not touch upon questions of metaphysics.

5. Conclusion.

The New Frontiers of Rights: Rights and Gen-Ethics

In this chapter I have presented a number of central features of rights, such as their structure, function and dimensions (legal and/or moral). The relevance of the distinctions here introduced is dependent upon the explicative force they maintain through ongoing progressions on the side of social arrangement and technological innovation. Therefore, right-categories not only *can* be revised whenever they become obsolete, but they *must* be modified in order to allow for a better grasp of the situation they aim at underpinning.

Take the present innovations in the medical field; the above-mentioned classifications are significant only as long as they can cope with the ongoing challenges on rights coming from recent developments in biotechnology. For this reason, yet further categories and notions that were not previously part of our understanding of rights have been adjoined. The *Unesco Universal Declaration on Bioethics and Human Rights* (2005) has attempted, indeed, to provide a guide to such new frontiers. One relevant case is that of research genomics, the medical branch concerned with the study of the genome and with those diseases connected to our genetic patrimony. When contextualizing rights in genetic practice, there is an unavoidable clash between scientific advancements and respect for patients' autonomy and dignity. Since science cannot operate outside an ethical covenant with society, ongoing involvement of individuals for the control and legitimation of medical practices is necessary. An interconnected issue is the balance between the respect of privacy and the right to health. Especially in research genetics, where analysis of the DNA is conducted purely for research purposes, it is very common to discover information pertaining to an individual's family group. This means that any conception of privacy based simply on individual privacy rights is inadequate for the protection of those people whose genetic information happens to be discovered through third party analysis. Further, even when explicit consent is sought, that to which the patient has consented is always characterized by *opacity*, or unforeseeable consequences[3]. This means that consent itself, while being a necessary requisite for legitimizing science research, can never be a sufficient criterion for the protection of patients' rights. To further the understanding of the limits of informed consent as an individual procedure of science legitimisation, different interpretive models of medical policy have been adopted. Some of the most successful have defended a notion of *deliberation* and suggested the integration of ethical committees on scientific boards. However, the problems connected to such practices are too complex to be introduced here. It suffices to know that genetic discoveries, while being of primary importance for the prevention and care of presently intractable diseases, expose us to possible risks of genetic manipulation and selection. A correct development of a theory of rights concerned with biotechnologies and genetic tests therefore has the primary task of avoiding such undesiderable risks without sacrificing the possible advantages one might enjoy through the improvement of his health.

BIBLIOGRAPHY

Aquinas, T. (1991 [1265-72]). *Summa Theologiae*, (McDermott, T., ed.). Allen Texas, Thomas More Publishing.

Aristotle (1998 [c. 350 B.C.]). *Nicomachean Ethics* (Ackrill, J.L., Ross, D.W. and Urmson, J. O., eds. and trans.). Oxford, Oxford University Press.

Cicero (2001 [c. 52 BC]). On the Laws. Book I. In Hayden, P. (ed.) (2001). *The Philosophy of Human Rights*, Paragon House, St.Paul.

Corradetti, C. (2009). *Relativism and Human Rights. A Theory of Pluralistic Universalism*. Berlin, Springer-Verlag.

Finnis, J. (1980). *Natural Law and Natural Rights*. Clarendon Press, Oxford, 1980.

Fuller, L. (1969). *The Morality of Law*. New Haven and London, Yale University Press.

Habermas, J. (1998a). *The Inclusion of the Other: Studies in Political Theory*. Cambridge, Mass., The MIT Press.

_____ (1998b). Remarks on Legitimation Through Human Rights. *Philosophy and Social Criticism,* 24, 113-36.

---

3   On this point see O'Neill, 2002, 44.

Hart, H.L.A. (1965). *The Concept of Law*. Oxford, Oxford University Press.

_____ (1982). *Essays on Bentham*. Oxford, Oxford Clarendon Press.

Henk, A.M.J. and M.S. Jean (eds.) (2009). *The Unesco Universal Declaration on Bioethics and Human Rights. Background, principles and application*. Paris, UNESCO Publishing.

Hobbes, T. (1998 [1651]). *Leviathan*. (Gaskin, J.C., ed.). Oxford University Press, Oxford.

Hohfeld, W.N. (1919). *Fundamental Legal Conceptions as Applied in Judicial Reasoning*. New Haven, Yale University Press.

Jones, P. (1994). *Rights*. New York, St. Martin's Press.

Kymlicka, W. (1995). *Multicultural Citizenship: A Liberal Theory of Minority Rights*. Oxford University Press.

Locke, J. (1954 [1660-64]). *Essays on the Law of Nature* (Von Leyden, W., ed.). Oxford, Oxford University Press.

_____ (1975 [1690]). *An Essay concerning Human Understanding* (Nidditch, P.H., trans.). Oxford, Oxford University Press.

_____ (1982 [1689]). *Second Treatise of Government* (Cox, R., ed.). Wheeling Ill., Harlan Davidson Inc.

McCormick, D.N. (1977). Rights in Legislation. In Hacker P.M.S. and Raz J. (eds.) (1977). *Law, Morality and Society*. Oxford, Oxford University Press.

McCormick, D. N. (1982). *Legal Right and Social Democracy: Essays in Legal and Political Philosophy*. Oxford, Oxford University Press.

Murphy, M.C. (2005). Natural Law Theory. In Golding, M.P. and Edmunson, W.A. (eds.). *The Blackwell Guide to the Philosophy of Law and Legal Theory*. Oxford, Blackwell Publishing.

O'Neill, O. (2005). *Autonomy and Trust in Bioethics*. Cambridge, Cambridge University Press.

Raz, J. (1985). Authority and Justification. *Philosophy and Public Affairs*, 14, 3-29.

Strauss, L. (1957). *Diritto naturale e storia*. Neri Pozza editore, Venezia.

Waldron, J. (1993). A right to do wrong. In Waldron, J. *Liberal Rights: Collected Papers 1981-1991*. Cambridge, Cambridge University Press.

11

Normative Ethics

Owen Anderson

1. Introduction

The study of ethics arises in relation to the reality of choice. As we make a choice, we are aware that there were other options and ask ourselves if we made the best choice. As we face future choices we ask "what ought I do?" The combination of this question and the realization that some choices are better than others leads to the study of ethics. Ethics seeks to answer this question by finding rational justification to answer the related question "what is the good" in order to know what choices are best for achieving the good. This field can be divided into branches based on different aspects of the question, such as *normative ethics* which simply studies the question itself (what ought I to do?), *descriptive ethics* which studies what answers people actually give to this question and how that affects their choices, metaethics which asks what we mean by terms like 'ought' and 'good', and *applied ethics* which seeks to discover if there is a moral law that can help solve concrete problems in contemporary choices. Although this chapter is about normative ethics, it is difficult to keep these areas distinct and we will of necessity ask about the meaning of key terms, think about how beliefs about what is good affect behavior, and seek to find solutions to difficult choices facing us in the contemporary world.

2. Objections to the Study of Ethics

This chapter will cover many different ideas without necessarily drawing the reader's attention to who said what and when. For instance, we will begin with the question "why study ethics at all?" Is it possible to make progress through this kind of study, and if it is, is it necessary or are there other better ways to proceed? An example of the claim that it is not possible to approach the subject in this manner is the view which says that the good cannot be known through reason.[1] This might be because it is believed that claims about the good are simply expressions of personal preference, or that reason is limited to the natural world and the good is not a natural object, or that the good is known through intuition (immediate perception) and not through rational reflection. Such objections are calling us to clarify what is meant by "rational justification."

When we speak about giving rational justification about what is the good, we are building on the reality that people give "reasons" for what they do. If a person has no reason for an action, simply a shrug, then such silence is not the basis for conversation. By contrast, we also recognize that not all *reasons*, are *reasonable*. That is, there is a standard for *rationality* by which we can judge competing *reasons*. If there is not, if every reason is equal, then, again, there is no basis for conversation and silence is the only option.

Given this, we can respond to the claim that the good is not known through reason but instead by intuition; by viewing it as one *reason* for a specific view of the good. Is "intuition" sufficient to justify a view of the good? What if others have competing intuitions? If there are competing intuitions, then the matter cannot be settled through intuition. A similar problem arises for those who claim that the good is simply an expression of personal taste or preference. It might be true that when a person says "I believe x is the good," that the person is expressing an unexamined personal preference, but can we go a step further and ask for justification? And are there competing personal preferences between which we must adjudicate? Any such adjudication or analysis presupposes that there is a standard for rationality that can be used.

And so we can respond to the claim that the study of ethics is not possible by noting that there are competing views of what is good, that not all views of the good are equal, and that people give reasons in support of their view and against other views. Yet there is still the claim that, even in such a process, we will never come to knowledge of the good. This might be due to the belief that knowledge is not possible at all, or that it is not possible in our present condition and we must wait until the afterlife. This raises the important question of responsibility and guilt. Do humans have a responsibility to believe and do anything? If we cannot know what is good, then we cannot know if our beliefs and actions conform to what is good, and so we cannot be held responsible for doing what is good. Therefore, consistency requires the person who says that we cannot know what is good to also maintain that there is no personal or communal responsibility. The reply might be that, while we cannot know, we can have probability or plausibility. Yet these become measurements of personal taste or opinion, and probability requires a known standard by which to judge what is and is not probable.

---

1   Popkin (2003).

3. Knowing the Good

Thus, we can proceed by assuming that it is possible to know what is good, and that the alternative is silence and loss of responsibility at any level. But is it really necessary to know the good? Examples of the viewpoints which say that it is not necessary to give rational justification for the good are the belief that the good can be achieved apart from reason (say, through faith where *faith* is defined as *blind belief*, or *belief without sufficiently supporting premises*), and the view that the intellect is not what is primarily important, but instead the problem is in the emotions or the will. The tension between *faith* and *reason* is an especially high profile and important problem and is worth spending some time considering.

It is often the case that the mere mention of *faith* and *reason* can lead to people taking sides based on other commitments. For instance, those in favor of this view of faith often hear the term *reason* as referring to how humans actually think apart from any religious commitments (natural reasoning about the material world). On the other hand, those who take the side of reason hear the term *faith* as mindless acceptance of superstition. We want to avoid both of these representations as straw men. Here we will distinguish between *faith*, *fideism*, and *reason*. Faith is the belief in what is not visible, but as such is not opposed to rational argumentation. Fideism is the acceptance of a conclusion on the basis of logically insufficient premises—it is often the result of accepting tradition or testimony. Reason can be defined in itself as the laws of thought (identity, non-contradiction, excluded middle); it can be defined in its use: we use reason to form concepts where we distinguish between 'a' and 'non-a', and then put these concepts into judgments and arguments; it can be defined in us: humans as rational animals form concepts, judgments, and arguments as part of their nature. Nothing in this definition of *reason* and *faith* places them in competition, although there are important tensions between *reason* and *fideism*.[2]

There may be times when people accept a conclusion based on authority, tradition, or testimony. The extent to which this is a problem is related to the level of importance of the conclusion. So, for instance, one may accept the authority of a newspaper on many topics. However, if the newspaper asks us to believe that the good is the acquisition of money, and what hangs in the balance is the very meaning of our lives, we would expect more proof than simple testimony. Thus, for that which is the most valuable and of highest importance (the good), we expect the highest level of proof (rational justification).

And yet, there are worldviews which maintain that the good cannot be known in this way, and yet if one does not accept certain beliefs or behave in specified ways one will suffer maximal consequences (for instance, eternal damnation).

---

2   Flew and MacIntyre (1955).

The contradiction is that while one ought to do x, one cannot do x. This is called the ought/can principle, and we will discuss it in more detail later. For many, this has been enough to abandon such worldviews. However, it is not necessary to abandon the worldview, but instead to abandon fideism, particularly in relation to what is of highest importance. If we cannot know the good then we cannot be held responsible for doing what is good. Therefore, if the failure to know and do the good results in maximal consequences, then the good must be maximally clear to all. This raises important questions about the ethics of belief.[3]

4. Culpable Ignorance

If it is clear what is good, and I do not know what is good, then I am guilty of culpable ignorance. Culpable ignorance affects making choices in two ways: first, the person involved is choosing what is believed to be good but is not actually good; secondly, and this is a mistake for which the person is responsible—the person could and should have known that what they are choosing is not actually good. This responsibility is inexcusable in that there is no one else to blame, or conditions that mitigate the guilt of this ignorance. An example of excuses that are offered for ignorance about what is good are that humans cannot really know what is good (we've sufficiently covered this already), or that beliefs about the good do not matter and that instead what is important is intuition, common sense, or some similar faculty. The problem with this excuse is that it misses the point that ethics is about choices, and that in choosing we reveal what we believe. So, it may be true that my choice is decided based on intuition, but this reveals my belief about the role and importance of intuition as an authority. I could believe differently about intuition and this would impact my choices. Another typical kind of excuse involves reference to the external conditions or environment, but this reduces to the assertion that the good is not knowable.

5. The Moral Absolute

If the good is readily knowable so that ignorance of the good is culpable and distorts all of our choices, then at this point we should be able to start discussing some formal features of the good to help us identify it. For instance, we should think about the good in relation to the other main concepts in ethics, virtue and happiness. As the end in itself, the good is the moral absolute—other ethical concepts are defined and understood in relation to the good.

There is a considerable tradition within ethical theory that focuses on "the right," or virtues. Virtues can be understood as a means to the good, and can

---

3   Dole and Chignell (2005).

be classified in various ways.[4] For instance, there are material virtues such as money or a car; and there are natural virtues such as a talent for music or physical strength. These are not ends in themselves but are means to ends. What about moral virtues, are they ends in themselves? Some thinkers, such as Immanuel Kant, have suggested that if a person is morally virtuous in order to gain something else then this takes away from the virtuous nature of the act. This is readily seen when the "something else" is a goal like money or fame. But is the problem in the pursuit of goals, or in the pursuit of the wrong goals? Money may not be an appropriate goal to justify behavior, but does that mean one should act without any goal or consequence? Rather, it seems that when humans act they act for some end (Aristotle), and the problem is not in this relationship (virtues for the good) but in a misconception of the good (the good is not money or fame).

Noting the necessity of acting for some end has lead thinkers like Aristotle to assert that all actions aim at the end of happiness. The idea of happiness has been understood in different ways, ranging from sensual pleasure to what is better understood as joy or contentment. Understanding happiness as a mental state keeps us from identifying it with sensual pleasure, but seeing instead that sometimes people are happy when they experience sensual pleasure (it is a means to being happy).[5] Indeed, this seems to uncover a truth about happiness, which is that it cannot be pursued directly but is instead the effect of possessing what one believes to be good. If a person believes sensual pleasures are the good, then that person will be happy when such experiences arise. If a person believes fame or power to be the good, then that person will be happy if fame or power are achieved.

These examples also bring to light another reality about happiness: there is a difference between lasting happiness and temporary happiness. A person who believes that sensual pleasures are the good will only be happy temporarily, because of the transient nature of such pleasures. The same is true of fame and power. And so, just as mistaken goals distort virtuous acts, so too mistaken beliefs about the good provide only temporary happiness. This is because these goals are not themselves lasting, and are not ends in themselves and so are not actually the good, or the highest good, the *summum bonum*. If a person knows and achieves the good as what is lasting then the effect would be lasting happiness.

6. Common Mistakes About the Good, the Right, and Happiness

The relationship between the good, virtue and happiness, if kept in mind, would prevent most mistakes that occur in ethical theory. For instance, it has

---

4 Gangadean (2008).
5 Aristotle, *Nicomachean Ethics*.

been common to search for a direct link between virtue and happiness. And yet it is commonly noted that the virtuous are often not happy, and the wicked are happy. The solution has been to postpone happiness until the next life, where the virtuous will be rewarded and the wicked punished. However, this solution concedes that there is no necessary relationship between virtue and happiness. Consequently, it has been the case that God, as a perfect judge, is invoked to guarantee the connection between virtues and happiness. This has led to another response where the supposed *virtues* that do not lead to happiness are rejected as slave-morality;[6] the lacuna that is left in the arena of virtues is then filled in various insufficient ways that are neither ends in themselves nor means to an end in itself as they are presented (power, authenticity, the absurd).

Building on skepticism about the good, or the belief that happiness is the good, some theories present an equation in which one should act so as to maximize happiness in the self and society (utilitarianism).[7] It is this view to which thinkers like Kant are responding because it seems to degrade virtue by making it something one does to be happy rather than valuable in itself.[8] This objection is recognizing that many things that are not virtuous seem to make people happy and so this equation undermines the value of virtue. However, even Kant reverted to some such equation in saying that our guiding principle should be to act in a way that we can will to be universal: this reduces how we should act to what we will, and since different people will to be universal different conditions, it does not provide a ground for a universal moral law.

Precisely because of this problem, the utilitarians will respond that our only option is to seek to maximize happiness, which seems to provide a universal ground for moral actions. And yet, if this approach is based on the assumption that we cannot know what is good, it becomes a kind of pragmatism where the maxim "whatever works/makes people happy" becomes the guide. As noted earlier, what makes people happy may not make them lastingly happy. Consequently, if people are encouraged to pursue what will only make them temporarily happy then the outcome is actually harm rather than good: people are pursuing what is not good as if it were good, and the result is that they achieve neither the good nor lasting happiness. The notion of "what works" does not make sense unless one knows the goal: "what works to achieve the goal?"

7. Identifying The Good

The mistakes of confusing the good with the right (virtue) and of pursuing

---

6 Nietzsche, *On the Genealogy of Morals and Ecce Homo*,
7 Mill, *Utilitarianism*.
8 Kant, *The Groundwork of the Metaphysics of Morals*

happiness directly rather than as an effect of the good can be avoided, but only if the good is knowable. In other words, it is not surprising that persons focus on being happy, or on traditional virtues, if the good cannot be known, although ultimately this failure to know the good also undermines the ability to know what is virtuous or what will provide lasting happiness.[9]

Until now we have discussed the insufficiency of skepticism but have not yet identified the good. In order to identify the good, we need to contextualize the question: we are asking *what is good for a human*? This requires us to know what it is to be a human, or *what is human nature*? Once again, we encounter objections before we have proceeded too far. These come in the form of denying that there is a human nature. This objection can arise for a number of reasons, including the belief that there are no natures or universals (nominalism),[10] or the belief that existence precedes essence (existentialism).[11] Without addressing these in detail, which would take us far afield of our current topic, we can note that *rationality* is a presupposition of any theory, including nominalism or existentialism. Both philosophies seek to present themselves to other humans, which presupposes that both the originator of the philosophy, and the audience, are rational. Rationality involves the ability to distinguish between a and non-a, and in practice as well as theory both nominalists and existentialists distinguish between humans and non-humans.

Consequently, when we are asking what is good for a human it is rationality that stands out as a demarcation of human nature. Although humans need food, water, shelter, clothes, relationships, etc., humans are also willing to abandon all of these and even kill themselves if they are not able to make sense of their lives. The use of reason to *make sense of, or understand, or find meaning in* life is an essential part of being a human in a way that food, shelter, water, etc, are not. We want food to stay alive and pursue meaning, if we are deprived of meaning we will push our food away, or it turns to ashes in our mouths. To argue otherwise is a self-contradiction: "let me help you understand why we don't need to understand."

Therefore, the good for humans is based on their nature as rational beings. As rational beings, humans try to make sense of the world, they seek for meaning. In doing this humans construct worldviews, and when these worldviews are challenged they will be justified or changed in an attempt to preserve meaning. A worldview is not merely a collection of details, but is an attempt to systematically understand reality; worldviews place details in relation to each other and to what is believed to be the highest reality. Thus, worldviews are constructed in response to the question: is there anything that is lasting, that is unchanging,

---

9   Aristotle, *Nicomachean Ethics*.
10 Oberman (2001).
11 Sartre (2001).

that is eternal?[12]

We can formulate an equation based on the above considerations: one's view of the good is determined by one's view of human nature, and one's view of human nature is determined by one's view of the real or eternal. We should expect, and indeed we find, that different worldviews will propose different views of the good, human nature, and the real. Even slight variations in belief about human nature or the real can produce significant differences in belief about the good, as is evidenced from quarrels about what ought to be done between sub-groups of a larger worldview (say, denominations within Christianity, or factions within Marxism).

8. Knowing The Good And Presuppositinal Thinking

For a variety of reasons, it has become a feature of the contemporary world to try to solve moral/social problems without addressing underlying differences about human nature or the real. Indeed, if one's attention was limited to the news media it would seem that the only differences that exist regard what ought to be done, and that these can be solved without addressing other more basic questions. We can identify questions about human nature and the real as "more basic" because they are presupposed by claims about what is good. Learning to "think presuppositionally" is resisted at many levels of our contemporary life and society.

One example of this is what has been classically called *akrasia*, or philosophical incontinence, but more commonly "a weak will." This problem arises when a person says "I knew what was right but I didn't do it," or "I knew it was wrong but I did it anyway." This reveals a kind of tension or disunity within the person. Although we cannot question that people believe this kind of tension occurs, we can ask about how it is interpreted. Is it possible to knowingly do evil? If our choices reveal our values, and we choose what we value in the given context, then it seems we not choose what we believe to be good. We may knowing act against what we earlier considered better judgment, or the advice of others, or our tradition's moral code. The tension then between our actual choice and what we claimed to have known reveals confusion about what is actually good; quite the contrary from knowingly doing evil, we reveal that we don't know what is good.

The good, as the highest value, provides unity to the diverse choices that face humans. This is true collectively and individually. Confusion about what is good, or changeableness over time, result in the statements noted above. This condition is due both to inconsistency on the part of persons (saying one thing

---

12   Aristotle, *Metaphysics*.

and doing another, believing contradictory propositions), and differing levels of awareness (to what extent is the person living the unexamined life). Tensions between societies, within a society, between individuals and within an individual, are traceable to competing visions of the good, and are therefore resolvable through coming to a common understanding of the good.

However, as we noted above, one's view of the good presupposes one's view of human nature and the real. As the moral absolute (virtue and lasting happiness are understood in their relation to the good), the good presupposes that there is a metaphysical absolute. If nothing is real then this includes the good and choices. Or if all is one and nothing is absolute, then there can be no meaningful distinction between good and evil since *all is one* translates into *good is evil*. This means that ethics as the study of the good must presuppose that there is a metaphysical absolute, there is something that is eternal and unchanging and something that is temporal and changing. Consequently, when we study applications below, the first will be about the relationship between ideas of God and ideas of the good.

9. Knowing The Moral Law And Free Will

Before considering applications, we must first ask if there is a moral law that humans can know about which explains the relationship between choices and the good. The first consideration is the knowability of the moral law and how this relates to human freedom. In speaking about freedom, we must distinguish between a free will (nothing hindering what is willed), and a will that could have done otherwise (no determining cause of the will). The former is compatible with pre-determination or causation because what is important is that the will is not hindered, whereas the ability to do otherwise requires that there is no cause. Thus, in speaking about a free will we are asking if there is anything that hinders the will so that the person cannot do what is wanted.

One way this has been expressed is as the *ought/can* principle. For thinkers like Kant this principle was used to argue that freedom requires the ability to do otherwise, since if one cannot do otherwise than one may not be able to do what ought to be done. When the consideration is limited to the will this is a problem. But as has been seen above, the will is affected by beliefs. Therefore, the first level of the *ought/can* principle is the level of what can be known. If a person ought to do something, then this *something* must be knowable to that person. If it is not knowable, then the person cannot will it.[13]

One objection to the idea that beliefs affect the will is that there does not

---

13   Augustine, *On Free Choice and the Will*, and Edwards, *The Freedom of the Will*.

always seem to be a one-to-one connection. That is, people report changing their beliefs (say, I now belief that smoking is unhealthy) without a corresponding change in the will (I still want to smoke). The problem is that this analysis is too superficial. Beliefs are connected to a larger worldview framework (which in the example may not have been changed), and they are related presuppositionally (the smoking example is not a basic example). So, while I might change my belief about smoking, I may not have changed my belief about the good—perhaps I believe the good is pleasure in some sense. Therefore, my will is not affected much by the new conviction about health because health is not my goal, pleasure is my goal. This robust analysis of a person's beliefs is much more fruitful in explaining the relationship between beliefs and actions, but it also faces the problem that people are not very conscious or consistent and so they may not be aware of their own beliefs - even to the extent they are aware they may hold contradictory beliefs.

The issue is therefore not whether one can do otherwise, since one does not want to do otherwise, but wants to do what is wanted. The issue is whether one wants what ought to be wanted, and how to change what is wanted if necessary. The *ought/can* principle is transformed into the *ought/can/want* principle which says "if I ought to do it then I must be able to do it, and if I can do it I must want to do it." But in order to want to achieve the good, one must know what is good. Therefore, freedom requires that the good and the moral law are knowable. This means that the following can all be true:

1. One cannot want otherwise than one does in fact want.
2. One is responsible because:
    a. The good is easily knowable.
    b. One does not want the good.

Indeed, this seems to be the central requirement for responsibility: one could know what is good, if one wanted to know what is good. In much discussion the energy is spent on whether one can want what is good if one cannot want otherwise; this is misspent energy if there is not a clearly knowable good. Freedom to want the good requires that the good is knowable. Freedom requires clarity.

10. Clarity, Responsibility and Human Nature

The need for clarity about what is good relates to the discussion earlier about rationality. There must be a distinction between what is good and what is non-good. If there is no such distinction then there can be no rational justification for which choice to make. This is the basic act of reason, distinguishing 'a' and 'non-a.' All other acts of reason presuppose this most basic act. So just as freedom requires clarity, so too clarity requires rationality. These three are related, so that if one cannot know the good, or the good is not clear to reason, or one denies rationality, then one is not free to want what is good and one cannot be held responsible. Furthermore, the reality that the good is clear to reason provides the foundation for responsibility: humans are inexcusable for not knowing what is clear about the good.

The ideas of clarity, responsibility, and inexcusability are directly related to the idea of a moral law.[14] The idea of a moral law initially can be confusing because it is asked "in what sense is it a *law* if it can be violated?" The purpose of articulating a law, such as the law of gravitation, is to understand an inviolable law of motion. The moral law is a *law* in precisely this way; it is a law of the human actions that are necessary to achieve the good, and therefore also a law about what happens when one does not achieve the good. In this sense, it is inviolable: if one wants the good one must know and do the moral law; if one does not follow the moral law one will not achieve the good and the consequences are predictable. The first question we must consider involves the very existence of such a law. Is there a moral law that governs which actions achieve the good?

One common objection to this idea is that it overlooks the particularity of each person and tries to generalize in a way that is unhelpful. This is an objection from Nietzsche and the existentialists, among others. Behind this objection is a belief that there are only particulars, a view called nominalism. In the medieval period this view, held by thinkers such as William of Ockham, led to the divine command theory. This theory says that humans cannot know *the good* because there are no universals, and therefore God must tell humans the moral law. In late modernity, Nietzsche also rejected universals, but since he rejected theism as well, he did not suggest divine command theory but instead the *will to power* (a view found in the interlocutor *Thrasymachus* from Plato's Republic). Although this involves important epistemological and metaphysical questions, for our purposes in normative ethics we can notice that it is a very unhelpful position. To answer the question "what ought I do" with some variation of "whatever makes you happy," "what will give you power over others to make you happy," "whatever best expresses your unique personality so that you will be happy" do not help in any way in settling the question "what can provide lasting happiness as opposed to only temporary happiness?"

Drawing out its implications, the view that there are no universals but only particulars must conclude that there is no good, there is no human nature, there are no universal situations, but only moments each different from the last. The implication for normative ethics is that there can be no rational justification to answer the question "what is the good, and what ought I to do?" Such a doctrine

---

14 Gangadean (2008).

cannot be articulated into a philosophy without becoming self-contradictory (relying on universals expressed in words). Indeed, adherents of such a view often argue that reason is useless and that instead one must rely on intuition. But if reason is that by which we make distinctions such as 'a' and 'non-a,' then the claim that we must go beyond reason cannot be distinguished from its opposite (we should not go beyond reason) and is therefore not communicating anything to the speaker or the listener. Reason, in this sense of the term, is inescapable.

This objection requires that extreme claim that there is no human nature, nothing that all humans share in common. This faces the problems just discussed. Most persons do not deny that there is common human nature. The implication is that there is one good. This is because what is good for human nature will be good for each individual that shares in this nature. Consequently, the moral law that describes how to achieve the good is applicable to each human as human. This does not deny that circumstances are variable. Indeed, there is a need for learning discernment in applying the moral law to particular cases. And yet there is a moral law that is applied, meaning that there is a description of how humans must act to achieve the good; not just any and every action results in what is good.

11. The Good and The Moral Law

The relationship between knowing and doing means that the moral law is both a guide to the good and a source of teaching about the good. The only way to know the good is to keep the moral law, and by observing the structure of the moral law we are taught about the nature of the good. Because we are seeking the good for humans, the moral law originates in human nature. So, we can speak about the first moral law as a law about the human good and the highest reality. As has already been noted, the basic question that is asked in Ethics is "what ought I do," and this is answered by knowing what is good for humans. Thus, the entire endeavor of Ethics is grounded in the reality of choice, and this reality is the beginning of the moral law. And so the beginning of the moral law draws our attention to the role of choices in our lives, and the need to know the good. Furthermore, since the good is grounded in the real, pursuit of the knowledge of the good requires that we know what is real.

The moral law, therefore, begins with the concepts of choice, the good, and the real. These are universal for humans and provide the foundation on which to discuss a universal moral law. All humans make choices, all choices assume the good, and the idea of the good is grounded in the idea of what is real. However, these formal concepts are given different content within different worldviews. In order to think about this content the moral law must address, in addition to the origin of the concepts within human nature, the nature of these concepts in order to give them content.

For instance, since there is one human nature, there is one good for all humans. This does not mean that there are not different personalities within the framework of human nature, but that those personalities, as human personalities, are pursuing the same good together. This means that the good is a source of unity within the reality of diversity, and that the failure to know the good is the source of disunity. In order to better understand this we can use the methodology we have used throughout this chapter and consider the alternative. What if there are a diversity of highest goods? (John Finnis). If these highest goods are incommensurable (as opposed to saying that they are really brought to unity under some higher good) then there can be no final unity within individuals, between individuals, or between groups. This incommensurable disunity, in the individual, would mean that there could be no rational justification for choosing one of these goods (and all the means required to achieve it) over another: the individual would be frozen in inaction. The very action of choosing is a witness to the fact that people believe there is a highest goal toward which they can make progress.

We can also consider the claim that the good is not achieved through reason, that it is not knowledge. In itself this is a knowledge claim about the good, and so it is claiming that some knowledge achieved through reason about the good is desirable. However, the crux of this objection is that it seeks to dichotomize *reason* and *intuition*, and assert that subjects such as goodness and beauty are best, or only, known through intuition. Of course, the problem would be that if this were true it could not be argued for or communicated without relying on reason. But it is also based on a superficial view of reason, where reason is limited to calculating or quantifying rather than being understood most basically as the laws of thought. Reason, understood in this latter way, is necessary for intuition itself since in intuition we distinguish between *beauty* and *non-beauty*, or *good* and *non-good*. Properly understood, there should be no tension here. Intuitions, as one source of information available to humans, must be subject to the same rational scrutiny as other sources of information such as common sense, tradition, and sense experience. It is this process that distinguishes humans from non-humans and helps us begin to define the good as the fulfillment of human nature in achieving knowledge.

12. The Ethics of Belief

Yet the good cannot simply be defined as knowledge. As we pursue knowledge of reality, we want to know not just about fleeting and changing aspects of reality, but about what is unchanging; we want to know the highest reality. In this way the ethics of choice begins immediately with the ethics of belief: what ought I to believe? What I believe about reality will shape what I believe is good, and this in turn will affect what I choose.

The first response by many has been either skepticism or fideism. We considered skepticism about the good earlier, but not about the human ability to know reality. Both skepticism and fideism (belief without sufficient proof—blind belief) agree that knowledge as inferential certainty is not possible. The skeptic says that therefore we should withhold belief (W.K. Clifford), and yet it has been pointed out that in some cases the choice is momentous and we must choose (William James). Consequently, the fideist says that although we cannot know we must believe. The problem is in choosing which of the various systems competing for our allegiance to believe in a fideistic manner.

We can unravel some of this problem using a similar methodology as above when discussing skepticism about the good. Does the reality of choice and the good tell us anything about knowing what is real? Can we know what is unchanging and eternal (without beginning)? Or is our knowledge limited to sense data which is by its nature temporary and impermanent? This quickly becomes a question about appearance and reality: everything that appears to me is changing, but I cannot conclude from there that everything is change and impermanence without committing the fallacy of overextension (concluding with a universal based on a particular—there may be more in reality that what appears to me).

We can formulate rules to guide us in the ethics of belief. For instance: First, we should not believe a contradiction. The use of reason to distinguish between *a* and *non-a* also helps us avoid confusing *a* and *non-a*. Thus, nothing is both *a* and *non-a* at the same time and in the same respect. Initially this will not seem helpful in the kinds of examples considered by many philosophers. For example, in the work that set the standard for discussing the ethics of belief, W.K. Clifford's *Ethics of Belief*, Clifford discusses the ethical nature of a belief held by a ship-owner about the seaworthy nature of his ship. He concludes that we should not believe anything without sufficient evidence. The kind of example used, and the notions of *sufficient* and *evidence* (coupled with the fact that Clifford was a mathematician) result in a kind of probabilistic analysis of the ethics of belief. The ship owner asks "have I performed all the necessary examinations of my ship, have I check the weather and carefully planned the voyage?" With these kinds of questions in mind, the ship-owner can conclude that there is a good chance the voyage will be safe. These kinds of choices are common and important, but how does this relate to our consideration of the basic question for normative ethics "what is the good?"

This leads us to our second rule, which is that we must learn to think presuppositionally. This means we must learn to identify what is presupposed in a belief, and know if those presuppositions are true, before we can speak about the belief being true. We notice that Clifford's example contains logical and ontological presuppositions. Some brief examples are that Clifford assumes some things exist. In Clifford's example the things that exist are temporal and changing.

Because they are temporal and changing they depend on previous changes and causes. Is there anything absolute? Anything that is eternal and unchanging?

There must be something eternal. If *none is eternal*, then this implies that all is temporal and changing, which implies that all had a beginning, which implies that all came into being, which implies that all came into being from non-being. To assert that *being* can come from *non-being* is to blur the most fundamental distinction there is, the distinction between existing and not existence, being and not being. An *a* can come from a *non-a* as in a chicken from an egg. But both of these are examples of beings, indeed, every distinction between *a* and *non-a* is a distinction between beings. If being can come from non-being then in this respect there is no distinction between being and non-being (they can both give rise to being); this is the blurring of what is fundamentally different, and this difference is a clear difference.

If it cannot be the case that *none is eternal*, another option is that *all is eternal*. This could mean an eternal series of temporal beings, or an unchanging being without beginning or end. An eternal series of temporal beings, like Nietzsche's eternal return, would make all choices meaningless: they have happened and will happen (much of the history of continental philosophy after Nietzsche is a coming to terms with this absurdity without questioning its presuppositions). If *all is one* in either sense above, then there is no real distinction between *good* and *evil*. If all is one, then good is evil. The implication is that no choice matters in that one cannot choose to do what is good, or achieve what is good, or even know what is good since this is not a real distinction.

The only alternative that preserves the meaning of choice is that only some is eternal. This leads to our third rule for the ethics of belief which is that we must have integrity, we must have consistency between our beliefs and between what we say we believe and what we do. If all is eternal and there is no distinction between good and evil, then a person that continues to argue for their position (implying it is the correct one) it no living with integrity. But if we conclude that *only some is eternal* can we know what is eternal? As we think about *being* we are aware of ourselves, personal being without extension, and we are aware of the world, non-personal being with extension.

The extended, or material, world is not eternal. If matter is eternal then it would be self-maintaining. The material world is not self-maintaining in that it tends toward sameness, and once at sameness it stays at sameness. And yet the material world is not currently in a condition of sameness (it is highly differentiated in terms of hot and cold). Therefore, the material world has not always existed. What is eternal is not material, but is instead personal and conscious (traditionally the term for this kind of being is *spirit*, in contrast to *matter*).

Although I am conscious, I am not eternal. If I were eternal then I would have all knowledge. Having existed without beginning, I would have had enough time to learn what can be learned, and after this amount of time if something has still not been learned then it cannot be known in any amount of time. And yet I do not have all knowledge. Therefore, I am not eternal.

Combining these, we get: *something is eternal, matter is not eternal*, and *the self is not eternal*. The implication is that what is eternal is a spirit with the qualities consistent with eternality. These include being infinite and unchanging (as well as eternal) in knowledge and power. Does it include goodness? In a recent debate with Alvin Plantinga, Daniel Dennett says that it just as possible that such a being is infinite in evil or indifference. And yet, if this being is the creator of what is not eternal (the temporal world), then this seems to rule out indifference as one cannot create with infinite deliberate wisdom and yet be indifferent. Similarly, infinite evil seems to be a contradiction in that evil is contrary to itself, and infinite evil would be infinitely contrary to itself—it could not continue to exist. The only option left is goodness.

13. The Good and God

These considerations bring us to what is called *Theism*. God exists, by which is meant a spirit who is infinite, eternal, and unchanging in power, knowledge and goodness. God is related to the good in that God, as the creator, is the determiner of human nature and therefore the determiner of what is good for human nature. Notice the methodology requires to get here: although it took steps, each step involved avoiding a contradiction and building to the next step. Sequentially, these were: something must be eternal, only some is eternal, matter is not eternal, the self is not eternal, what is eternal is a spirit that is infinite and unchanging in power, knowledge and goodness. Should a rational being know this? Clifford, the "father" of the ethics of belief, rejected belief in God because he said there was not enough evidence, where by *evidence* he meant sense data. However, this criterion rules out belief in God from the beginning since the changing world of sense data is by its nature temporal, and the question of God's existence is about what is not changing and is eternal. On the other hand, William James allowed for belief in God as the result of some experiences. But, again, these experiences as such are not able to prove that there is something eternal. So while these thinkers came up short, it seems they should have known that only God is eternal through the process of reason.

We can contrast knowing God as the determiner of good and evil for humans with the many other ethical theories that have been discussed in the history of philosophy. For instance, divine command theory also claims that God determines the good, but says this occurs apart from the nature of things. In this view, God's will determines the good to be whatever God wills it to be.

Consequently, humans cannot know the good apart form divine revelation. In order to avoid this consequence, there are many ethical theories that seek to ground the good in some aspect of human nature so that the good is knowable by all.

One example is utilitarianism and deontology (Bentham/Mill and Kant, respectively). These seek to ground the good in, respectively, pleasure and virtuous behavior. Or there is ethical egoism (personal pleasure, Freud), naturalism (individual instinct, Rousseau and Lao-Tzu), tradition (collective instinct, Confucius), existentialism (will apart from essence, Sartre), humanism (the good as actualization of potential, Maslow), and contemplation (the good in exercise of the intellect, Aristotle).[15] In pursuing the good as some aspect of human nature each of these affirms the universality of the good. However, in doing so apart from the metaphysical absolute each of these isolates and therefore distorts the good. For instance, in humanism the good is human excellence—the actualization of human potential. Yet without knowing what is the metaphysical absolute, one cannot know what it is to be excellent because different visions of the absolute produce different views of excellence. Or, in contemplation, the act of the intellect is understood to be an immediate perception of the forms or the unmoved mover. This view says that the good is difficult to attain because the desires of the body keep us from this vision; therefore, the body must be left behind and then the direct vision can be attained in the next life. Consequently, the knowledge of God is not through the nature of what God has made, but apart from it.

It may seem at first that the diversity of these moral theories makes for an overwhelming job in adjudicating which to select to think about the good and choice. However, this task becomes readily understandable when we keep in mind two matters we have discussed previously: thinking presuppositionally, and the metaphysical absolute. Each of these makes some aspect of human nature and personality absolute and then develops a moral theory around that feature. However, the manner in which each theory understands the human personality is grounded in more or less consciously held beliefs about the metaphysical absolute. In order to make this more clear we can examine each of these theories in terms of which personality trait they focus on and what this reveals about their view of the metaphysical absolute.

In utilitarianism, the good is equated with happiness. This view is sometimes called conseqentialism and can be confused with teleology because both argue that the question of what ought to be done must be answered in relation to the end that is being sought. However, consequentialism focuses on the outcomes (consequences) of achieving the end, which is important different than teleology

---

15   See Gangadean (2008) for more discussion on these views and the relationship between God and the good.

which pursues the end in itself (which should be valued not for its consequences but for itself). This view is called utilitarianism because it assess choices in terms of their utility in maximizing desires outcomes or consequences. Thus, its motto has come to be "the greatest good for the greatest number of people."

Utilitarianism is helpful in noting this relationship between choice and goals. However, it faces problems when it confuses the good (the end in itself) with happiness. Happiness as a consequence will only be as permanent as is the good to which it is linked. Thus, a mistaken good will not result in lasting happiness. Nor is it sufficient to act so as to maximize happiness since this might be to maximize a happiness that is not related to the actual good but is based on a misunderstanding or on culpable ignorance. Furthermore, when utilitarianism becomes pragmatism (do whatever works) it becomes emptied of helpful content. Either the phrase "whatever works" means "whatever satisfies" and is therefore no longer part of an objective discussion about the end in itself and what will bring lasting happiness, or it presupposes knowledge of what is good (whatever works means do what achieves the good).

By way of contrast, deontology has set itself up as a solution in contrast to the failures of utilitarianism. Deontologists like Immanuel Kant assert that the only good thing is a good will (in contrast to a good outcome). This is to say that we should *will* what is our duty apart from what we will get as a consequence. It was noted by Kant that doing one's duty, or being virtuous, does not always result in happiness in this life. Thus, we must postulate God's existence and immortality to guarantee the relationship between these in the next life. Another way to solve this problem is to notice that the move from virtue to happiness is skipping the good; virtue as a means to the good, once achieved, will result in happiness.

Thus, whereas utilitarianism absolutizes happiness (as the consequence of right action), deontology absolutizes virtue or duty. The rest of each respective system is centered on these as the moral absolute. However, this emphasis on either virtue/duty or happiness has been noticed by other moral theories and the attempt is made to fill the lacuna by relying on an aspect of human personality to know the good.

For instance, in ethical egoism personal pleasure is said to be the deciding factor in an individual's choices. This is something of a reaction to both utilitarianism and its concern for the whole, and deontology in its disconnect from personal pleasure, although this is not to suggest a chronological development in such a manner. Beginning with Sigmund Freud, contemporary psychology has analyzed personal choice in terms of what will bring about pleasure. Indeed, Freud discussed the development of the *self* in terms of internal and unconscious conflict and the tension between personal pleasure and social norms. One notable problem is that pleasure is not the same as happiness, and not all happiness is lasting. Thus, if the individual wants lasting happiness the solution is to know the good which is common to all humans and not limited to any individual.

Naturalism also emphasizes the individual, although in this case stressing the individual's uncorrupted intuition. This has been expressed in the West by thinkers like Rousseau and in the East by thinkers like Lao Tzu. The individual's natural intuitions are a source of guidance, but can become flawed due to interaction with society. Social constraints cause persons to ignore their natural intuitions and this gives rise to social evils. Of course, a problem for naturalism is that people often have competing intuitions which must be adjudicated, and intuitions change over time (in maturation hopefully). Thus, that one has an intuition does not guarantee that the intuition is aimed at the good as opposed to an immature misunderstanding.

By way of contrast, tradition emphasizes the collected wisdom passed down through the generations. While individuals are prone to error, such errors are often caught and corrected over time. The best ideas and best solutions to problems persevere and survive. The sum total of this, expressed in a culture's canonized tradition, is the high point of wisdom about how to behave. However, not unlike the problems facing naturalism, there are many competing traditions with diverse and contradictory solutions to life's problems. Furthermore, each tradition is based on differing views of what is real, what it is to be a human, and what is good. Thus, it seems that traditions must be judged based on their beliefs about these, rather than beliefs about these being determined by what a tradition says.

Where an emphasis on tradition can cause an individual to feel that one's entire life is pre-determined, existentialism absolutizes freedom and authenticity. If an act is not authentically yours, then you cannot take credit or accept blame. An act cannot be authentically yours unless you did it freely. Thus, one must reject any predetermination from society or human nature. The motto for existentialism is that existence precedes essence; this means that although one exists, one is not predetermined by an essence but must choose an essence. A problem arises when one considers this view of freedom. If freedom requires that there is no cause, then freedom requires an uncaused event. And yet, if one's choice is uncaused then it is not clear that one can accept credit or blame for what is not caused. However, if one does cause the action for reasons or intentions one deems important, then predetermination arises because the manner in which one decides on reasons or intentions is wrapped up in one's personality and background. Some existentialists see this problem and argue that one must accept the contradiction and live in the absurdity—this absurdity includes the need for reason and reason's inability to provide a solution, as well as the need for meaning in the fact of no meaning. An alternative to accepting a contradiction is to re-evaluate the presuppositions that lead to the contradiction; in this case, one can re-evaluate the claim that freedom requires no predetermination or cause. One need to settle on this libertarian view of freedom, and indeed the fact that it leads to such a contradiction is one indication of why to reject it.

Whereas these previous moral theories have emphasized an act of will guided by one aspect of human personality (intuition, tradition, authenticity), humanism emphasizes a general striving toward excellence. This is the view presented by Aristotle in the first 9 parts of his book *Nicomachean Ethics*. It comes to highest expression in the *polis*, or human society, where all the virtues necessary for a shared life can be expressed in excellence. A problem that arises is that one must know what is real in order to know what is excellent. So, for instance, Aristotelianism will yield a different view of excellence than will Marxism or Hinduism. Before one can be excellent, one must settle this question of what is real, which settles the question of what is human nature and what is the human good.

Finally, contemplation asserts that the highest goal of human life is the contemplation of the highest reality. This came to expression in Plato's allegory of the cave, and in the last part of Aristotle's *Nicomachean Ethics*. This contemplation takes place apart from the bodily senses by a direct/immediate act of the mind. In Thomism it is identified with the beatific vision, which was given dramatic expression in Dante's *Paradiso*. In popular culture this has come to be expressed as the doctrine of heaven, where the goal of life is to lead a sufficient virtuous existence so as to be granted access to heaven at death. This view avoids some of the mistakes of previous views by connecting the highest good to the highest act of humans in knowing and specifically to knowing the highest reality. However, a problem arises in claiming that reality can be known immediately, rather than through an act of the mind such as inference. Understanding the meaning of an experience requires interpretation which requires inference, whereas an immediate but uninterested experience is not meaningful. The body becomes an obstacle to knowing the highest reality rather than the means through which the highest reality is revealed.

An emphasis on one aspect of human choice or personality apart from defining the good as the end in itself also faces the problem of being too narrow and not sufficiently comprehensive. To avoid this we will need to explore the concept of a *moral law*, which define human choice in relation to the good based on human nature. If the good is correctly identified, and since it is based on human nature, it will not single out any one part of human nature to the detriment of the others. Such a moral law would be clear (because it is based on human nature and it is clear what is a human), comprehensive (applying to all aspects of human personality and choice), and critical (because it is a matter of achieving the good it is a matter of life and death).

14. Developing The Moral Law

What we have considered thus far in the ethics of belief provides us with a foundation about the good and God on which to build in considered specific applications of the moral law. For instance, if we by-pass these considerations and attempt to directly solve problems such as piracy in the Indian Ocean, problems that contain many presuppositions, we will fail. We can apply various moral theories to the situation, but as long as these are incommensurable this will simply be an academic exercise. If we wish to arrive at unity we must have a common good that can serve as the foundation of knowing what we ought to do. Furthermore, this good must be grounded in the nature of things, particularly in the source of the nature of things—the metaphysical absolute. The alternative is that the good is not grounded in the nature of things and become arbitrary and subjective.

There are consequences to not having this foundation for the moral law in place. Specifically, since the moral law began with the use of reason to distinguish between *good* and *non-good*, and between the *eternal* and the *temporal* (non-eternal), the consequences relate to what happens when we fail to use reason. We use reason to find meaning, to understand what *is* and what *is not*. When we fail to reason we fail to draw appropriate distinctions and we will not find meaning. In failing to find meaning we fail to see a purpose and this results in boredom. As we seek to avoid boredom we generally go to excess which results in a sense of guilt. As these three combine (meaninglessness, boredom, and guilt), we spiral further into non-rational or irrational behavior as we attempt to fill our lives and avoid the lack of meaning.

The alternative is a return to the life of reason in the pursuit of meaning. This is a return to distinguishing between the creator and the created. And yet even this move can be clouded. Francis Bacon identified *idols* that keep humans from attaining knowledge. These are misrepresentations of reality. Idols involve a reversal of thinking: rather than thinking of the less basic in light of the more basic (the creation in light of the creator), an idol is the most basic in light of the less basic (the creator in light of the creation, or God in light of man). Thus, although the theistic religions recognize the reality of the metaphysical absolute as creator, they each understand the justice and mercy of God differently. Conflicts between the theistic religions are global and have persisted for centuries. Yet, the common approach to solutions is to think only of the less basic; if unity is to be reached it must first occur at the most basic level. What is required by divine justice? Can God's justice be set aside by his mercy? Can humans satisfy divine justice by their own suffering or good works? Or must divine justice and mercy be reconciled in one event of atonement? The consequence of not addressing these questions is continued disunity at every level of human civilization.

The resistance on the part of humans to thinking presuppositionally, and instead focusing normative ethics on practical and psychological problems, is a problem of integrity. Integrity begins as consistency within our own nature as rational beings. Attempting to solve moral problems apart from thinking presuppositionally is a denial of our natures. Attempting to solve moral problems at only the practical and psychological levels, and not the logically basic and philosophical, is a denial of rationality. Integrity requires thinking about what is most basic first, and then drawing out consistent implications for the other areas of life. If a person had integrity then that person would know what is clear at the most basic level. The consequence of not having integrity is confusion and mental impression.

The goal of integrity is knowledge of what is lasting, and humans can have hope that this knowledge is attainable. This is a knowledge that comes through knowing the nature of things, which in turn reveals the nature of the creator. Therefore, the work of pursuing the good is a goal for humans that spans individual lives, cultures, and civilizations. It is a goal that requires all of humanity contributing to the outcome. It is a knowledge that is too grand for any individual to attain apart from the work of the whole. In contrast to contemplation where the individual thinker is alone in the vision of God, this is a knowledge of all aspects of reality which cannot be attained through individual effect. Consider the many diverse dimensions and levels of reality, and the effort needed to uncover each and explain it to others. This is a work that calls everyone to give their best and develop their excellence toward the goal of fullness. The reality of moral evil adds to the work in that the knowledge attained is not only of the world, but also of the conflict between good and evil in history, and the justice and mercy of God in providing redemption. Hope that the goal will be achieved can be seen on many levels, including success thus far, and the purposes of God in human history. The failure to think of one's work in terms of this goal is that work becomes empty and meaningless—at best one works for self-pleasure which is fleeting.

Once we have discussed the concepts of work and excellence we naturally begin to think about authority. Authority in any given area of life must be based on insight into how that area achieves the good. This kind of authority is rational and not personal, it can be demonstrated through objective questions and cannot be defended based on personality or charisma alone. The quality of rationality, or the potential for rationality, can be more broadly applied as what gives human dignity. If the potential for rationality is denied to a person, then their human dignity has been denied and they have effectively been treated like an animal. There are many applications that can be drawn from this to contemporary issues such as abortion and euthanasia. Similarly, as humans each of us is the product of parents, a male and female. This is the immediate origin of our being which carries with it the responsibility both to care for those brought into being and to learn how to lasting love the other with whom one is united.

The moral law must also address issues of value and justice. If value is assessed in a multilevel system then stealing from others can also occur at many levels. That is, while physical possessions can be of value and therefore might be stolen, so too one's talents are of value to others and therefore the failure to develop these in service to others is a kind of theft. Ultimately, it is the failure to know the good and seek the good for self and others that is the highest form of theft. This relates to justice because justice requires the truth, the whole truth, and nothing but the truth. This truth must not be only a partial truth related to limited events, but the whole truth about the good and the real. If one does not know what is good, or what is real, then one cannot seek for full justice. This level of justice requires addressing culpable ignorance about what is good and not only conflicts over resources. To be a faithful witness about the good is to seek full justice.

And yet, even in light of these considerations, one might ask if the good is really attainable given all the suffering in the world. Therefore, the moral law must conclude by discussing how the good can be attained in the face of suffering. Suffering is not primarily physical or environmental; that is, suffering is not primarily due to lack of resources or commodities. Rather, the deepest suffering arises in relation to perceived lack of meaning. As one comes to believe that life is not meaningful, one suffers. Therefore, to alleviate this most devastating level of suffering one must attain meaning. Since subjective claims to meaning will be tested by objective trials, it is not sufficient to be satisfied with fideism. Rather, one must be able to show what is good and how this relates to the human good and the real. Once this happens, nothing can occur to keep one from the good, indeed all events including suffering can be understood to deepen the good.

We can continue to draw out applications of the moral law to many other areas of human life. These include the need for authority that is based on insight into the good rather than physical power or personality; the need to affirm human dignity and hold others accountable for their humanity; the relationship between the good, friendship, and marriage as well as our origin in the union of male and female; the role of value and talent in human society as we learn to demand what is good and value those who produce the good; the need for the whole truth as a basis for justice, including truth at the most basic level; and finally the role of suffering in the pursuit of the good such that for those who understand the good all things are seen to work together.

One inevitable objection to proceeding in this presuppositional manner is that it is not quick enough in settling problems that occupy our attention. For instance, how does this apply to the problem of piracy, or terrorism, or hunger? However, it is not true that presuppositional thinking does not apply to these matters. Rather, the approach is to build on a lasting foundation rather than working toward solutions that are either not permanent or not helpful. A lasting foundation must first take into account what is actually good and the source of the good. Then we can ask "how does this apply to piracy?" Where are the pirates at in their thinking about the good? From the interviews I've heard they are skeptics about the good, and have said that since we cannot know what is good they will focus on getting money to lead a more comfortable life. But perhaps their country is war-torn precisely due to this kind of skepticism: if we cannot know what is good then what is the point of building a peaceful civilization as opposed to simply doing whatever it takes to get ahead? If we want to provide a lasting solution to these kinds of problems we must be able to show that humans can know the good, and that humans can make progress in achieving the good. As long as we ignore these questions we are really accepting the skepticism of the pirates.

15. Conclusion

Needless to say, there is much more work to be done in the study of normative ethics. What we have done here is to formulate a foundation on which this work can be done in a way that lasts. This foundation includes identifying basic concepts in the study of ethics, considered how mistakes about these concepts have led to problematic ethical theories, thinking about the relationship of the good, human nature, and God, and drawing out some implications from this relationship to a moral law. We also spent time on problems of skepticism and fideism, responded to objections from these positions, and thought about the nature of a free will. In order to understand where to begin, we articulated some rules for the ethics of belief—these rules were based on the nature of rationality at its most basic level, and in the need to know what is basic if we are to know anything else. We can end with an encouragement to begin—that is, we can summarize the above as an attempt to lead the examined life. Therefore, as we conclude we can also begin this process, a process of curiosity of what is good, and fear of not attaining or knowing the good.

BIBLIOGRAPHY

Augustine (2001). *Political Writings* (Atkins, E.M. and Dodaro, R. J., eds.). Cambridge, Cambridge University Press.

Aquinas, T. (2002). *Political Writings* (Dyson, R.W., ed.). Cambridge, Cambridge University Press.

Aristotle (1952). Metaphysics. In Ross, W. D. (trans). *Aristotle: 1*, Vol. 86, 499-626. New York, *Encyclopedia Britannica*.

_____ (1952). *Nicomachean Ethics*. In *Aristotle: II.* Translated by W. D. Ross. Vol. 21, 339. New York, Encyclopedia Britannica.

Dole, A. and Chignell, A. (2005). *God and the Ethics of Belief.* Cambridge, Cambridge University Press.

Dyson, T and R. W. (2002). *Political Writings.* Cambridge Texts in the History of Political Thought. Cambridge, Cambridge University Press.

Finnis, J. (1980). *Natural Law and Natural Rights.* Oxford, Oxford University Press.

Flew, A.G.N. and MacIntyre, A. (1955). *New Essays in Philosophical Theology.* New York, Macmillan

Gangadean, S. (2008). *Philosophical Foundation: A Critical Analysis of Basic Beliefs.* Lanham, University Press of America.

Jopling, D. A. (1992). Sartre's Moral Psychology. In Howells, C. (ed.). *The Cambridge Companion to Sartre.* Cambridge, Cambridge University Press.

Kant, I. and Paton, H. J. (2005). *The Moral Law: Groundwork of the Metaphysic of Morals.* London, Routledge Classics.

Mill, J. (2007). *Utilitarianism.* New York, Dover Publications.

Nietzsche, F. (1989 [1886]). *Beyond Good and Evil: Prelude to a Philosophy of the Future.*(Kaufmann, W., trans.). New York, Vintage.

_____ (1989). *On the Genealogy of Morals and Ecce Homo.* New York, Vintage.

Oberman, H. (2001). *The Harvest of Medieval Theology: Gabriel Biel and Late Medieval Nominalism.* Grand Rapids, Baker Academic.

Plato. (2008). *Republic.* In Cooper, J. (ed.). *Plato: Complete Works.* Grube, G. M. (trans.). Cambridge, Hackett Publishing Company.

Popkin, R. H. (2003). *The History of Skepticism: From Savonarola to Bayle.* New York, Oxford University Press.

Sartre, J.-P. (2000). *Existentialism and Human Emotions.* New York, Kensington Publishing Corporation.

Sartre, J. P. (2001). *Basic Writings.* London, Routledge.

12

Utilitarian Ethics

Joakim Sandberg

1. Introduction

Is it morally permissible to lie when people's lives are at stake? Say that you could save two people's lives by telling a flagrant lie; would it be morally correct to do so? What about killing one to save five – can this sometimes be morally obligatory? Say that the only way in which you could save a *million* people's lives were to kill one? Finally, think of all the people that presently are dying in developing countries around the world. Are we doing something wrong when we fail to help them? Is doing nothing here just as wrong as killing them?

Utilitarianism is the moral theory which suggests that the answer to these questions depends on what action would have the best consequences in the situation. What we should be asking ourselves, then, is what would happen if we lied, killed or helped, and compare it to what would happen if we refused to do so. Even though lying has bad consequences in most situations, and we for this reason probably should teach our children not to lie, it would be morally correct to lie in some extraordinary situations when people's lives are at stake. Likewise, killing one to save five may be morally obligatory in some situations, although the best rule of thumb (which will produce better consequences in most situations) certainly is to respect people's autonomy and right to life. According to utilitarianism, there is no genuine moral difference between killing someone and letting someone die, so we are probably at fault if we do nothing to help the starving people in Africa. However, there may be indirect or social reasons for viewing these kinds of actions differently – while society should convict murderers, for instance, it may be counterproductive to prosecute or blame those who give nothing to charity.

The theory of utilitarianism was first introduced by the British philosophers Jeremy Bentham and John Stuart Mill in the late 18th and early 19th century. Both of these were political thinkers and used their account of utilitarianism primarily to justify certain legal and social reforms, which were generally considered radical at the time – Bentham is, e.g., most famous for his arguments for a special kind of prison (the 'panopticon') and Mill is sometimes regarded as the father of political liberalism. However, both Bentham and Mill suggested that they in utilitarianism had found the ultimate principle of ethics. Variously referring to it as 'utilitarianism', 'the principle of utility' or 'the greatest happiness principle', Bentham's and Mill's credo is often restated as "the greatest good for the greatest number of people" (a formulation which we will have reason to return to below).

Even though far from all contemporary moral philosophers agree that Bentham and Mill had found the ultimate principle of ethics, the merits and demerits of their utilitarianism are still widely discussed. In fact, utilitarianism is generally considered to be one of the main contenders in normative ethics (the debate over general moral theories), and it seems fair to say that any book on moral theory would be incomplete without a treatment of it. In this chapter, I will outline some of the basic elements of utilitarian ethics and discuss what I take to be the most common moral arguments for and against it. I will primarily discuss problems internal to the theory, but towards the end I will also discuss some external criticisms. Much attention will be given to the apparent *flexibility* of the utilitarian framework, and I take this flexibility to consist in two things: Firstly, I will show how utilitarianism actually could be seen as a *group* of moral theories rather than a single theory. Secondly, I will try to show how even classical utilitarianism can employ a number of tricks to incorporate moral ideas which initially may seem inconsistent with it. It is perhaps this flexibility which explains utilitarianism's longstanding place as one of the main contenders in normative ethics. Whether this flexibility shows that utilitarianism is the *best* theory, however, is an issue which I leave to the reader to decide.

2. The Basic Elements of Utilitarianism

A great deal has been written about utilitarianism, both for and against it, since the days of Bentham and Mill. Furthermore, as we will soon see, different utilitarians actually tend to defend somewhat different versions of the theory. For these reasons, it is not easy to give a simple characterisation of what utilitarianism says, but I take the following five elements to roughly outline the basic tenets of utilitarian ethics:

Firstly, utilitarianism is normally conceived of as a theory of the morality of *actions* – that is, of what actions are morally right (correct, obligatory) and what actions are morally wrong (incorrect, impermissible). The question of the morality of actions is perhaps only a part of what moral philosophy can be about. Moral philosophers can scrutinise a lot of things – intentions, motivation, character, actions, social structures, etc. – and maybe utilitarianism can be extended to cover all of these things. Indeed, there are examples in the literature where philosophers defend, for example, a utilitarian account of character or utilitarianism as a political philosophy. First and foremost, however, utilitarianism is a theory of what makes correct actions correct and wrongful actions wrong.

Secondly, as already noted, utilitarianism characteristically holds that the correctness of actions ultimately is determined by *consequences*. This is what most markedly separates utilitarianism from some of its main contenders – for example, Kantianism or Aristotelianism. According to utilitarianism, whether a certain action is right or wrong does not depend on what kind of action it is (whether, e.g., it is a case of lying or killing) or with what intention it is performed (whether, e.g., it is performed with good or bad intentions). Rather, the central issue is what consequences or outcomes different actions produce, i.e. what the results of different actions are.

It may be noted that utilitarians typically give a very broad definition of what counts as consequences or results of actions: The consequences of action A is sometimes defined as basically all events which succeed A, i.e. everything that happens after A in time. While this kind of definition initially may seem extreme, it is important to see the reasoning behind it. Say for instance that I have the possibility of stopping person X from killing person Y, but that I for some reason fail to do so. We may not in ordinary language say that the death of person Y is a consequence of *my* behaviour in this case – rather, we might say that it is more naturally understood as a consequence of the actions of person X, i.e. the person actually doing the killing. But according to utilitarianism, as I have said, there is no genuine moral difference between killing someone and letting someone die. Utilitarians would thus hold that Y's death *is* a consequence of my behaviour – after all, Y would *not* have died if I had acted differently, i.e. if I had intervened. It is partly because utilitarians make no moral difference between *actions* and *omissions*, then, or because inaction only is viewed as a special form of action, that they typically give a very broad definition of what counts as consequences of actions.

Thirdly, utilitarianism characteristically holds that what determines the correctness of a particular action are not only the consequences of that *distinct* action, but also what the consequences would be of *all other actions open to the agent in the situation*. Utilitarianism could be said to rest on the idea that there in most situations in our ordinary lives are more than one line of action "open" to us, i.e. there are a lot of (perhaps quite different) things that we could do (if only we wanted to). Instead of reading this book, for example, you could go and buy some coffee, or take a nap, or call a distant relative, or something else still. According to utilitarianism, then, morally correct actions are not simply all actions with (in some sense) *favourable* consequences, but the morally correct action is the one which produces the *best* consequences – best here understood in relation to the consequences of all of the other actions open to the agent in his or her situation. It is sometimes said that utilitarianism confers on moral agents the obligation to *maximise* the positive contribution of their actions. Of course, if two or more alternative actions in a certain situation produce equally good outcomes, it may be morally permissible to choose any of these. Interestingly, this seems to be the only case in which utilitarianism gives room for extended moral choice. If there is only one action which produces the best outcome, namely, it is not only morally correct but *obligatory*.

Fourthly, utilitarianism suggests that it is roughly how *well* people are made which determines how good the consequences of a certain action are. Utilitarianism is sometimes said to be a moral theory which "derives the right from the good" – that is, that it ultimately is the issue of what is (morally) valuable which determines what is morally right (since the right thing to do simply is to maximise whatever is valuable). In order to be neutral about what is to count as valuable in the relevant sense, Bentham and Mill sometimes spoke about *utility* as whatever makes people's lives go well, and this is what has given utilitarianism its name. In the end, however, they both equated utility with *happiness* or *pleasure*. To what extent the consequences of a certain action should be regarded as good, then, they thought depends on how happy or unhappy people are made by it or, as it is sometimes formulated, the 'balance of pleasure over pain' produced by the action. Now, not all utilitarians agree with this, and I will return to the idea of happiness as the only value below. Suffice it to say that most utilitarians hold that what makes consequences good or bad roughly is how well off people are made.

Finally, utilitarianism characteristically holds that *all people's welfare matters equally* in making consequences good or bad. In a sense, utilitarianism could be seen as the middle ground between egoism and altruism. It may be noted that, at least on one interpretation, these stances are quite similar to utilitarianism – what makes actions right or wrong, on both stances, is namely the utility of their consequences. But according to egoism the only thing that matters is *my* welfare, and according to altruism, conversely, it is only *other people's* welfare that matters (and I should sacrifice my own well-being for that of others). Utilitarianism is the middle ground between these two extremes in so far as it holds that *all* people's welfare matters, both my own and that of others, and the welfare of each person counts *just as much* in making outcomes good or bad. This feature is sometimes formulated as the idea that utilitarianism cares about the *overall* or *aggregate* balance of pleasure over pain 'in the universe as a whole'. However, exactly how different people's well-being should be weighed against each other's is a rather complicated and contentious issue, and I will return to this below.

If we put these five elements together, we get the following rough first formulation of the core idea of utilitarianism:

> Classical Utilitarianism: *An action is right if and only if there was nothing else which the agent could have done in the situation which would have produced a greater overall balance of pleasure over pain in the universe.*

What is striking by this position, according to most proponents of utilitarian ethics, is, among other things, its immense simplicity. All that matters is people's happiness, and actions are morally right or wrong in so far as they maximise this kind of moral value. According to Bentham and Mill, utilitarianism should also be the moral theory of choice for people in our kind of post-religious and scientific society, since it essentially poses a challenge to all those philosophers promulgating, e.g., a sacred right to life or a list of the 'natural rights of men'. Before we believe in such things, Bentham and Mill suggested, we must be presented with some idea as to how they connect with what people actually value – that is, with people's happiness. According to the many critics of utilitarianism, however, the theory's simplicity is one of its main weaknesses. Although how well off people are made as a result of a certain action certainly may be morally *relevant*, other relevant factors seem to be, e.g., justice, autonomy, human rights, the sanctity of life, etc. etc.

I will return to these kinds of external criticisms of utilitarian ethics below. Before that, however, we may discuss some problems more *internal* to the theory – that is, criticisms to the effect that the position outlined above doesn't make sense, or builds on mistaken presuppositions.

3. Evaluating Consequences

At the core of utilitarian ethics lies an appeal to utility or happiness. Morally correct actions are those that maximise overall happiness in the universe, and all people's happiness should be given equal weight when calculating this overall happiness. Some critics suggest, however, that utilitarianism basically gets it wrong from the start here. In this section, I will discuss three kinds of recurrent criticisms directed against utilitarian ethics: According to some, (1) it is simply mistaken to equate utility, or more generally moral value, with happiness. According to others, (2) the way in which utilitarianism aggregates different people's happiness into one overall measure is morally problematic. According to yet again others, the problem is actually even more fundamental than this: (3) it just isn't possible to compare different kinds of happiness with each other or to combine the welfare of different people into one single measure. By discussing these criticisms, I hope to shed further light on how proponents of the kind of classical utilitarianism outlined above generally reason, but also to introduce some more recent variations on this view.

3.1. Theories of Value

The classical utilitarian view of what makes outcomes good or bad or, more generally, what has (morally relevant) value, as noted above, is that only happiness or pleasure matters. What this means, it should be added, is that only pleasure is *intrinsically* good (and that only pain is intrinsically bad). Many things can be *instrumentally* good in the sense that they *lead* to happiness. So, for instance, knowledge and virtue can be instrumentally good in so far as they tend to lead to happiness, both for the one who attains them and for people around them. Similarly, torture will almost always be instrumentally bad in so far as it leads to pain and suffering in the victim. But torture would not be bad, and knowledge and virtue would not be good, or so the idea goes, if they didn't have these relations to pleasure and pain. According to classical utilitarianism, then, the only thing which is good *in itself* is pleasure. This view is sometimes referred to as *hedonism*, or *hedonistic* utilitarianism, from the Greek work *hédoné* (pleasure).

Many philosophers regard hedonism as a fundamentally problematic doctrine. A first problem which sometimes is stressed in this context is that it seems plausible to treat different instances, or kinds, of pleasure rather differently. This was a problem which Mill himself anticipated. Mill famously suggested that "it is better to be a human being dissatisfied than a pig satisfied; better to be Socrates dissatisfied than a fool satisfied". According to Mill, then, it seems plausible to say that certain kinds of pleasures (the more intellectual ones) actually are infinitely more valuable than others (the more brute ones). So perhaps the happiness gained from going to the opera, say, is infinitely more valuable than the pleasure derived from eating or engaging in sexual intercourse. Even more radically, Mill toyed with the idea that certain kinds of pleasure may have no value whatsoever. Say that a group of torturers happen to be so sadistic that they take enormous pleasure from torturing one poor innocent soul – what should we make of this kind of pleasure? Perhaps this kind of pleasure actually has no value at all, Mill suggested, or at least we should give very little attention to it when morally evaluating the torturers' activity.

While these examples seem problematic for the hedonist, a more fundamental problem with his or her view is brought out by an oft-cited example from the more contemporary philosopher Robert Nozick. Nozick asks us to consider a fantastical case where a group of scientists offers us the possibility of placing our brains in a sophisticated kind of neurological machine. If we do so, the scientists assure us that they would be able to stimulate our brains so that we come to experience life exactly as we do now – that is, we wouldn't be able to tell the difference between being in the machine and going on living. Our experiences would remain the same (and we would not know that we were in the machine) but with one exception – they would give us considerably more pleasure, so our lives would feel a lot better. Would anyone be interested in taking the scientists up on their offer? Nozick suggests that the answer is a resounding no, and this shows that having pleasurable experiences clearly is not all that matters to us. Besides happiness, Nozick says, things such as having contact with reality and not being systematically deceived also have morally relevant value.

The considerations above are clearly problems for the classical or hedonistic form of utilitarianism. Before considering what proponents of this kind of utilitarianism can say in reply, however, we may ask whether they are also problems for utilitarianism as such. Actually, the received view on this matter is that they are not. As noted above, utilitarianism can be seen as the general idea that we have an obligation to maximise whatever is valuable. Even though hedonism may be fundamentally problematic, then, this may only be thought to show that utilitarians have reasons to opt for some alternative and different theory of value. Indeed, many well-known utilitarians defend theories of value quite different from that of Bentham and Mill. According to one theory, for instance, defended by G. E. Moore, such things as knowledge and virtue should actually be regarded as good *in themselves*, and not only as instrumentally good. This is sometimes referred to as the *Objective List* theory, which yields the following form of utilitarianism:

> Ideal Utilitarianism: An action is right if and only if there was nothing else which the agent could have done in the situation which would have produced a greater amount of objective good in the universe.

Another kind of popular value theory is slightly more reductionist, although not as reductionist as hedonism. According to this theory, defended by, e.g., Peter Singer, knowledge and virtue are only valuable to the extent that they lead to people getting what they want – that is, to satisfaction of preferences. What Nozick's example of the 'experience machine' shows, according to proponents of this view, is not that it is bad in itself to be systematically deceived, but rather that very few of us want this. However, to the extent that some people actually *want* to be systematically deceived, taking the scientists up on their offer could actually be a good thing. This view is called *preferentialism* and yields the following form of utilitarianism:

> Preference Utilitarianism: An action is right if and only if there was nothing else which the agent could have done in the situation which would have produced a greater amount of preference satisfaction in the universe.

By opting for one of these alternative theories of value, then, utilitarians seem able to avoid the problems connected with the classical hedonistic account. But, of course, there are problems attached to these theories as well and it is not clear whether they really are improvements on the classical form of utilitarianism. Hedonists typically suggest that there is something odd with making the issue of how much value a certain person's life contains depend on something quite outside the person him- or herself. Say, for instance, that one of your deepest wishes is to be regarded as one of the world's greatest writers, and it just so happens that one year the Swedish Academy seriously considers giving you the Nobel Prize in Literature. However, since the Academy's proceedings are secret, you never find out about this. It may seem problematic to say that *your* life contains more value because of this – after all, your life feels just the same *to you* as it did before.

In response to Nozick's example with the experience machine, the hedonist's standard reply is that the example just is too fantastical. We quite naturally, but entirely mistakenly, think that the experiences which the scientists would induce in us would be of lesser quality, and it is difficult to let go of the fact that we know that they are unreal. In a sense, then, our hesitation about taking the scientists up on their offer may be based on things quite external to the issue at stake, and thus it just says very little. The hedonist might add that we don't strictly know whether we are in the machine or not right now, but – apart from some sci-fi-writers and metaphysicians – no one seems to care very much about this matter. Whether the hedonist's reply ultimately is successful, and whether he or she has access to good replies to the other problems noted above, are issues I leave to the reader. Would you take the scientists up on their offer?

3.2. Total Versus Average Utilitarianism

So far we have only discussed what makes *one* person's life go better, but utilitarians are typically interested in the *overall balance* of pleasure over pain, 'in the universe as a whole' as they say. How should this be understood? Well as noted at the outset, Bentham's and Mill's credo is often restated as "the greatest good for the greatest number of people". But we may now note a certain ambiguity in this credo. In certain situations, your only options may be to either give a *greater* benefit to *fewer* people or to give a *smaller* benefit to *more* people. That is, you may have to choose between the greatest good, on the one hand, and the greatest number of people, on the other. What should you choose?

The classical utilitarian answer to this question is that you should try to find the best *mix* between the two, i.e. that it is the *total amount* of utility which matters. This is what it means to say that utilitarianism cares about the *overall* or *aggregate* utility in the universe. In the case above, the total amount of utility is most easily calculated by taking the size of the benefits distributed and multiplying this by the number of people who get it. If the number of people to which you can give the smaller benefit is sufficiently large, then, this may outweigh the fact that the benefit is smaller and you should then go for the smaller benefit. However, if the size of the greater benefit is sufficiently great, this may outweigh the fact that fewer people get it and you should go for the greater benefit. By caring about the total amount of utility in the universe, classical utilitarians suggest that they strike a reasonable balance between the quality of benefits and the quantity of people enjoying them.

Since it appeals to the total amount of utility in the universe, classical utilitarianism is often referred to as *total* or *quantitative* utilitarianism. Some philosophers have suggested, however, that total utilitarianism is morally problematic, often building on an ingenious example from Derek Parfit. According to Parfit, those who believe in total utilitarianism actually have two ways in which they can make the universe a better place: either by making *existing* people *happier*, or by simply *adding* more *happy people* (that is, by being more sexually active in the right kind of way). In today's world, Parfit suggests, it seems plausible to assume that most people we could add would live lives that are worth living, i.e., that their existence would increase the total amount of utility in the universe. The *average* quality of life would probably go down as we continued to add people, but we may assume that the total amount of utility would continue to go up for quite some time. Now, if this is this case, Parfit says, total utilitarianism seems to push us towards thinking that the *best* world would be the one in which we've simply added so *extremely* many new people so that there is no way of continuing doing so without making the average standard of living completely *hostile* (so that people's lives would cease to be worth living, and thus decrease the total amount of utility in the universe). But Parfit calls this 'the *repugnant* conclusion' – it just seems absurd to say that such a world would be better than a world in which a fewer amount of people enjoyed a higher average quality of life.

Parfit's line of reasoning above makes the classical form of utilitarianism morally problematic. It may be noted again, however, that this need not be a problem for utilitarianism as such. Persuaded by similar kinds of reasoning, some utilitarians abandon Bentham's and Mill's appeal to the total amount of utility in the universe and appeal instead to the following kind of theory:

> Average (or Qualitative) Utilitarianism: An action is right if and only if there was nothing else which the agent could have done in the situation which would have produced a greater average balance of pleasure over pain in the universe.

Interestingly, however, Parfit has counterexamples to this kind of theory as well, so it is once again not clear whether we have found an improvement on classical utilitarianism. Consider the more fantastical case of a hundred people having been condemned to the biblical hell for a hundred years. One day Satan arrives and gives the hundred an offer: He can reduce their stay in hell with one year, so that they only would have to spend ninety-nine years there, he says, if they would accept that he added a million further people to share their destiny. These further people are not alive yet, but Satan can just snap his fingers and bring a million new people into existence to suffer ninety-nine years of hell. Parfit suggests that average utilitarianism seems committed to saying that the hundred should take Satan up on his offer, since the world which he proposes clearly would have a higher average quality of life. But this is also an absurd position, Parfit suggests – surely, the addition of a million further people suffering the torments of hell has moral relevance.

In the end, Parfit argues that some middle position needs to be found, but finds himself struggling with the issue of exactly what this position could be.

It seems fair to say that most contemporary utilitarian thinkers stick with the appeal to the total amount of utility in the universe (the classical view); and this view may indeed have an intuitive advantage. After all, utilitarianism rests on the idea that all people's happiness should be given equal weight, and it may seem inconsistent with this to make the moral import of one person's quality of life depend on whether it is greater or lesser than the average quality of life of others. Whether proponents of classical utilitarianism have access to good reasons for fending off Parfit's repugnant conclusion, however, is a complicated issue which we cannot go into here but which I challenge the reader to ponder some more.

3.3. The Problem of Incommensurability

In the two sections above, I have outlined some recurring moral criticisms directed against classical utilitarianism. According to some further criticism, however, this theory has problems even more fundamental than so: it just doesn't seem possible to compare different kinds of happiness with each other, or to combine the welfare of different people into one single measure, as utilitarianism does.

To understand where this kind of criticism is coming from, we may go back to Mill's observation of the seeming difference between, for example, intellectual experiences like going to the opera and more brute pleasures like eating or having sex. Say that you one night are deciding between either going to the opera or staying in and enjoying a bit of sex and a nice fruitcake. According to utilitarianism you are to choose the action which maximises the amount of pleasure you get out of your night. But what does this mean more exactly? How are you to choose? Critics of the present kind suggest that utilitarianism actually gives you no guidance in this situation, because the two kinds of experiences seem so fundamentally different from each other. While they both may be enjoyable, the pleasure you would get from going to the opera is of an intellectual and sublime kind, while culinary and sexual pleasures arguably are more carnal and bodily. Since it just seems so difficult to find a meaningful way of comparing them, the critics say, perhaps we should simply say that they are *incomparable* or *incommensurable*. The present line of thinking is sometimes referred to as the *problem of incommensurability*.

The problem is exacerbated when we consider interpersonal value comparisons, especially utility sums. Say that you could give a certain benefit either to person A or to B and C together. Utilitarianism suggests that the right thing to do here is to distribute the benefit so that the total amount of happiness is as large as possible. But how can we make sense of the idea that there is some uniform scale along which person A's happiness may be greater or smaller than that of person B or person C? Furthermore, how can we make sense of the idea that giving the benefit to B and C may be better because the *sum* of their pleasures may be greater than A's? According to its critics, utilitarianism seems to assume that we can apply a kind of simple mathematics to moral dilemmas and just count people's pleasures in terms of whole numbers. But reducing morality to simple mathematics may seem impossible, or it may seem insensitive to the full complexity of the moral realm.

I cannot say much more about the problem of incommensurability in the present context since this would take us too far from the subject at hand. However, it may be fruitful to distinguish between two quite different worries which the criticisms above could be taken to express. On one interpretation, the critique is primarily of a *practical* nature – that is, that it seems difficult for most moral agents to *know* how to make both intra- and interpersonal value comparisons. On a more radical interpretation, however, the critique basically amounts to saying that it is completely *impossible* or *nonsensical* to make such comparisons. I believe the literature from proponents of utilitarianism contains many suggestions which could be used in attempts to reply to the more radical interpretation of the critique above. According to Bentham himself, for instance, while different pleasures certainly may feel quite differently, they could all be understood as having a certain *intensity* and *duration*. Now, perhaps this suggestion is all that is needed to make sense of the idea that it is at least *theoretically* possible to compare the hedonic value of different kinds of experiences.

Another suggestion in this context is that utilitarians may cease to talk about the qualities of *distinct* experiences and instead focus on how people value their experiences *as a whole*, or what we may call 'happiness states'. According to this suggestion, there is a sense in which we could be said to be at different general states of happiness at different times of our lives, or even different times of the day. I may now feel that life is a bit more enjoyable than how I experienced it when I woke up this morning, so I am in a higher happiness state now than I was this morning. If there is such a thing as the 'smallest detectable difference between different happiness states', perhaps this can be the currency in which utilitarianism should be expressed. While different people may experience life rather differently, there may be a sense in which we all enjoy our lives so and so much more or less than we would have enjoyed not existing.

Well, if any of these suggestions work, it is at least not completely nonsensical to talk about the 'total amount of happiness of universe' and so utilitarianism is not nonsensical. But obviously, the practical problem of trying to calculate this amount remains and we may now turn to this problem.

4. Applying Utilitarianism

Say that you've taken a university course on normative ethics and for some reason, perhaps because of its simplicity, you have become convinced of the correctness of utilitarianism. On the first day of your summer break, you decide that you shall start to live by your new creed – that is, you decide that you want to become a practicing utilitarian. So what are you to do now? Well in one sense you obviously know what to do: you are to maximise the overall happiness in the universe. But the obvious problem is: How are you to know how to do that? Should you give all of your money away to homeless people on the street, or perhaps move to a developing country and dedicate your life to helping people there, or should you simply give all of your money to cancer research? Perhaps you actually contribute the most by going on living exactly like you did before?

There are many reasons for why it seems almost impossible to know what action utilitarianism favours in any given situation, and so what actions are morally right and wrong. Consequences are by definition things that happen in the future, and only seldom will we know for certain what even the most immediate and local outcome of a specific action will be. But, of course, utilitarianism does not only care about the *immediate* consequences of an action, but everything which happens as a result of this action *until the end of time*. Nor does it only care about *local* outcomes, but how the *universe as a whole* is affected by a certain action. What utilitarianism asks us to keep track of is how the total amount of *happiness* in the universe is affected by our actions and, as we have already seen, this seems extremely difficult to evaluate. Finally, to establish whether a certain line of action is right or wrong we need not only estimate the probable consequences of *that* action, but also of *all alternative actions* open to us in the situation.

Many critics suggest that the considerations above show how utilitarianism actually never can be used to give practical recommendations to real people in the real world, and so it seems to be useless as a moral theory. One of the main things that we want out of a moral theory, it is suggested, is exactly practical action-guidance – that is, a moral theory is supposed to be practically usable as a guide to what we should and should not do. Utilitarians have responded in many quite different ways to this critique. Two rather popular responses, however, are the following: Firstly, some utilitarians question the idea that moral theories need to be practically action-guiding. What utilitarianism is supposed to be, they say, is first and foremost a *criterion of rightness* – that is, a criterion which says that actions are right and wrong, respectively, exactly when we on best reflection hold that they are right and wrong. In order to succeed as a criterion of rightness, a moral theory does not have to be practically action-guiding but what is more important is that the theory withstands theoretical counterexamples and moral arguments.

Secondly, utilitarians generally suggest that their criterion of rightness easily can be supplemented by a distinct kind of *decision procedure* which then can be used to make decisions in practical circumstances. In what follows, I will outline two of the most popularly suggested utilitarian decision procedures, and through this I hope to further illuminate the distinction between decision procedures and criteria of rightness.

4.1. Calculating Expected Utility

The most popular and probably most straightforward utilitarian decision procedure is one which appeals to calculations of so-called expected utility. Since we in real life have no way of knowing what the *actual* consequences of acting in a certain way will be, nor the *actual* utility of these consequences, utilitarians typically suggest that we may act on expectations of what *might* happen and evaluations of *expected* utility. To see how this is supposed to work, consider the following case: You work the nightshift at a nuclear power plant and are trying to decide whether to stay awake or go to sleep. You are awfully tired, so going to sleep certainly would feel better for you personally. However, there is a small risk that something might go wrong during the night – as things have been known to do in nuclear power plants – and if this were to happen, you are the only one around who could prevent a major catastrophe. Utilitarianism here, as always, tells you to choose the action which produces the best outcome, but the problem is obviously that you don't know whether your skills will be needed during the night or not. If they won't, you might as well go to sleep. So what are you to do?

According to proponents of the present kind of decision procedure, you may decide what to do by carefully working out the expected utilities of your options, and the first stage of this is pondering the probability of different possible outcomes. If you stay awake, you are quite confident that the only thing that would happen is that you would lose a good night's sleep. If you go to sleep, however, you know that you would feel much better, but you also estimate that there is a 1% risk of a nuclear catastrophe happening. The second stage involves estimating the expected utilities or values of these outcomes: that is, estimating roughly how good or bad the outcomes would be in utilitarian terms. Let's say that you estimate that the catastrophe would roughly be a million times worse than your losing the sleep. If your losing the sleep is -1 in utility, then, the catastrophe would be -1.000.000, say. Compared to this, you further estimate that getting a good night's sleep would give you the positive utility of 10.

You are now in the position to calculate the expected utilities of your options, which is the final stage of the decision procedure. The expected utility of a certain action is simply the sum of the expected probabilities of its possible outcomes multiplied by their expected utilities. The expected utility of staying awake, then, is 1 * -1 (you are certain that you will lose your sleep) = -1, and the expected utility of going to sleep is .99 * 10 (quite probable that you will get a good night's sleep) + .01 * -1.000.000 (the small risk of nuclear catastrophe) = -9.990,1. Since the expected utility of staying awake is greater than that of going to sleep, the procedure of calculating expected utility tells you to stay awake.

According to classical utilitarians, calculating expected utility will often be a useful tool in deciding what to do. Remember, however, that they only regard this as a decision procedure – that is, you are not *guaranteed* to choose the morally right action even if you go through the procedure. What ultimately matters to the correctness of actions, according to classical utilitarianism, is still the *actual* utility of its consequences, not the expected utility at the time of action. Some utilitarians have suggested that, in order to avoid the problem of practical action-guidance completely, utilitarianism may be reformulated to incorporate an appeal to expected utility directly in its criterion of rightness. These utilitarians defend the following view:

> Probabilistic Utilitarianism: An action is right if and only if there was nothing else which the agent could have done in the situation which would have produced a greater expected balance of pleasure over pain in the universe.

It should be noted, however, how this view is different from classical utilitarianism and, furthermore, how it comes with problems of its own. The estimations of both risks and utilities in the example above are obviously extremely subjective and arbitrary, and at least some deal of subjectivity in calculations of expected utility seems impossible to avoid – after all, we have agreed that the true utilities of the true consequences of actions are impossible to know in advance. But what happens if you have grossly misunderstood your situation? Say that you decide to stay awake but that, unbeknownst to you, some scientists actually have stopped the nuclear activities of the power plant – so there was really no risk of a catastrophe after all. Furthermore, say that your staying awake not only causes yourself some slight inconvenience but actually seriously affects people around you (perhaps because of the horrible state you are in the next day). In this case, some proponents of probabilistic utilitarianism may still want to say that your staying awake was the right thing to do, since you chose the action with the highest expected utility based on your subjective estimations of the situation. But is this really plausible? What you really have done, many people would say, is to cause people around you great harm for absolutely no use.

Other proponents of probabilistic utilitarianism may be tempted to say that your staying awake was morally wrong, since you didn't choose the action with the highest expected utility based on the *best* estimations of the situation (estimations based on full knowledge of, for example, what the scientists had done). But an interesting feature of this suggestion should be noted: As we keep adding restrictions on how objectively justified the estimations of expected utility involved need to be, we seem to get closer and closer to classical utilitarianism and the problem of practical action-guidance obviously seems to resurface – that is, how are we to know the *true* risks and chances of situations? In any case, if we really care about people's happiness, classical utilitarians argue, we should care about how the world *actually* goes and not how some people may *expect* it to go. While calculating expected utility may be a useful heuristic under certain circumstances, then, what matters to the correctness of actions is actual utility.

4.2. Rules of Thumb

Some utilitarians suggest that calculating expected utility is not always an appropriate decision procedure. In situations where immediate action is required, for instance, one may simply not have the time to go through all of the necessary calculations. In other situations, going through the necessary calculations may be too costly and so ultimately not worth it. Interestingly, it has been suggested that even the most conscientious person may find it difficult to avoid letting bias or wishful thinking affect his or her estimations of expected utility. When we have had a bit too much to drink and are considering whether to walk or drive home, for example, it is easy to falsely estimate the probability of an accident happening as rather insignificant and therefore conclude that it is okay to take the car. In all of these situations, the idea goes, it may be better to make decisions according to more crude *'rules of thumb'* – that is, more straightforward decision rules which will be easier to implement. One such rule of thumb may be "don't drink and drive".

The introduction of rules of thumb into utilitarian thinking is quite interesting. Many proponents of utilitarianism suggest that this feature is likely to bring utilitarianism much closer to some of its rivals than what is generally appreciated. Some quite useful rules of thumb, namely, may be the rules "never actively kill someone" and "never lie". Since the situations in which the action which maximises happiness will be an instance of killing or lying are likely to be uncommon, namely, it may be better to never even consider such actions as viable alternatives than to do so and sometimes kill or lie when it has disastrous consequences. It may here be argued that these decision rules seem quite different from the core idea of utilitarianism, and so there seems to be some tension between going for maximising happiness and abiding by these rules of thumb. But we may now generalise over the issue of suitable decision procedures and ask on what grounds utilitarians may prefer one over the other.

A first thought may be that the best decision procedure simply must be the one which leads you to perform morally correct actions as often as possible. But this is actually not how utilitarians generally frame the issue of appropriate decision procedures. In a sense, utilitarians suggest, the choice of decision procedure is just like any other choice of what to do, except that it concerns how to form decisions over a longer period of time. The idea that most utilitarians defend here, then, is quite simply that you should adopt the decision procedure which, if you followed it over a longer period of time, has the *best consequences* compared to (your following) other such decision procedures. And this best decision procedure may very well involve certain quite anti-utilitarian rules such as "don't kill" and "never lie". Some utilitarians, like, e.g., Henry Sidgwick, go even further and suggest that it may actually never have good consequences to *think directly like a utilitarian* – that is, to ponder what line of action would maximise overall happiness. Or at least, it may never have good consequences to *tell others* that you are thinking like a utilitarian, so perhaps utilitarianism should be kept a secret. According to Sidgwick, then, we may have utilitarian reasons for not acting like utilitarians.

Many philosophers suggest that the kind of reasoning invoked above is absurd. Some proponents of utilitarianism try to avoid the seeming absurdity of Sidgwick's suggestion above by once again asking us to reconsider the formulation of utilitarianism. If following certain non-utilitarian rules of thumb really has such good consequences, they say, perhaps right and wrong should be defined more straightforwardly exactly as following such rules. These philosophers defend the following view:

> Rule Utilitarianism: An action is right if and only if it conforms to the set of rules which are such that there is no other set of rules which, if everyone followed it, would produce a greater overall balance of pleasure over pain in the universe.

But is this view plausible? The standard argument from proponents of classical utilitarianism, or *act* utilitarianism as it is often called, is that rule utilitarianism is an unstable mix between utilitarian and non-utilitarian moral thinking. If you take any more rigid rule, it seems plausible to say that there will be exceptional cases where it would be better in utilitarian terms if agents didn't follow the rule. Even though killing normally has bad consequences, for instance, it seems downright anti-utilitarian to say that one should not kill one where this is the only way in which one could save five others. But as we keep adding exceptions to the rules, the idea goes, rule utilitarianism – just like probabilistic utilitarianism – simply seems to collapse back into classical act utilitarianism, i.e. the idea that we always should maximise the positive contribution of individual *actions*.

Once again, the classical utilitarian would not say that you have acted morally rightly just because you managed to follow the best decision procedure. The classical utilitarian would say that the rightness of an action is determined by the consequences of the action itself. However, following certain rules of thumb may sometimes be *practically* useful – that is, it may be a good way of making decisions. In fact, even when following such rules of thumb leads you to do the wrong thing, this may be a case of what utilitarians call *blameless* wrongdoing (which I will explain further below). Furthermore, this is probably how we should try to make people *think* about moral issues in general. Doing so, as I have said, may have better consequences than trying to make everyone think in direct utilitarian terms.

5. External Criticisms of Utilitarianism

In whatever way you formulate it, utilitarianism is surely a controversial moral theory. While proponents of utilitarianism often hold out the simplicity of the theory as one of its principal strengths, as noted above, critics generally argue that this is one of its principal weaknesses. For evident reasons, I cannot give justice to the enormous literature for and against utilitarianism in the present context. Simplifying matters tremendously, however, we may separate the external criticisms of utilitarianism into two main groups: One the one hand, it is often argued that utilitarianism is too *permissive*, and on the other, it is sometimes argued that utilitarianism is too *demanding*.

The argument that utilitarianism is too permissive takes as its starting point the idea that utilitarianism basically can approve of *all* kinds of actions, however crude or morally abhorrent they may seem to be, as long as they happen to maximise happiness. As noted at the outset, a fundamental tenet of utilitarianism is that whether a certain action is right or wrong does not depend on what kind of action it is (whether, e.g., it is a case of lying or killing) or with what intention it is performed (whether, e.g., it is performed with good or bad intentions) but the only interesting issue is what consequences different actions produce. Here are some things which utilitarianism often is thought to be unable to accommodate for: Firstly, the idea that human beings have certain fundamental *moral rights* seems to sit uneasily with utilitarianism. Utilitarians may respect such rights when nothing can be gained by violating them, but as soon as one can maximise happiness by violating such rights this is morally obligatory. Secondly, the fact that I have *promised* someone to do X is never directly or *in itself* a reason for doing X. Since utilitarianism only cares about consequences or, we may say, *forward*-looking considerations, *backward*-looking considerations like the fact that I have promised something are never morally important in themselves.

Thirdly, utilitarianism is sometimes said to be at odds with some of our most basic intuitions about *distributive justice*. Say that I can take all of the resources of one person and distribute them to enough other people so that the total sum of enjoyment is greater than before. If this is possible, utilitarianism suggests that I have every reason to do so. I may even have reason to do so if the first person dies as a result of my redistribution, and the people to which I give the resources were quite well-off to start with. Fourthly, utilitarianism seems to sit uneasily with our intuitions about *retributive* justice as well. While it most often may be best to punish the guilty for offenses, there is nothing in principle which prevents utilitarianism from accepting punishment of the innocent. In fact, utilitarianism seems to imply that sentencing an innocent person to death may be justified as long as it prevents enough other people from committing serious crimes.

The considerations above can obviously be multiplied. Utilitarianism is not only criticised for being too *permissive*, it may be noted, but sometimes it is criticised for being too *demanding* as well. While utilitarianism says very little about exactly what kinds of actions may be called for in the pursuit of maximising happiness, there is one thing which utilitarianism is quite insistent on: that we ought to dedicate our entire lives to maximising overall happiness in the universe. But what this means, critics say, is that we are obliged to give up all of the life projects we currently are engaged in and completely dedicate ourselves to the serving of others. Some critics suggest that this in a sense means giving up our very *identity*, since we to a large degree tend to identify ourselves with our personal projects. According to others, what is most problematic here is that utilitarianism is at odds with the value of personal relationships. At the very core of utilitarianism lies the idea that we should pay equal attention to how everyone's happiness is affected by our actions. However what this means in practice, it is argued, is that I must care just as much about, for example, other people's children as my own, and as much about other people's spouses as my own. It is not difficult to see why this result has been thought to be deeply counterintuitive.

Once again simplifying things enormously, one could say that utilitarians generally have presented three main kinds of responses to the criticisms above: First of all, as already noted, many utilitarians suggest that utilitarianism actually is much closer to some of its rivals than what is generally appreciated. Even though the theory *in principle* accepts that even quite horrific actions could be justified if and when they maximise happiness, such actions will quite seldom be the best alternative *in the real world*, utilitarians say. Punishing innocent people will seldom lead to very good consequences, for instance, because the fact that they are innocent will most often come out in the end. And redistributing wealth from the poor to the rich will almost certainly never be a good thing, because the poor simply get more happiness out of a given amount of resources than the already well-off do (in terms borrowed from economic theory, this is sometimes referred to as the *law of diminishing marginal utility*). In any case, since it is impossible to *know* exactly what action maximises general happiness in real life scenarios, utilitarianism – just like its rivals – suggests that the reasonable thing to do probably is to follow a *rule of thumb* which says that no horrific actions are to be performed.

Secondly, utilitarians sometimes put their appeal to rules of thumb to use in a further and quite ingenious way, which we have yet to discuss. According to some utilitarians, the issue of whether a certain line of action is *blameworthy* or not is actually not the same issue as whether it is morally right or wrong. Whereas proponents of other moral theories typically see blameworthiness as something fundamentally connected to wrongness, and praiseworthiness as something fundamentally connected to rightness, these utilitarians suggest that blaming and praising people simply should be regarded a special kind of actions. So whether we should blame someone for, for instance, not keeping her promises, ultimately depends on the consequences of the *act of blaming*. And it may very well be so, as we have seen that utilitarians sometimes argue, that we should try to instill non-utilitarian values in people around us. This will simply have better consequences than making these people direct utilitarians.

While actions such as killing, lying, not respecting people's rights and breaking one's promises may be morally obligatory under certain circumstances, then, utilitarianism may hold that many of these actions actually are blameworthy. And while it never is morally correct to act on a greater consideration of the happiness of people closer to us than that of more distant people, doing so may sometimes be blameless or even praiseworthy. This is so because there seldom will be any point in blaming people for caring more about their own children or spouses than that of others – after all, doing away with personal relationships will make us all very unhappy. By separating the issue of blame and praise from the issue of right and wrong, then, utilitarians seem able to cater for a whole range of quite non-utilitarian moral ideas. Whether such a separation really makes sense, however, is obviously not clear.

If or when all of the above fails, utilitarians typically resort to a final way of responding to the criticisms outlined above; namely to fully *embracing* the supposedly counterintuitive implications of their theory. Most of the criticisms above are based on intuitions, it may be noted. Critics say that it just seems so counterintuitive to say that killing innocent people sometimes may be morally obligatory, or that we ought to dedicate our entire lives to the serving of others. But some utilitarians respond to this simply by saying that it may be some of our intuitions which are faulty, and not utilitarianism. Why do we think that killing always must be morally wrong? According to one suggestion, this may in fact just be *squeamishness* on our part – that is, we hesitate to do the right thing when it calls for actions which we find unpalatable or unpleasant. Similarly, some suggest that our aversion against dedicating our lives to serving others may just be *self-indulgence*. When our intuitions clash with the recommendations of utilitarianism, then, perhaps we must simply modify our intuitions. Indeed, we may note that political liberalism seemed too radical and counterintuitive to people in Mill's days. But most people now think that this is just because those people knew too little about justice and fairness.

6. Conclusion

In this chapter I have outlined some of the basic elements of utilitarian ethics and discussed what I take to be the most common moral arguments for and against it. Much attention have been given to what we may call the apparent *flexibility* of the utilitarian framework, which I take to consist in two things: Firstly, I have shown how utilitarianism actually could be seen as a *group* of moral theories rather than a single theory. Secondly, I have tried to show how even classical utilitarianism can employ a number of tricks to incorporate moral ideas which initially may seem inconsistent with it. I have said that it perhaps is this flexibility which explains utilitarianism's longstanding place as one of the main contenders in normative ethics. Whether this flexibility shows that utilitarianism is the *best* theory, however, is an issue which I leave to the reader to decide.

While the utilitarian framework indeed is rather flexible, it should be noted that the theory cannot be made compatible with just about everything. It still has a rather precise core in the suggestion that what ultimately matters is how people's well-being is affected by actions. Whether this general idea is correct, and whether utilitarianism can avoid the problems it is said to have, will probably be central issues in moral philosophy for centuries to come. I encourage the reader to discuss these issues with his or her peers. When discussing this issue, however, I suggest that the reader also takes some time to think through the last of the issues discussed above: Just because some of our intuitions go against the tenets of utilitarianism, does this mean the theory is wrong? Could not the fault instead rest in *ourselves*? Perhaps we should simply revise some of our moral intuitions in light of utilitarianism?

BIBLIOGRPAHY

Notes on the Bibliography

Bentham's classic statement of utilitarianism can be found in his *Introduction to Principles of Morals and Legislation* (originally published in 1789). However, Mill's *Utilitarianism* (originally published in 1859) is probably more informative of the reasoning of the early utilitarians. Other classic works are Sidgwick's *The Methods of Ethics* (1874) and Moore's *Principia Ethica* (1903). All of these books can be found in many more modern editions, and some of them are also for download.

Nozick discusses the example of the experience machine in a short section of his *Anarchy, State, and Utopia* (Basic Books, 1974) and Parfit gives his examples in *Reasons and Persons* (Oxford University Press, 1984). The latter book not only contains an ingenious discussion of the issue of total versus average utilitarianism, but also gives insightful comments on so-called blameless wrongdoing and the issue of what has value – in short, it is a modern classic. Singer elaborates extensively on how his version of preference utilitarianism can be applied to real-life moral dilemmas in his *Practical Ethics* (Cambridge University Press, second edition 1993), and a version of rule utilitarianism is defended by Brad Hooker in *Ideal Code, Real World* (Oxford University Press, 2000).

An outstanding example of the debate between utilitarians and non-utilitarians can be found in J. J. C. Smart's and Bernard Williams' *Utilitarianism: For and Against* (Cambridge University Press, 1973). However, the utilitarian thinker from which I probably have taken most inspiration in this chapter is Torbjörn Tännsjö, my former professor. His main work is *Hedonistic Utilitarianism* (Edinburgh University Press, 1998), but an eloquent introduction to utilitarianism can also be found in his *Understanding Ethics* (Edinburgh University Press, second edition 2008). Tännsjö defends classical utilitarianism with no fear whatsoever of embracing counterintuitive implications – indeed, he accepts many implications much more counterintuitive than the ones outlined in this chapter.

Bentham, J. (2009 [1859]). *Introduction to Principles of Morals and Legislation*. Mineola, N.Y., Dover Publications.

Hooker, B. (2000). *Ideal Code, Real World*. Oxford, Oxford University Press.

Mill, J. S. (2001 [1859]). *Utilitarianism*. Indianapolis, Hackett.

Moore, G. E. (2004 [1903]). *Principia Ethica*. Mineola, N.Y., Dover Publications.

Nozick, (1974). *Anarchy, State, and Utopia*. New York, Basic Books.

Parfit, D. (1984). *Reasons and Persons*. Oxford, Oxford University Press.

Sidgwick, (1981 [1874]) *The Methods of Ethics*. Indianapolis, Hackett.

Singer (1993). *Practical Ethics (2nd Edition)*. Cambridge, Cambridge University Press.

Smart, J.J.C. and Williams, B. (1973). *Utilitarianism: For and Against*. Cambridge, Cambridge University Press.

Tännsjö, T. (1988). *Hedonistic Utilitarianism*. Edinburgh, Edinburgh University Press.

_____ (2008). *Understanding Ethics (2nd Edition)*. Edinburgh, Edinburgh University Press.

13

Virtue Ethics

Richa Yadav

1. Introduction

The Meaning and Scope of Virtue Ethics

The word 'Ethics' is very much in vogue in today's extremely conscientious and vigilant consumerist global market. Ethical issues have become a focal point for social workers, academicians, politicians, doctors, environmentalists, industrialists and the owners of multi-national companies. 'Ethics' aims at creating an 'awareness' among people so that they might become better citizens, employers, employees and so forth, which in turn ensures the smooth fabric of society. This is the lay-man's way of understanding ethics. However, ethical philosophers have tradtionally also offered various ethical theories to help people attain the 'correct' line of thinking and behavior. Various modern and contemporary ethical theories have focussed on the problem of practical judgment, elaborating on its philosophical implications and practical ramifications for the various social concerns of society. Most contemporary theories focus on guiding humanity with regard to what it 'ought' to do by analyzing and redefining moral concepts - defining how one ought to behave in a society. Thus, the thrust is on being 'ethical' rather than being 'moral'. The aim has also been to define the correct ethical code of conduct, our obligations and what we personally ought do.

However, if we trace the roots of such ethical theories we find that in ancient times their formation was less driven by social concerns and focused more on individual reform. Its primary thrust was to see how an individual could become a better person by inculcating inner virtue. Classical ethicists aimed at the personal transformation of the individual. They believed that ethical behaviour cannot become manifest unless one tries to become virtuous from the core of one's heart. They believed that ethical protocols could be better nurtured when a person inculcates the virtues as his second nature. The focal point of much of historically early ethics revolves around the concern with individual excellence. Although this concern for virtue appears in several philosophical traditions, in the West the first thinkers to emphasize such rational thinking emerged in the ancient Greek world in the 6th century B.C.

If we look at the political scene of 5th and 6th century (B.C.E.) Greece, we find that the Greeks lived in relatively small city-states, which were frequently in conflict over territory. This background of war set the stage for the development of virtues that would promote civic harmony. This was the time when philosophers like Socrates, Aristotle and Plato made a great break with the past. They tried to understand the world through the use of reason and taught others to do the same. They were the first teachers who did not try to pass on the body of knowledge by appealing to their religion, authority or tradition. Instead, they encouraged their pupils to try to understand what was good and right for them and to adopt virtue as their second nature. These Greek philosophers laid the foundation of rational thinking and established the first form of virtue ethics through their understanding of the individual as an important unit of society, who should try to act virtuously as a moral agent.

The foundation of virtue ethics laid by these Greek philosophers has been influential on much subsequent moral philosophy. For them, ethics was a reflective study involving an analysis of what is good or bad in a human character and describing how one can lead a virtuous and moral life by using one's capacity for reason and sense of personal responsibility. They believed that this would ultimately contribute to one's own well being.

The term 'virtue' cannot denote a mere natural feeling or susceptibility to feeling, such as anger, fear or pity. It rather denotes a settled habit, formed by a course of action in which vicious excess and deficiency have been avoided. Virtue is a quality of mind that we acquire by our own efforts. It denotes those characteristics that enables an individual to live well - in harmony with himself and his community. Classical virtue theorists believed that the key to one's real happiness (*eudaimonia*) is a matter of one's personal choice. It also teaches us what good conduct, nobility of character and readiness to lead a virtuous life with moral values involves.

2. Classical Virtue Ethics: Tracing its Development

Although Greek philosophers did not propound any explicitly unified ethical theory, their views have been grouped together under the heading of 'virtue ethics' by various authors and commentators, in an attempt to organize them within a coherent theoretical framework. In this section, we will the trace the development of virtue ethics by exploring the views of Socrates, Plato and Aristotle. We will begin with certain basic questions and consider the answers of the Greeks. Any ethical theory makes an attempt to answer questions such as what is the meaning of virtue, which character traits are properly called virtues, what does virtue consists in, and why should one consciously work on inculcating virtue in oneself? Socrates, Plato and Aristotle have each considered these questions in their own way. For virtue ethicists, any attempt to answer these qeustions must begin with the exploration of the concept of 'virtue' itself.

2.1. Socrates and Plato

We will begin with Socrates, as he can be regarded as the origin of virtue ethics. Socrates does not provide us with a complete theory, but his contribution is nevertheless significant, as he is the first to raise key philosophical questions - such as what moral concepts should be used and what criteria should we apply for their use?

There is no written manuscript left to us by Socrates himself. His pupil Plato elaborates the views of his master in his early works. The 'Socratic Method' of inquiry is unique, in that it poses simple questions to common people, like what is pity, courage and justice? Socratic questioning is designed to arouse interest in fundamental philosophical questions. He believed that by employing this strategy one could reach the true knowledge, which lies within each individual person. If one knows what the best way is, one would not intentionally commit errors. For instance, if we know the true meaning of justice, we would by default become a just person - for to be otherwise would not be rational. Following from this, Aristotle later concludes that if men do what is wrong it is through intellectual error- and not solely through moral weakness. One can overcome one's moral weakness through attaining the right knowledge, which itself is a virtue. Socrates concludes that any moral virtue is a form of knowledge. The knowledge that constitutes virtue involves not only the beliefs that such and such should be the case, but also a capacity to distinguish good from bad and an ability to act appropriately.

Socrates was the first to teach the priority of personal integrity in terms of a person's duty to himself rather than to a god, the law or any other authority. He encouraged people to preserve the integrity of their souls, because real personal catastrophe consists in the corruption of the soul. This is the primary reason why we should refrain from doing any injustice to another. But how can one be honest to one's soul? Socrates professes a deep belief in the maxim 'Know thyself'. For Socrates, the most important knowledge always stems from self-knowledge. Hence, in so far as virtue is knowledge, and virtue implies self-knowledge, virtue must involve both knowledge of, and care for, oneself and one's soul.

Socrates believed that all the moral virtues are rooted in practical wisdom. He emphasized the importance of self-examination, observation of other worthy men, reflection on the meaning of our moral convictions and moderation in feelings and action. Socratic well-being consists in the actual doing of what is good. This gives rise to a dynamic theory of happiness and moral success; to do good is to fare well. He avoided offering a formal standard for the determination of what is good, but insisted that through reflection one could discover the ideals of temperate justice and courageous living. He argued that no man voluntarily chooses evil, as to prefer evil to good is not constitutive of human nature. The implication is that one will always do what one *thinks* good - and that education helps one to make reliable judgment regarding what is good. For Socrates, the concept of good is necessarily bound to the concept of observing a limit. He suggests that limitless desire is insatiable.

Anything that is to be demarcated as a proper way of living must have a form that allows us to distinguish it from other less appropriate ways of living. Furthermore, if anything is to be termed good, and has the possibility of being known as desirable, then it must be specifiable in terms of some set of rules which might govern behavior.

In the above discussion, we have seen that for Socrates virtue is knowledge. This answers our the first question that we set ourselves - 'what is virtue?' Our next question will be: what does virtue consists in (or what character traits are virtues)? For Socrates, virtue consists in being good. And this is possible only through knowing one's soul and showing concern for one's real self.

The work of Socrates is further developed by his student Plato. Both argue that the ultimate good for any individual is his own welfare or well-being. Plato believes that the just life is a happier life than the unjust one. The unjust man does not set any limits on his desires, and as he always keeps himself engaged in the effort to satiate his unfulfilled desires, he ends up always being discontented. A person who knows the difference between the pleasure of reason and the satiation of desires is a happy one. Rational intellectual pleasure is deemed genuine and appropriate.

The ultimate object of Plato's philosophical contemplation is 'the good'. In *The Republic* he presents his idea of the good. It is conceived as the ultimate ground of all being and knowledge, although it is not knowledge itself. He defines this ultimate object of knowledge as the essence of all virtue.

He maintains that such knowledge is the actual measure of pleasure and pain. Plato believes that all things really were, "realized their ideal", proportionately to the extent that they accomplished the special end or good for which they were adapted. But this special end can only be really good in so far as it is related to the ultimate end or good of the whole, as one of the means or particulars by or in which this is partially realized. If then the essence, or reality, of each part of the organized world is to be found in its particular end or good, the ultimate ground of all reality must be found in the ultimate end or good of the universe. And if this is the ground of all reality, the knowledge of it must also be the source of all guidance for human life. Man's goodness is derived from the good and the being of the universe - the ground of all things, i.e. the good as the knowledge of good includes all other knowledge.

Plato talks about four kinds of excellences that were already recognized in the moral consciousness of Greece, which later became known as the cardinal virtues- (1) Wisdom (2) Courage or Fortitude (3) Temperance or Orderliness (4) Justice or Uprightness. The two most important of these are wisdom, which implies the full possession of knowledge that the philosopher seeks, and justice, which is the harmonious and regulated activity of all elements of the soul. In Plato's view the two fundamental virtues, in their highest form, are mutually involved. A wise soul would necessarily be one in which all elements operate in harmonious activity, and this activity cannot be perfect unless the rational and governing element is truly wise. Plato is of the view that all branches of civic duty would be regulated in minute detail by a wise government aiming at the promotion of moral excellence in its subjects as the main element of their well being. Especially in the ideal state of his *Republic*, where division of sentiment and life would be excluded, and relation of the sexes ordered with a single eye to perfection of breeding and distribution of functions according to fitness, and where obedience to rules laid down by the government would constitute the whole sphere of ordinary virtue.

In Plato's *Republic*, the notion of well-being or *eudaimonia* (to be discussed in further detail later) is retained and explored. His ethics are fundamentally *eudaimonistic*. He sees the good life for man in terms of the personal attainment of well being. In the ideal condition, man's reason would regulate and order all the functions of his irrational appetites. The movement within each man towards the ideal personality is an original version of self-perfection ethics. The development of virtues is a personal process, which varies from one person to another. Plato is also aware of the social dimensions of human life and well being. A good life requires association with other persons. Ethics is but a dimension of politics, which deals with how to live well in a state. Plato maintains a general coextension between personal moral goodness and political good order, but stresses throughout the superiority of political virtue over the attainments of the individual. Since state morality is identified with the divine good, *The Laws* offer a suggestion of totalitarianism. This is one of the least attractive features of Plato's social ethics.

Plato regards knowledge as the essence of all virtues. He holds that such knowledge is really mensuration of pleasure and pain and that the most important element of the good life for ordinary men consists in doing well. So we see that Plato attempts to identify fullness of being (unity) with moral perfection (good) and is thus inaugurating a type of self-perfection ethics. When discussing what is good for man, Plato suggests that there is an objective criterion available. He believes that this criterion cannot be derived from social structures and institutions, or from our deires - as we use our evaluative concepts to criticize these. Hence, it must be derived from an order that exists independant of human life.

2.2. Aristotle's Theory of Virtue

For Plato, the meaning of the word 'good' is defined as knowledge of the form of the Good. But Aristotle argues that Plato's good is not explanatory, as it cannot account for the diversity of our uses of the term. Where Plato sees the criterion of well-being as transcendent, Aristotle sees it as embedded in a particular type of practice and social arrangement. He is less other-worldly than Plato and more naturalistic. He thinks that the world of sensible things is the real world and that there is no realm of unintelligible entities. Aristotle's two main works in ethics are the *Eudemian Ethics* and *Nicomachean Ethics*.

According to Aristotle, all human beings pursue a chief good and achieving this is their ultimate aim. He calls this principal good *eudaimonia*. *Eudaimonia* is achieving one's full potential - thereby making one's life worth living. To live a life which can be characterized by *eudaimonia* is precisely the aim of morality. *Arête* is another word used by Aristotle, which is translated as 'excellence' or 'virtue'. For someone to possess *arête* is for that person to be good at something, to possess a certain skill - although this term is not always used in a moral sense. Different translators have used different words to translate *eudaimonia*, depending on the context of its usage, such as 'happiness', 'fulfillment' or even 'human flourishing' and words like 'virtue', 'excellence', 'skill', 'being good at' for *arête*.

Aristotle is the first philosopher to ground morality in nature, and human nature in particular. The *eudaimonia* of Aristotlian ethics is teleological. It stresses the purposiveness of human nature. For him, the goal of moral activity is achieved when man develops control of his unrestrained and appetitive powers, so that he can habitually act in accordance with moral virtue. He claims that in every action there is a subordination of ends. Most of our actions are directed at some purpose and, since all actions are purposeful, there must be some final goal towards which all actions are directed. And this final end of the things that we do, must not be aiming at achieving something else. This goal must be what we desire for its own sake (everything else being desired for the sake of this), and this must be the chief good. There can be no higher aim than this.

Aristotle discusses two main characteristics of *eudaimonia* or a fulfilled life - (i) it is the most complete end and (ii) it is sufficient in itself. The former characteristic means that it is sought after for its own sake and not for the sake of anything else. If one has a fulfilled life, then nothing more is required and hence no further end needs to be pursued. The feature of completeness denotes that such happiness is by definition the most desirable of all things, so it logically cannot have any goods externally added to it. All goods lie within its borders. This happiness is actually the final end or goal. We may choose to pursue intelligence, honor, wealth and so forth for the sake of happiness, but we could not choose to pursue happiness in order to secure intelligence, honor or wealth. The second characteristic of *eudaimonia* is self-sufficiency. Happiness is a self-sufficient good. It is not a component in some other state of affair. This means that nothing can be further added to *eudaimonia*, because it contains all the other goods for the individual. Self-sufficiency is defined by Aristotle as that which, when attained, makes life desirable and lacking in nothing. An individual can become self-sufficient in two ways, either by lowering one's need or by producing more than required. Aristotle maintains that nothing needs to be added to the highest good or happiness from outside - not because of low internal demand, but because of ample internal supply.

However, a question may be asked regarding whether we really know the way to attain *eudaimonia*. Aristotle suggests that we will discover what fulfillment consists in, if we can grasp the essential function of human beings. He proposes the *ergon* or function argument, which is based on the consideration of the function or characteristic activity of man in order to explain how his greatest good can come to be specified. Aristotle thus lays the foundation of his ethical system by assuming that human good consists in the proper exercise of the characteristic activity or work of man. To do something well, and to do it according to virtue or excellence, are synonymous expressions. For Aristotle, to function properly, and hence to attain a fulfilled life, is to exercise the capacities to be found in the human soul and to exercise them well. Thus, the human good turns out to be activity of the soul in conformity with excellence or virtue (*arête*). What makes us good human beings, according to this definition, is action in accordance with the standards for the good use of reason.

Aristotle gives *eudaimonia* a dynamic signification. Aristotelian *eudaimonia* is (1) that to which all men aspire as a fulfillment (2) a continued and perfect activity (3) a whole human life embodying this activity in a favorable context of possessions and friends. He emphasizes that human happiness is an activity and not a habitual state. Then he argues that it is an activity of intellectual understanding (*nous*), continuous, pleasant and sufficient unto itself. He suggests that it is a high an ideal for man, but that we should try to cultivate it. He distinguishes three factors within the human soul - emotions (*pathe*), powers (*dunameis*), and habitual states (*hexeis*) - and concludes that virtues are good habits. Vices are bad habits.

Virtue has its origin in the Latin word *vir* and refers to strength and manliness. For Aristotle virtue is *arête*. It refers to excellence of various kinds. The term 'virtue' denotes a settled habit formed by a course of action, under rule and discipline, avoiding extremes. The virtuous man is a man without any internal conflict, and the one who wills action that accomplish the happy mean in their effects. According to Aristotle, there are two basic kinds of virtues - intellectual and moral. Intellectual virtue is excellence of mind - for example, the ability to understand and reason. These traits are learned from teachers. The growth of these virtues depends on the way they are taught. On the other hand, moral virtues are dispositions; they dispose one to act well. These virtues are learned not by being taught, but by repetition or practice. For instance, by practicing courage or honesty we become more courageous and honest. If one repeats the practice of certain virtues often, it becomes one's second nature. We adapt these virtues from nature and then perfect them by inculcating them in ourselves as habits.

Aristotle does not believe in taking any action or habit to its extreme level. Unrestrained self-indulgence and self-assertion will bring us into perpetual conflict with other people, and it will also leave us unhappy with ourselves. Similarly, even an excessive inhibition to do what is best for us is not a very positive trait for the development of our character. So inhibition is not recommended. Aristotle develops his theory of moral virtues as a *golden mean* between the extremes of vice as excess and deficiency, according to which a virtue is a perfect midway point. For instance, generosity is the mean between profligacy and meanness. The aim always is to be a balanced personality. This, he thinks, is the way to achieve happiness. The Aristotelian golden mean is concerned with the object of virtuous choice; we act virtuously when we choose a mean between two extremes which constitute the corresponding vices. The notion of a mean is quantitative. It is based on the belief that in passions and actions we can distinguish between excess and deficiency. But still we cannot have a mathematical calculation about the same. Subjective conditions vary widely, and so the moral agent has to think and to decide.

The list of virtues in 'ethics' is not a list resting on Aristotle's own personal choice, but rather it reflects what he takes to be the code of the gentleman in contemporary Greek society. Aristotle analyses some virtues and shows how they represent the mean of the two extremes. For instance, what would be an ideal behavior for a soldier during the war? If he shows bravery and enters into the war alone then he has a chance of losing his life. This will be foolhardiness on his part, not bravery. And if he does not face his enemies and runs away from the battle field, then he would be known as a coward. The golden mean between these two extremes is to use one's reason and moral sensibilities and fight for one's country. This would require a lot of courage. So courage is the mean between foolhardiness and cowardice. Following, is a brief list of some other qualities suggested by Aristotle as the golden mean between two extremes. Courage and temperance are concerned with the regulation of the primitive or animal aversions and appetites. Aristotle gives two pairs of virtues which are occupied respectively with the two chief objects of man's more refined and civilized desire for, and pursuit of, wealth and honor.

Excess	Mean	Defect
Foolhardiness	Courage	Cowardice
Licentiousness	Temperance	Insensibility
Vanity	High-mindedness	Small-mindedness
Boastfulness	Truthfulness	False modesty
Envy	Righteous indignation	Spite

According to him right, actions are performed in accordance with the corresponding moral virtue. Virtuous action requires knowledge, choice and a steadfast way of reacting to passions or affections. The central element of virtuous action is choice, and specifically the choice of something for its own sake. This reinforces the view that the right is conceived of as the good in itself, and not as something conducive to some further first-order good. Excellence is a state or habit concerned with choice, that lies in a mean relative to us - as determined by reason and the way in which the man of practical wisdom would determine it. One striking thing about Aristotle's moral philosophy is that it has little moralizing. The aim is essentially practical. He argues that it is impossible to be practically wise without being good, so there is a role of prudence in morally right action.

3. Objections to Greek Virtue Ethics

Greek virtue ethics has been widely criticized by various authors and ethical theorists. Socrates thinks that if one has proper knowledge, one will have all the virtues. He seems to be saying that if one knows what is right and good one will do it. It is argued that this sort of moral intellectualism is probably over optimistic in its view of human conduct. One need not always follow the virtuous path, even though one knows what the right path is. He presents a very intellectual view of moral thought, hence failing to provide any ground for morality.

It is pointed out by some contemporary philosophers that any moral question can be raised only in the light of how one has to behave when one is in a social context or community. Morality is always understood in the context of self versus others. And if we look at the crux of virtue ethics, we realize that it seems to be essentially interested in the acquisition of the virtues as part of the agent's own well-being and flourishing. It can be accused of being too self-centered, because its primary concern is with the agent's own character. It does not seem to consider others. The idea of one's own well-being as a moral notion sounds very selfish. However, this objection fails to appreciate the role of the virtues within the theory. All the virtues one would have would be ultimately beneficial to others as well. Kindness, for example, is about how we respond to the needs of others. With this in mind, a reply to this objection can be given as follows - the account of virtue ethics claims that the good of the agent and the good of others are not two separate aims. Therefore, instead of being too self-centered, virtue ethics unifies what is required by morality and what is required by self-interest.

Another major objection to the theory is that simply delineating some general principles of virtue cannot give concrete guidelines for behavior. This theory seems weak because it does not offer clear direction for resolving concrete ethical dilemmas, and if a theory fails to be action-guiding, it is of no use as a moral theory. The main response to this criticism is to stress that knowing what to do is not a matter of internalizing some set rules and manners, but is rather a long process of moral learning. It makes a person think about what would be the best action to do in a particular situation. One must learn to internalize goodness in such a way that one can perceive a situation ethically and give one's best moral judgment. Virtue ethics does not delineate any hard and fast rules because it is more flexible and situation-sensitive. It can be action-guiding, if we understand the role of the virtuous agent and we have faith that virtue actually consists of the right reason and the right desire. Hence, we should follow it's commands. A person with fair understanding of the virtues, and who has practical wisdom, will perceive that virtues do not give rise to any contrary alternatives regarding ethical action and that there are no irresolvable dilemmas in the path of virtue.

Aristotle's treatment of ethics has been criticized as highly unsystematic and confused. He is said to commit the naturalistic fallacy, which is a mistaken attempt to define something in terms of something else. In this case it would be the attempt to define what would be morally worthwhile in terms of the biology or psychology of human beings. In other words, it has been claimed that Aristotle is trying to assign moral responsibility to human beings because they have certain biological structures and because they have a soul. G. E. Moore holds that the sense of a moral term is irreducible to the sense of any non-moral term. No moral property can be identical to any non-moral property.

Another criticism of Aristotle's theory of virtue is that it does not seem to be based on any serious attempt to consider human conduct exhaustively. It is undoubtedly important to express the need of limitation and regulation, but his quantitative statement of the relationship of virtue to vice is misleading. There is also a great deal of disagreement within virtue ethics over what are virtues and what are not. There are also difficulties in choosing and defining virtue in the ways that the Greek philosophers have suggested.

Aristotle has also been accused of favouring some sort of maximisation doctrine, in other words, if contemplation is the greatest good then it would have to be secured at any price, even if one has to pay a very high-price for it. The reply to this objection is that Aristotle's ethics is not an ethics of maximization of some commodity either for the individual or for the greatest number. It is a prudential ethics, a guide to action which stresses that what ought to be done is determined by what, in the given circumstances, appears to be the appropriate good to be pursued.

Despite the fact that the ethical theories we have so far examined have problems, it cannot be denied that Greek philosophers have been instrumental in laying the foundation of virtue ethics. In the next section we shall look at the development of virtue ethics in modern and contemporary ethical philosophy.

4. Modern Ethics and the Re-emergence of Virtue Ethics

Aristotle says that the good person is the virtuous person. The central idea of Greek virtue ethics has been that understanding human nature enables us to see what we ought to do for our own well-being and happiness. Ever since then, Western ethics' emphasis on morality kept growing until ethical views gradually came to be seen as universal truths. Western ethics reached the status of becoming normative ethics. That is, given the appropriate inquiry into, and understanding of, the good or right action or conduct, a moral theory could set the standard for others to behave accordingly. Theories like utilitarianism and consequentialism laid so much stress on human goodness that they started taking it as a human being's duty, to which all men are bound. Immanuel Kant (1724-1804) universalized moral judgments. His idea was that you should always act in such a way that the maxim of your action can become a universal law. He initiated the trend of 'cognitivism', which is the view that there exists knowledge or the human capability of acquiring knowledge, relative to some field of inquiry, and that knowledge can be seen as action guiding for the agent.

Kant's morality gradually changed the focus of ethics from voluntarily chosen virtues to the rational notion of the categorical imperative. An imperative is a statement of *ought* - what ought to be done. There are two kinds if imperatives according to Kant- hypothetical and categorical. The former kind of imperative is based on the function of cause and effect. It gives humans some liberty to decide whether one wants to follow it or not. For instance, if one wants to buy a burger from McDonalds, one 'ought' to go to a nearby McDonald's restaurant. In this example of an imperative statement, the key word which makes a statement an imperative is the word 'ought' or 'should'. These rules are not necessarily binding, but are contingent on certain things, as in the example, the desire to eat a McDonald's burger is the contingent factor for going to a nearby McDonald's. If you do not, in fact, wish to go, then the 'ought' statement is unnecessary. For Kant, it is the categorical imperative that is relevant for morality. A moral categorical imperative is a rule which must be followed universally and without exception. Changing circumstances and beliefs do not modify the rules of action governed by a categorical imperative. A Kantian does not examine the possible outcomes of a situation when he or she is determining an action. A rule such as 'one ought to speak the truth' would hold true for him all of the time.

Where does this categorical imperative come from? Are they features of the world? No says Kant. They are features of our own rationality which help us to bring morality into this world. We discover the moral imperatives through use of our rational faculties; we make our moral rules as universally applied rules. Kant emphasizes that following these moral rules is one's duty. For example, a Kantian might argue that lying is always wrong, regardless of any potential good that might come from lying.

Thus, this form of modern ethics tried it's best to neatly define its ethical terms and rules. Classical moral philosophers have apparently had no difficulty in picking up universal moral truths and defining terms like 'good'. Although there were a multitude of incompatible views being presented. However, a contemporary philosopher, G.E Moore (1973-1958), set a new trend in ethical philosophy by formulating his doubt that it is really possible to define ethical terms like 'good'. He begins by doubting whether philosophers really knew what they were doing when they attempted to define terms like 'good'. He reaches the conclusion that there is nothing ethical to know, for knowledge aims to track or represent independent truths about things.

In the mid-20th century a whole group of theorists known as 'non-cognitivists' started arguing that there is no possible body of knowledge about moral distinctions and relations. Therefore, they contended that there was no basis upon which one person could legitimately give moral instruction or guidance to another, or upon which moral institutions of right and law could be maintained. They argued that ethical statements do not express factual claims or beliefs; they do not assert propositions, and therefore they are neither true nor false. Ethical propositions do not have any cognitive, epistemic, or truth values. It may be that they represent a non-cognitive state of mind which involves no knowledge or cognition of any kind. Had ethical properties existed, they would have been different from any other thing in the universe. Since a proposition about an ethical property would have no referent, ethical statements must be something else. The non-cognitive approach has been taken by many philosophers like Hume, A.J Ayer, R. M. Hare, and R. L. Stevenson.

Logical positivists hold that statements about value—including all ethical and aesthetic judgments—are, like metaphysical claims, literally meaningless and therefore non-cognitive; that is, incapable of truth or falsity. Emotivists suggest that ethical statements are expressions of emotions and attitudes. Similarly, prescriptivism interprets ethical statements as commands or prescriptions. A person telling another that 'killing is wrong' probably does not want the other person to kill someone, and may be explicitly attempting to stop him from doing so. Thus the statement 'Killing is wrong', calculated to prevent someone from killing, can be described as an exhortation not to do so. Expressivism defends the view that non-cognitive attitudes underlie moral discourse and that this discourse therefore consists in non-declarative speech acts. Moral claims are called 'non-declarative speech acts' because moral claims are neither true nor false and so on and so forth.

However, some contemporary moral philosophy emphasizes character and human excellence or virtue, as opposed to moral rules or consequences. With the ascendancy of cognitive theories which highlight human cognition and rationality, like utilitarianism and deontology, closely followed by the various forms of non-cognitive theories, virtue theory moved to the margins of Western philosophy. Philosophers turned the direction of their ethical theories to either normative ethics or descriptive ethics proposed by non-cognitivists. Contemporary virtue theory again returned to prominence in Western philosophical thought in the twentieth century, specifically in the late 1950's in Anglo-American philosophy. The contemporary revival of virtue theory is pioneered by the works of the philosopher G. E. M. Anscombe (1919-2001). She changed the way many think about normative theories. She criticised modern moral philosophy's pre-occupation with a law conception of ethics, which deals exclusively with obligation and duty. She was critical of utilitarian and deontological theories (i.e. Mill's Greatest Happiness Principle and Kant's Categorical Imperative) that rely on rules of morality, which are claimed to be applicable to any moral situation. She believed that universal principles in ethics can only give rigid moral codes that are based on a notion of obligation which is meaningless in modern, secular society because they make no sense without assuming the existence of a lawgiver–an assumption that we no longer necessarily make.

In its place, Anscombe calls for a return to a different way of doing philosophy. Taking her inspiration from Aristotle, she appeals for a return to concepts such as character, virtue and flourishing. She recommends that we should place virtue more centrally in our understanding of morality. This idea is taken up by a number of philosophers and the consequence is the emergence of 'contemporary virtue ethics'. Anscombe's critical and confrontational views set the scene for way in which virtue ethics would develop. The philosophers who took up Anscombe's call for a return to virtue saw their task as defining virtue ethics in terms of what it is not; that is by delineating how it differs from and avoids the mistakes made by normative theories and descriptive theories. Philosophers like Phillipa Foot, Rosalind Hursthouse, Julia Annas and Alasdair MacIntyre, have made an effort to reconstruct a virtue-based theory in dialogue with the problems of modern and postmodern thought. They have not only revived Greek virtue ethics, but have given a new interpretation to the non-cognitivist approach. Virtue theorists agree upon one thing - that morality comes as a result of intrinsic virtues. The basic idea of virtue ethics is to promote inner virtue in a person, so that one's actions become a reflection of one's inner morality. One follows a virtuous path not because one is aware of the ethical norms of the society, or one feels obligated to be ethical, but because one possesses some inner virtue. Thus, virtue is not just about choosing and doing the right action, but is also about a way of being that causes the person exhibiting the virtue to make the right choice consistently in each situation. Whereas, on one hand, normative ethics focuses on how things 'ought' to be, and the descriptive theories of non-cognitivists explains the way ethical terms are to be understood, on the other hand, virtue ethics focuses on the character traits of the individual. A theory of virtue is a systematic, comprehensive framework for thinking about the moral evaluation of character which conceives virtue as an intrinsic moral excellence.

We shall now briefly look at the ideas of two main contemporary virtue theorists, Foot and Annas, in order to see how, like Anscombe, they were also instrumental in changing our understanding of moral philosophy. They argued for a radical change in the way we think about morality. They call for a change of emphasis from moral obligation, or moral decision making, to a return to a broader and deeper understanding of ethics, or a unifying tradition of practices that generate virtues.

4.1. Phillipa Foot

Philippa Foot (1920-) is a central figure in the revival of ethical naturalism and character-based ethics. She is one of the philosophers responsible for the turn away from non-cognitivist, descriptive theories like emotivism and prescriptivism, subjectivism and the entire anti-naturalist movement. Her work may be seen as a revival of Aristotelian philosophy, because she defends the cognitive and truth-evaluable character of moral judgment, bringing the question of the rationality of morality to the fore. Instead of further discussing fact/value distinction about ethical claims, she finds room for a sophisticated kind of ethical naturalism, which is a version of an Aristotlian ethic in which the nature of human beings is itself a determinant of their good.

Foot criticizes Kant's categorical imperative which gives a notion of blind fulfillment of one's duty, without being convinced by one's reason or revelation. Her approach requires firm connections between one's virtue, rationality, and self-interest. The central idea of her thesis is that although human beings are basically rational, and they have a reason to act morally and behave virtuously, we should still appreciate their virtuosity. This is because one's virtuosity does not soley result from the the fact that one has a reason to be so, but also because one has the inner motivation to be virtuous. She argues that even though everyone has reason to cultivate virtues such as courage, temperance and prudence, the rationality of just and benevolent acts must turn on one's contingent motivations. If one goes out of one's way to help someone, or fights for the security of one's country and gives away one's life, it is not just because one is a rational human being but also because one made a choice based on one's own personal motivation. Foot's idea seems to be the reversal of Kant's categorical imperative. In a famous inversion of a remark of Kant, she says that "we are not conscripts in the army of virtue, but volunteers". Philippa Foot cannot find any reason in Kantian thinking for why moral imperatives should be held in any higher esteem than the categorical imperatives of etiquette and club membership rules. Foot seems to be suggesting that all categorical imperatives are the same, leaving us with a morality which is no more moral than any other type of rule following. We do, in fact, hold rules such as 'do not kill anybody' in higher esteem than rules such as 'do not make noise from your mouth while you eat'. We do not normally think of the rules of etiquette as moral rules. However, they are phrased in much the same way situationally and linguistically as we would phrase moral rules, yet "I ought not to make noise while eating' is not a statement of morality, normally understood, but is at the same time a rule to follow for no other reason than it's own existence.

For Foot, goodness is not a kind of property to which we could give judgments and decisions like '*x* is good'. Her thesis is that moral judgment of human actions and dispositions is one example of a genre of evaluation. This evaluation itself is actually characterized by the fact that its objects are living things. She believes that evaluations of human will and actions share a conceptual structure with evaluations of characteristics and operations of other living things, and can only be understood in these terms. She gives a naturalistic theory of ethics opposed to the anti-naturalism of Moore and others. For moral evaluation, something conative has to be present as well as belief in matters of fact. Furthermore, if we are to characterise the motivation behind following club rules as that of wanting to be a member of a club, we must also consider the possibility that the motivation for following Kantian categorical imperatives is the motivation to be a good person.

4.2. Julia Annas

Julia Annas (1946-) is also one of the few modern writers on virtue who has attempted to recover the ancient idea of virtue. She explains how happiness and morality are closely associated in Greek morality. She argues that the Greek philosophers' ethics of the good life is in fact compatible with the morality of right conduct, and their ethical theories are in fact more wholesome, as they keep in view the final end of human life while propounding their ethical views. She contends that ancient ethics is 'agent-centered' (not 'act-centered' like much of modern ethics) and that Aristotle also agrees that 'the agent's life has a unitary structure which is provided by the formal constraints required of a final end of human life that it should be complete and self-sufficient'. Annas holds that a grasp of the structure and status of the Greek virtues is necessary for an agent to adequately understand his final end, because this helps one see the good of one's life as a whole.

A second important point that Annas makes about Greek philosophy is that happiness involves a significant degree of concern for the good of others for their own sake. She contends that the scope of ancient ethics is larger than that of modern ethics. Aristotle's virtues emanate from the whole fabric of ancient social life, which is the necessary context for an agent's understanding of his final end; bringing the whole of our lives into reflective focus cannot be done in isolation. Since the virtues have to be developed as a whole, and these include justice, courage, and the like, the good of others is immediately implicated. Therefore, ethics of virtue is at most formally self-centered or egoistic, but its content can be as fully other-regarding as that of other systems of ethics. There is nothing structural in *eudaimonistic* theories separating morality and self-interest. There is merely a 'superficial' philosophical tension existing between my own interests and the interests of others.

Annas concludes that acting virtuously is the way to the successful attainment of the final good, and that the virtues are dispositions to do what is right - as established independently of the agent's interests. Therefore, even though ancient ethical theories are formally agent-centered, they are not necessarily self-centered and egoistic. She also addresses the question of how ethical judgments are to be grounded or justified. Ancient philosophers regularly sought justification by appeal to nature, and nature forms a common element in ancient *eudaimonistic* ethical theories. In Aristotle's teleological view, human nature is not just a starting point but something which provides ethical goals. This perspective is eventually refined by the Hellenistic schools, most notably the Stoics, into a coherent ethical argument that equates the agent's final end to a life lived in accordance with nature. In Greek ethics, Nature functions as an ethical ideal attainable by the agent possessing the necessary skills in practical decision making. Her final thesis is that in Greek philosophy there is a significant role that morality plays in happiness, which reflects the role that morality plays in the good life.

4.3. Critical Comments on Contemporary Virtue Ethics

Contemporary approaches to virtue ethics have been criticized for different reasons. Although it has grown remarkably in the last twenty years, it is still very much in the minority. One failing is that it does not explain in detail how it is possible for a person to act morally in all practical situations. Some critics have shown dissatisfaction over the inability of much of contemporary ethics, despite technical sophistication and logical rigor, to make clear what it takes to live a moral life.

Some criticize the theory in its modern form in relation to the difficulty involved in establishing the nature and meaning of the virtues, as perceptions of virtue change according to the era, customs and institutions of a society. It is difficult to give a concrete account of virtues because different people, cultures and societies often have vastly different opinions on what constitutes a virtue. Not only this, virtues are also numberless. Every situation brings in some special adaptation of disposition. No social group could be maintained without patriotism and chastity, but the actual meaning of chastity and patriotism is widely different in contemporary society from what it was in the ancient period. Proponents of virtue theory sometimes respond to this objection by arguing that a central feature of a virtue is its universal applicability. In other words, any character trait defined as a virtue must reasonably be universally regarded as a virtue for all sentient beings. Other proponents of virtue theory, notably Alasdair MacIntyre, respond to this objection by arguing that any account of virtues must be based on the community in which those virtues are to be practiced. That is to say that the virtues are, and necessarily must be, grounded in a particular time and place. What counts as virtue in fourth-century Athens, might not have any relevance in the twenty-first century. It would be improper to understand virtues to be static. Our moral activity should be such that it attempts to contemplate and practice the virtues, which can provide the cultural resources that allow people to change, albeit slowly, the ethos of their own societies.

Another response to this objection is that experimental results from social psychology concerning 'helping' behavior are best explained not by appealing to so-called 'global' character traits like compassion, but rather by appealing to external situational forces. Some individuals 'locally' also possess such traits. A number of philosophers have argued that virtue ethics can accommodate the empirical results in question. And the literature of social psychology does indeed show evidence which suggests that many people do possess one or more robust global character traits pertaining to helping others in need.

Another short-coming of virtue ethics is it does not give any account of moral obligation. There is a disagreement between modern moral philosophers and some virtue ethicists about a theory of right action. The two parties respond to two very different questions. Whereas virtue ethicists tend to use 'right' as interchangeable with 'good' or 'virtuous' and as implying moral praise, other modern moral philosophers use it as roughly equivalent to 'in accordance with moral obligation.' One implication of this is that virtue theory ignores the importance of moral obligation. It believes that being virtuous is sufficient to lead a moral life. It completely ignores the need for discussing 'moral obligation'. A common response to this is that virtue ethics bases the rightness of action in the motive from which it proceeds.

A frequent objection to agent-based nature of virtue is that it does not allow us to draw the commonsense distinction between doing the right thing and doing it for the right reasons, that is, between act-evaluation and agent-appraisal. A possible reply to this objection is that one can solve this problem by supplementing an agent-based criterion of right action with a hypothetical-agent criterion of action guidance. Another objection raised against virtue ethics is that it is not always possible for a virtuous agent to maintain his virtuosity. Sometimes people are forced to compromise on their virtues during times of difficulty. Virtuous agents in such instances may not fare well due to adverse circumstances, or through lack of knowledge.

Virtue ethics has also proven vulnerable to criticisms that it is essentially dependent on an erroneous, folk-psychological, notion of character and, so, must either abandon its characteristic notion of virtue or forego any pretensions to psychological realism.

One major objection to Phillipa Foot's thesis, is that she proposes an uncomfortable and unrealistic notion of morality, as we would not normally think of our morality as simply a list of polite rules to follow. Her reduction of moral language to the language of etiquette does not appear to clarify in any way what in fact does constitute a moral *ought*.

5. Conclusion

Relevance of Contemporary Virtue Ethics in Today's' World

This section aims to throw light on the transition of ideas of ethical value from the classical to the contemporary, with an added explanation of how and why this change of focus occured, and to explain why virtue ethics as a philosophy is highly relevant for modern times and for the future.

To begin with, it is noted that one's own good and the good of others are construed differently by moderns than by the ancients. In ancient philosophy an ethical system is based on the perspective of a whole life. It looks at morality in a more wholesome way, as the final goal of life. Moreover, Greek ethics is about happiness, not obligation or duty. It is about natural deliberation on the part of human beings instead of simple rule following and abiding by law. It is grounded in experience, not moral theory. And the motivation for being ethical comes from the deepest of human desires - the desire to make our lives go well. On the contrary, the seminal ethical notion today is that ethics is about obligations arising from moral laws or principles. People do not agree on where these moral laws come from. It is a debatable question as to whether we should go back to the Greeks and center our ethics on the quest for virtue, which is concerned with happiness, rather than on questions of right as suggested by many modern ethicists.

What should guide our action and behavior in today's world - exclusively duty based morality or exclusively virtue based morality? Is there a way to strike a mean between them? Is it that the two types of morality should compliment rather than compete with each other? Contemporary virtue theories are formulating an answer. These theories recognize the importance of the agent's own reasoning in the practice of virtue. They claim that the virtues benefit the agent by leading to flourishing; and stress that the virtuous person does far more than conform to the conventions of her society. Moreover, they explore a form of naturalism which locates humans in the biological universe in a scientifically sound way. These theories can guide today's generation in its attempt become a better citizens and balanced dwellers on the earth who think they have certain duties not only towards themselves, but also society and for the environment as a whole. Contemporary analysis of virtue calls for more self-motivated, applied virtue ethics, for example, application to the field of environmental ethics, which may prove particularly fruitful. Taking lessons from Greek virtue ethics, contemporary virtue ethics teaches us the value of moral education, not as the inculcation of rules, but as the training of character.

BIBLIOGRAPHY

Adler, M. J. (1978). *Aristotle for Everybody: Difficult Thought Made Easy*. New York, McMilan Publishing.

Annas, J. (1993). *The Morality of Happiness*. New York, Oxford University Press.

Anscombe, G. E. M. (1958). Modern Moral Philosophy. *Philosophy*, 33, 1–19.

_____ (1999). *Platonic Ethics Old and New*. USA, Cornell University Press.

Cavalier, R. J., Gouinlock. J., and Sterba, J. P. (eds.) (1989). *Ethics in the History of Western Philosophy*. New York, St Martin's Press.

Dewey, J. and Tufts, H. J. (1908). *Ethics*. New York, Henry Holt And Company.

Foot, P. (1978). *Virtues and Vices and Other Essays in Moral Philosophy*. California, University of California Press.

_____ (2001). *Natural Goodness*. USA, Oxford University.

Frankena, W. K. (1963). *Ethics*. USA, Prentice Hall.

Hamlyn, D.W. (1987). *A History of Western Philosophy*. New York, Viking.

Hughes, G. J. (2001). *Routledge Philosophy Guidebook to Aristotle on Ethics.* London and New York, Routledge.

Higgins, T. J. (1968). *Basic Ethics.* Milwaukee, The Bruce Publishing Company.

MacIntyre, A. (1966). *A Short History of Ethics: A History of Moral Philosophy from the Homeric Age to the Twentieth Century.* New York, Touchstone.

MacKinnon, B. (2007). *Ethics Theory and Contemporary Issues.* Thomson Wadsworth. California, Wadsworth Publishing Company.

Magee, B. (1998). *The Story of Philosophy: The Essential Guide to the History of Western Philosophy.* New York, DK Publishing.

Schollmeier, P. (2006). *Human Goodness: Pragmatic Variations on Platonic Themes.* New York, Cambridge University Press.

Sidgwick, Henry. (1988). *Outlines of the History of Ethics.* Indianapolis/Cambridge, Hackett Publishing Company.

Sober, E. (2005). *Core Questions in Philosophy : A Text With Readings.* New Jersey, Pearson Prentice Hall.

14

Ethics and Well-Being

Mark Piper

1. Introduction

Philosophy is sometimes criticized for being too far divorced from matters that really concern most of us – and for some philosophical inquiries this criticism might be justified. But this isn't the case with the inquiry into well-being. *Everyone* cares about living a good life. Of course people differ in their ideas of what a good life involves, but everyone agrees that living a good life is desirable and important. And if we combine this universal interest in well-being with the nearly universal agreement that people can make *mistakes* about what is involved in living well, then we have very good reason to take the philosophical investigation into the nature of well-being seriously. Although some might say that what is involved in living well is obvious, a moment's reflection should cast doubt upon this claim. After all, don't many of the things that are commonly considered important for living well – fame, money, power, and so on – often lead to harm for those who get them? And isn't it the case that some peoples' lives would go better *without* these things? As with many philosophical concepts, the question of the nature of well-being seems clear at first, but the more one thinks about it, the more this confidence is shaken. Despite this, the payoff gained from answering the question of well-being correctly is potentially enormous: it can make the difference between living well and living poorly.

In addition, just about everyone thinks that well-being is or should be considered important for ethics. Most would agree, that is, that at least part of what it means to be an ethical person is to take the well-being of others into consideration: to help others to live well (or at least to avoid preventing them from doing so). This is especially the case when we consider relations of care. Few would deny that a fundamental part of being a good (ethical) parent, sibling, or friend is to take special concern for the well-being of one's children, siblings, or friends. On the other hand, it seems reasonable to hold that being ethical can't be *only* about making others' lives go better. Many would argue, for example, that although someone's life would go better if she won the lottery, this doesn't mean that cheating the system to ensure that she wins it would be the ethical thing to do. In short, it's fairly clear that well-being has an important place in ethics, but it is less clear what that place should be. If we care about being ethical persons, then, we should also care about trying to understand the relative importance of well-being for ethics. And this requires an understanding of what well-being *is*.

This chapter is concerned with addressing these important topics. I should make it clear from the outset, however, that my purpose here is not so much to give my answers to these questions as to familiarize readers with the range of ways in which philosophers have sought to answer them. My hope is that those who read this chapter will find themselves in a position to come to their own informed views about these pivotal issues.

The next several sections are devoted to doing some important preparatory work for the discussion that follows. Although this might seem somewhat tedious, it is vital to any inquiry – as it is vital to almost any undertaking (performing surgery, building a house, etc.) – to prepare well in advance in order to avoid confusion and mistakes down the road. Firstly, then, we have to separate the concept of well-being from other related concepts that are often confused with it. Doing this will ensure that we're all talking about the same thing when we talk about well-being. Secondly, we will clarify the notion of well-being further by elaborating on the kind of value that is at stake when we talk about well-being and by separating this from other forms of value. Again, this will help to ensure that we don't confuse or conflate well-being with something that it is not. Thirdly, we will make a very important distinction between two different sorts of theories about well-being: 'substantive' theories of well-being, and 'formal' theories of well-being. Fourthly and lastly, we will consider four criteria that a good theory of well-being should satisfy. This will give us a set of standards with which to assess the satisfactoriness of competing theories of well-being. With these aids in hand, we will then (in section 6) canvass the leading theories of well-being, the arguments in favor of them, and the common objections leveled against them. From there we will turn (in section 7) to a consideration of the ways in which well-being is incorporated into the four leading ethical theories (consequentialism, deontology, virtue ethics and pluralist ethics). We will see that there is considerable disagreement about how important well-being is considered in relation to the determination of right action and ethical agency. Lastly (in section 8) I will give my final comments.

2. Well-Being and Related Concepts

Well-being, like many central philosophical concepts, is fairly ambiguous. The most basic meaning of 'well-being' is 'living, being, or doing well'. This isn't very helpful. And the situation isn't helped by the fact that there are several other concepts that are quite similar. Here I would like to say a bit more about what 'well-being' means (while still leaving plenty of work to do regarding how to understand the concept in a more detailed way), and to clarify the concept by distinguishing it from a number of other concepts that are closely related to it.

Traditionally, philosophers conceive 'well-being' as what people have when their lives are going well *for them*. The italicized qualification sounds rather obvious, but it introduces a very important component into the analysis of well-being: *subject-relativity*. The basic idea is highly intuitive: there may be many things in my life that are good in some sense – I may own a good lawnmower; I may be the intended beneficiary of a morally good action; I may have a secret admirer – but *my* well-being isn't enhanced unless they make *my* life go better in some way. To say that well-being is subject-relative, then, is to say that judgments about well-being must be made relative to individual subjects: Claire has well-being to the extent that her life is going well *for her*; Simon lacks well-being to the extent that his life is going poorly *for him*, and so on. Most philosophers agree that subject-relativity is the conceptual core of well-being. Indeed, it is usually considered the assumed starting point for those who theorize on well-being ("We all agree that well-being is subject-relative – now what can we say about it more precisely?"). In what follows I will maintain this traditional practice.

Now there are a number of concepts that are very similar to 'well-being'. Perhaps the most similar is 'happiness'. Many people would consider these to be synonyms, in fact. After all, if I'm happy with my life, then it certainly seems that my life is going well for me, doesn't it? Yet well-being and happiness are not exactly the same, for a few reasons. First, happiness usually refers to a short-lived psychological state, whereas well-being refers to how well a person's life is going as a whole. In more technical terms, we may say that happiness usually refers to a *local* phenomenon that can fluctuate a great deal from day to day (e.g. you might be happy about winning at poker one night, and unhappy about having to wake up early the next day), whereas well-being refers to a more *global* phenomenon that encompasses how a person's life is going as a whole (e.g. you might be happy about winning at poker very often, but your life still may be going poorly for you on the whole). So this is one difference between the two concepts. A second difference is that talk about 'living and doing well' – that is, talk about well-being – seems to apply not only to humans, but to other living things as well, and in some of these cases it is odd to use the term 'happiness'. There is a perfectly clear sense, for example, in which I might say that my cat, or a squirrel, or some tomato plants aren't doing well (they might be diseased, for instance). Although we might find it acceptable to say that my cat is unhappy, it seems too much of a stretch to say that the tomato plants are unhappy. So the concept of well-being is typically distanced from the concept of happiness as a broader notion, both in the sense of referring to a more global judgment about how a life is going for its possessor, and in the sense of referring to most (or perhaps all) living things. Now, on further examination, it might turn out that the best way to understand well-being is to relate it in some way to happiness, but given these points of difference, this cannot be assumed without argument.

Another concept that is very close to well-being is the concept of 'flourishing'. Unlike 'happiness', 'flourishing' seems to involve both a global judgment and seems to apply easily to all living things. It makes perfect sense to say that my cat or a tree or even a virus is flourishing. But there is at least one important difference between the two that should prevent us from assuming without further argument that they are synonyms. To say that a living thing is flourishing is usually to say that it is functioning very well in an *organic* sense – as when we say, for example, that one's garden is flourishing (Indeed, the etymological root of the word 'flourishing' is the Latin 'florēre', meaning 'to bloom' or 'to blossom'). This is the most intuitive and natural sense of the term. Following from this, we can also say that a person is flourishing when she is physically and mentally healthy. But just because someone is physically and mentally healthy doesn't necessarily mean that the person's life is going well for her as a whole. We can imagine, for example, someone who is physically fit and mentally sound but who lives under the shadow of some great regret or remorse. Here we may say that although that person may be flourishing in an organic sense, her life isn't going well for her – and hence that she lacks well-being. Now the term 'flourishing' is also used in a wider sense that is synonymous with 'prospering' or 'thriving', and it might be said that *this* sense of 'flourishing' nicely captures the notion of well-being. The problem with this move, however, is that it is *possible* – at least it cannot be assumed otherwise without argument – that some peoples' lives go better for them when they are lazy or submissive or always left alone. And while it is not a stretch to say that those sorts of lives are going well for those persons, it is a stretch to say that lives of that sort are *flourishing* lives. So, without further argument at least, there are good reasons to hold that 'well-being' and 'flourishing' are not necessarily synonymous.

As a last note, sometimes people use the term 'welfare' as a synonym for 'well-being'. As long as we're not thinking about social welfare programs or anything of that sort, this usage is both common and acceptable. In what follows I will use the term 'well-being', but 'welfare' would be equally acceptable.

3. The Kind of Value at Stake in Well-Being is Prudential Value

There are many kinds of values that should be kept distinct from one another. Things can be 'valuable' in different ways. Fertilizer has value for helping a garden to grow, but has little value as baby food. An aphrodisiac may have sexual value, but it may be detrimental to one's health. There is certainly a kind of value at stake in well-being, and philosophers call this *prudential value*. Because prudential value is the value at stake in well-being, prudential value is also subject-relative. We say, then, that a life has high prudential value if it is going very well for its possessor, and we also say that certain objects or events have (or lack) prudential value to the extent that having them conduces (or fails to conduce) to a person's life going well for her. Now, just as it is important to keep the concept of well-being separate from related concepts, it is also important to keep prudential value – the kind of value at stake in well-being – separate from other forms of value. Here I would like quickly to distinguish prudential value from three other forms of value with which it is sometimes confused: ethical value, perfectionist value, and aesthetic value.[1]

Ethical value is the value that is at stake in the determination of right action, usually insofar as it impacts the lives of others. Arguably the two primary ethical values are justice and compassion, and, assuming that this is roughly correct, we can say that actions, events, and persons possess ethical value to the extent that they manifest these values. We might say, for example, that the act of saving a life has high ethical value, or that a person's life has high ethical value to the extent that that person is consistently just and compassionate.

Perfectionist value is the value that is at stake in the determination of the extent to which something is a good specimen of its species – that is, the extent to which something manifests the excellences characteristic of its nature. Tigers, for example, are by nature predators. A tiger that possesses all of the attributes for it to be a good hunter would manifest perfectionist value as a tiger. Many philosophers have contended that *rationality* is a characteristic *human* excellence. If this is correct, then we can say that humans who possess a high amount of rationality manifest perfectionist value as a human. It should be noted that the determination of perfectionist value is relative to species or groups of similar things, and therefore that what is a perfectionist value for one type of creature (e.g. being very aggressive) might not be for another type.

Aesthetic value is the value that is at stake in the determination of what is beautiful or sublime. We most commonly speak of objects (paintings, sculptures, etc.) possessing aesthetic value, but we can also speak of lives as having aesthetic value. A life that is marked by style, elegance and symmetry may manifest a high degree of aesthetic value, for instance.

There are many other kinds of value (this list is not exhaustive by any means), but these four forms of value deserve special mention here because they are so often associated with the determination of *the quality of a person's life*. The important point here is that these different forms of value should be kept distinct. More specifically, just because a person's life has high prudential value doesn't necessarily mean that that person's life also has high ethical, perfectionist, or aesthetic value. Remembering that well-being is subject-relative, it must be

---

1   In what follows I am indebted to L.W. Sumner's discussion (1996) of the same in *Welfare, Happiness, and Ethics* (Oxford, Oxford University Press, 20-25).

admitted as at least possible that a life that goes best for a person will be a life that lacks these other forms of value. Imagine, for example, the case of a person whose most satisfying life is to be left alone to read lewd comic books in her apartment. Such a life is deficient aesthetically (it is colorless and repetitive, lacking in dynamism), morally (it is devoted to the satisfaction of lewd forms of personal pleasure, without care for justice or sympathy for others), and perfectionistically (it hinders cognitive and social development), yet it is prudentially valuable for her. Now, there may be strong correlations between prudential value and these other forms of value – that is, it may be the case that very often lives that go best for their possessors will be lives that manifest these other values – but these connections are never entailed. It will be important in what follows to keep this conclusion firmly in mind to avoid conflating prudential value (and hence well-being) with other forms of value.

4. Substantive Vs. Formal Theories of Well-Being

The discussion to this point has been devoted to specifying the object of inquiry in order to ensure that we are all on the same footing and that we avoid conflating well-being (and prudential value) with something that it is not. Let us now turn our attention more closely to theorizing about well-being.

There are two different types of theory at stake when one seeks to give a philosophical account of well-being. On the one hand, one can develop a *substantive* theory of well-being. A substantive theory of well-being is a theory about the things that need to be in a person's life in order for it to go well for him or her. The content of a substantive theory is thus essentially a list of the elements of well-being. Such a list might include the following: financial success, close personal relationships, some measure of fun and excitement, and so on.

On the other hand, one can develop a *formal* theory of well-being. A formal theory of well-being is a theory about *what qualifies the objects on the substantive list to be there*. A formal theory provides an answer to the question, "What is it about those items (success, close personal relationships, etc.) that make them elements of well-being?"

It is very important to see that providing a complete philosophical account of well-being requires providing *both* a substantive *and* a formal theory. When asked what is best in life, Conan the Barbarian unhesitatingly replied, "To crush your enemies, see them driven before you, and to hear the lamentation of their women!" This is certainly a substantive theory of well-being, but most of us wouldn't buy it – at least not without some exceptionally strong supporting reasons: that is, not without a very strong formal theory. If we wish to have a full theory of well-being, we have to have an account of both what a life of well-being consists in and why that is the case.

5. Criteria for a Good Theory of Well-Being

We are almost ready to look at the leading accounts of well-being, but before doing that we need to determine the criteria or standards that we will use to judge which one is best. Many of these criteria are intuitive, but making them explicit should be helpful.[2]

Four criteria are especially important for judging the quality of a theory of well-being. They are: formality, fidelity, generality and neutrality. In what follows I will expand upon each of these.

First, a good theory of well-being will be *formal*. This is basically the requirement just mentioned above: a good theory of well-being will give an account of why the items on a (substantive) list of the elements of well-being deserve to be there.

Second, a good theory of well-being will manifest *fidelity* to our most fundamental intuitions regarding the nature of well-being. Now this will certainly be a rough measure, and will not always be decisive, but it will help us in some cases. A theory of well-being that implies that one's life can only be going well for one at night, or when intoxicated, etc. simply cannot be right. Conversely, if a theory of well-being gives no weight to health or close personal relationships, we have good reasons to be suspicious of it on grounds of fidelity alone. Again, the criterion of fidelity will be a crude measure, and will usually only be helpful in defeating some of the more implausible theories of well-being, but it has a central role to play in keeping our theorization suitably grounded.

Third, a good theory of well-being will be *general* in scope. The basic idea here is that a good theory of well-being will show how it is possible to make the many kinds of judgments that we make about well-being. For example, we want to be able to say that someone's well-being is high or low; moreover, we want to be able to say that someone's well-being can improve or worsen. In addition, we want to be able to say that a certain range of creatures can be evaluated in terms of their well-being, including humans and other animals at least, if not flora as well. A good theory of well-being will capture these features.

Lastly, a good theory of well-being will be largely substantively *neutral*. This means that a good theory will not include a bias towards one particular kind of life. This criterion is important, both because a good theory of well-being will apply across many different species (in accordance with the criterion of

---

2 Again, in what follows I am indebted to L.W. Sumner. See Sumner (1996), 10-20.

generality), and because it is simply highly unlikely, when speaking of human well-being alone, to assume that there is one best form (or only a few best forms) of life for all persons.

Much more could be said about these criteria, but hopefully enough has been said to suggest that they are all reasonable. We can now move (at long last!) to a consideration of the leading contenders amongst theories of well-being.

6. Theories of Well-Being

As we have seen, well-being is what a person possesses when her life goes well *for her*. In this section I will canvass the leading theories of well-being, clarifying what distinguishes them, and mentioning what is in their favor and what common objections are leveled against them. Before proceeding, it should be mentioned again why it is necessary to discuss theories of well-being at such length. After all, it might be said, isn't this chapter primarily about well-being as it applies to *ethics*? Yes, it is – but it is impossible to assess the place of well-being in ethics without having an idea of what *well-being is*. So it is logically necessary to get a grasp on well-being before we can properly understand its place in ethics.

6.1. Subjective, Objective, and Hybrid Theories

Theories of well-being can be helpfully divided into two major camps: subjective theories and objective theories. Subjective theories of well-being hold that an account of what it is for a person's life to go well for her must be based in some way on her *attitudes, concerns, feelings or thoughts about her life*. We call these theories 'subjective' because they are based in some way on the mental states of a subject. The basic intuitions behind subjective theories of well-being are twofold. First, it is reasonable to hold that in order for something to make a person's life go better or worse, that thing should *matter* to the person in some way: the person should have some concern for (or against) it, or some attitude towards (or against) it. Second, it is reasonable to think that persons know best what is best for them, and a subjective account captures this nicely.

On the other hand, objective theories of well-being hold that an account of what it is for a person's life to go well for her *need not make any reference* to the person's attitudes, concerns, or feelings about her own life. The basic intuitions behind objective theories are also twofold. First, it stands to reason that certain things are good for *all* people no matter what they think about them, or even if they think about them at all (good health might be an example of this). Second, it stands to reason that some *specific* things are good for certain people even if they don't have any attitude towards or thoughts about them at all (for example, being an astronaut might be good for me even though I've never given it a moment's thought).

Some philosophers also defend hybrid accounts. I'll discuss those at a bit more length below. Before getting to those, however, I will say a bit more about specific leading objective and subjective accounts. Because I wish to leave a good deal of space for discussing how well-being considerations are incorporated in the leading ethical theories, I will only provide sketches of the leading well-being theories here. Those interested in reading about these theories in more detail are advised to consult the bibliography for more literature on them.

Before proceeding, one quick word is in order. It's important to keep the *subject-relativity* of well-being separate from *subjective* theories of well-being. Although the terms are similar, their meanings are quite different; and the difference is this. *All* theories of well-being are subject-relative: that is, all theories of well-being attempt to capture what it is for a person's life to go well *for her*. But only *some* theories of well-being are subjective: that is, only some theories of well-being hold that the best way to understand what it is for a person's life to go well for her is to base the account (in some way) on the person's attitudes, feelings, concerns and thoughts about her life. Keeping this distinction firmly in mind will help to avoid confusion.

6.2. Objective Theories

There are many different versions of objective theory of well-being. Here I would like briefly to mention four of them: objective list theories, need-based theories, functioning and capability theories, and teleological theories. Along the way I will note the major strengths and weaknesses of each. It should be remembered that these theories are *objective* because they hold that giving an account of what it is for a person's life to go well for her doesn't require making any reference to that person's subjective states (concerns, attitudes, desires, etc.).

(i) *Objective list* theories of well-being consist in a list of supposed elements of well-being that all or most people should possess or experience if they wish to live well. Common elements on these lists include such items as knowledge, close personal relationships, creative expression and accomplishment. What distinguishes objective list theories is that they usually consist merely in a substantive list of elements of well-being but lack a developed formal theory of what justifies those as part of well-being (beyond perhaps a claim that these elements can intuitively be seen as constitutive of well-being). The strength of this account is that the items mentioned by most objective list accounts usually *are* intuitively compelling (after all, aren't knowledge and accomplishment important for living well?), but the primary problem with objective list theories is fairly clear: by failing to give a developed formal theory of well-being, they come across as mere assertions without any justification.

(ii) *Need-based* theories of well-being are based on the idea that in order to live well, persons must have their basic needs satisfied. The theory is objective because it holds that satisfying basic needs is what is crucial for well-being – whether people realize or want or seek this or not (Note that this account, unlike mere objective list accounts, does indeed provide a formal theory: it attempts to explain *why* certain things are good for us – namely, because they satisfy our basic needs). The strength of this account is that it does seem to capture something important for well-being – after all, almost everyone would agree that we can't live well if our basic needs aren't being satisfied. The weaknesses of this account are twofold. First, even though satisfying basic needs seems important for well-being, it also seems like satisfying important *wants* is important too. So it might be said that the basic needs account is incomplete. And second (and relatedly), it is arguable that at least some peoples' basic needs will be subjectively determined: that is, they will be based on peoples' most important desires or wants. And if this is the case, then a purely objective need-based account won't work.

(iii) *Functioning and capability* theories of well-being are quite similar to need-based theories, but instead of focusing on needs as the key to well-being, they hold that what is crucial for well-being is that one is able to function in certain ways and to have certain capabilities for functioning (a capability is the ability to function in some way if one desires). 'Functioning' is to be understood in a very broad sense, to cover things that people can do or ways that they can be. So, for example, being well nourished or being able to walk in public without shame would be considered functionings that are important for well-being. One of the strengths of this account is that it can capture things that intuitively seem very important for well-being but which do not seem to be basic needs in a strict sense – for example, being able to read and write and count. The weaknesses of this account, however, are twofold. First, the account seems to be too indeterminate. There are billions of possible kinds of functionings (and related capabilities), and not all of them seem important for well-being (e.g. having a pet salamander). Without a determinate way to specify which functionings are important for well-being, the theory seems hollow. And second, when we try to determine which functionings are important for well-being, it seems that at least some functionings will be important for the well-being of some persons because of their connection with their wants and desires. And if this is the case, then a purely objective functioning and capability theory might not work.

(iv) *Teleological* theories of well-being are primarily based on the work of Aristotle. They hold that well-being is a matter of fulfilling one's nature. This can be understood in a 'species' sense (e.g. fulfilling one's nature as a human) or an 'individual' sense (fulfilling one's nature as this or that particular person). These accounts are objective to the extent that the relevant sense of 'nature' is determined independently of a person's thoughts, attitudes, or concerns. This immediately suggests that the individual sense of fulfilling one's nature is problematic as an objective account, since it seems hard to see how it would be possible to flesh out an individual's nature in a way that makes no reference to that person's attitudes or concerns. This leaves us with the 'species' interpretation of the teleological theory – which is indeed the most popular form of the theory. The strengths of this account are threefold. First, it is at least arguable that we can defend an objective account of human nature, so that the account will remain purely objective. Second, it captures the subject-relativity of well-being nicely, insofar as it makes sense to hold that how well one's life is going for one is determined by the extent to which one fulfills or fails to fulfill one's nature as a human. And third, it seems intuitively satisfying to hold that our lives go better for us to the extent that we actualize or fulfill our human nature: that is, to the extent that we develop our specific human excellences to the highest degree. There are two major weaknesses with the teleological account, however. First, some might argue that there is no such thing as an objective account of human nature. A number of philosophers have disputed this based on the fact that human beings have free will. If we have free will, they argue, our nature is not predetermined. And second, it seems strained to say that just because we develop our characteristic human excellences to a high degree that our lives will necessarily be going better for us. Let us suppose, for example, that our characteristic human excellences are rationality and creativity. It might be the case that some persons at least would find their lives highly unsatisfying despite having well-developed rational and creative abilities. These cases might be quite rare, but they do seem possible. And if they are possible, then it is false to say that well-being is entirely a matter of developing our species excellences to a high degree. Here it should be remembered – as mentioned above – that prudential value and perfectionist value (the value at stake in determining whether something is a good specimen of its species) probably do not always coincide. If this is correct, then it is possible to be a good specimen of one's species, and yet for one's life to go poorly for one – say, from one's point of view. Despite these weaknesses, however, many philosophers would agree that the teleological theory of well-being is the best chance for defending a purely objectivist account.

6.3. Subjective Theories

As with objective theories, there are many different types of subjective theory. Here, as before, I will sketch the leading contenders. There are three of them: desire-satisfaction theories, hedonistic theories, and life satisfaction theories. Also as before, I will note the major strengths and weaknesses of each. It should also be kept in mind that these theories are *subjective* because they are in some way based on the notion that understanding what it is for a person's life to go well for her requires making some reference to that person's subjective states (desires, wants, concerns, attitudes, etc.).

(i) *Desire-satisfaction* theories hold that a person's life goes well for her to the extent that her desires are satisfied. There are two major variants on this theory: *actual* desire-satisfaction theories and *informed* (or ideal) desire-satisfaction theories. Actual desire-satisfaction theories hold that a person's life goes well for her to the extent that her actual desires are satisfied. This account might seem initially plausible (after all, don't our lives go better for us when we get what we want?), but a moment's reflection should uncover the major weakness of this theory: namely, there are many cases where it seems obvious that getting what we want causes our lives to go worse. Many people, for example, wish to be famous. Yet many who wished for fame and subsequently got it found that their lives went worse for them because of the added pressures and public scrutiny that attends being famous. So the actual desire-satisfaction account isn't very plausible. In response to this, many philosophers have developed informed desire-satisfaction theories. These accounts hold that a person's life goes well for her to the extent that a privileged subset of her desires – desires that are suitably 'informed' in some way – are satisfied. Informed desires are not the desires that people *actually* have, but the desires that people *would have* if they were *fully informed* both about themselves and about all the possible options in their lives.

The informed desire-satisfaction theory has attracted the support of many leading philosophers, and there are two main reasons why. First, it corrects for the faults of the actual desire-satisfaction theory while retaining all of its intuitive appeal (it certainly does seem plausible to hold that our lives go better when we get what we would want if we were fully informed). And second, it very nicely captures the subject-relativity that is the conceptual core of well-being (different people will have different informed desires).

The account does have weaknesses, however. First, it might be argued that satisfying our informed desires will not make our lives go better if we aren't actually in an informed state. Unbeknownst to me, the best life for me might be the life of a farmer, but in my current (uninformed) condition, that seems like a very unsatisfying life. In response to this problem, it has been suggested that the informed desire-satisfaction account should be this: our lives go better for us to the extent that the desires that our 'fully informed self' would want are satisfied for us *in our current condition*. But a second problem looms. There might be desires that I don't have and would never consider having (e.g. becoming a father), but which, if satisfied, would make my life go considerably better. The qualification just introduced doesn't seem to capture this, since it indexes well-being to the set of desires that our fully informed self would want for us in our current condition – and my current condition (let us say) doesn't include any desire for being a father. So it seems that desire-satisfaction – even informed desire-satisfaction – isn't the whole story about well-being. Then there is a third notable problem. What if our properly 'informed' desires are satisfied, but we're not aware of it? I might have an informed desire that my brother gets a secret admirer, and he may in fact get one. According to the theory, this makes my life go better. But this seems like a very odd thing to say, if I'm not *aware* of the satisfaction of the desire. Some philosophers have responded to this worry by introducing an 'experience requirement'. This is basically a provision that the only informed desires whose satisfaction contributes to our well-being are those that are in some way experienced by us. The problem with this move, however, is that it seems to shift what is important for well-being from *satisfying a desire* to *having a favorable experience* of some kind. And if it is having favorable experiences that really matters, then whether these experiences satisfy a desire or not seems irrelevant. On the basis of these reasons, a number of philosophers have expressed deep skepticism about the (informed) desire-satisfaction theory of well-being.

(ii) *Hedonistic* theories of well-being hold that a person's life is going well for her to the extent that her life is filled with a predominance of pleasure over pain. This is a very old theory that goes back at least as far as Epicurus. The basic idea is highly intuitive: what counts in having a good life is pleasant experience and the absence of pain: the more that pleasure outweighs pain, the better one's life is going for one. This account does an excellent job of capturing subject-relativity (since different things can be pleasant or painful for different persons), while remaining broad enough to apply to almost all living things. There are, however, two main problems with it. First, hedonism is often associated primarily with sensual pleasure of some kind: the pleasure we feel, for example, when having fun playing a game, or eating a delicious meal. Some have argued that although these things are important for our well-being, they aren't the whole story. Some have even argued that a life that is primarily filled with *pain* can *still* be a life of high well-being. Many people live highly meaningful lives that are filled with pain – consider, for example, the life of a medical missionary ministering to the indigent in a poor country. His life may be filled with all sorts of pain, and yet this might be the best and most meaningful life for him. If this is the case, then a hedonistic theory of well-being isn't telling us the whole story. The second main problem with the theory is that it entails that whether someone's life is going well for her or not is entirely a matter of how she experiences it – in other words, it's all a matter of her having positive mental states. But many would argue that this can't be right. Imagine, for example, the case of a married woman who *experiences* her marriage as wonderful when *in fact* her husband is just play-acting his affection, and in truth doesn't even like her, and is cheating on her regularly. Many would say that even though her life is dominated by the experience of pleasure, her life is not going well for her. Insofar as hedonism would claim that her life is going well for her, it seems to be an unacceptable theory.

(As a side-note, this problem with hedonism had led some philosophers to accept some kind of desire-satisfaction theory because, on that theory, whether someone's life is going well for her isn't just a matter of what's going on in her head; it's also a matter of whether what she desires – say, a faithful and loving husband – is *actually* satisfied.)

(iii) *Life satisfaction* theories of well-being are similar to hedonistic theories, but differ from them in one important respect. According to this theory, one's life is going well to the extent that one experiences one's life as both affectively *and evaluatively* satisfying. Hedonism, with its focus on pleasure, concentrates upon the presence of affective pleasure, and therefore can't capture cases where a life that lacks such pleasure seems to be going well for the person anyway (as in the case of the medical missionary). Life satisfaction theories make up for this by holding that well-being is *also* a matter of how worthwhile one judges that one's life is. In other words, this account adds a qualitative dimension to the subjective account of well-being: well-being isn't just about how one feels, it's also about how one judges the quality of one's life. The advantages of this addition are greatly increased flexibility, and perhaps an even *better* capturing of subject-relativity (since people have widely differing notions of what kinds of lives are worthwhile for them). This account also has its drawbacks, however. First, like hedonistic theories, life satisfaction theories entail that well-being is solely a matter of what is going on in a person's head, so to speak. Many people think that this leads to counterexamples of the sort mentioned above (the deceived wife who thinks and judges that her marriage is excellent), and therefore that it can't be right. And second, it has been argued that people are not always the best judges of how well their lives are going. For example, some people who are brought up in conditions of extreme deprivation get habituated to those conditions, and, if asked how well their lives are going, would say that they are (both affectively and evaluatively) very satisfied. Yet this seems very counterintuitive, especially when it seems obvious that their lives would be going much better if their living conditions were improved.

6.4. Hybrid Theories

Faced with the challenges to the leading objective and subjective theories of well-being, some philosophers have speculated that the best account of well-being should contain the best of both theories. A popular view in this vein is that persons' lives are going well for them to the extent that they (subjectively) want what is truly (objectively) valuable. So, for example, if knowledge and close personal relationships are objectively valuable, someone's life is going well for her to the extent that she desires these things, or has a positive attitude towards them, and possesses them. This might seem to capture what is most appealing about both sorts of accounts, and thus to be the most appealing view. The primary objections to hybrid theories of this sort, however, are threefold. First, it is argued that combining the two approaches, rather than reducing the problems that have been canvassed above, actually multiplies the problems, by bringing both sets of problems on board (the problems with objective and subjective accounts), and by having to find a way to reconcile all of them. Second, it can be argued that there are many cases of people who live lives of great relish and enjoyment that have nothing to do with what is objectively valuable (however that is unpacked). Imagine, for example, a porn star who absolutely loves her life, but who doesn't care about knowledge or close personal relationships or anything of that sort. Many would say that it is too much of a stretch to say that she has *no* well-being at all, yet this is what a hybrid account of the sort just mentioned entails. And third (and relatedly), making well-being dependent upon having just the right subjective states towards just the right objective values would seem to make well-being a fairly rare occurrence. Yet this seems to be too austere: surely most people have at least *some* well-being.

6.5. Which Theory is Best?

After reviewing all of the different well-being theories and considering how all of them seem to attract notable difficulties, you might be thinking that there is no way to decide which is best. Now it is true that the question of well-being – like most philosophical questions – is a very difficult one. But there are resources at hand to aid us in determining which theory is to be preferred. For starters, we have the four criteria mentioned above: formality, fidelity, generality, and neutrality. Some of the theories fall by the wayside – or at least are rendered unlikely – by applying these criteria carefully, and others begin to look more attractive.

But most importantly, I would suggest, the key to determining which theory of well-being is right is to keep firmly in mind that what we're looking for is the best account of what it is for someone's life to go well *for her*. Subject-relativity is the conceptual core of well-being, and it might well be the case that the best we can do is to try to find the account that best captures subject-relativity – even if that account has other problems that have to be dealt with.

7. Well-Being and Ethical Theory

We come at last to a consideration of the importance of well-being for ethics. Well-being is certainly important for ethics. Most philosophers would agree that any acceptable ethical theory has to take well-being into consideration in some way. But there are important differences between the ways in which different ethical systems do this. In this section I would like to explore those differences. In what follows I will examine the place of well-being in four leading ethical theories: consequentialism, deontology, virtue ethics, and pluralist ethics.

7.1. Well-Being and Consequentialism

Roughly speaking, consequentialism is the ethical theory that holds that the ethically right action is the action that conduces to, or brings about, the best consequences, or the most good. This is of course a very general definition; and there are as many different particular forms of consequentialism as there are different ways of unpacking the notion of 'the best consequences' or 'the good'. Certainly many of the possible forms of consequentialism are silly or implausible (e.g. holding that the good that is to be maximized is furniture preservation or torture). The most appealing and influential form of consequentialism is utilitarianism. As we will see, utilitarianism has traditionally placed great importance on well-being. A theory that places even greater importance on well-being is known as welfarism. We will examine both of these theories below.

7.1.1. Utilitarianism

Utilitarianism is a consequentialist ethical theory that holds that the ethically right action is the action that brings about the greatest amount of good for the largest number of people, where 'good' is understood either as pleasure, happiness, or well-being. Arguably the most common way to understand 'the good' is as well-being, though, so it can immediately be seen that well-being has a central place in most versions of utilitarianism. This won't necessarily be the case, however. Some utilitarians may accept a pluralist theory of what is good. They may agree that well-being is important, but also say that equality and justice are important as well. But the most common and basic version of utilitarianism is based upon the importance of maximizing general well-being.

The basic idea behind utilitarianism, then, is that well-being should be maximized. If I have a choice between two courses of action, and I want to find out which is the ethical (or more ethical) action, I should, according to utilitarianism, try to determine which of the two actions will lead to the greatest potential increase in well-being for the largest number of people affected by the action (or, as it the case may be, the smallest potential decrease in well-being for the largest number of people affected by the action). Certainly this will often be difficult to determine with precision. But in some cases the probable outcomes of actions are fairly clear. If, for example, I have 100 Euros of disposable income and would like to give it to a charity, and of the two charities that I investigate, charity A will be able to feed 10 families with the money, and charity B will be able to feed 5 families with the money, then, according to utilitarianism, I should give my money to charity A. Other cases will be somewhere between easy and difficult to determine. Imagine a case in which a politician proposes a ban on internet gambling. Should you support the ban or not? According to utilitarianism, you should support it if doing so will lead to the greatest increase (or the smallest decrease, if that's the best option available) in well-being. But will it? Well, probably – given that the loss in well-being suffered by those who lose their money consistently to card sharks is probably weightier than the loss in well-being that would be suffered by people being disappointed at not being able to gamble online anymore. We can't be sure about this, but it seems probable that banning internet gambling will have the best results for aggregate well-being.

Utilitarianism certainly has intuitive appeal (after all, isn't being ethical in large part about helping people?). But utilitarianism has also been criticized in many ways. I will not discuss these criticisms here. Readers who are interested in finding out more about the merits and demerits of utilitarianism are advised to consult the chapter on utilitarianism in this book. What I would like to discuss, however, is how utilitarianism looks when we construe well-being in different ways. We must keep in mind that *what it means to maximize general well-being* will be different depending on the conception of well-being that we employ. More specifically, what I would like to suggest below is that utilitarianism will look stronger if an objective theory of well-being is correct, and weaker if a subjective theory of well-being is correct.

Let's start with a subjective theory of well-being. According to the three leading subjective theories, well-being consists in either desire-satisfaction, pleasure, or experienced life satisfaction (both affective and evaluative). Now it is notable that all of these categories are extremely open-ended in the sense that one can desire almost anything, one can take pleasure in almost anything, and one can experience affective and evaluative satisfaction in almost any kind of life. Certainly there will be some limits here: it doesn't make much sense to say that people could desire (or take pleasure in, or experience life satisfaction in) a life of pure pain for its own sake. But beyond this, the field is more or less wide open: Matthew desires enlightenment; Mary desires intoxication; William desires to be left alone; Jill takes pleasure in hiking; Bob takes pleasure in fasting; Neal takes pleasure in burglary; Carolyn experiences life satisfaction from being a successful executive; and David experiences life satisfaction from being the most feared gangster in town. And so on and so forth. For each category, what a life of well-being will look like will be extraordinarily variable from person to person (and culture to culture); and for a subjectivist about well-being, this will all be quite right and proper. I wish to suggest, however, that utilitarianism looks much less promising if well-being subjectivism is true.

The primary problem is that on any subjective theory of well-being, peoples' well-being might well consist in terrible things. I might, for example, desire to kill innocent people in the name of God. Or I might take pleasure in raping women. Or I might find the most affectively and evaluatively satisfying life to be that of a successful con man. Now utilitarianism holds that the right action is the action that brings about the greatest amount of well-being for the largest number of people. And it is possible that in some situations, the greatest amount of well-being might be brought about by satisfying some terrible desires, or allowing some terrible pleasures, etc. Imagine, for example, that an extremist religious group has captured an enemy soldier. The soldier recently found out that his wife is divorcing him, and because of this he's deeply depressed and really doesn't want to live anymore. He's so devastated by the divorce that he doesn't really care what the terrorists to do him. The terrorists, however, are all fervently committed to torturing and killing the soldier (they desire it intensely; or it would give them great pleasure; or they find it a very important part of living a satisfying life). Let's further assume that the captured soldier is, because of a past indiscretion, very unpopular at home, and no one would really miss him much. In a case such as this, it seems that a utilitarian who accepts a subjective theory of well-being will have to conclude that maximizing well-being requires allowing (or possibly even helping) the terrorists to torture and kill the soldier. But this seems unacceptable. An acceptable ethical theory, we tend to think, can't allow for *that*. But this seems to be entailed by combining utilitarianism with a subjective theory of well-being.

It may be said that an informed desire-satisfaction theory could avoid this problem. This would be the case if the only desires that would count as 'informed' would be ethically acceptable ones. But this seems unlikely to work. It certainly seems possible that some persons at least could informedly desire things that most of us consider terrible. So the problem remains.

Let us now look at objective theories of well-being. In contrast with subjective theories, objective theories usually have a more fixed notion of what it is for persons to live well – we find this, for example, in need-based theories and in (species-based) teleological theories. Moreover, the substantive items on these lists are usually ones that don't arouse any suspicion or discomfort. A need-based theory might say that our basic needs include food, water, air, self-esteem, close personal relationships, and some amount of freedom. A teleological theory might say that a good life for a human involves the development of rationality and sociality. These don't strike us as objectionable – on the contrary, they strike us as acceptable and indeed important. Assuming, then, that one holds an objective theory of well-being whose substantive components (the specific items on the list of what one needs to live well) are widely ethically acceptable, a utilitarian theory looks much stronger. For it does seem to be ethically important to increase peoples' well-being in these ways.

Before proceeding, it should be stressed that just because accepting an objective theory of well-being might have these beneficial results (in terms of fitting in nicely with an ethical theory), that doesn't give us any reason to accept that theory of well-being as true. To do this would be putting the cart before the horse. We must first determine which theory of well-being is the best in its own right, and then we can see what implications follow in our ethical theory from accepting that theory of well-being.

7.1.2. Welfarism

As we saw above, it is possible to be a utilitarian but to conceive of 'the good' as something other than well-being. True, most utilitarians hold well-being as the good that should be maximized, but not all do. Some say that happiness is 'the good'; others have pluralist notions of 'the good'. There are some consequentialists, however, who hold that promoting well-being (and avoiding harm to well-being) is *the whole point of ethics*, and hence the only thing that should be considered when determining right action. These people are known as welfarists, or supporters of welfarism. According to welfarists, right action must involve some kind of well-being benefit to persons, or at least the prevention or avoidance of well-being harm.

Welfarism definitely has some intuitive weight. It has also attracted a number of criticisms. I will only mention two of them quickly. First, as we saw above, if we are welfarists (that is, if we hold that the whole point of being ethical is increasing the well-being of others) and if we are subjectivists about well-being, then we're going to run into the same problem explored above: namely, we might find that, in some circumstances at least, maximizing well-being will involve doing or allowing some horrible things. As we saw above, this problem will be alleviated if one can defend an objective theory of well-being whose substantive components are ethically acceptable. Second, many philosophers believe that there are important ethical considerations that are *not* ultimately related to well-being. Some would say, for example, that considerations of justice are of this sort. Imagine, for example, that I lend you 100 Euros and you promise to pay me back in a week. You subsequently learn that I'm using all of my money on very harmful drugs, and so you have good reason to believe that I'll use the 100 Euros you give back to me to buy them. What should you do? A welfarist would probably say that you shouldn't give me back the money, as doing so will likely result in a loss of my (and possibly your) well-being. But some philosophers would argue that even though giving the money back to me will probably have bad well-being results, you should do it anyway because it is the just thing to do, or because you made a promise. Considerations like these (and others) are brought forward by philosophers to suggest that although well-being may be important for ethics, it is not the whole story.

7.2. Well-Being and Deontology

Deontological ethical theories determine right action by specifying a rule or principle that constitutes right action, where that rule or principle has no connection to bringing out (or avoiding) certain consequences. Deontological ethical theories thus hold that some actions are right or wrong in and of themselves, and hence must be done or not done, regardless of the consequences that come about as a result of doing (or not doing) those actions. For example, one kind of deontological ethical theory is called *divine command theory*. On this theory – to give a rough characterization – right and wrong actions are determined by God's commands: if God approves of an action, it is right, and must always be done; and if God doesn't approve of an action, it is wrong, and must never be done – regardless of the consequences. If one of God's commands is never to steal, then stealing is wrong in itself, and must never be done, even if stealing would bring about wonderful results (The most influential deontological theory in the history of ethics was developed by Immanuel Kant).

Now it can at once be seen that considerations of the importance of bringing about an increase in well-being (or of avoiding a decrease in well-being) cannot have a fundamental place in deontological ethics. In other words, deontologists cannot say that a *fundamental* ethical reason for doing certain things (or refraining from doing certain things) is *because doing so will bring about an increase (or avoid a decrease) in the well-being of others*. If a deontological theory holds that lying is wrong, then one must never lie, even if lying would, in the circumstances, lead to a massive increase (or avoid a massive decrease) in the well-being of others.

This is not to say, however, that deontological ethical theories cannot make any room at all for the promotion of the well-being of others. From what I have just said, it might seem as though this is the case, but it is not. Deontological ethical theories can incorporate rules that call for the promotion of others' well-being – as long as these rules are *derived from* more basic rules or principles that are themselves not based on the ethical importance of bringing about certain consequences. This may sound confusing, but an example may help. Let's use the divine command theory example once again. According to (our simplified) divine command theory, the fundamental way to determine ethically right and wrong action is to see what God commands and forbids. On this theory, the *fundamental reason* why some actions should be done and other actions shouldn't be done is *because God wills it* – not because doing or not doing those actions will, in consequence, lead to an increase or prevent a decrease in well-being. Now let us suppose that God wills that we must promote the well-being of others when we can. We now have ethical reason to try to bring about an increase in others' well-being. But the theory remains a deontological theory because the fundamental reason why we should promote others' well-being is because God wills it, *not* because promoting others' well-being has any independent ethical value *in its own right*. If, say, God changed its mind, and commanded that we must decrease the well-being of others if we can, then this would be our duty. So the point is that deontological ethical theories *can* include provisions about promoting the well-being of others, but that these provisions will always be secondary and derived from more basic ethical principles that give *no* independent weight to bringing about good consequences for its own sake. What distinguishes deontological ethical theories, then, is that they give no basic or fundamental or independent weight to the ethical importance of bringing about good consequences.

One of the important criticisms of deontological ethical theories is related to the fact that they give no basic ethical weight to bringing about good consequences. Because we are primarily discussing well-being in this chapter, let us speak in terms of it. According to deontological ethics, we should give no basic or fundamental ethical weight to promoting the well-being of others for its own sake. If doing the right thing leads to an increase in others' well-being, that's great, but if it leads to a decrease in others' well-being, we should still do it. Even in deontological ethical theories that incorporate a secondary principle about promoting the well-being of others, there can still be cases where more fundamental duties should be followed that entail a subsequent decrease in others' well-being (to take the divine command theory example: we may have a divine command to promote others' well-being, but we may also have a more fundamental duty never to lie, so that sometimes we will have to tell the truth when lying would bring about a massive increase in well-being). The problem with this is that it seems unacceptable to many that doing the ethical thing could involve intentionally hurting people or ignoring their well-being.

There is also a second important criticism that is closely related. As we have seen, deontological ethical theories give no *basic* or *fundamental* weight to ethical reasons of the following sort: 'I should do X *because it will make Tim's life better*', or 'I shouldn't do Y *because it would make Christy's life worse*'. Instead, deontological ethical theories might say something like the following: 'Doing X will make Tim's life better, but the basic reason I should do it is *because God commands me to*', or 'Doing Y will make Christy's life worse, but the basic reason I shouldn't do it is *because Christy is an end-in-herself*'. The objection to this feature of deontological ethics is that it seems too cold and too severe – especially when the people that we can potentially help or harm are ones we care about. According to this objection, there must be some cases (again, especially when loved ones are involved) when considerations of benefitting or harming them are ethically fundamental. Ethics, it could be said, is not just about fulfilling our duties strictly – it is also about having sympathy and compassion for people, and in some cases the most important ethical consideration should be based on the importance of helping others (or not harming them) for its own sake.

One of the main challenges for deontological ethics to face, then, is to explain in a convincing way why ethics has nothing to do at a *fundamental* level with promoting others' well-being (or bringing about good consequences generally), and to show how our intuitions that considerations of well-being are ethically fundamental can be satisfyingly incorporated within a theory that gives such considerations no basic ethical importance.

Finally, it should be mentioned that, as in consequentialism, the ethical importance of well-being in deontological ethics well may fluctuate depending on the theory of well-being that one holds. As before, if one accepts a subjective theory of well-being, then there may be many instances in which promoting the well-being of others (even as a secondary or derived duty) will seem ethically very problematic; and yet if one can defend an objective theory of well-being whose elements are ethically acceptable, the demands associated with promoting others' well-being can seem stronger. Also as before, it should be remembered that we should not choose a theory of well-being based upon how well it fits in with an ethical theory that one finds attractive. We must first decide which theory of well-being is preferable on its own grounds (that is, which theory gives the best account of what it is for someone's life to go well for her), and then we can see how that theory affects (or doesn't affect) the ethical theory that we find most plausible.

7.3. Well-Being and Virtue Ethics

Virtue ethics is the ethical theory that holds that right action is action that springs from good or virtuous character. Consider, for example, the act of telling the truth. A consequentialist might argue that telling the truth is (usually) the right thing to do because truth-telling reliably leads to the best results. A deontologist might argue that telling the truth is the right thing to do because it is a fundamental duty (regardless of the consequences). A virtue ethicist might argue that telling the truth is the right thing to do *because it is what a virtuous person would do* – or, more specifically, because it would be the *honest* thing to do. Consequentialists and deontologists often theorize about the virtues, but they hold that the virtues have derivative importance, insofar as what the virtues are is determined by a more basic idea about 'the good' or about one's duties. But virtue ethicists argue that this is a mistake: they argue that considerations of virtue are ethically fundamental in the determination of right action, and stand as an alternative to the other two sorts of ethical theory. According to virtue ethics, we should explain both what is good about good results and what our duties are by reference to the more fundamental notion of virtuous or ethical character.

Almost no one doubts that philosophizing about ethics requires talking about virtue. But there are many who doubt that virtue ethics has the fundamental status that its proponents say that it has. I will not enter into these debates here except to say the following: it seems hard to see how virtuous character could be ethically fundamental because there is a natural tendency to explain what makes one's character virtuous by referencing the good results that such a character brings about (consequentialism) or fact that a virtuous character is one that does its duty (deontology). In other words, there is a natural tendency to explain virtue in terms of good results or duties, which suggests that explaining good results and duties in terms of virtue gets things backwards. But for present purposes let us suppose that virtue ethics can respond satisfactorily to this challenge.

The relation between virtue ethics and well-being is a complex one. Part of the complexity lies in the fact – as we have seen – that well-being is understood in many different ways. The situation is made even more complex by the fact that virtue has also been understood in many different ways. Given this complexity, I cannot hope to cover all of the theorization on the relations between well-being and virtue here. But I can provide a rough division that should help to order matters better. Virtue ethicists generally come in two stripes: those who (more or less) follow Aristotle and those who do not. The former seek to reintroduce a virtue ethics that follows from the writings of Aristotle. The basic ideas behind this movement are that a person has virtue to the extent that she fulfills her human nature and has the practical wisdom to live virtuously (in thought, action, emotion, and so on) in all of the differing situations in which she finds herself in life. By contrast, the latter defend versions of virtue ethics that place virtue at the center of ethics, but do not tie virtue to the possession of species excellences. *Neo*-Aristotelian virtue ethics is therefore more perfectionist in character than *non*-Aristotelian virtue ethics.

One of the advantages of virtue ethics (of either sort) is that they can consistently make room for the view that ethics isn't just about promoting others' well-being. A neo-Aristotelian virtue ethics, for example, might hold that promoting others' well-being is part of being a good human, but might also hold that being just can be more excellent (as it were) in some situations, even if this means a net loss in well-being. Similarly, a non-Aristotelian virtue ethics can hold that virtue consists in more than just promoting others' well-being. If we think that ethics involves more than just a concern for others' well-being, this will be an attractive feature of virtue ethics.

While acknowledging this flexibility, it is clear that both of these types of virtue ethics can consistently hold that at least part of what it is to be a good (virtuous) person is to have concern for the well-being of others. But can either type of virtue ethics hold that promoting another's well-being can be a fundamental moral reason for action in its own right?

Neo-Aristotelian virtue ethics will have a hard time with this. According to (most versions of) this theory, actions are right to the extent that they are virtuous, and they are virtuous to the extent that they are an expression of, or conduce to, species excellence. On this account, promoting others' well-being may be the right thing to do, but only because it is a part of species excellence, not because it is valuable in itself. Non-Aristotelian virtue ethics might not have such a hard time with this, however. On one version of non-Aristotelian virtue ethics, for example, being a virtuous person is largely a matter of being a caring and benevolent person: of having caring attitudes and motives towards others. On this theory, it seems possible to say that promoting the well-being of others can be a basic moral reason for action in its own right. If you lean towards the view that a proper ethical theory should allow for promoting others' well-being to be a basic moral reason in its own right, then this might be a reason to prefer a non-Aristotelian virtue ethics.

One other issue on the relation between virtue ethics and well-being deserves mention. According to many neo-Aristotelian virtue ethicists, persons who have the virtues (again, understood as species excellences) will, because of this, possess well-being themselves. As argued above, however, this is a debatable view. It isn't at all clear that just because someone is flourishing as a human being means that her life is going well *for her*. This might be the case, but it requires argument. Similarly, a non-Aristotelian virtue ethicist might claim that a person possesses well-being to the extent that he possesses the virtues (such as benevolence, a sense of justice, and so on). The problem with this suggestion is similar to that just mentioned: namely, as we also saw above, just because someone manifests a great deal of moral value does not mean that that life also possesses high prudential value for the person. At least this cannot be assumed without argument.

Lastly it should be mentioned that, as with consequentialism and deontology, the ethical importance of well-being in virtue ethics will fluctuate depending on the theory of well-being that one accepts. Generally speaking, the more subjectivist one's account of well-being, the more likely it is that promoting others' well-being will sometimes be ethically problematic; and the more objectivist one's account of well-being, the stronger the demands of well-being will be (at least where the list of items that comprise well-being is ethically acceptable).

7.4. Well-Being and Pluralist Ethics

Lastly, some philosophers defend a pluralist theory of ethics, according to which considerations of consequences, duties, and virtue (or perhaps two of these three, or more) can all be fundamental, depending on the circumstances. The advantages of this kind of theory are twofold. First, such a theory can support a much wider array of our ethical intuitions. Second, such a theory is far more flexible than the three major theories just covered. The primary problem with a pluralist theory, however, is that while it is easy to say that it is right, it is difficult to defend a well-developed pluralist account that provides a principled account of when different moral reasons are in play.

Because pluralist ethical theories can take many different forms, it is difficult to make any general statements about their relation to considerations of well-being. But this at least can be said: almost all pluralist ethical theories will allow that considerations of the promotion of others' well-being can sometimes be fundamental, and will also allow that such considerations can be outweighed (or 'trumped') in other circumstances. But the precise importance that well-being considerations will have will be determined by the exact makeup of the pluralist theory and the specific understanding of well-being that one brings to the table.

8. Conclusion

Well-being is important both personally (we *all* want to live well) and ethically (being ethical must have at least *something* to do with concern for the well-being of others). But it is not obvious what well-being is or involves, and it is not clear exactly how much importance well-being considerations should have in ethical theory. Addressing these important issues with the care that they deserve requires engaging in a sustained philosophical examination. In this chapter I have attempted to provide an inroad into these debates by providing an overview of contemporary theorization on well-being and its importance for ethics. As mentioned at the beginning of the chapter, these issues are difficult – our pre-theoretical intuitions can be overturned surprisingly easily, and matters quickly become very complicated – but I think almost no one would disagree that having the right answers to these questions is extremely important. With this in mind, we should conclude that careful thought about these matters, while difficult, is eminently worthwhile.

BIBLIOGRAPHY

Annas, J. (2003). Should Virtue Make You Happy? In Jost, L.J. and Shiner R.A.(eds.). *Eudaimonia and Well-Being: Ancient and Modern Conceptions.* Kelowna, British Columbia, Academic Printing and Publishing, 1-19.

Aristotle (1999) (Irwin, T., trans.). *Nicomachean Ethics.* Indianapolis, Hackett.

Bentham, J. (1970). An Introduction to the Principles of Morals and Legislation. In Burns, J.H. and Hart, H.L.A. (eds.). *Collected Works of Jeremy Bentham.* London, Athlone Press.

Brandt, R. B. (1998). *A Theory of the Good and the Right.* Amherst, NY, Prometheus Books.

Darwall, S. (2002). *Welfare and Rational Care.* Princeton, Princeton University Press.

Epictetus (1925). *The Discourses as Reported by Arrian, The Manuel, and Fragments.* Cambridge, MA, Harvard University Press.

Finnis, J. (1980). *Natural Law and Natural Rights.* Oxford, Clarendon Press.

Griffin, J. (1986). *Well-Being: Its Meaning, Measurement, and Moral Importance.* New York, Clarendon Press.

Haybron, D. (2008). *The Pursuit of Unhappiness: The Elusive Psychology of Well-Being.* Oxford, Oxford University Press.

Hurka, T. (1993). *Perfectionism.* New York, Oxford University Press.

Kant, I. (2002 [1785]). *Groundwork of the Metaphysics of Morals* (Zweig, A., trans.)., Oxford, Oxford University Press.

Kraut, R. (2007). *What is Good and Why: The Ethics of Well-Being.* Cambridge, MA, Harvard University Press.

Mill, J. S. (1979). *Utilitarianism.* Indianapolis, Hackett.

_____ (1997). *On Liberty.* New Jersey, Prentice-Hall.

Nussbuam, M. (1988). Nature, Function, and Capability: Aristotle on Political Distribution. In *Oxford Studies in Ancient Philosophy,* suppl. vol. I, 145-184.

_____ (2000). *Women and Human Development: The Capabilities Approach.* New York, Cambridge University Press.

Paul, E.F., Miller, F.D., and Paul, J. (eds) (1999). *Human Flourishing.* New York, Cambridge University Press.

Raz, J. (2004). The Role of Well-Being. *Philosophical Perspectives,* 18, 269-294.

Scanlon, T. (1998). *What We Owe To Each Other.* Cambridge, MA, Belknap Press.

Sen, A. (1993). Capability and Well-Being. In Nussbaum, M. and Sen, A. (eds.). *The Quality of Life.* Oxford, Clarendon Press, 30-53.

Sidgwick, H. (1962). *The Methods of Ethics.* London, Macmillan.

Slote, M. (2001). *Morals From Motives.* Oxford, Oxford University Press.

Sobel, D. (1994). Full Information Accounts of Well-Being. *Ethics,* 104, 784-810.

_____ (1997). On the Subjectivity of Welfare. *Ethics,* 107, 501-8.

_____ (1998). Well-Being as the Object of Moral Consideration. *Economics and*

Philosophy, 14, 249-281.

Sumner, L.W. (1996). *Welfare, Happiness, and Ethics*. Oxford, Oxford University Press.

Thomson, G. (1987). *Needs*. London, Routledge and Kegan Paul.

Index

A

Acatalepsia 6
Activism 61, 103, 181, 182
Agency 31, 124, 310
Ahimsa 22, 27, 28, 34, 35, 162
Akrasia 16, 29, 243, 298
Altruism 67, 68, 135, 136, 137, 138, 139, 140, 141, 143, 145, 146, 147, 148, 149, 150, 151, 152, 297, 302, 304
Altruistic 67, 68, 135, 136, 137, 138, 139, 140, 141, 143, 145, 146, 147, 148, 149, 150, 151, 152, 297, 302, 304
Animal 1, 6, 10, 11, 28, 29, 32, 34, 48, 56, 73, 114, 115, 147, 148, 187, 189, 194, 195, 199, 203, 207, 208, 211, 212, 213, 214, 218, 222, 223, 226, 228, 258, 291, 293, 299, 300, 301, 302, 306, 328, 329, 330, 331
Annas 301, 302, 303, 304, 307, 333
Anscombe 301, 302, 307
Anthropocentrism 158
Appetite 109, 110, 115, 116, 117, 118, 128, 133, 137, 155, 191, 257, 259
Aquinas 8, 24, 26, 50, 195, 235, 236, 238, 264
Augustine 7, 8, 14, 18, 24, 26, 38, 52, 94, 158, 159

B

Belief 7, 12, 21, 23, 25, 26, 31, 32, 54, 70, 80, 139, 166, 194, 242, 243, 244, 246, 247, 248, 250, 251, 253, 254, 255, 256, 261, 264, 291, 296, 303
Bentham 1, 6, 10, 11, 28, 29, 32, 34, 48, 56, 73, 114, 115, 147, 148, 187, 189, 194, 195, 199, 203, 207, 208, 211, 212, 213, 214, 218, 222, 223, 226, 228, 258, 291, 293, 299, 300, 301, 302, 306, 328, 329, 330, 331
Bible 50, 158, 159
Biblical 158, 159
Business 31, 124, 310

C

Care 59, 79, 80, 85, 86, 89, 92, 93, 94, 96, 97, 99, 100, 101, 102, 103, 104, 105, 106, 107, 333
Carroll 31, 124, 310
Carson 56, 83, 161, 163, 164, 165, 167, 207, 212, 257, 258, 301, 310, 323, 331, 332
Categorical Imperative 1, 6, 10, 11, 28, 29, 32, 34, 48, 56, 73, 114, 115, 147, 148, 187, 189, 194, 195, 199, 203, 207, 208, 211, 212, 213, 214, 218, 222, 223, 226, 228, 258, 291, 293, 299, 300, 301, 302, 306, 328, 329, 330, 331
Christian 7, 8, 14, 18, 24, 26, 38, 52, 94, 158, 159
Christianity 7, 8, 14, 18, 24, 26, 38, 52, 94, 158, 159
Church 8, 24, 109
Cicero 235, 236, 238
Civil Rights 31, 124, 310
Claims 222, 225, 226, 227, 239
Communitarianism 186, 187, 190, 193
Community 109, 110, 115, 116, 117, 118, 128, 133, 137, 155, 191, 257, 259
Conscsciousness 1, 6, 10, 11, 28, 29, 32, 34, 48, 56, 73, 114, 115, 147, 148, 187, 189, 194, 195, 199, 203, 207, 208, 211, 212, 213, 214, 218, 222, 223, 226, 228, 258, 291, 293, 299,

300, 301, 302, 306, 328, 329, 330, 331
Consequences 1, 6, 10, 11, 28, 29, 32, 34, 48, 56, 73, 114, 115, 147, 148, 187, 189, 194, 195, 199, 203, 207, 208, 211, 212, 213, 214, 218, 222, 223, 226, 228, 258, 291, 293, 299, 300, 301, 302, 306, 328, 329, 330, 331
Consequentialism 1, 6, 10, 11, 28, 29, 32, 34, 48, 56, 73, 114, 115, 147, 148, 187, 189, 194, 195, 199, 203, 207, 208, 211, 212, 213, 214, 218, 222, 223, 226, 228, 258, 291, 293, 299, 300, 301, 302, 306, 328, 329, 330, 331
Constitution 110, 121, 122, 123, 124, 125, 126, 127, 128, 131, 132, 133, 272, 273, 274, 286
Contract 9, 25, 26, 51, 63, 76, 109, 110, 111, 112, 113, 114, 115, 116, 119, 120, 121, 127, 132, 133, 135, 136, 149, 154, 194, 229, 231, 239
Control 109, 110, 115, 116, 117, 118, 128, 133, 137, 155, 191, 257, 259
Corporations 31, 124, 310
Correlativity 222
Corruption 2
Cosmopolitanism 186, 187, 188, 189, 190, 193, 199, 204
Cruelty 1, 6, 10, 11, 28, 29, 32, 34, 48, 56, 73, 114, 115, 147, 148, 187, 189, 194, 195, 199, 203, 207, 208, 211, 212, 213, 214, 218, 222, 223, 226, 228, 258, 291, 293, 299, 300, 301, 302, 306, 328, 329, 330, 331
Cynic 4, 5, 188

D

Dante 16, 29, 243, 298
Deceipt 7, 13
Deception 7, 13
De George 31, 124, 310
Democracy 109, 110, 115, 116, 117, 118, 128, 133, 137, 155, 191, 257, 259
Democritus 3, 4
Deontological 56, 83, 161, 163, 207, 212, 257, 258, 301, 310, 323, 331, 332
Deontology 56, 83, 161, 163, 207, 212, 257, 258, 301, 310, 323, 331, 332
Descartes 1, 6, 10, 11, 28, 29, 32, 34, 48, 56, 73, 114, 115, 147, 148, 187, 189, 194, 195, 199, 203, 207, 208, 211, 212, 213, 214, 218, 222, 223, 226, 228, 258, 291, 293, 299, 300, 301, 302, 306, 328, 329, 330, 331
Desire 2, 3, 4, 6, 12, 14, 24, 26, 32, 33, 54, 87, 138, 140, 141, 142, 144, 236, 257, 258, 292, 306, 317, 318, 320, 321, 322, 325, 326
Diogenes 4, 188
Distributive Justice 110, 126, 127, 199, 200, 201, 202, 203, 283
Double Effect 196
Dualism 9, 98, 117, 125, 129, 131, 132, 135, 137, 139, 140, 141, 142, 143, 152, 153, 268, 302, 303, 306
Duty 1, 6, 10, 11, 28, 29, 32, 34, 48, 56, 73, 114, 115, 147, 148, 187, 189, 194, 195, 199, 203, 207, 208, 211, 212, 213, 214, 218, 222, 223, 226, 228, 258, 291, 293, 299, 300, 301, 302, 306, 328, 329, 330, 331

E

Ecology 160, 161, 163, 165, 166, 183
Economics 48, 51, 73, 96, 157, 166, 167, 170, 175
Ego 1, 6, 10, 11, 28, 29, 32, 34, 48, 56, 73, 114, 115, 147, 148, 187, 189, 194, 195, 199, 203, 207, 208, 211, 212, 213, 214, 218, 222, 223, 226, 228, 258, 291, 293, 299, 300, 301, 302, 306, 328, 329, 330, 331
Egoism 1, 6, 10, 11, 28, 29, 32, 34, 48, 56, 73, 114, 115, 147, 148, 187, 189, 194, 195, 199, 203, 207, 208, 211, 212, 213, 214, 218, 222, 223, 226, 228, 258, 291, 293, 299, 300, 301, 302, 306, 328, 329, 330, 331
Emotion 1, 6, 10, 11, 28, 29, 32, 34, 48, 56, 73, 114, 115, 147, 148, 187, 189, 194, 195, 199,

Index

203, 207, 208, 211, 212, 213, 214, 218, 222, 223, 226, 228, 258, 291, 293, 299, 300, 301, 302, 306, 328, 329, 330, 331
Enlightenment 186, 187, 190, 193
Environment 61, 103, 181, 182
Environmental 61, 103, 181, 182
Epicureans 4, 19, 24
Epicurus 5, 18, 321
Equality 109, 110, 115, 116, 117, 118, 128, 133, 137, 155, 191, 257, 259
Ethical Egoism 67, 68, 135, 136, 137, 138, 139, 140, 141, 143, 145, 146, 147, 148, 149, 150, 151, 152, 297, 302, 304
Eudaimonia 2, 3, 5, 7, 290, 293, 294, 295
Evil 2, 4, 6, 9, 13, 42, 44, 62, 64, 70, 72, 111, 189, 211, 236, 248, 249, 255, 256, 262, 292
Excellence 16, 29, 243, 298
Existential 1, 6, 10, 11, 28, 29, 32, 34, 48, 56, 73, 114, 115, 147, 148, 187, 189, 194, 195, 199, 203, 207, 208, 211, 212, 213, 214, 218, 222, 223, 226, 228, 258, 291, 293, 299, 300, 301, 302, 306, 328, 329, 330, 331
Existentialist 1, 6, 10, 11, 28, 29, 32, 34, 48, 56, 73, 114, 115, 147, 148, 187, 189, 194, 195, 199, 203, 207, 208, 211, 212, 213, 214, 218, 222, 223, 226, 228, 258, 291, 293, 299, 300, 301, 302, 306, 328, 329, 330, 331

F

Faith 16, 29, 243, 298
Feminist 79, 90, 93, 99, 100, 101, 102, 103, 104, 105, 106
Fideism 16, 29, 243, 298
Foot 301, 302, 303, 306, 307
Freedom 110, 126, 127, 199, 200, 201, 202, 203, 283
Free Will 110, 126, 127, 199, 200, 201, 202, 203, 283
French 31, 124, 310
Freud 1, 6, 10, 11, 28, 29, 32, 34, 48, 56, 73, 114, 115, 147, 148, 187, 189, 194, 195, 199, 203, 207, 208, 211, 212, 213, 214, 218, 222, 223, 226, 228, 258, 291, 293, 299, 300, 301, 302, 306, 328, 329, 330, 331

G

Gaia 56, 83, 161, 163, 207, 212, 257, 258, 301, 310, 323, 331, 332
Gandhi 1, 6, 10, 11, 28, 29, 32, 34, 48, 56, 73, 114, 115, 147, 148, 187, 189, 194, 195, 199, 203, 207, 208, 211, 212, 213, 214, 218, 222, 223, 226, 228, 258, 291, 293, 299, 300, 301, 302, 306, 328, 329, 330, 331
Gilligan 79, 80, 81, 82, 83, 84, 88, 89, 99, 100, 104, 105, 106
Global Ethics 50, 52, 59, 61, 72, 76, 77, 78, 102, 157, 159, 170, 171, 173, 174, 175, 176, 180, 181, 182, 185, 186, 203, 204, 205, 206
Global Warming 158
God 7, 8, 9, 10, 14, 24, 26, 29, 47, 158, 162, 235, 236, 246, 249, 251, 256, 257, 258, 261, 262, 264, 265, 325, 328, 329
Government 110, 121, 122, 123, 124, 125, 126, 127, 128, 131, 132, 133, 272, 273, 274, 286

H

Habermas 102, 229, 230, 231, 238
Happiness 2, 3, 4, 5, 6, 7, 10, 11, 12, 136, 139, 149, 160, 187, 189, 190, 213, 214, 215, 216, 218, 219, 244, 245, 246, 247, 249, 251, 257, 258, 268, 270, 271, 272, 276, 277, 278, 280, 281, 282, 283, 284, 285, 290, 291, 294, 295, 296, 299, 303, 304, 306, 311, 312, 324, 327
Heaven 147, 150, 154, 275, 276, 286, 287
Hedonism 3, 272, 273, 319, 321, 322

Hedonistic 3, 272, 273, 319, 321, 322
Hegel 186, 187, 190, 193
Hell 147, 150, 154, 275, 276, 286, 287
Hobbes 9, 25, 26, 51, 63, 76, 109, 110, 111, 112, 113, 114, 115, 116, 119, 120, 121, 127, 132, 133, 135, 136, 149, 154, 194, 229, 231, 239
Hohfeld 222, 225, 226, 227, 239
Holism 56, 83, 161, 163, 207, 212, 257, 258, 301, 310, 323, 331, 332
Humanitarian 196, 197, 203
Human Nature 16, 29, 243, 298
Human Rights 222, 225, 226, 227, 239
Hume 1, 6, 10, 11, 28, 29, 32, 34, 48, 56, 73, 114, 115, 147, 148, 187, 189, 194, 195, 199, 203, 207, 208, 211, 212, 213, 214, 218, 222, 223, 226, 228, 258, 291, 293, 299, 300, 301, 302, 306, 328, 329, 330, 331

I

Ignorance 2, 244
Immunities 222, 225, 226, 227, 239
Impartialism 67, 68, 135, 136, 137, 138, 139, 140, 141, 143, 145, 146, 147, 148, 149, 150, 151, 152, 297, 302, 304
Incommensurability 276
Individualism 56, 83, 161, 163, 207, 212, 257, 258, 301, 310, 323, 331, 332
Industrial Revolution 158
Inequality 186, 187, 190, 193
Instinct 109, 110, 115, 116, 117, 118, 128, 133, 137, 155, 191, 257, 259
Intention 2, 3, 7, 18, 25, 45, 67, 73, 195, 269, 283
InterestTheory 222, 225, 226, 227, 239
Intuitionism 1, 6, 10, 11, 28, 29, 32, 34, 48, 56, 73, 114, 115, 147, 148, 187, 189, 194, 195, 199, 203, 207, 208, 211, 212, 213, 214, 218, 222, 223, 226, 228, 258, 291, 293, 299, 300, 301, 302, 306, 328, 329, 330, 331

J

Jus ad bellum 195
Jus in bello 196
Justice 79, 80, 81, 82, 83, 84, 88, 89, 99, 100, 104, 105, 106

K

Kant 11, 23, 26, 38, 66, 80, 161, 163, 164, 166, 182, 188, 189, 195, 204, 207, 208, 209, 210, 211, 212, 213, 214, 215, 216, 217, 218, 219, 220, 245, 246, 249, 257, 258, 265, 299, 300, 301, 302, 328
Knowledge 1, 2, 3, 4, 7, 10, 18, 81, 121, 125, 139, 172, 176, 208, 211, 224, 242, 252, 253, 254, 256, 257, 258, 261, 262, 272, 273, 280, 290, 291, 292, 293, 294, 297, 299, 300, 306, 317, 322, 323
Kohlberg 79, 80, 81, 82, 83, 84, 88, 89, 99, 100, 104, 105, 106
Kymlicka 224

L

Land Ethic 160, 161, 163, 165, 166, 183
Law 31, 124, 310
Legislation 109, 110, 115, 116, 117, 118, 128, 133, 137, 155, 191, 257, 259
Legislative 98, 113, 208, 221, 222, 227
Leopold 160, 161, 163, 165, 166, 183

Index

Liberty 110, 121, 122, 123, 124, 125, 126, 127, 128, 131, 132, 133, 272, 273, 274, 286
Locke 1, 6, 10, 11, 28, 29, 32, 34, 48, 56, 73, 114, 115, 147, 148, 187, 189, 194, 195, 199, 203, 207, 208, 211, 212, 213, 214, 218, 222, 223, 226, 228, 258, 291, 293, 299, 300, 301, 302, 306, 328, 329, 330, 331

M

MacIntyre 94, 104, 193, 243, 265, 301, 305, 308
Marx 1, 6, 10, 11, 28, 29, 32, 34, 48, 56, 73, 114, 115, 147, 148, 187, 189, 194, 195, 199, 203, 207, 208, 211, 212, 213, 214, 218, 222, 223, 226, 228, 258, 291, 293, 299, 300, 301, 302, 306, 328, 329, 330, 331
Marxist 1, 6, 10, 11, 28, 29, 32, 34, 48, 56, 73, 114, 115, 147, 148, 187, 189, 194, 195, 199, 203, 207, 208, 211, 212, 213, 214, 218, 222, 223, 226, 228, 258, 291, 293, 299, 300, 301, 302, 306, 328, 329, 330, 331
Maxim 110, 126, 127, 199, 200, 201, 202, 203, 283
McMahon 31, 124, 310
Medical 2, 9, 11, 22, 26, 28, 31, 33, 36, 41, 42, 44, 45, 46, 47, 48, 53, 54, 58, 59, 60, 61, 63, 64, 66, 67, 69, 70, 71, 72, 83, 85, 86, 88, 89, 91, 92, 96, 109, 118, 123, 127, 130, 135, 137, 138, 140, 141, 146, 148, 149, 152, 166, 172, 174, 188, 190, 191, 192, 195, 208, 209, 210, 211, 212, 213, 214, 215, 216, 217, 218, 219, 221, 226, 228, 235, 237, 241, 242, 243, 245, 246, 248, 250, 253, 258, 259, 267, 268, 270, 271, 272, 273, 274, 275, 276, 277, 278, 280, 282, 283, 284, 285, 286, 289, 291, 296, 304, 305, 306, 309, 311, 312, 316, 317, 318, 320, 321, 322, 323, 324, 325, 326, 327, 329
Mercer 67, 68, 135, 136, 137, 138, 139, 140, 141, 143, 145, 146, 147, 148, 149, 150, 151, 152, 297, 302, 304
Mill 1, 6, 10, 11, 28, 29, 32, 34, 48, 56, 73, 114, 115, 147, 148, 187, 189, 194, 195, 199, 203, 207, 208, 211, 212, 213, 214, 218, 222, 223, 226, 228, 258, 291, 293, 299, 300, 301, 302, 306, 328, 329, 330, 331
Moore 1, 6, 10, 11, 28, 29, 32, 34, 48, 56, 73, 114, 115, 147, 148, 187, 189, 194, 195, 199, 203, 207, 208, 211, 212, 213, 214, 218, 222, 223, 226, 228, 258, 291, 293, 299, 300, 301, 302, 306, 328, 329, 330, 331
Moral Imperative 110, 126, 127, 199, 200, 201, 202, 203, 283
Motivation 9, 74, 98, 99, 117, 125, 129, 131, 132, 133, 135, 137, 139, 140, 141, 142, 143, 152, 153, 203, 238, 268, 302, 303, 306, 307, 333
Motives 31, 124, 310

N

Naess 160, 161, 163, 165, 166, 183
Nationalism 186, 187, 190, 193
Naturalism 1, 6, 10, 11, 28, 29, 32, 34, 48, 56, 73, 114, 115, 147, 148, 187, 189, 194, 195, 199, 203, 207, 208, 211, 212, 213, 214, 218, 222, 223, 226, 228, 258, 291, 293, 299, 300, 301, 302, 306, 328, 329, 330, 331
Naturalistic Fallacy 1, 6, 10, 11, 28, 29, 32, 34, 48, 56, 73, 114, 115, 147, 148, 187, 189, 194, 195, 199, 203, 207, 208, 211, 212, 213, 214, 218, 222, 223, 226, 228, 258, 291, 293, 299, 300, 301, 302, 306, 328, 329, 330, 331
Natural Law 8, 230, 238, 265
Natural Rights 110, 121, 122, 123, 124, 125, 126, 127, 128, 131, 132, 133, 272, 273, 274, 286
Neoplatonist 1, 6, 10, 11, 28, 29, 32, 34, 48, 56, 73, 114, 115, 147, 148, 187, 189, 194, 195, 199, 203, 207, 208, 211, 212, 213, 214, 218, 222, 223, 226, 228, 258, 291, 293, 299, 300, 301, 302, 306, 328, 329, 330, 331
Newton 1, 6, 10, 11, 28, 29, 32, 34, 48, 56, 73, 114, 115, 147, 148, 187, 189, 194, 195, 199, 203, 207, 208, 211, 212, 213, 214, 218, 222, 223, 226, 228, 258, 291, 293, 299, 300, 301, 302, 306, 328, 329, 330, 331
Newtonian 1, 6, 10, 11, 28, 29, 32, 34, 48, 56, 73, 114, 115, 147, 148, 187, 189, 194, 195, 199,

203, 207, 208, 211, 212, 213, 214, 218, 222, 223, 226, 228, 258, 291, 293, 299, 300, 301, 302, 306, 328, 329, 330, 331
Nietzsche 1, 6, 10, 11, 28, 29, 32, 34, 48, 56, 73, 114, 115, 147, 148, 187, 189, 194, 195, 199, 203, 207, 208, 211, 212, 213, 214, 218, 222, 223, 226, 228, 258, 291, 293, 299, 300, 301, 302, 306, 328, 329, 330, 331
Noddings 79, 80, 81, 82, 83, 84, 88, 89, 99, 100, 104, 105, 106
Normative 79, 80, 81, 82, 83, 84, 88, 89, 99, 100, 104, 105, 106
Nozick 110, 121, 122, 123, 124, 125, 126, 127, 128, 131, 132, 133, 272, 273, 274, 286

O

Obligation 31, 87, 90, 91, 98, 124, 310
Obligatory Ends 110, 126, 127, 199, 200, 201, 202, 203, 283
Ontological 16, 29, 243, 298

P

Pacifism 196
Pacifists 196
Pain 5, 6, 12, 22, 25, 27, 30, 32, 33, 34, 136, 199, 215, 270, 272, 274, 275, 280, 282, 292, 293, 321, 325
Pantheism 9, 10
Pantheistic 9, 10
Parfit 67, 68, 135, 136, 137, 138, 139, 140, 141, 143, 145, 146, 147, 148, 149, 150, 151, 152, 154, 275, 276, 286, 287, 297, 302, 304
Passions 1, 6, 10, 11, 28, 29, 32, 34, 48, 56, 73, 114, 115, 147, 148, 187, 189, 194, 195, 199, 203, 207, 208, 211, 212, 213, 214, 218, 222, 223, 226, 228, 258, 291, 293, 299, 300, 301, 302, 306, 328, 329, 330, 331
Pelagius 8
Perfectionist Fallacy 31, 124, 310
Pets 1, 6, 10, 11, 28, 29, 32, 34, 48, 56, 73, 114, 115, 147, 148, 187, 189, 194, 195, 199, 203, 207, 208, 211, 212, 213, 214, 218, 222, 223, 226, 228, 258, 291, 293, 299, 300, 301, 302, 306, 328, 329, 330, 331
Plato 1, 2, 5, 19, 28, 44, 50, 77, 191, 251, 260, 265, 290, 291, 292, 293, 294
Pleasure 4, 6, 12, 213, 245, 272, 276, 277, 326
Pojman 158
Politics 31, 47, 48, 50, 89, 191, 244, 247, 248, 254, 284, 293
Pollution 52, 170, 171, 174, 175
Porphyry 1, 6, 10, 11, 28, 29, 32, 34, 48, 56, 73, 114, 115, 147, 148, 187, 189, 194, 195, 199, 203, 207, 208, 211, 212, 213, 214, 218, 222, 223, 226, 228, 258, 291, 293, 299, 300, 301, 302, 306, 328, 329, 330, 331
Positivism 18, 230
Possessions 110, 121, 122, 123, 124, 125, 126, 127, 128, 131, 132, 133, 272, 273, 274, 286
Poverty 14, 35, 44, 52, 73, 97, 177, 186, 187, 193, 199
Power 109, 110, 115, 116, 117, 118, 128, 133, 137, 155, 191, 257, 259
Privileges 222, 225, 226, 227, 239
Profit 31, 124, 310
Proletariat 1, 6, 10, 11, 28, 29, 32, 34, 48, 56, 73, 114, 115, 147, 148, 187, 189, 194, 195, 199, 203, 207, 208, 211, 212, 213, 214, 218, 222, 223, 226, 228, 258, 291, 293, 299, 300, 301, 302, 306, 328, 329, 330, 331
Property 110, 121, 122, 123, 124, 125, 126, 127, 128, 131, 132, 133, 272, 273, 274, 286
Punish 110, 121, 122, 123, 124, 125, 126, 127, 128, 131, 132, 133, 272, 273, 274, 286
Pyrrho 6

Index

R

Racism 56, 83, 161, 163, 207, 212, 257, 258, 301, 310, 323, 331, 332
Rawls 79, 80, 81, 82, 83, 84, 88, 89, 99, 100, 104, 105, 106
Reason 6, 26, 102, 103, 105, 154, 208, 243, 252, 253
Regan 56, 83, 161, 163, 207, 212, 257, 258, 301, 310, 323, 331, 332
Relational View 87, 90, 91, 98
Relationships 87, 90, 91, 98
Resolution 87, 90, 91, 98
Retaliation 110, 121, 122, 123, 124, 125, 126, 127, 128, 131, 132, 133, 272, 273, 274, 286
Revelation 7, 8, 27, 88, 260
Reward 110, 121, 122, 123, 124, 125, 126, 127, 128, 131, 132, 133, 272, 273, 274, 286
Rights d, 1, 9, 22, 26, 27, 32, 33, 34, 43, 47, 49, 53, 56, 57, 58, 59, 62, 73, 81, 82, 83, 84, 87, 88, 90, 91, 94, 95, 97, 98, 109, 110, 112, 113, 115, 117, 118, 120, 121, 122, 123, 125, 126, 127, 128, 132, 161, 162, 165, 168, 169, 171, 186, 188, 189, 192, 193, 194, 195, 196, 197, 198, 203, 221, 222, 223, 224, 225, 226, 227, 228, 229, 230, 231, 237, 238, 271, 283, 285
Rousseau 109, 110, 115, 116, 117, 118, 128, 133, 137, 155, 191, 257, 259

S

Sartre 1, 6, 10, 11, 28, 29, 32, 34, 48, 56, 73, 114, 115, 147, 148, 187, 189, 194, 195, 199, 203, 207, 208, 211, 212, 213, 214, 218, 222, 223, 226, 228, 258, 291, 293, 299, 300, 301, 302, 306, 328, 329, 330, 331
Scanlon 110, 121, 122, 123, 124, 125, 126, 127, 128, 131, 132, 133, 272, 273, 274, 286
Schweitzer 160, 161, 163, 165, 166, 183
Science 10, 32, 102, 103, 158, 172, 179
Scientific 158, 159, 173
Self-Interest 67, 68, 135, 136, 137, 138, 139, 140, 141, 143, 145, 146, 147, 148, 149, 150, 151, 152, 297, 302, 304
Sensitivity 87, 90, 91, 98
Sidgwick 67, 68, 135, 136, 137, 138, 139, 140, 141, 143, 145, 146, 147, 148, 149, 150, 151, 152, 297, 302, 304
Singer 1, 6, 10, 11, 28, 29, 32, 34, 48, 56, 73, 114, 115, 147, 148, 187, 189, 194, 195, 199, 203, 207, 208, 211, 212, 213, 214, 218, 222, 223, 226, 228, 258, 291, 293, 299, 300, 301, 302, 306, 328, 329, 330, 331
Skepticism 6, 7, 204, 265
Skeptics 6, 7
Social Contract 9, 25, 26, 51, 63, 76, 109, 110, 111, 112, 113, 114, 115, 116, 119, 120, 121, 127, 132, 133, 135, 136, 149, 154, 194, 229, 231, 239
Socrates 1, 2, 4, 18, 44, 272, 290, 291, 292, 297
Solomon 31, 124, 310
Soul 3, 4, 5, 10, 23, 29, 272, 291, 292, 293, 295, 298
Speceism 22, 27, 28, 34, 35, 162
Spinoza 9, 10, 25, 66, 162
Stakeholders 31, 124, 310
Standards 31, 124, 310
State 110, 121, 122, 123, 124, 125, 126, 127, 128, 131, 132, 133, 272, 273, 274, 286
Stoicism 5, 6, 7, 8, 19, 24, 188, 304
Stoics 5, 6, 7, 8, 19, 24, 188, 304
Summum Bonum 7, 8, 14, 18, 24, 26, 38, 52, 94, 158, 159

T

Technology 77, 174

343

Theism 16, 29, 243, 298
Theology 7, 157
Thomism 16, 29, 243, 298
Truth 6, 7, 8, 15, 71, 136, 138, 140, 141, 143, 146, 152, 153, 162, 171, 173, 207, 210, 211, 214, 217, 236, 237, 245, 263, 299, 300, 302, 321, 329, 330

U

Universal 110, 126, 127, 199, 200, 201, 202, 203, 283
Universalization 110, 126, 127, 199, 200, 201, 202, 203, 283
Universal Law 1, 6, 10, 11, 28, 29, 32, 34, 48, 56, 73, 114, 115, 147, 148, 187, 189, 194, 195, 199, 203, 207, 208, 211, 212, 213, 214, 218, 222, 223, 226, 228, 258, 291, 293, 299, 300, 301, 302, 306, 328, 329, 330, 331
Utilitarianism 1, 6, 10, 11, 28, 29, 32, 34, 48, 56, 73, 114, 115, 147, 148, 187, 189, 194, 195, 199, 203, 207, 208, 211, 212, 213, 214, 218, 222, 223, 226, 228, 258, 291, 293, 299, 300, 301, 302, 306, 328, 329, 330, 331
Utility 1, 6, 10, 11, 28, 29, 32, 34, 48, 56, 73, 114, 115, 147, 148, 187, 189, 194, 195, 199, 203, 207, 208, 211, 212, 213, 214, 218, 222, 223, 226, 228, 258, 291, 293, 299, 300, 301, 302, 306, 328, 329, 330, 331

V

Value 1, 6, 10, 11, 28, 29, 32, 34, 48, 56, 73, 114, 115, 147, 148, 187, 189, 194, 195, 199, 203, 207, 208, 211, 212, 213, 214, 218, 222, 223, 226, 228, 258, 291, 293, 299, 300, 301, 302, 306, 328, 329, 330, 331
Vegetarianism 22, 27, 28, 34, 35, 162
Veil of Ignorance 109, 110, 115, 116, 117, 118, 128, 133, 137, 155, 191, 257, 259
Vice 2, 6, 58, 69, 296, 298
Virtue 1, 2, 3, 4, 5, 6, 7, 10, 11, 12, 34, 36, 49, 56, 93, 94, 96, 101, 130, 149, 177, 188, 190, 191, 199, 217, 218, 227, 244, 245, 246, 249, 258, 272, 273, 289, 290, 291, 292, 293, 294, 295, 296, 297, 298, 299, 301, 302, 303, 304, 305, 306, 307, 310, 323, 330, 331, 332
Vivisection 158

W

War 110, 121, 122, 123, 124, 125, 126, 127, 128, 131, 132, 133, 272, 273, 274, 286
Welfarism 327
Well-Being j, 180, 309, 310, 312, 314, 315, 316, 323, 324, 327, 330, 332, 333
Will Theory 222, 225, 226, 227, 239
World Bank 196

Z

Zeno 5, 6, 7, 8, 19, 24, 188, 304

www.ingramcontent.com/pod-product-compliance
Lightning Source LLC
Chambersburg PA
CBHW060939230426
43665CB00015B/2004